THIRD PARTY LITIGATION FUNDING

THIRD PARTY LITIGATION FUNDING

Nick Rowles-Davies

Consultant Editor
Jeremy Cousins QC

UNIVERSITY PRESS

Great Clarendon Street, Oxford, OX2 6DP,
United Kingdom

Oxford University Press is a department of the University of Oxford.
It furthers the University's objective of excellence in research, scholarship,
and education by publishing worldwide. Oxford is a registered trade mark of
Oxford University Press in the UK and in certain other countries

© Oxford University Press 2014

The moral rights of the author have been asserted

First Edition published in 2014

Impression: 1

All rights reserved. No part of this publication may be reproduced, stored in
a retrieval system, or transmitted, in any form or by any means, without the
prior permission in writing of Oxford University Press, or as expressly permitted
by law, by licence or under terms agreed with the appropriate reprographics
rights organization. Enquiries concerning reproduction outside the scope of the
above should be sent to the Rights Department, Oxford University Press, at the
address above

You must not circulate this work in any other form
and you must impose this same condition on any acquirer

Crown copyright material is reproduced under Class Licence
Number C01P0000148 with the permission of OPSI
and the Queen's Printer for Scotland

Published in the United States of America by Oxford University Press
198 Madison Avenue, New York, NY 10016, United States of America

British Library Cataloguing in Publication Data
Data available

Library of Congress Control Number: 2014942234

ISBN 978–0–19–871592–4

Printed and bound by
CPI Group (UK) Ltd, Croydon, CR0 4YY

Links to third party websites are provided by Oxford in good faith and
for information only. Oxford disclaims any responsibility for the materials
contained in any third party website referenced in this work.

FOREWORD

There is no access to justice if parties cannot afford to bring meritorious claims or to defend unmeritorious claims. If civil justice is to be affordable, it is necessary (a) that there be rules in place to control the costs of litigation and (b) that methods of funding meritorious claims or defences be available to parties of limited means. These objectives are simple to state, but far from simple to achieve. The civil justice reforms of 2013 represented a serious attempt to achieve those objectives, so far as it was practicable to do so. Unfortunately the cutbacks in legal aid which were introduced in the same year (indeed on the same day) had the effect of diminishing access to justice.

This book deals with one important aspect of the 2013 civil justice reforms, namely means of funding civil litigation. The book concentrates in particular on third party funders, who are also referred to as litigation funders. The book recounts the history of third party funding both before and after the 2013 reforms. It looks at the position in several overseas jurisdictions. There is also discussion of other means of funding litigation, such as conditional fee agreements (CFAs) and damages based agreements (DBAs). The authors rightly draw attention to problems with the present DBA Regulations.

This book is a clear and helpful guide to litigation funding. It will be of considerable assistance, not only for legal practitioners but also for court users and for those who are contemplating litigation.

Sir Rupert Jackson
12th August 2014

PREFACE

The idea to write this book seemed a good one at the time. The reality of doing it proved rather more difficult than I had imagined.

The world of litigation funding has developed considerably in the last few years and even whilst this book was being written. The market has matured in many ways and the use of litigation finance has become far more commonplace. Litigation funding can mean many things—not just the funding of one-off large cases. The industry has become sophisticated in meeting the needs of clients and lawyers and has developed products to meet those needs.

Consequently, two important caveats apply to this book.

First, after writing the book but before it was published, I became a Managing Director at Burford Capital, the world's largest litigation funder. The opinions and perspective in this book are mine, not necessarily Burford's.

Secondly, my main focus in this book has been the funding of single litigation matters in the courts of England and Wales by dedicated, professional litigation funders.

There are clearly many other ways to provide for litigation expenses, ranging from a litigant's existing resources to law firms taking risk on matters to hedge and other types of non-dedicated investment funds. Those existed long before the advent of dedicated litigation funders and continue to exist today. The 'market' is not limited to the small number of firms that only engage in litigation finance, and indeed those firms make up a small minority of the capital devoted to litigation 'funding'.

It is also notable that litigation finance firms, like Burford, do much more than single-case litigation funding. The industry has moved to encompass a wide range of corporate finance and insurance products, including portfolio financing and recourse lending. I touch on these items briefly but the principal focus of this book is single-case funding.

I would like to take this opportunity to thank my consultant editor, Jeremy Cousins QC, without whom the task of completing this publication would have been impossible. I am extremely grateful for his advice, insight, and invaluable edits.

I am grateful also to Kerry Jack, who instigated this project and worked tirelessly to persuade the Oxford University Press of its merit. Thanks must also go to Rachel Holt at Oxford University Press, who remained calm despite missed deadlines. Additionally, thanks to Anne Evans for her research and assistance' to Neil Purslow of Therium Capital Management for his help with case studies, in providing invaluable documentation and for proofreading and editing, and to the management of Vannin Capital and my colleagues at Burford for their assistance with the case studies.

Above all I thank my wife, Rebecca, for her support throughout this project, during which, undoubtedly, I would have tried the patience of a saint.

Nick Rowles-Davies
July 2014

CONTENTS

Table of Cases — xv
Table of Legislation — xix
List of Abbreviations — xxi

1. Introduction and Background — 1
   - A. Introduction and Background — 1
   - B. What is Litigation Funding? — 4
   - C. History — 5
   - D. How does it Work? — 6
   - E. What Type of Case can be Funded? — 9
   - F. Why is the Use of Third Party Litigation Funding Increasing? — 12
   - G. The Effect of the Jackson Reforms — 19

2. History and Development — 22
   - A. History, Champerty, Evolution — 22
     1. History and development — 22
     2. Champerty and maintenance — 23
     3. Evolution — 25
   - B. Case Law — 26
     1. *Giles v Thompson* — 27
     2. *Stocznia Gdanska SA v Latreefers Inc* — 28
     3. *The Eurasian Dream (No 2)* — 30
     4. *Hamilton v Al-Fayed (No 2)* — 30
     5. *R (on the application of Factortame) v Secretary of State for Transport, Local Government and the Regions (No 2)* — 33
     6. *Gulf Azov Shipping Co Ltd v Idisi* — 36
     7. *Arkin v Borchard Lines Ltd & Ors* — 38
     8. *London & Regional (St George's Court) Ltd v Ministry of Defence* — 42
     9. *Merchantbridge & Co Ltd v Safron General Partner 1 Ltd* — 43
     10. *Sibthorpe and Morris v Southwark London Borough Council* — 45

	11. *Jennifer Simpson (as assignee of Alan Catchpole) v Norfolk & Norwich University Hospital NHS Trust*	47
	12. *Cecil & others v Bayat & others*	49
	13. *Tinseltime Ltd v Eryl Roberts & Ors*	50
	14. *Flatman v Germany*	52
	15. *Harcus Sinclair (a Firm) v Buttonwood Legal Capital Limited & Ors*	53
	16. *Excalibur Ventures LLC v Texas Keystone Inc.; Gulf Keystone Petroleum Ltd; Gulf Keystone Petroleum International Ltd; Gulf Keystone Petroleum (UK) Ltd*	54
C.	Conclusions	56

3. Use of Funding 60
   A. Use of Funding 60
   B. Why is Funding Used? 61
   C. Which Cases? 64
      1. Subject matter 66
      2. Client 66
      3. Merits 67
      4. Value 67
      5. Forum/venue/jurisdiction/applicable law 68
      6. Enforceability 68
   D. Lower Value Cases 69
   E. Alternative Methods 72
      1. Portfolio funding 72
      2. Basket of cases 74
      3. Hybrid DBA funding 75
      4. Alternative business structures 75
   F. International Landscape 76
      1. United States 76
      2. Australia 79
      3. New Zealand 82
      4. South Africa 82
      5. Canada 83
      6. France 83
      7. Germany 83
      8. Caribbean 84
      9. Channel Islands 84
      10. Dubai and Qatar 84
      11. Ireland 85
      12. Hong Kong 85
      13. Singapore 85

4. Funder Models — 87
- A. Funder Models — 87
- B. 'Case by Case' Funding — 88
    1. 'One-off' funders — 89
    2. 'Fund raiser' funders — 90
- C. Family Office — 93
- D. Private Equity — 95
- E. Investment Fund — 95
- F. Publicly Listed — 97
- G. Case Study: Burford Capital — 98
- H. Case Study: Therium Capital Management Limited — 100
- I. Case Study: Vannin Capital — 102
- J. Conclusion — 103

5. The Funding Process — 104
- A. The Funding Process — 104
- B. Brokers or Direct Approach to Funders? — 106
- C. Key Areas — 108
    1. Merits and quantum — 109
    2. Budget — 110
    3. Strategy — 111
- D. Intake Review and Assessment — 111
- E. Indicative Terms — 112
- F. Negotiation — 113
- G. Term Sheet — 114
- H. Exclusivity — 114
- I. Due Diligence Assessment — 116
- J. Pricing — 117
- K. Retainers — 119
- L. ATE — 119
- M. The Litigation Funding Agreement — 120
    1. Section Two—'Agreement to Fund' — 121
    2. Section Three—'Payment Terms and Interest' — 121
    3. Section Four—'Changes to Project Plan' — 121
    4. Section Five—'Excluded Costs and Liabilities' — 121
    5. Section Six—'Conditions Precedent and Warranties' — 122
    6. Section Seven—'Payment of Reasonable Costs' — 122

	7. Section Eight—'Adverse Costs'	122
	8. Section Nine—'Claimant's Obligations'	122
	9. Section Twelve—'Security for Costs'	122
	10. Section Thirteen—'Treatment of Claim Proceeds'	123
	11. Section Fourteen—'Confidentiality'	123
	12. Section Fifteen—'Termination'	123
	13. Section Twenty-Five—'Dispute Resolution'	124
	14. 'Schedule'	124
	15. Appendix 1—'Project Plan'	124
	16. Appendix 2—'Reliance Letter'	124
	17. Appendix 3—'Priorities Agreement'	124
N.	Conclusion	125

6. Costs and Insurance — 127
   - A. Costs and Insurance — 127
   - B. ATE Insurance — 128
   - C. Payment of the Insurance Premium — 129
     1. Payment in full on inception — 131
     2. Deposit premium — 132
     3. Fully deferred premium — 133
   - D. Security for Costs — 134
   - E. Costs of Setting up Funding and ATE — 138
   - F. Funders' Costs Risk — 139
   - G. *Excalibur* — 140
   - H. Conclusion — 141

7. Group Litigation — 142
   - A. Group Litigation — 142
   - B. England and Wales — 143
   - C. Issues for Litigation Funders — 149
   - D. Conclusion — 152

8. Jackson and DBAs — 154
   - A. Jackson and Damages Based Agreements — 154
   - B. Outline of the Changes — 155
     1. Conditional fee agreements — 155
     2. ATE insurance premium recoverability — 156
     3. Increase in general damages — 156

4. *Simmons v Castle*		156
5. Increased sanctions under Part 36		159
6. Proportionality		160
7. Costs management orders		163
C. Damages Based Agreements		168
1. The DBA Regulations		171
2. Practicalities		174
D. The Effect of Jackson on Third Party Litigation Funding		176
1. Lawyers' costs immunity, DBAs, and third party funding		176
2. Hodgson immunity		176
3. Alternative business structures		179
E. Conclusion		179
9. Professional Obligations		**182**
A. Introduction		182
B. The Association of Litigation Funders		182
1. Membership		183
2. Code of conduct		183
C. Solicitors		192
1. Conduct rules		194
2. Solicitors' duties		196
D. Conclusion		203
10. Funding and the Future		**205**
A. Introduction		205
B. Regulation and Self-Regulation		208
C. Education		211
D. ABS		214
E. Jurisdictions		216
F. Evolution		217
G. Conclusion		218
Appendix 1. Litigation Funding Agreement		221
Appendix 2. Preamble		248
Appendix 3. A Procedure to Govern Complaints Made against Funder Members by Funded Litigants		252

Appendix 4. Articles of Association of the Association of Litigation Funders of England & Wales	260
Appendix 5. Code of Conduct for Litigation Funders	273
Appendix 6. The Association of Litigation Funders of England and Wales	277
Index	285

TABLE OF CASES

UNITED KINGDOM

Adris and others v RBS and others [2010] Costs LR 598, [2010] EWHC 941 .... 8.131, 9.73, 9.74, 9.76
Aiden Shipping Co Ltd v Interbulk Ltd [1986] AC 965, HL............................. 2.37
Arkin v Borchard Lines [2005] 1 WLR 3055, [2005] EWCA Civ 655 ...... 1.08, 2.59–2.67, 2.78, 2.79, 2.122, 5.90, 6.13, 6.58, 6.59, 6.62, 6.66, 7.43, 8.119, 8.121, 8.123, 9.90

Bremer Vulkan Schiffbau und Maschinenfabrik v South India Shipping Corporation Ltd
  [1981] AC 909 .... 1.54
Bristol & West BS v Mothew [1998] Ch 1.................................... 1.59, 8.91
Brown v Innovator One plc [2012] EWHC 1321 (Comm)........................... 10.41

Carver v BAA [2008] EWCA Civ 412... 8.30
Case of Barratry (30 Eliz) 8 Rep 36, 77 ER 5.................................. 2.06
Cecil & others v Bayat & others [2011] 1 WLR 3086, CA...................... 2.95–2.101
Cooper v Maxwell (unreported) 20 March 1992 (Court of Appeal (Civil Division))
  Transcript No 273 of 1992 .... 2.37

Devlin v Baslington [1994] 1 AC 142... 2.20
Dymocks Franchise Systems (NSW) Pty Ltd v Todd (Costs) [2004] UKPC 39; [2004]
  1 WLR 2807.. 2.63, 2.64, 2.67, 2.106, 8.116, 8.124

Excalibur Ventures LLC v Texas Keystone Inc.; Gulf Keystone Petroleum Ltd; Gulf Keystone
  Petroleum (UK) Ltd [2013] EWHC 2767 (Comm); EWHC 4278 (Comm)....... 2.115–2.122, 6.62–6.66, 10.10, 10.41

Factortame Limited v Secretary of State for the Environment, Transport and the Regions
  (No 2) sub nom. R (on the application of Factortame and others) v Secretary of State
  for Transport, Local Government and the Regions [2002] EWCA Civ 932, [2002]
  4 All ER 97, [2003] QB 381.. 2.43–2.53, 2.64
Factortame Limited v Secretary of State for the Environment, Transport and the Regions
  (No 8)) sub nom. R (on the application of Factortame and others) v Secretary of
  State for Transport, Local Government and the Regions [2002] EWCA Civ 932,
  [2002] 4 All ER 97 [2003] QB 381.. 2.123, 2.132
Flatman v Germany [2013] 1 WLR 2676, CA................................. 2.108–2.110

Garrett v Holton Borough Council [2007] 1 WLR 554........................ 9.67, 9.69, 9.71
Geophysical Service Centre Co v Dowell Schlumberger (ME) Inc [2013] EWHC 147
  (TCC), HT-12-168 .... 6.50, 6.55
Gibbon v Manchester City Council [2010] 1 WLR 2081 .... 8.30
Giles v Thompson [1993] UKHL 2, [1994] 1 AC 142......... 2.08, 2.10, 2.13, 2.20–2.25, 2.45, 2.46, 2.123
Globe Equities Ltd v Globe Legal Services Ltd [1999] BLR 232, CA.................... 2.37
Greene Wood McLean LLP (In Administration) v Templeton Insurance Limited
  [2010] EWHC 279, [2011] Lloyd's Rep IR 557 .... 9.85–9.87

Greenwood & Ors v Goodwin & Ors [2014] EWHC 227 (Ch) 7.05, 7.18–7.25, 7.38–7.41
Gulf Azov Shipping Co Ltd v Idisi [2004] EWCA Civ 292 . . . . 2.54–2.58
Guy Churchill (1888) 40 Ch D 481 . . . . .2.17

Hamilton v Al-Fayed [2002] CA Civ 665 . . . . .8.116
Hamilton v Al-Fayed (No 2) [2003] QB 1175. . . . . . . .2.35–2.42, 2.51, 2.55, 2.57, 2.58, 2.63, 2.76
Harcus Sinclair (a Firm) v Buttonwood Legal Capital Limited & Ors [2013]
    EWHC 1193 (Ch) 2.111–2.114, 9.27
Harold v Smith (1860) 5 H & N 381; 157 ER 1229 . . . . .8.108
Heron v TNT (UK) Limited [2013] EWCA Civ 469 . . . . 9.73, 9.75
Hill v Archbold [1968] 1 QB 686, CA 1.23, 2.87
Hodgson v Imperial Tobacco [1998] 1 WLR 1056 . . . . 2.104, 8.114, 8.115, 8.120, 8.123,
                                                                                  8.124, 8.127, 10.55
Home Office v Lownds [2002] EWCA Civ 365 . . . . 8.33, 8.37
Horrocks v Ford Motor Company Ltd, The Times, February 15, 1990 . . . . .7.22

Jefferson v National Freight Carriers Ltd [2002] EWCA Civ 365. . . . . .8.33

Kelly v Cooper [1993] AC 205, PC. 9.82
Knight v FP Special Assets Ltd (1992) 174 CLR 178. . . . . .2.63

London & Regional (St George's Court) Ltd v Ministry of Defence [2008]
    EWHC 526 (TCC). 2.68–2.72
Lownds v Home Office [2002] 1 WLR 2450. . . . . 8.32, 8.39

Martell v Consett Iron Co [1955] Ch 363, CA 2.29
Merchantbridge & Co Ltd v Safron General Partner 1 Ltd [2011] EWHC 1524 . . . . . . .2.73–2.80,
                                                                                  2.94, 2.132, 6.61
Metalloy Supplies Ltd v MA (UK) Ltd [1997] 1 WLR 1613 . . . . .2.63
Michael Phillips Architects Ltd v Riklin & Riklin [2010] EWHC 834 (TCC). 6.49
Mitchell v News Group Newspapers Ltd [2013] EWCA Civ 1537, [2013]
    6 Costs LR 1008 . . . . 8.57, 10.07
Motto v Trafigura Limited [2011] EWCA Civ 1150 . . . . .6.56
Murphy v Young & Co's Brewery plc [1997] 1 WLR 1591, CA. 2.37
Myatt v National Coal Board [2007] 1 WLR 554, [2007] EWCA Civ 307 . . . . .8.118, 8.124,
                                                                                        9.67, 9.71

Papera Traders Co Ltd v Hyundai Merchant Marine Co Ltd (The Eurasian Dream)
    (No 2) [2002] Lloyd's Rep 692, Commercial Court. 2.31–2.34, 2.123
Photo Production Ltd v Securicor Transport Ltd [1980] AC 827, HL 9.30

R v Supreme Court Office, ex p John Singh and Co [1997] 1 Costs LR 49. . . . . .8.44

Sarwar v Alam [2002] 1 WLR 1217 . . . . .9.67
Seear v Lawson (1880) 15 ChD 426 . . . . 1.08, 2.17
Sibthorpe and Morris v Southwark London Borough Council [2011]
    1 WLR 2111, CA. 2.81–2.87
Simmons v Castle [2012] EWCA Civ 1039, [2012] EWCA Civ 1288, [2013]
    1 WLR 1239. . . . . .8.13, 8.15–8.24
Simpson (Jennifer) (as assignee of Alan Catchpole) v Norfolk & Norwich University
    Hospital NHS Trust [2012] QB 640, CA 2.88–2.94
Smart v East Cheshire NHS Trust [2003] EWHC 2806 . . . . .8.51
Stocznia Gdanska SA v Latreefers Inc [2000] EWCA Civ 36, [2001] 2 BCLC 116 . . . . . 2.26–2.30
Symphony Group plc v Hodgson [1994] 179, CA. 2.37, 8.116

TGA Chapman Ltd v Christopher [1998] 1 WLR 12 ....2.63
Tinseltime Ltd v Eryl Roberts & Ors [2013] PNLR 4, [2012] EWHC 2628
 (TCC) 2.102–2.108, 2.122
Tolstoy v Aldington [1996] 1 WLR 736 .... 2.104, 8.114
Trendtex Trading Corporation & another v Credit Suisse [1980] 1 QB 629, CA 1.24, 2.06,
 2.16, 2.24, 2.45
Trepca Mines Ltd (No 2), Re [1963] Ch 199.................................. 2.06, 2.45

Willis v Nicholson [2007] EWCA Civ 199 ....8.51

INTERNATIONAL

Australia

Arundel Chiropractic Centre Pty Ltd v Deputy Comr of Taxation (2001) 179 ALR 406 .....2.63

Brookfield Multiplex Limited v International Litigation Funding Partners Pte Ltd
 (No 2) [2009] FCAFC 3.120

Campbells Cash & Carry Pty Ltd v Fostif Pty Ltd [2006] 229 CLR 386, [2006] HCA 41.......1.25,
 2.129, 3.116, 3.117, 3.118, 3.123, 10.13, 10.73

Fostif v Campbells Cash and Carry [2005] 63 NSWLR 203 ....3.118

International Litigation Partners Pte Ltd v Chameleon Mining NL (Receivers and
 Managers Appointed) [2012] HCA 45 .... 3.121, 3.122

Jeffrey & Katauskas Pty Limited v SST Consulting Pty Ltd (2009) 239 CLR 75, [2009]
 HCA 43 .... 3.119, 6.59

Kebaro [2003] FCAFC 5 ....2.63
Kirby v Centro [2008] FCA 1505..3.118

McNamara Business & Property Law v Kasmeridis (2007) 97 SASR 129............. 9.78–9.78
Mobil Oil Australia Pty Limited v Trendlen Pty Limited [2006] HCA 42 ....3.116

QPSX Limited v Ericson Australia Pty Ltd [2005] FCA 933 ....3.118

Canada

Buday v Location of Missing Heirs Inc [1993] 16 OR (3d) 2.124

Dugal v Manulife Financial Corporation [2011] ONSC 1785 (SCJ)....................3.130

E. Eddy Bayens and others v Kinross Gold Corporation and others (2013) ONSC 4974 .....3.131

Caribbean

Hugh Brown & Associates (Pty) Ltd v Kermas Limited [2011] (BVIHCV(COM)) 3.137

(1) Massai Aviation Services (2) Acrostar Limited v (1) Attorney General (2) Bahamasair
 Holdings Limited [2007] UKPC 12 ....3.135

Stiftung Salle Modulable and Rutti Stiftung v Butterfield Trust (Bermuda) Limited [2014]
 Bda LR 13...3.136

Table of Cases

Channel Islands

(The) Valetta Trust [2011] JRC 3.139, 10.57

Hong Kong

Po Yuen (To's) Machine Factory Limited, Re [2012] HKCU 816 .... 3.146

Winnie Lo v HKSAR [2011] FACC 2/2011 .... 3.144

Ireland

Thema international Fund plc v HSBC Institutional Trust Services (Ireland) Limited
    [2011] IEHC 357 .... 3.143

New Zealand

Saunders v Houghton [2010] 3 NZLR 331 .... 3.125

South Africa

PriceWaterhouseCoopers Inc and Others v National Potato Co-operative Ltd [2004]
    (6) SA 66 (SCA) 3.126

United States

Kelly, Grossman & Flanagan LLP v Quick Cash, Inc, No 04283-2011, 2012 WL
    1087341 (Suffolk Co 2012) 3.102

Leader Technologies, Inc v Facebook, Inc 719 F Supp 2d 373, 376 (D Del 2010) 3.101

Miller UK Ltd v Caterpillar, Inc, ND Ill, no 10 C 3770, 1/6/14 .... 3.103–3.105
Mondis Technology Ltd v L G Electronics Inc No 2:07-cv-565, 2011 WL 1714304,
    at *3 (ED Tex 4 May 2011) 3.101

TABLE OF LEGISLATION

TABLE OF TREATIES

EC Treaty
- Art 81 .... 2.59
- Art 82 .... 2.59

TABLE OF STATUTES

Access to Justice Act 1999 .... 2.127, 9.47
- s 27 .... 8.06
- s 28 .... 4.33, 10.24
- s 29 .... 6.14, 6.16, 8.07

Arbitration Act 1950
- s 13A 1.54
- s 41 .... 1.54

Bankruptcy Act 1869 .... 2.17
Civil Procedure Act 1997 .... 8.32
- s 6 .... 9.01

Courts and Legal Services Act 1990 ..... 2.127
- s 58 .... 2.49, 2.85, 8.04, 8.06
- s 58AA 8.78, 8.85
- s 58B 4.33, 10.24
- s 58B(3)(a) 4.33
- s 58B(4) 4.33
- s 102 .... 1.54

Criminal Law Act 1967 .... 1.23, 2.16
- s 13(1)(a) 2.15
- s 13(1)(b) 2.15
- s 14(1) 2.15
- s 14(2) 2.15
- Sch 4 .... 2.15

Financial Services and Markets Act 2000
- s 90(1)(b)(i) 7.18
- Sch 10 .... 7.18

Legal Aid, Sentencing and Punishment of Offenders Act 2012 .... 3.59, 8.08, 8.11, 8.14, 8.123
- Pt 2 .... 1.86, 3.09, 8.02
- s 44(6) 8.18, 8.22, 8.23
- s 45 .... 8.85
- s 55 .... 8.26
- s 58C(1), (2) 6.14

Legal Services Act 2007 .... 3.89, 10.20, 10.48
Senior Courts Act 1981
- s 51 .... 2.73, 5.90

Statute of Westminster I (1275)
(3 Edw. I, C25, 28, and 33) 2.14
Supreme Court Act 1981
- s 51 .... 2.36, 2.54, 2.61
Third Party (Rights Against Insurers) Act 1930 .... 6.50

TABLE OF STATUTORY INSTRUMENTS

Civil Procedure (Amendment) Rules 2000 (SI 2000/221) 7.13
Civil Procedure Rules 7.48, 8.02, 8.40
- r 1.1 .... 8.45
- rr 3.12–3.18 .... 8.55
- rr 3.12–3.19 .... 7.50
- r 3.12(1) 8.70
- r 3.12(1)(a) 1.62
- r 3.12(1)(b) 1.62, 8.56
- r 3.12(1)(c) 8.57
- r 3.13 .... 8.57
- r 3.14 .... 8.57
- r 3.15 .... 8.59, 8.69
- r 3.16 .... 8.59
- rr 3.19–3.21 .... 8.51
- PD 3E 8.55, 8.72
- rr 19.10–19.15 .... 7.14
- r 19.11 .... 7.14
- r 19.11(2) 7.17
- r 19.11(3) 7.17
- r 19.12(1) 7.17
- PD 19B 7.14
- PD 19B, para 2.1 .... 7.17
- PD 19B, para 3.1 .... 7.15
- PD 19B, para 3.3 .... 7.15
- PD 19B, para 3.5 .... 7.15
- PD 19B, para 3.6 .... 7.15
- PD 19B, para 13 .... 7.17
- Pt 23 .... 7.15
- r 25.13(2)(f) 2.63
- r 26.3(1) 8.57
- Pt 36 .... 8.25–8.30
- r 36.14(1A) 8.29
- r 36.14(3) 8.30
- r 44.3 .... 8.45

r 44.4(1) 8.45
r 44.5(3) 8.34, 8.44
rr 44.18–44.20 . . . . 8.51
r 44.18(2) 8.89
r 46.6 . . . . 7.19
r 46.6(2) 7.22
r 46.6(3) 7.22, 7.40
r 46.6(4) 7.22, 7.40
r 48.2(1)(a) 2.54
Conditional Fee Agreements Order
   2000 (SI 2000/823) 8.06
Conditional Fee Agreements
   Regulations 1995 . . . . 2.49
Conditional Fee Agreements Regulations
   2000 (SI 2000/692) 2.49, 8.06
Damages Based Agreements (DBA)
   Regulations 2013 . . . . . 8.86, 8.87, 8.125
   reg 1 . . . . 8.93
   reg 3 . . . . 8.90
   reg 4 . . . . 3.79, 8.90, 8.92, 8.94
   reg 4(2) 8.96
   reg 4(3) 8.96
   reg 4(4) 8.96, 8.97

Legal Aid, Sentencing and Punishment of
   Offenders Act 2012 (Commencement
   No. 5 and Saving Provision) Order 2013
   Art 4 . . . . 3.80
Offers to Settle in Civil Proceedings
   Order 2013 . . . . 8.26

OTHER LEGISLATION

Netherlands

Collective Settlement of Mass Claims
   Act 2005 . . . . 7.11

South Africa

Contingency Fees Act 66 of 1997 . . . . . . 3.127

INTERNATIONAL INSTRUMENTS

Convention on the Recognition and
   Enforcement of Foreign Arbitral
   Awards 1958 . . . . 3.53

LIST OF ABBREVIATIONS

ABI	Association of British Insurers
ABS	alternative business structure
AIM	Alternative Investment Market
ALF	Association of Litigation Funders
ASX	Australian Securities Exchange
ATE	after the event
BLC	Buttonwood Legal Capital Limited
BTE	before the event
CAT	Competition Appeal Tribunal
CCA	consumer credit agreement
CFA	conditional fee agreement
CJC	Civil Justice Council
CJ	Lord Chief Justice
CLSA	Courts and Legal Services Act 1990
CMC	claims management company
CPR	Civil Procedure Rules
DBA	damages based agreement
DIFC	Dubai International Financial Centre
FSMA	Financial Services and Markets Act
GLO	group litigation order
GWM	Greene Wood McLean
HH	Her Highness's
IP	intellectual property
IPO	initial public offering
J	judge
JA	judge of appeal
LASPO	Legal Aid, Sentencing and Punishment of Offenders Act
LFA	litigation funding agreement
LJ(J)	Lord Justice(s)
LLC	Limited Liability Company
MOD	Ministry of Defence
MPC	Managers and Processors of Claims Ltd
MR	Master of the Rolls
MRSA	meticillin-resistant staphylococcus aureusis
PD	Practice Direction
PR	Practice Rule

List of Abbreviations

PSC	President of the Supreme Court
QC	Queen's Counsel
QFC	Qatar Financial Centre
RBS	Royal Bank of Scotland
SRA	Solicitors Regulation Authority
TCC	Technology and Construction Court
TPF	third party funding
V-C	Vice-Chancellor

1

INTRODUCTION AND BACKGROUND

A. Introduction and Background	1.01	E. What Type of Case can be Funded?	1.45
B. What is Litigation Funding?	1.18	F. Why is the Use of Third Party Litigation Funding Increasing?	1.56
C. History	1.23		
D. How does it Work?	1.28	G. The Effect of the Jackson Reforms	1.86

A. Introduction and Background

1.01 The question of how to fund any litigation is not a new one. Litigation has always been expensive and the cost has always been an important consideration for any potential litigant. In many situations the cost is prohibitive and the action is never commenced. In some of these cases, a valid and meritorious claim may never be pursued simply because of the cost.

1.02 Risk is an equally important factor in the decision making process of whether to embark on litigation. There are those who can afford to run a claim, but choose not to risk their money. They do not wish to throw good money after bad, or they simply have other things they prefer to spend their funds on. There are also, of course, those who cannot afford to run a claim at all, and their decision has historically been made for them.

1.03 These two very rudimentary factors of cost and risk are the two most often cited by potential litigants as having been critical in a decision to look for an alternative method of financing a case.

1.04 Third party litigation funding is a relatively new phenomenon in the contentious world; however, its use is very much on the rise. Whilst it cannot yet be regarded as commonplace across all litigation, there are certain areas where it is very much part of the fabric.

1.05 This rapid ascent from an industry peculiarity, which is confined to overseas jurisdictions and limited to certain practice areas, to the mainstream of litigation practice is something that has forced litigators to make it their business to understand third party litigation funding.

1.06 In this book we shall concentrate on the commercial world, which is where the majority of litigation funding takes place. Whilst a lot of what we shall discuss applies equally to civil and consumer litigation, mainstream third party litigation funding operates (save for perhaps some very high value professional negligence actions for individuals) almost entirely in the commercial sector and funds commercial cases. (When we refer to 'commercial cases' we do so in a broad sense, not being confined simply to the work of the Commercial Court. Much funded litigation is conducted in the Chancery Division, or Mercantile Courts.)

1.07 Funding is a relatively new phenomenon on the legal landscape in England. However, with the endorsement from Sir Rupert Jackson[1] and the increase in the number of funders, its use is increasing and litigators need to be fully acquainted with its implications, and to understand the changes it is bringing to the market. This is so whether advising prospective claimants, the viability of whose litigation might depend upon obtaining funding, or advising parties against whom funded claims are to be brought. In this chapter we shall put into context the use of funding in England and Wales today, including a short overview of other funding options, and explain why this book is important to today's litigator.

1.08 We shall then look at the history and background, including the legitimacy and restrictions, of third party litigation funding and follow its development and growth over the years from a seldom mentioned oddity to a very significant element of commercial litigation in the English legal system today. In explaining from where the use of funding derived, we consider funding from its beginnings in the nineteenth century in *Seear v Lawson*[2] right up to the modern day, including the case of *Arkin*[3] and beyond. We consider in detail the ongoing issues of champerty and maintenance. As well as examining historic developments, this book aims to provide a clear understanding of what is and is not permitted and what the practitioner should be looking out for when considering litigation funding.

1.09 Chapter 3, 'Use of Funding', including the international landscape, deals with how funding is actually exploited by claimants and practitioners in its full range of applications, including international arbitration and smaller value claims. We examine where it is potentially helpful, and consider a range of scenarios including the types of cases suitable for funding, and where it can be used successfully. This chapter also provides an overview of the international funding market, paying particular attention to the United States and the real birthplace of litigation funding—Australia.

---

[1] Rupert Jackson LJ, *Review of Civil Litigation Costs: Final Report*, 9 December 2009, Ch 11.
[2] *Seear v Lawson* (1880) 15 Ch D 426.
[3] *Arkin v Borchard Lines* [2005] EWCA Civ 655.

Introduction and Background

1.10 Chapter 4 is concerned with Funder Models, examining the many forms of third party funder entities and options available to solicitors and their clients including: venture capital, family office, listed funders, hedge funds, one-off funders, and private individuals. The characteristics of each are discussed, together with the merits and disadvantages of all funding options available.

1.11 The Funding Process is considered in Chapter 5 which deals with the A–Z of arranging funding. We look at a typical funding process, aiming to make practical suggestions with a view to maximizing the prospects of achieving funding. We consider how best to prepare a funding request, how to choose a funder, and what to look out for, as well as presenting a sample funding agreement in the appendices. All too often funding applications are delayed, and some fail, because there has been insufficient attention paid to assembly and persuasive presentation, of the material which enables a funder, or any independent adviser whom it consults, to form an adequate, let alone, favourable view of the case. Topics addressed in this chapter include budgeting and strategy, indicative terms, exclusivity arrangements, term sheets, due diligence (and the function of independent counsel), and after the event legal expenses insurance.

1.12 In Chapter 6 we consider what solicitors need to address concerning costs and insurance. A full market assessment of the options available is provided addressing insurance versus no insurance, upfront premium, no premium, fully deferred premium, bonds and deeds of guarantee, including the key characteristics of each option. We also look at the duties of solicitors when funding is being, or should be, considered, the merits and issues of the various options, who pays the costs of setting up the funding, after the event policies, general protection against adverse costs, and negotiation with providers.

1.13 The Jackson reforms have had a huge impact on the litigation landscape in England. Chapter 7 examines the impact of Jackson and provides a detailed assessment of damages based agreements ('DBAs').

1.14 Recent cases, particularly including actions by shareholders against major banks, and aggrieved investors looking to obtain compensation in relation to failed investment schemes, have been brought with the aid of third party funding. In Chapter 8 we consider the use of third party funding in group actions and the necessity for group litigation orders.

1.15 Chapter 9, 'Professional Obligations', looks at all aspects of a solicitor's professional and regulatory obligations as regards funding options. As well as containing a thorough outline of the obligations, this chapter seeks to offer practical help and advice to avoid pitfalls, particularly in negotiations with clients, funders, and brokers.

1.16 Without question, funding is here to stay but it will face many challenges including whether it should be subject to voluntary regulation as against self-regulation, and the degree to which it becomes an indispensable part of the litigator's toolbox. We believe that consolidation will be a feature of the future litigation funding market, with fewer but larger players competing with non-traditional funders and facing competition direct from law firms. The final chapter, Chapter 10 ('Funding and the Future') assesses what the future may hold for third party litigation funding.

1.17 Before that, we shall look at some of the fundamentals of third party litigation funding, what it is, how it works and why it has become a necessity for litigators to be familiar with the industry.

B. What is Litigation Funding?

1.18 What is third party finance of litigation? Simply put, litigation funding, or third party funding, is the process whereby an entity, a 'funder', that has no direct interest in a piece of litigation, pays the legal fees for one of the parties. For reasons that will become clear later in this book, the party that is funded is, in almost every case, the party bringing the action.

1.19 In return for the payment of the party's legal fees, the funder receives a return on their investment. In the most common form of litigation funding, the return received is conditional on the success of the case and is paid to the funder from the proceeds of the action.

1.20 It is usual for the return on the funder's investment to be a multiple of the amount which they advanced, or a percentage of the proceeds. It may be a combination of these methods or some other calculation made with reference to the risk involved, the amount of money at stake or the time the money is at risk. Even at this early stage in the development of the funding market, it is obvious that very great flexibility exists in terms of funding models. Over time, it is to be anticipated that the market will respond to client demand by developing an ever greater range of options for funding methods and terms.

1.21 Most litigation funding models used in commercial cases are on a non-recourse basis, so that the amount that is advanced or borrowed is only repayable if the case is successful and an award of damages is received, and paid. This is a significant advantage to any borrower or would-be litigant and obviously, a major distinguishing factor when this type of funding is compared to any other sort of finance or borrowing that could be used to fund litigation. As the investment made by a third party funder is on a non-recourse basis and is potentially a high risk investment, the return that a funder seeks on their investment is going to be high, and proportionate to the perceived risk. Most mainstream third party funders would expect a minimum of three times their money by way of return; some may expect a higher return than that. The reason for this, other than the high risk, is that all mainstream funders operate a portfolio of investments, a range of cases that they have invested in. The portfolio approach allows a funder to set off the losses which will inevitably be incurred, given the nature of the investment, against the high returns on winning cases. For this reason the winning cases have to provide a sufficiently high return to absorb the losses and then make a profit across the entire scheme or business.

1.22 There are a number of different sorts of funding model and we shall review a number of them in Chapter 4. The most common in the commercial litigation and arbitration world is the one described in paragraph 1.19.

C. History

1.23 Litigation funding is a relatively new phenomenon for the majority of litigators and arbitrators in England and Wales. Historically its development was seriously restricted. Legal policy was hostile to both maintenance and champerty. A person was guilty of maintenance if he supported 'litigation in which he has no legitimate concern without just cause and excuse'.[4] Both were crimes and torts at common law, and under statute. Champerty, explained Lord Denning MR in *Trendtex Trading Corporation & another v Credit Suisse*,[5] was a 'particularly obnoxious form of [maintenance]. It exists where the maintainer seek to make a profit out of another man's action—by taking the proceeds of it, or part of them, for himself.'[6] The Criminal Law Act 1967 abolished the common law torts of maintenance and champerty, but legal policy remained, in principle, hostile to both maintenance and champerty. However, both before and after the enactment of the 1967 Act, legal policy developed, by stages, so as to accommodate certain arrangements whereby genuine claims would not be stifled by reason of want of means to litigate.

1.24 The litigation funding industry has developed with most pace in Australia. Unsurprisingly, the duties of any liquidator or other insolvency office holder in Australia are broadly similar to those of their equivalent in England. They are required to maximize the assets available to the creditors. If the main asset is a piece of litigation, which is either under way, or still to be commenced, then there is a duty to examine the financial benefit to the insolvent company and to its creditors of continuing with or issuing the claim in order to realize the financial award.

---

[4] See per Lord Denning MR in *Hill v Archbold* [1968] 1 QB 686, CA, at 694. However, as Lord Denning recognized in his judgment, there were ill-defined exceptions, and the law had developed significantly over the years; see pp 693–6. Danckwerts and Winn LJJ both delivered concurring judgments, in which they expressed full agreement with Lord Denning.

[5] [1980] 1 QB 629, CA, at 654. The Court of Appeal's decision was unsuccessfully appealed to the House of Lords, [1982] AC 679. In his speech, Lord Wilberforce (at 694) paid acknowledged indebtedness to the Court of Appeal judgments for their examination in depth of the English law of maintenance and champerty, describing them as 'this still obscure subject'.

[6] See his judgment in *Trendtex Trading Corporation & another v Credit Suisse* [1980] 1 QB 629, CA, at 654.

1.25 Despite the generally held view that litigation funding started in Australia, it was actually first used in England. However, until recently, the Australian market has grown faster and with greater speed than in England and Wales. That market is far more mature than its English equivalent. The Australian courts have made a number of important decisions, particularly the *Fostif*[7] decision, which was a watershed for funders in Australia.

1.26 The case, which is looked at more fully in Chapter 3, was decided by Australia's High Court. The court held, by a majority of 5 to 2, that litigation funding was not an abuse of process and that litigation funding agreements were enforceable notwithstanding the facts that the lawyers in the case were retained by the funder and not the client, and that the funder could even settle the case without reference to the client.

1.27 This was a significant decision for the Australian market allowing funders practically to take control of, and run, the litigation. The English funding market has not developed to that extent, nor has it disposed of the torts of maintenance and champerty.

D. How does it Work?

1.28 Litigation funding can take many forms as has been stated earlier. We review the various different funding options and litigation funding arrangements later in the book. There are a number of methods and schemes which have been developed over the years. However the purest, and most common form, of third party funding is where a claimant pursuing a commercial litigation action receives a non-recourse loan facility to be drawn upon for the purposes of paying the legal bills in the case.

1.29 In such a typical case, the client (almost invariably the claimant), enters into a contractual arrangement with a funder at the very start of the case using a Litigation Funding Agreement. (Funding is, however, often sought and provided at different stages in litigation.) This contract is designed to govern the way the conduct of the funding process is to work, and usually includes reference to some standard matters:

(a) The lawyers involved in running the case (including counsel) are generally parties to the agreement, and if not then they are defined as the appointed legal representatives.
(b) The amount of the facility needed to fund the litigation is a key element. The lawyers and client agree the extent of the budget needed, and on what the funds are to be expended.

---

[7] *Campbells Cash & Carry Pty Ltd v Fostif Pty Ltd* [2006] 229 CLR 386.

(c) The definition of success is recorded. Whilst the funding loan is almost always on a non-recourse basis in the event that the case is not successful, if the case is won, the funds are repayable, in most circumstances, and depending upon the level of success. It is clearly important for there to be clarity as to what amounts to success, and the circumstances in which the funder is entitled to be repaid their loan with a return on their investment.
(d) The funder's success fee is defined so that everybody is aware of what is to be repaid to the funder on a successful outcome.
(e) There are provisions as to when and how the agreement can be terminated by either of the parties.

1.30 Once the agreement has been concluded and the case is under way the litigation proceeds as it would in any case, funded or otherwise. The solicitors run the case, counsel is used as and when appropriate, and instructions are given by the client to the lawyers.

1.31 There are, of course, certain differences between funded litigation and other cases. Quite obviously, a fundamental difference is that in a funded case each month the legal bill raised by the client's solicitors is paid by the funder rather than the client. Some funders deposit the full amount of the facility into the solicitors' client account once the funding agreement is signed; others pay on a monthly or other regular drawdown request. Either way, the whole essence of the arrangement is that the funder pays the legal bills.

1.32 One of the key areas of funded cases which is often misunderstood is the extent to which the funder can influence the decision making process in a case. For example, it is regularly suggested that if a client decides to make use of funding, then they will lose control of the key decisions in the action. This is simply not the case in traditional third party funded litigation in England and Wales. It cannot be. As we shall see when we look at the history and development of the subject matter in Chapter 2, there are historic and more contemporary legal and public policy reasons for this. Litigation funding has a long history, from the ancient Greeks and medieval England via twentieth-century Australia. However, its use in modern day litigation in England is tolerated as it provides 'access to justice'.

1.33 As explained in paragraph 1.23, whilst the historic ancient crimes and torts of maintenance and champerty have been abolished, the public policy which lay behind them, and which continues to inform the law, has survived though in an ever developing form. If a funder in England were de facto, to take over conduct of a piece of litigation, seeking to impose directly its instructions to the lawyers in a case, then that could well be held to go beyond permissible bounds. It might well result in a finding that the arrangement between the funder and the client was in fact champertous being contrary to public policy, whereas usually normal third party funding arrangements are acceptable. This fear was expressly recognized in Sir Rupert Jackson's Preliminary Report, at paragraph 15.3.2.

1.34 A third party litigation funder cannot impose their will on a client. They cannot have the final decision making authority which remains with the client. The relationship between the solicitor and the client does not change, although under the terms of a funding agreement, the client's solicitors will usually be required to report regularly on developments and progress to the funder. Some funders will take a keen interest in such matters, which is to be expected since the funder is often making a substantial investment in the litigation.

1.35 The author's experience, personal and anecdotal, is that in most funded cases the solicitors and clients are happy to allow the funder to be involved in the regular client updates on the case. Similar experience is that many clients and their legal advisers welcome the contribution made by a funder's representatives who can sometimes introduce additional experience, perceptions, knowledge, and assessments.

1.36 The client will be bound by the funding agreement to cooperate fully with the funder's requests for information. Additionally, the agreement usually allows the funder to be notified of all offers received and to have the choice of whether to be present at any appropriate meetings, for example, consultations with leading counsel, strategy discussions, or mediations.

1.37 In usual circumstances these matters will have been discussed at the outset. One factor that a funder will consider, when deciding whether or not to fund a case, is the strategy that is proposed to be employed to win the case. This strategy forms part of the case assessment that the funder carries out.

1.38 In addition to other due diligence, the funder will assess the proposed client and how they behave, what motivates him/them, what they are looking to gain or obtain from the litigation, and most importantly the funder considers whether they feel 'comfortable' with the prospective client and his case. Given that the funder is likely to be making a sizeable investment, and that the funder cannot control the client's decision on whether to accept or reject an offer or whether to plough on to trial, then the funder needs to be satisfied that the client is likely to make a sensible commercial decision based upon the facts of the case, the merits and any offer made.

1.39 A litigation funder's position is not dissimilar to that of an after the event (ATE) legal expenses insurer. Indeed, the funder's process of assessment of the case is very much the same as the ATE insurer's. They both review the merits, look at the quantum, and decide if the proposed budget for the case (whether their own side's costs budget or the proposed cover for the opponent's costs) can be justified in the light of their own assessment of the likely award. Additionally, it is very normal practice during the course of a case for an ATE insurer to receive regular case updates as to progress, and to be invited to attend conferences with counsel and mediations.

1.40 In short, therefore, a funder will be kept up to date throughout the course of the case by way of regular meetings and discussions with the client and the lawyers instructed. As and when a decision is required over a strategic step or whether to make or accept an offer the funder will be consulted, but the client will always have the final decision and give the instructions to the legal team. The funder is an interested observer in much the same way as a legal expenses insurer.

1.41 There are two occasions when a funder may become involved in the case in material fashion: first, if there are settlement negotiations and the client, lawyers, and the funder have agreed that the funder should be involved in any settlement discussions, and if so to what extent; and secondly, if the merits of the case have deteriorated and the funder decides that it wishes to terminate the funding agreement. In this situation the process is governed by the Association of Litigation Funders' (ALF) Code of Conduct, if the funder is a member of the ALF. This is discussed in detail in Chapter 9.

1.42 When the case has concluded, either at trial or by settlement, and as long as the award is sufficient the funds are distributed in accordance with previously agreed ratios as recorded in the funding agreement.

1.43 In the event that there are insufficient or less than the anticipated amount of damages available at the conclusion of the case, the sums actually available are distributed in accordance with the priorities agreement established at the outset, either within the funding agreement or by a separate deed of priorities. This document sets out the ranking of the various parties upon division of a sum which is insufficient to give the parties concerned what they had hoped to achieve financially with a successful outcome. In a situation where there is a 'drop hands' settlement, or a payment of a nominal amount or a nuisance payment, it is often the case that there is only sufficient to repay the funder's initial investment, and on occasions even that amount will not be recovered. Others whose interests rank behind the funder's will recover nothing.

1.44 If the claim fails, whether at trial, or by withdrawal because it is discontinued following an adverse reassessment of its prospects, then the litigation funder 'walks away' and writes off their investment.

E. What Type of Case can be Funded?

1.45 It is very clear that litigation funding in its usual format is not suitable for every case. In this book we concentrate on commercial litigation and commercial clients rather than on consumer litigation. Currently, to the vast majority of cases that are issued in the courts of England and Wales, litigation funding is irrelevant. Its reach is expected to widen and deepen, however, as the litigation community learns more of its application and uses, and as different schemes develop which are suitable for smaller value cases. This is something which is already happening and, additionally, the pressures of cash flow and tightening of legal budgets has meant that law firms and clients are looking for ways to make their legal budget go further.

1.46 Civil and commercial litigation cases in the county court system and the lower value cases in the High Court are not of sufficiently high quantum to justify the use of mainstream third party litigation funding. More importantly, on their own, those individual cases would be of no interest to mainstream commercial third party litigation funders. Whilst there are other schemes available, some of which we shall look at in Chapter 4, that are specifically designed for lower value cases or a combination or 'basket' of lower value cases, most of what we shall consider in this work relates to higher value one-off cases.

1.47 A critical consideration in this connection is the amount that a funder requires in return for their high risk investment. Invariably the return is as stated previously, either a multiple of the facility provided or funds invested, or a percentage of the award, or both. Something that is well known to all litigators practising in England is that it often costs a similar amount of money to fight a case for £1m in value as it does to fight a case for £3m. However, a funder will be acutely aware that in a £1m case there is unlikely to be enough money available with a successful outcome to ensure that the funder receives the return they will expect or need and for there still to be sufficient damages left for the client to feel that the process was worthwhile and financially rewarding. The budgets are very similar. Accordingly, in relatively modest or low value cases, there is unlikely to be a sufficient recovery for the funder to be repaid their investment, then paid a success fee for taking the risk, whilst also leaving enough for the client to remain incentivized in the process, or satisfied that it was a worthwhile exercise and use of their time.

1.48 In most cases a litigation funder would look to ensure that the ratio of likely quantum of damages to the budget is a minimum of one to four, with most looking at a more likely ratio of one to ten. If the budget to trial for a proposed case is £1m then the likely quantum needs to be a minimum of £10m for a funder to be satisfied that it is a case to fund. Again, this is not a strict rule, but it is, in the author's experience, an industry norm.

1.49 Whilst most funded cases are high value, that alone does not mean that a case satisfies a funder's criteria. Indeed, there are some cases concerning very high values and subject matters which are not fit for the purposes of funding. For a case to be suitable for and likely to benefit from litigation funding, it needs to have an outcome which will result in the payment of money to the winning claimant. By the very nature of the arrangement, a funder wants to be repaid at the end of the case with a return on the investment, from the proceeds of the case.

1.50 For this reason, claims for declaratory relief or specific performance are unlikely to be attractive to a third party funder. That does not mean that a funder would never look at any case which is not a straightforward claim for damages, indeed some funders are more flexible than others and as long as an arrangement can be made that provides for the repayment of the advance and the return in short order or security for its payment is provided, then it may be possible to fund a case that does not perfectly satisfy the normal criteria.

1.51 Taking these matters into account, the most likely cases to be accepted for funding by a litigation funder are commercial disputes where it is likely that a financial award is to be expected. But funders do not just look at the value of the likely award. They will pay close attention to, and carry out careful due diligence on, the likelihood that the proposed defendant can satisfy any financial award, whether damages, debt, equitable compensation, or costs. Pyrrhic victories are not something that litigation funders are very keen on, so a defendant who cannot pay a judgment made against them is unlikely to be a defendant in a funded case. Quite obviously, that assessment should be carried out, in any event by any lawyer who is proposing to act for a client in any piece of litigation before embarking on litigation and incurring costs. But, given the size of the cases that most funders consider, the necessity for this examination and due diligence, by the funder, is of great importance.

1.52 It is for this reason that funders look with interest at cases where the proposed defendant is likely to have the benefit of professional indemnity insurance. This term is used in a wider than conventional sense, and so it will include cases against directors and senior corporate executives, because it is commonly the case that such persons have the benefit of indemnity cover. In recent times there has been a number of third party funders particularly interested in funding professional negligence and liability claims, whether against solicitors, accountants, valuers and surveyors, or directors. The availability of the indemnity insurance that covers claims against such professionals means that, subject to matters which may lead to a denial of cover, there is unlikely to be a difficulty regarding satisfaction of any judgment or award or the ability of the defendant to make payment.

1.53 Funders look for cases that will produce a result that enables them to be paid back as swiftly as possible. The funding world is predicated on an investment in the right case producing a healthy return on investment in the shortest time possible, in order to show a very successful return on funds deployed. In other words, a quick result with a good return is the perfect case for a funder.

1.54 From this it follows that litigation funders are not attracted to cases which give rise to doubtful legal issues which will make the outcome of a case particularly uncertain, with the added disadvantage of a likelihood of an appeal or appeals, with consequent delay and expense. A case that it will take many years to conclude is, therefore, not likely to interest a funder unless they can be compensated by reference to a corresponding increase in return. Even then it is not the funder's preferred kind of investment. For this reason the world of international arbitration divides opinion among the funding community. In arbitration matters, whether an investment treaty case or otherwise, the level of damages sought by the party bringing the case tends to be of a very high level and often of the order of many millions of pounds. It is no surprise that these levels of quantum would be attractive to funders. The third party funding option is often attractive to clients bringing an arbitration claim as the legal budget for such cases can be extremely high and run into several million pounds. Accordingly, third party litigation funding and arbitration cases are reasonably well suited. However, there is at least one negative factor for funders in such cases, namely the length of time those cases take to conclude. Whilst arbitration is supposedly a quicker route to resolving a dispute, and indeed it may once have been, it certainly is not always so now,[8] in comparison to a case issued in the High Court in London.

1.55 In conclusion, third party litigation funders look for three specific elements when they decide upon whether or not a case is one that they would like to fund. First, will a successful outcome in the case produce a monetary payment? Secondly, is the legal budget one which is sufficiently proportionate in size to the amount of damages likely to be awarded? Thirdly, can the defendant pay the damages which are likely to be awarded? In practice, many funders will consider these questions in reverse order, because unless there is likely to be a fund from which recovery can be effected, and cost is proportionate to the risk undertaken and the likely reward, the merits of the case could not justify investigation, let alone an investment.

F. Why is the Use of Third Party Litigation Funding Increasing?

1.56 The rise of litigation funding in the last few years is the result of a number of different factors, including the fact of its widespread availability, and also the general non-availability of public funding. However, people and organizations that make use of litigation funding fall into two categories: users of funding by choice, and users of funding by necessity. Litigation is expensive and risky and if third party litigation funding can mitigate that risk, whether a claimant

---

[8] Delay in arbitral proceedings was recognized as a problem by the courts as long ago as the late 1970s; see the observations in judgments in the Court of Appeal, and speeches in the House of Lords in *Bremer Vulkan Schiffbau un Maschinenfabrik v South India Shipping Corporation Ltd* [1981] AC 909. The particular problem highlighted in that case was the absence of a power in an arbitrator to dismiss for want for prosecution, contrary to the position in litigation in the courts. That particular problem was addressed by the insertion (by s 102 of the Courts and Legal Services Act 1990) of s 13A of the Arbitration Act 1950, now s 41 of the Arbitration Act 1996. Matters of concern affecting arbitral delay today are more likely to be issues in connection with the challenge to the agreement, disputes as to appointments, coordinating availability of the tribunal especially where there is more than one arbitrator, and disputes as to enforcement of the award. Such considerations will, of course, be entirely absent in the case of many commercial arbitrations.

is pecunious or impecunious, it is something that any litigant should consider. Litigation funding comes at a cost, represented by the deduction from any recovery that the funder makes. In exchange for incurring that cost, however, the client lays off the risk of expending his own funds in pursuing the claim, and exposure to his opponent's costs.

It would be very unusual for a party to litigation to be ignorant of the risks involved. Even the most regular or serial litigators, large entities with many matters running at one time, are acutely aware of the potential pitfalls and financial exposure assumed in fighting a case in the English legal system. **1.57**

The majority of litigants are averse to the risks that are present and are keen to protect themselves against such risks; to do otherwise would be reckless or foolish. This aversion to the risk, and not merely inability to fund, is one reason that litigation funding is on the increase. An increasing general awareness of the ability to use third party funding and how it may protect a claimant is something that is changing people's attitudes. The latest version of the Solicitors Code of Conduct 2011, released in April 2014, specifically requires solicitors to provide clients with information that they need to make informed decisions about the services they require, how they will be delivered, and at what cost. Specifically, in relation to Outcomes, the Code requires that clients be informed about services that they need, and options available to them. In relation to Indicative Behaviours the Code provides that solicitors should discuss how the client will pay, including whether public funding may be available, whether the client has insurance that might cover the fees, and whether the fees may be paid by someone else. The previous Code of Conduct, in 2007, contained similar provisions.[9] It has been suggested, in the light of these requirements, that solicitors may be under a duty to disclose funding options.[10] **1.58**

Solicitors are not required to recommend any particular funding option, but it would be likely to amount not merely to professional negligence, and a breach of professional duty, but also a breach of fiduciary duty,[11] if a solicitor were for reasons of his own interest to fail to mention relevant options available to a client; but the client has to be given enough information to make a choice. The obligation to discuss funding options exists even in respect of options which the solicitors firm concerned may not be prepared to offer itself. It would not be a good reason for a solicitor to refrain from mentioning an option simply because his firm does not like it, or offer it. **1.59**

There has been a significant increase in the general awareness, by solicitors, of the funding options available to clients. The availability of a whole range of funding options has **1.60**

---

[9] IB 1.16 SRA Code of Conduct 2011, Rules 2.03(1) (d)(ii) & (g) SRA Code of Conduct 2007.
[10] See the article by John Hyde in the Law Society's *Gazette* of 10 May 2012 'Solicitors have "duty" to disclose funding options', in which this issue is discussed.
[11] This is because a fiduciary must not prefer his own interests over those of his client; see the discussion of this topic in the judgment of Millett LJ, as he then was, in *Bristol & West BS v Mothew* [1998] Ch 1, at 16–19.

been promoted particularly since the coming into force of the Jackson reforms, not merely by funders, but in the legal press and many widely publicized lectures and seminars organized by leading legal training organizations. However, there is still a sizeable sector of the profession which is slow to embrace it as an option and to explain its availability to clients. The necessity to advise clients on the funding options, and, whilst the evidence is only anecdotal, particularly the availability of legal expenses insurance has supposedly seen a rise in potential claims against solicitors from aggrieved clients who have discovered, after the event, that they could have benefited from cover in relation to their adverse costs liability and possibly not have had to pay their legal bills.

1.61 Independently of solicitors raising the issue of funding options, there has been an increase in the sophistication of many, especially commercial and corporate, clients, when purchasing legal services, in their awareness and understanding that there are several options available to them. They are likely to raise the subject even if their legal advisers do not.

1.62 Over many decades the cost of litigation has continued to increase. At the time of writing, it is too early to make an assessment as to whether the changes made to the Civil Procedure Rules in April 2013, including as to costs budgeting, introduced pursuant to the Jackson Final Report, actually have an impact upon this apparently unstoppable tendency. (The author doubts that the impact on costs will be significant in relation to most cases suitable for litigation funding because pursuant to CPR 3.12(1)(a), the costs management provisions of the Rules do not apply to cases in the Admiralty and Commercial Courts, unless the court otherwise orders. Similarly, pursuant to CPR 3.12(1)(b), the Chancellor of the High Court, and the President of the Queen's Bench Division, directed respectively on 18 February 2013, that (i) in the Chancery Division, and (ii) the Technology and Construction Courts, and the Mercantile Courts, costs management would not apply to cases where at the date of the first case management conference the sums in dispute exceed £2,000,000, excluding interests and costs, except where the court so orders.)[12] Whilst the world of commerce and industry has struggled with deep recession over recent years, the hourly rates charged by most of the top London, and provincial, firms has increased. London has succeeded in establishing itself as the litigation capital of the world. The Rolls Building and the Royal Courts of Justice are the venue of choice for many litigants in the highest value, most expensive, most complex, and highest profile cases in the world. The expertise of the judiciary in these courts is undoubtedly a dominant consideration, but so is the high quality of counsel and solicitors representing parties in such cases. This increased demand for

---

[12] The 72nd Update to the CPR came into force on 22 April 2014. This limited the costs budgeting provisions to Part 7 Multi-track claims except where the claim is valued at £10m or more. In other types of case the court will have the discretion to implement costs management and parties will be able to apply for costs management if it is deemed appropriate by the circumstances of the individual case.

the highest quality legal services, combined with a relatively inelastic supply of them, has contributed to rising costs.

1.63 This costs pressure, for clients own fees and the consequent risks of adverse costs, under the costs shifting principles of English law, means that the budgets for running high value cases are substantial. Inevitably it is likely to remain the case that many large corporate entities that can afford to fund their own litigation, with all attendant costs risks, will continue to do so, because they consider that the costs associated with litigation funding outweigh the benefits of laying off risk. In 2009, at the time of his Preliminary Report, Sir Rupert Jackson noted (at Chapter 15, paragraph 2.8) that in the Commercial Court, use of funding was 'still very rare', citing research by Ipsos MORI, that 74 per cent of FTSE 350 businesses were 'fairly unlikely' or 'very unlikely' to use it. However, he cited evidence that it was becoming more common. In his Final Report (at Chapter 11, paragraph 1.2) he expressed the view that it would become 'even more important as a means of financing litigation if success fees under CFAs become irrecoverable'. It is equally inevitable that many litigants, even in very substantial cases, including insolvency office holders, do not have funds to embark on litigation, however meritorious their claims may be. Between these two extremes, it is likely that some substantial prospective claimants, well able to afford the risks of litigation, will prefer to pursue claims with funding, and accept the cost of doing so, in order not merely to lay off risk, but so as to avoid tying up capital.

1.64 The inability to adhere to the budget estimate given at the outset of a case is often cited as a reason for complaint by clients. In defence of the lawyers giving those estimates, litigation is not an exact science and a budget is only as good as the assumptions upon which it is based. They are the key. If the assumptions need to be amended, then of course the budget will change. It rarely reduces, but the increases are acceptable if they are based on sensible changes to the assumptions which have a consequential effect of increasing the budget.

1.65 The state of the economy has led to a change in attitude over legal spending. Many large organizations have cut their legal budgets substantially and are not embarking on litigation other than out of necessity. Whilst this attitude is changing with an upturn in the state of the economy, the choice as to whether to spend money or not remains.

1.66 Cash flow will always be the lifeblood of a business. For any business to choose to use that important resource to fund litigation is a difficult decision. Litigation is a risky and unwanted distraction for any business. It is a process that most wish to avoid. Occasionally though, litigation is the only choice if a difficult customer or client is to be forced to pay what is due, or a supplier is to be compelled to compensate the business for losses it has caused.

1.67 If litigation is the route that is chosen, then a prudent claimant will wish to consider all available means of protecting the business against the potential financial risks that the business may be exposed to during the process. This will involve a discussion over the various methods of funding the case. In addition to the need to pay their own lawyers (even if it is a proportion of the fees, rather than all of them, under some form of discounted or hybrid CFA) the claimants will need to consider the risk of having to pay the opponent's costs, should the case not go as planned.

1.68 The most effective method of insulating the business against these risks is to consider the use of third party funding combined with an ATE policy. With the use of third party litigation funding, the funder pays the legal fees as they are incurred throughout the case. The purchase of an ATE policy with an adequate limit of indemnity will protect a claimant against paying most if not all of a defendant's legal costs, should the case be unsuccessful.

1.69 Litigation funding is not the only solution. The lawyers may be able to work on a full CFA, where no fee is due to them unless they are successful and then they are paid only at the end of the case. Some claimants may take the view that it is not a cheap solution either. The funder will require a percentage of the proceeds of the case or a multiple of their investment—the claimant may receive only 60 to 70% of the damages due. The premium payable for the ATE policy could be considered expensive, particularly as the premium will also be payable from the damages.

1.70 Litigation funding is an attractive proposition, financially at least. Admittedly, financial reasons are not the only driver in making a decision over whether to litigate. However, from a financial perspective it is easy to see why the litigation funding argument is attractive to that sort of client and why it is being used in more cases.

1.71 Another reason for growth in the use of funding is that it is enabling the investigation and bringing of cases that previously were unlikely to be viable. This is so particularly in relation to group litigation[13] where very large numbers of prospective claimants have individually suffered losses as a result of alleged connected wrongdoing by a single prospective defendant, or group of prospective defendants. Since each prospective claimant's claim is relatively small in relation to the very considerable costs of pursuing it, it is likely that such claims would not be brought without some form of litigation funding.

1.72 A large number of clients have become less willing to accept a standard retainer and are increasingly looking for their lawyers to offer something different. The general awareness among commercial clients that there are risk based retainers that may provide a better option for them has meant that more and more claimants are enquiring what the alternatives are to the standard retainer. There will always be those clients who have the necessary resources to pay their lawyers to do the job needed at the normal hourly rate that prevails, but not every lawyer is in the comfortable position of having clients that both can do that and are prepared to do so. Solicitors are required to explain that there are other funding options available, even if that particular firm is not prepared to offer an alternative form of retainer.

---

[13] As early as 2009, Sir Rupert Jackson noted in his Preliminary Report at Ch 15, para 2.14 that the use of third party funding was growing in group actions.

1.73 Of course there are many alternatives today to hourly based billing. These include risk based retainers such as conditional fee agreements, hybrid or discounted conditional fee agreements, and damages based agreements. Clients are increasingly aware of the ability for them to enter into retainers providing that their lawyers be paid some or all of their fee contingent on success. The reduced financial commitment throughout the case is an obvious attraction for the client. Alternatives to risk based retainers are fixed fees, discounted rates, or a standard hourly based retainer.

1.74 Third party litigation funding can be combined with any of these retainers. Whilst litigation funding is most commonly used with a discounted rate conditional fee agreement (often called 'hybrid CFA' or 'a no win—some fee agreement') it is rarely a condition of funding that the lawyers work on some form of contingent based retainer. However, when a litigation funder is assessing a case for funding, the willingness of the law firm to take some risk on the case is often an advantage. A funder may well consider that to be a positive factor—albeit it will not be decisive. It is not at all uncommon for solicitors to accept a risk element in respect of remuneration, but for counsel in the same case to be remunerated on the traditional basis that their fees are payable irrespective of outcome. Litigation funding works well with the discounted conditional fee agreement as the monthly invoice delivered by the law firm, comprising a percentage (often 60 to 75 per cent of the usual hourly rate) is met by the litigation funder. The balance of the fees (the 40 or 25 per cent discount) is held over until the end of the case when that amount plus an uplift of the full hourly rate is payable in the event that the case is successful. Obviously with a standard retainer, the law firm is paid for their monthly, hourly based, billing.

1.75 The advantages of litigation funding combined with any retainer but particularly the discounted conditional fee agreement are easy to explain to clients who are keen to reduce the financial burden of litigation. Additionally lawyers have realized that offering third party litigation funding as an alternative to other methods of financing litigation—particularly the clients paying for it themselves as they go along—can set the law firm apart from the opposition. A number of litigation teams are now offering a litigation funding option and using it to market themselves. Some firms have 'white labelled' the products of litigation funders and are using them to attract clients. Other law firms have set up a panel of third party litigation funders offering strict service levels.

1.76 There are many good law firms that offer dispute resolution services. The majority of the lawyers are perfectly capable of handling a particular case with skill and efficiency and will produce the right result for the client. The use of litigation funding is a way for these very similar practices to set themselves apart from the opposition by creating the perception that they are offering something different.

1.77 Realistically there is very little for the lawyers not to like about litigation funding. One big attraction is the guarantee, subject to certain caveats, that each month their bill will be paid. That is an extremely important consideration. The rise, certainly from 2008 until April 2013, of the use of the discounted conditional fee agreement as opposed to the use of the straight no win no fee based conditional fee agreement, was partially down to the necessity of law firms to meet overheads on a monthly basis. Regardless of the retainer, the knowledge that the monthly invoice will be discharged on a funded case can only be of benefit to a law firm's cash flow. There is a certainty which is not always there when the client is paying the bill.

1.78 Another aspect of a funded case is the ability to plan and budget as regards cash flow. As the litigation funder requires a budget for the case and also requires it to be regularly updated, and adhered to, a funded case is one where financial planning and projection for the lawyers is much easier.

1.79 The same can be said for counsel's clerks and for counsel themselves. In a funded case the budget for counsel and leading counsel will have been agreed, to a very large extent, in advance. In fact it may well have been fixed or capped. A number of litigation funders will append the budget documentation and an equivalent of Form H to the Litigation Funding Agreement. It is for this reason that counsel and their clerks will know well in advance what fees are to be available to counsel, billed and paid on a particular case if it is funded. They know, again subject to certain caveats, that the solicitors instructing them are in funds and will be able to pay them. In funded cases, there is no need for counsel's clerk to be chasing the solicitors for payment and asking for reassurances that they are in funds and that all is well financially. In a case backed by litigation funders solicitors and counsel can concentrate on running and winning the case rather than having the unwelcome distraction of worrying whether or not their client will or will not have the financial wherewithal to fund the case to its conclusion.

1.80 The positive benefits that third party litigation funding can bring to a law firm's and to counsel's cash flow, and the ability for law firms to reference the use of funding in their marketing, have had an impact on the take-up and use of litigation funding. But aside from these reasons, third party funding has grown as a result of the very simple and straightforward benefits that it provides. It allows access to justice. Sir Rupert Jackson was convinced when he said in his *Review of Civil Litigation Costs: Final Report*, 'I expressed the view that the institution of third party funding was beneficial in that it promoted access to justice.'[14]

1.81 Third party litigation funding can help to 'level the playing field' between a defendant with great financial resources and a less well placed claimant, with limited or no funds to spend on the litigation. It reduces the scope for a defendant of great means, as a matter of tactics, to outspend the claimant by a significant factor. Funding for a case reduces the scope for deploying such tactics.

---

[14] Jackson, *Review of Civil Litigation Costs*, Ch 11, p 117, para 1.2.

Introduction and Background

1.82 Aside from the fact that the resources of the litigation funder would then be behind the claimant, in many cases the knowledge that a litigation funder has decided to back a particular case can change the defendant's attitude to settlement. Litigation funding tends to bring about an equality of arms. In his Preliminary Report, Sir Rupert Jackson noted (at Chapter 15, paragraph 3.1) that the experience of funders was that funding can promote settlement, first because of the appreciation that the claimant has the resources to see the case through, and secondly, because it is appreciated that an independent party (the funder) has objectively assessed there to be good prospects of success.

1.83 Sir Rupert Jackson went further in his endorsement of third party litigation funding in his Final Report:

> I remain of the view that, in principle, third party funding is beneficial and should be supported, essentially for five reasons:
> (i) Third party funding provides an additional means of funding litigation and, for some parties, the only means of funding litigation. Thus third party funding promotes access to justice.
> (ii) Although a successful claimant with third party funding foregoes [sic] a percentage of his damages, it is better for him to recover a substantial part of his damages than to recover nothing at all.
> (iii) The use of third party funding (unlike the use of conditional fee agreements ('CFAs')) does not impose additional financial burdens upon opposing parties.
> (iv) Third party funding will become even more important as a means of financing litigation if success fees under CFAs become irrecoverable.
> (v) Third party funding tends to filter out unmeritorious cases, because funders will not take on the risk of such cases. This benefits opposing parties.[15]

1.84 It would be inappropriate for any text on litigation funding to ignore the fact that the industry has its critics. Litigation funding is not universally applauded. Indeed it has been suggested that litigation funding increases the number of cases brought that lack merit.

1.85 The US Chamber of Commerce through its Institute of Legal Reform has published a number of reports on litigation funding around the world. In particular, *Selling Lawsuits, Buying Trouble* in 2009 warns against the perceived risks of litigation funding.

G. The Effect of the Jackson Reforms

1.86 The merits, or otherwise, of third party litigation funding were considered in some detail in both Sir Rupert Jackson's Preliminary Report and his Final Report.

---

[15] Jackson, *Review of Civil Litigation Costs*, Ch 11, p 117, para 1.2.

The recommendations that he made in his Final Report that were accepted were enacted into law by Part 2 of Legal Aid Sentencing and Punishment of Offenders Act 2012 and came into force on 1 April 2013.

1.87 A package of reforms was implemented, some of which will have more impact on the world of third party litigation funding than others. The ending of recoverability of ATE legal expenses insurance premiums and conditional fee agreement success fees have so far had limited effect at the third party funding end of the legal market, namely the higher value cases.

1.88 With the very high value cases, the insurance premium can often be lost in a global settlement and will now become a cost or overhead of running the litigation, and a price for peace of mind in respect of adverse costs.

1.89 In anticipation of these changes, from some time prior to their implementation, some legal expenses insurers had been looking for full or partial upfront premiums to be paid when there is a funder involved. It is possible that insurers will continue to press for upfront premiums when recoverability ends. It is possible that third party funders will use the existing legal expenses markets less, and offer indemnities within their funding agreements, or set up their own captives, as some do already. The non-recoverability of premiums, it must be recognized, will, averaged across the industry, tend to increase costs of funding, and it is therefore likely to exert upward pressure on the cost of funding to clients.

1.90 If there continues to be an increase in the demand for upfront legal expenses premiums then funding for those premiums is one solution, either from the third party funding market or from law firms raising their own capital to use for funding of their cases. There have been examples of this happening already.

1.91 A significant change to the funding options available to litigators and clients arrived with the advent of damages based agreements. For the first time, from April 2013, English lawyers are able to share in the proceeds of litigation with their clients, as has been the case for many years under the contingency fee retainers commonly used in the United States. These will have an impact on the litigation funding market but the extent of that remains to be seen. It would be a surprise to most members of the legal profession if lawyers and law firms suddenly changed their appetite for risk and flocked to do DBAs just because the upside is slightly or even significantly better than under pre-Jackson retainers. Any sensible law firm works on a carefully managed risk based case load in both volume and exposure and that is unlikely to change with DBAs.

1.92 An attractive combination is that of third party litigation funding and DBAs. This seems to be a very good solution.

1.93 However, the use of DBAs in England and Wales has so far been hampered by the perceived ambiguity in the DBA Regulations. The general view from the legal profession appears to be that the use of a hybrid DBA is not permitted by the current wording of Regulation 4. In other jurisdictions clients are used to sharing damages and once it becomes more prevalent here in England and Wales, litigation funding is likely to increase further. In any event, someone still has to pay the base costs under a DBA and litigation funders present a useful way of doing that. Indeed, in the United States litigation funders frequently see situations where they are asked to fund base costs or discounted fees with the litigation funder taking a percentage of the contingency fee that has been agreed between the law firm and the client. For example, if the agreed contingency fee is 45 per cent of damages on success, the litigation funder may fund a sum equivalent to 70 per cent of the law firm's hourly rate in return for 35 per cent of the damages on success, leaving the law firm a 10 per cent contingency fee for their risk in deferring the balance (30 per cent) of their fees.

As far as growth in the third party funding sector is concerned, the most activity in the next few years is likely to be in mainstream commercial litigation as clients and lawyers learn more about what funding can do to assist them. Sir Rupert Jackson noted in paragraph 11.2.4 of his Final Report that third party funding is 'still nascent in England and Wales'. The knowledge gap is closing, albeit slowly. The existing areas of high activity for litigation funders such as patents and international arbitration are continuing to thrive. The mainstream English High Court commercial cases have increased in their use of litigation funding, and the use of DBAs and funding will continue to support that increase. Whilst the real effects of the Jackson reforms will take time to be seen, it seems unlikely that they will do anything to dampen the buoyant third party funding marketplace and, so far, the view from the funding profession is that they have not. **1.94**

2

HISTORY AND DEVELOPMENT

A. History, Champerty, Evolution	2.01	9. *Merchantbridge & Co Ltd v Safron General Partner 1 Ltd*	2.73
1. History and development	2.01		
2. Champerty and maintenance	2.05	10. *Sibthorpe and Morris v Southwark London Borough Council*	2.81
3. Evolution	2.14		
B. Case Law	2.19	11. *Jennifer Simpson (as assignee of Alan Catchpole) v Norfolk & Norwich University Hospital NHS Trust*	2.88
1. *Giles v Thompson*	2.20		
2. *Stocznia Gdanska SA v Latreefers Inc*	2.26	12. *Cecil & others v Bayat & others*	2.95
		13. *Tinseltime Ltd v Eryl Roberts & Ors*	2.102
3. *The Eurasian Dream (No 2)*	2.31	14. *Flatman v Germany*	2.109
4. *Hamilton v Al-Fayed (No 2)*	2.35	15. *Harcus Sinclair (a Firm) v Buttonwood Legal Capital Limited & Ors*	2.111
5. *R (on the application of Factortame) v Secretary of State for Transport, Local Government and the Regions (No 2)*	2.43	16. *Excalibur Ventures LLC v Texas Keystone Inc.; Gulf Keystone Petroleum Ltd; Gulf Keystone Petroleum International Ltd; Gulf Keystone Petroleum (UK) Ltd*	2.115
6. *Gulf Azov Shipping Co Ltd v Idisi*	2.54		
7. *Arkin v Borchard Lines Ltd & Ors*	2.59		
8. *London & Regional (St George's Court) Ltd v Ministry of Defence*	2.68	C. Conclusions	2.123

A. History, Champerty, Evolution

1. History and development

2.01 This chapter is concerned with how litigation funding has developed and explains the difficulties that have been part of its evolution into the position it now occupies in mainstream litigation in England. Funding has taken some time to become accepted. The interference in someone else's litigation, with no interest other than for commercial gain, which is essentially what litigation funding is, has been frowned upon from medieval times. To do so was to face criminal and civil penalties up until the late twentieth century.

2.02 Historically, the development of litigation funding has been restricted by hostile legal policy and the principles of maintenance and champerty. Its transformation has been a relatively slow process until recent years, when various interventions have accelerated the use and acceptance of funding as an option in litigation.

Third party litigation funding has recently developed to become an integral part of the mainstream litigation process.

In order to gauge the progress of funding, it is important to be aware of the historic issues it has faced and the relevance of those objections to modern day litigation. Maintenance and champerty (and barratry) were the difficulties, and to a certain extent they remain an issue. Traditionally under common law, the involvement of a third party in litigation was illegal under the doctrine of champerty and its related concepts of maintenance and barratry. **2.03**

Over time the complete prohibition has been relaxed. In modern day litigation, in England, certain allowances are made with regard to the historic doctrines and public policy has become receptive to funding. It has now found a balance between the need to protect against potential for unjustified, and unpalatable, interference in litigation and the need to allow for access to justice in the interests of the litigants. **2.04**

2. Champerty and maintenance

'A person is guilty of maintenance if he supports litigation in which he has no legitimate concern without just cause or excuse.'[1] It is 'the procurement, by direct and indirect financial assistance, of another person to institute, or carry or defend civil proceedings without lawful justification.'[2] **2.05**

Champerty is an aggravated form of maintenance, in which the maintainer receives 'a share of the proceeds of the action or suit or other contentious proceedings where property is in dispute'.[3] It is defined by Lord Denning MR in *Trendtex Trading Corporation & another v Credit Suisse*,[4] as a 'particularly obnoxious form of [maintenance]. It exists where the maintainer seeks to make a profit out of another man's action—by taking the proceeds of it, or part of them, for himself.' Detractors of litigation funding have no difficulty in making it fit neatly into these definitions. Barretry is a form of maintenance. 'A common barrator is a common mover or stirrer up or maintainer of suits, quarrels, or parties, either in Courts, or in the country, in Courts of Record, and in the County, Hundred, and other Inferior Courts.'[5] **2.06**

A helpful assessment of the area can be found in 'Litigation Funding: Status and Issues': 'the rules of champerty and maintenance were intended to retain the purity of the litigation process. They were also to prevent speculation in litigation by parties who have no interest in the legal proceedings and whose activities might **2.07**

---

[1] *Chitty on Contracts* (28th edn, 1999), Vol 1, para 17-050.
[2] Law Commission, *Proposals for the Reform of the Law Relating to Maintenance and Champerty* (1966) at [9].
[3] *Re Trepca Mines Ltd (No. 2)* [1963] Ch 199 at 224; *Trendtex Trading Corp v Credit Suisse* [1980] 1 QB 629 at 663.
[4] *Trendtex Trading Corp v Credit Suisse* [1980] 1 QB 629 at 663.
[5] *Case of Barratry* (30 Eliz) 8 Rep 36, 77 ER 5.

amount to an abuse of process....The courts believed that they were capable of protecting against the obvious biases of the parties themselves, but not against external and possibly less visible commercial influences.'[6]

2.08 The prohibition on maintenance, champerty, and barratry has a long history.

> The crimes of maintenance and champerty are so old that their origins can no longer be traced, but their importance in medieval times is quite clear. The mechanisms of justice lacked the internal strength to resist the oppression of private individuals through suits fomented and sustained by unscrupulous men of power. Champerty was particularly vicious, since the purchase of a share in litigation presented an obvious temptation to the suborning of justices and witnesses and the exploitation of worthless claims which the defendant lacked the resources and influence to withstand. The fact that such conduct was treated as both criminal and tortious provided an invaluable external discipline to which, as the records show, recourse was often required.[7]

2.09 The development of maintenance and champerty in England began in mediaeval times.'Maintenance originates from a time when interference in litigation was widespread, practiced by royal officials and nobles to subvert justice and oppress vulnerable litigants. Its survival in modern law has been attributed to a persisting fear that it is still needed as a safeguard against blackmail and speculation in lawsuits prone to increase litigation.'[8]

2.10 As and when conflicts arose between feudal barons they were settled by a 'private war'.[9] Eventually these battles were replaced by courtroom trials, judges, and juries. The result was a process involving bribery, intimidation, and corruption. Holdsworth observed, 'when those who are wronged are compelled to have recourse to the law, much of the unscrupulousness and trickery which accompany the waging of a war are transferred to the conduct of litigation. The courts are besieged with angry litigants who fight their lawsuits in the same spirit as they would have fought their private or family feuds. This...was especially apparent in medieval England...contemporaneously with the growth of the power of the royal courts, we get the growth of many various attempts to pervert their machinery...'[10]

2.11 The doctrines of maintenance and champerty were designed to combat these historic abuses. By the 1800s there were those who felt that they were unnecessary. Their existence was always based upon public policy; originally to protect against the barons and latterly to protect against individuals stirring up litigation at no risk to themselves.

---

[6] Christopher Hodges, John Peysner, and Angus Nurse, 'Litigation Funding: Status and Issues', Oxford Legal Studies Research Paper No. 55 (2012), 12.
[7] *Giles v Thompson* [1994] 1 AC 142 at 153.
[8] J G Fleming, *The Law of Torts* (9th edn, 1998), 689.
[9] W Holdsworth, *A History of English Law* (4th edn), Vol 3 at 394–395.
[10] W Holdsworth, *A History of English Law* (4th edn), Vol 3.

Jeremy Bentham observed that these restrictions on the funding of litigation were a 'barbarous precaution' born out of a 'barbarous age'.[11] He thought that the judiciary was able to cope without these principles:

2.12

> A mischief, in those times it seems but too common, though a mischief not to be cured by such laws, was, that a man would buy a weak claim, in hopes that power might convert it into a strong one, and that the sword of a baron, stalking into court with a rabble of retainers at his heels, might strike terror into the eyes of a judge upon the bench. At present, what cares an English judge for the swords of a hundred barons? Neither fearing nor hoping, hating nor loving, the judge of our days is ready with equal phlegm to administer, on all occasions, that system, whatever it be, of justice or injustice, which the law has put into his hands.[12]

The historic necessity for protection had passed. The court system became resilient and consistent. 'As the centuries passed the courts became stronger, their mechanisms more consistent and their participants more self-reliant. Abuses could be more easily detected and forestalled, and litigation more easily determined in accordance with the demands of justice...'[13] The need to ensure there was equality before the law was greater. The continued existence of maintenance and champerty and their prohibition against funding undermined equality before the law or 'access to justice'.

2.13

3. Evolution

Historically, maintenance and champerty were criminal offences. They were declared to be unlawful in 1275 by the Statute of Westminster,[14] which prohibited court clerks from providing maintenance or champerty.

2.14

The Criminal Law Act 1967 provided, by section 13(a), for the abolition of the crimes of maintenance and champerty at common law, and, by section 13(1)(b) and Schedule 4, for the abolition of the statutory offences. By section 14(1) the Act abolished the common law torts of maintenance and champerty, but, significantly, section 14(2) provided that the 'abolition of criminal and civil liability under the law of England and Wales for maintenance and champerty shall not affect any rule of that law as to the cases in which a contract is to be treated as contrary to public policy or otherwise illegal'.

2.15

The effect was that a contract could be ruled unenforceable as a matter of public policy if the champerty is not justifiable.[15] Legal policy remained, in principle, hostile to both maintenance and champerty, as was demonstrated in the judgments of the Court of Appeal, and speeches in the House of Lords in *Trendtex Trading*

2.16

---

[11] Letter XII: Maintenance and Champerty.—Jeremy Bentham, *The Works of Jeremy Bentham*, Vol 3 [1843].
[12] Letter XII: Maintenance and Champerty.—Jeremy Bentham, *The Works of Jeremy Bentham*, Vol 3 [1843].
[13] *Giles v Thompson* [1994] 1 AC 142 at 154.
[14] Statute of Westminster I (1275) (3 Edw. I, C 25, 28, and 33).
[15] Sections 13 and 14 of the Criminal Law Act 1967.

Corporation v Credit Suisse[16] in 1982. However, both before and after the enactment of the 1967 Act, legal policy developed, by stages, so as to accommodate certain arrangements whereby genuine claims would not be stifled by reason of want of means to litigate. A good illustration of such evolution of policy arose in the field of insolvency practice, in which, commonly, financial resources are limited for an office holder, a liquidator, or trustee. In many insolvency situations there are assets, requiring realization, including debts that need to be called in and collected. It may be that the only asset in an insolvent company is a right of action or a claim. It is also very likely that there is little or no money available to pay lawyers either to evaluate and assess the merits of the case, or to run it in the event it has already been assessed as having reasonable prospects of success.

2.17 In *Seear v Lawson*[17] in 1880, the Court of Appeal, upholding a decision of Bacon V-C, held that even assuming that at common law it would not have been possible for a person to assign an action against a grantee of a conveyance for a declaration that the same was a mortgage, following the grantor's bankruptcy, it was permissible (having regard to the provisions of the Bankruptcy Act 1869) for the trustee in bankruptcy of the grantor to assign for value the cause of action concerned. This decision was soon followed by that of Chitty J, as he then was, in *Guy v Churchill*[18] in which it was held that it was permissible for a trustee in bankruptcy to assign a cause of action which had previously vested in the bankrupt, to a creditor of the bankrupt who was to conduct the litigation at his own expense, but upon terms that any recoveries should be divided in agreed shares between the creditor and the trustee. Chitty J, upon the foundation of *Seear v Lawson*, held that the law as to maintenance and champerty was not engaged in the transaction because it was lawful to maintain an action 'where the person maintaining it have an interest in the thing in variance.' He cited examples of beneficiaries funding a claim by a trustee, and commoners maintaining an action where one of their body sues in respect of the common right.

2.18 Since the middle of the twentieth century there have been important amendments to the basic policy which was historically used to justify the prohibitions on maintenance and champerty. There have been significant changes in the attitude of the courts and legislature in regard to their attitude towards litigation funding and progress over the last few years has been very fast.

B. Case Law

2.19 There are many cases which could be said to have influenced and guided the acceptance of third party litigation funding over the last few years. The cases which

---

[16] *Trendtex Trading Corporation v Credit Suisse* [1982] AC 679.
[17] *Seear v Lawson* (1880) 15 Ch D 426.
[18] *Guy v Churchill* (1888) 40 Ch D 481.

follow are the key decisions that have driven that change in attitude, and represent landmark decisions in the law's development. Additionally, these cases set out some of the boundaries for third party litigation funders and examine key issues of liability for adverse costs, pure as opposed to commercial funders, the extent of a funder's influence, and the division of the proceeds of litigation.

1. *Giles v Thompson*

This is one of the first cases of the modern era to consider funding arrangements. The case,[19] heard with the conjoined appeal in *Devlin v Baslington*, examined whether the agreements between motorists and their credit hire companies were contrary to the contemporary public policy and therefore unlawful due to champerty.   **2.20**

In that case the plaintiffs, motorists involved in accidents (the fault for which lay with other drivers, the defendants), sought compensation for loss of use of their vehicles. The plaintiffs entered into agreements with credit hire companies for the hire of substitute vehicles whilst their own were being repaired. The plaintiffs' claims included sums which represented the care hire charges which they had incurred. The contractual arrangements between the credit hire companies and the plaintiffs provided that the credit hire company should make a charge for the loan of the replacement car, which was to be reimbursed from that part of the damages recovered by the plaintiffs from the respective defendants or their insurers, which reflected the loss of use of the plaintiffs' respective vehicles. Until such recovery was effected, the plaintiffs were under no obligation to pay for the use of the replacement car. These arrangements were conditional on the cooperation of the motorist in pursuing the claim and any resulting legal proceedings.   **2.21**

The only fully reasoned speech was that of Lord Mustill (with whom Lords Keith, Ackner, Jauncey, and Lowry agreed). The questions of relevance to later judicial assessment of issues regarding litigation funding were focused on the arrangements between the credit hire companies and the plaintiffs in the action, their customers.   **2.22**

The House of Lords considered, first, whether the credit hire companies had obtained any direct rights over the fruits of the plaintiffs' claims, and secondly, whether the degree of control exercised by the companies over the conduct of the litigation was objectionable. Their lordships concluded, on the first question, that the credit hire companies had had no interest in giving them a claim to the proceeds, since their profits came from the hiring of vehicles, rather than from the litigation.[20] On the second issue, they held that there was nothing objectionable because there was not 'anything officious or wanton about the intervention of the hire company' in the litigation, and there was not a realistic possibility that   **2.23**

---

[19] [1993] UKHL 2 (26 May 1993) [1994] 1 AC 142.
[20] At 161F–G.

the administration of justice might suffer,[21] concluding that the 'perils to the proper administration of justice' were 'much exaggerated'.[22]

2.24 The defendant, in the *Giles v Thompson* case, had submitted that the agreements were unlawful prompting a three-stage review by the court: first, an analysis of whether the credit hire companies as strangers to the underlying disputes had agreed to involve themselves in the litigation in a way which yielded a financial benefit from a successful outcome; at the second stage, whether the companies had an interest in the transaction which legitimated what would otherwise have been unlawful, and finally whether aside from special rules concerning champerty, the relationships had features which made it contrary to public policy, and hence unenforceable. Lord Mustill rejected this approach, paying close regard to the decision of the House of Lords in *Trendtex Trading Corporation v Credit Suisse*.[23] Referring to Steyn LJ's judgment in the case under appeal, he said that the law on maintenance and champerty had not stood still, but had accommodated itself to changing times, and that the law on those topics could

> ... best be kept in forward motion by looking to its origins as a principle of public policy designed to protect the purity of justice and the interests of vulnerable litigants. For this purpose the issue should not be broken down into steps. Rather, all the aspects of the transaction should be taken together for the purpose of considering the single question whether ... there is wanton and officious intermeddling with the disputes of others where the meddler has no interest whatever, and where the assistance he renders to one or the other party is without justification or excuse.

2.25 In deciding that the arrangements were not unlawful or against public policy, their lordships had express regard to the commercial reality that 'there are many motorists who lack the inclination or the ready cash to hire a substitute on the chance of recovering reimbursement from the defendant's insurers. Thus, there exists in practical terms a gap in the remedies available to the motorist, from which the errant driver, and hence his insurers, frequently profit.'[24]

2. *Stocznia Gdanska SA v Latreefers Inc*

2.26 This decision of the Court of Appeal[25] was concerned primarily with the winding up of Latreefers, a Latvian company, by the English court. A secondary point is of particular note from the litigation funding perspective. One aspect of the appeal was to decide whether or not an agreement between Stocznia and a third party litigation funder, providing for the payment of the legal costs incurred in prosecuting

---

[21] At 164D–G.
[22] At 165B.
[23] *Trendtex Trading Corporation v Credit Suisse* [1982] AC 679.
[24] At 154H–155A.
[25] [2000] EWCA Civ 36, [2001] 2 BCLC 116.

the petition to wind up Latreefers and related proceedings in the Commercial Court, was champertous.

2.27 Once the existence of a funder became known to the defendants, they applied for a stay of proceedings. The application was dismissed and this decision was appealed. The agreement with the funders was that in return for 55 per cent of the proceeds of the litigation they would finance the legal fees incurred in pursuing the action. They also agreed to pay any adverse costs ordered as against Stocznia.

2.28 The funders had a pre-existing interest in that they were already owed money under an agreement which successful litigation would enable them to recover. The defendants' case was that the funding agreement was champertous because the share of the proceeds of the litigation for which the funders had contracted (55 per cent) was disproportionate to its genuine commercial interest.

2.29 The issue raised in this case is one of importance for funders, namely, to what extent does the amount of the funder's interest affect the legality of the arrangement? It was noted that it is in the public interest for impecunious litigants with genuine claims to be able to bring them. But, equally it is in the public interest to protect litigants against exploitation by funders. The suggestion here was that the funders had an interest in the litigation deriving from their contractual commission arrangements, but that their share of the potential proceeds was disproportionately large in comparison with that pre-existing interest. Accordingly, it was argued for the defendants that the funders had no legitimate interest to 'intermeddle'. They sought a stay of the proceedings on the basis that the funding agreement was champertous. Although the Court of Appeal did not have to decide the issue (because, on the basis of previous authority, the fact that an action was funded by a champertous agreement did not in itself render the action an abuse, even though the champertous agreement would not be enforceable itself[26]) it was strongly of the view that it was not champertous. The alleged disproportion was substantial, but not grossly so; the real chance that the pleaded claim might succeed in full must have been seen as doubtful, and therefore the disproportion was more theoretical rather than real. A large disproportion might contribute to a finding of abuse, but would not necessarily do so.

2.30 Additionally, in undertaking to meet their own side's and any adverse costs, the funders were taking on a substantial costs liability. The funders had a pre-existing interest in the subject matter of the claim and they would not be able to influence the conduct of the litigation because, including any settlement negotiations, it was in the hands of experienced solicitors. The court said (at paragraph 62) that these features 'make it plain that this funding agreement was not trafficking in litigation and came nowhere near being wanton and officious intermeddling

---

[26] See para 59 in particular, and *Martell v Consett Iron Co* [1955] Ch 363, CA.

with the disputes of others'. There was no abuse of process. It is notable that in this case, the arrangement concerned was one which conferred a direct interest in a share of proceeds.

3. *The Eurasian Dream (No 2)*

2.31 This well known and often quoted case[27] arose from damage by fire to Papera's cargo of cars on board the defendants' ship *The Eurasian Dream*.

2.32 Marine claims assessors, Websters, carried out work at the request of Papera's insurers on a 'no cure, no pay' basis under which they would be entitled to a fee of 5 per cent of the recovered amount. Their task was to conduct recovery services. The liability of the defendants was established at trial in the court's first judgment,[28] and following this Papera's insurers sought to recover Websters' fees for recovery services as damages, or alternatively, as costs. Cresswell J, at paragraph 39 of his judgment, described the issues raised as 'novel and important'. The defendants alleged that the arrangement was champertous and therefore unenforceable, and even if that was not the case, then any sum was recoverable as costs of the action and would be subject to assessment in the usual manner.

2.33 Cresswell J specifically acknowledged that a contingency fee agreement which entitled those providing litigation services to a percentage of anything recovered might give rise to a particular objection on the ground that it posed a temptation to act in an unethical manner so as to maximize recovery, so that it was necessary to consider the role played by Websters to see whether the nature of their interest in the outcome of the litigation carried with it any tendency to 'sully the purity of justice on the facts of this case'. Cresswell held that because he regarded the Websters' fees to be recoverable as a costs item, rather than damages, the defendants were protected by the provision that costs would be subject to assessment under CPR 47, and that the fees would be considered on an hourly rate basis, with the 5 per cent agreement operating as a cap on fees.

2.34 Websters' ability to influence the outcome of the litigation was limited, as solicitors and counsel were instructed. It was relevant, further, that it was the practice in this market to be remunerated on a similar basis, and that the agreement was not exclusively concerned with litigation.

4. *Hamilton v Al-Fayed (No 2)*

2.35 This case[29] is the most recent, and clearest, review of the distinction between a 'pure' funder and a 'professional' funder of litigation.

---

[27] *Papera Traders Co Ltd v Hyundai Merchant Marine Co Ltd (The Eurasian Dream) (No 2)* [2002] Lloyd's Rep 692, Commercial Court (Cresswell J).
[28] [2002] EWHC 118 (Comm).
[29] [2003] QB 1175.

2.36 Mr Neil Hamilton, a former Member of Parliament, brought and failed in a libel action against Mohammed Al-Fayed arising out of the 'cash for questions' scandal. The court ordered Mr Hamilton to pay the costs which were assessed, following Mr Hamilton's unsuccessful application for permission to appeal, in the sum of £1,467,576, of which £1.19m remained unpaid. Mr Hamilton was subsequently adjudged bankrupt. A sizeable part of Mr Hamilton's legal fees had been funded by a number, some 484, of anonymous contributions amounting to £466,320, on the basis that if the action were to be successful, the monies were to be returned, but not otherwise. Most of the contributions were for modest sums, but the 18 largest contributors were for £5,000 or more. The trial judge (Morland J) required the identities of those contributors to be revealed, and Mr Al-Fayed sought an order for costs against them under s 51 of the Supreme Court Act 1981. Morland J declined to make such an order, holding that the contributors were pure funders, and thus not liable. He observed that the donations had not been made as a result of any obligation to Mr Hamilton, but as an act of charity through sympathy with his predicament and in some instances from political affinity with the Conservative Party. He said that the donors had no control over how the donation was spent, and contrasted this with the position of the professional funder who exercises considerable control, management, and supervision of the litigation. Morland J said that it 'will be rare or very rare that it will be just and reasonable' to make a costs order against a 'pure' funder, whereas in the case of a professional funder it would be 'very exceptional' where it would not be just and reasonable to make an order under s 51.

2.37 All three members of the Court of Appeal (Simon Brown, Chadwick, and Hale LJJ) agreed that the appeal should be dismissed. Simon Brown LJ observed that conflicting principles were in play 'and only one can prevail. Should the law accord priority to the funded party gaining access to justice or to the unfunded party recovering his costs if he wins?'[30] Having reviewed a great many authorities on the topic[31] he concluded that:

> ...on balance [the authorities] clearly favour the respondents' argument and that the unfunded party's ability to recover his costs must yield to the funded party's right of access to the courts to litigate the dispute in the first place. That seems to me to be the essential policy underlying the cases. Perhaps most conspicuously this is so in two of the categories of case discussed above: the CFA cases and those concerning security for costs. The respondents' argument arising out of the CFA ruling is really a very powerful one: if in these cases solicitors (or, indeed, barristers)

---

[30] At para 44.
[31] Including *Aiden Shipping Co Ltd v Interbulk Ltd* [1986] AC 965, HL, *Cooper v Maxwell* (unreported) 20 March 1992 (Court of Appeal (Civil Division)) Transcript No 273 of 1992, *Symphony Group plc v Hodgson* [1994] 179, CA, *Globe Equities Ltd v Globe Legal Services Ltd* [1999] BLR 232, CA, and *Murphy v Young & Co's Brewery plc* [1997] 1 WLR 1591, CA.

2.38 At paragraph 47 he continued:

> ...the pure funding of litigation (whether of claims or defences) ought generally to be regarded as being in the public interest providing only and always that its essential motivation is to enable the party funded to litigate what the funders perceived to be a genuine case.

2.39 He identified a powerful logical justification for the conclusion at paragraph 48:

> So long as the law continues to allow impoverished parties to litigate without their having to provide security for their opponent's costs, those sympathetic to their plight should not be discouraged from assisting them to secure representation. Thus is access to justice promoted and, another benefit too—fewer litigants in person.

2.40 Chadwick LJ had no doubt as to how the conflicting principles highlighted by the case had to be resolved. He said, at paragraph 63:

> The starting point, as it seems to me, is to recognise that, where there is tension between the principle that a party who is successful in defending a claim made against him ought not to be required to bear the costs of his defence and the principle that a claimant should not be denied access to the courts on the grounds of impecuniosity, that tension has to be resolved in favour of the second of those principles.

2.41 As for the position of the 'pure funder', he added at paragraph 71:

> It follows that I would hold that—in the interests of justice generally—fairness to the successful defendant does not, as a general rule, require that where a pure funder provides financial support towards the litigation costs of an impecunious claimant, he should contribute to the costs which that defendant will (by reason of the claimant's impecuniosity) be unable to recover under an order for costs against the claimant alone. In that context I use the expression 'pure funder' to denote a person who provides funds to meet the litigation costs of a claimant in circumstances in which he, himself, has no collateral interest in the outcome of the claim—other than as a source of reimbursement of the funds which he has provided.

2.42 Hale LJ was 'reluctantly persuaded to agree' with the other members of the court, warning, however, at paragraph 86 of 'exceptional cases':

> On balance, the arguments in favour of a general approach that 'pure' funders should not be expected also to fund the opposing party's costs outweigh the arguments in favour of a general approach that they should. There must, however, be exceptional cases where it would be quite unjust not to make an order: principally where the litigation was oppressive or malicious or pursued for some other ulterior motive. The fact that it was quite unmeritorious would be powerful evidence of ulterior motive but neither a necessary nor a sufficient criterion in itself.

---

[32] Para 45.

5. R (on the application of Factortame) v Secretary of State for Transport, Local Government and the Regions (No 2)

2.43 *Factortame*[33] was another important decision in the development of third party litigation funding. In this case, the claimants were Anglo-Spanish fishing companies which triumphed by demonstrating both that they had been unlawfully excluded from fishing in British waters, and that they were entitled to damages to compensate them.

2.44 The proceedings were protracted and the finances of the claimant group were poor. One of the creditors of the claimant group was Grant Thornton, which had carried out complex and time consuming work in establishing the quantum of damages suffered by the claimants. They agreed to prepare and submit the claims for loss in return for 8 per cent of the final settlement received. They were not the experts in the case and their work consisted largely of important back-up services for the two independent experts. Sensibly, they considered that they were precluded, by their interest in recovering their outstanding accountancy fees from their clients' damages, from acting as independent experts in the case. In fact Grant Thornton paid the fees of the two retained expert witnesses in the case.

2.45 The judgment, of the particularly strongly constituted court (Lord Phillips of Worth Matravers MR, Robert Walker and Clarke LJJ), handed down by Lord Phillips, examined the development of the law in relation to maintenance and champerty, referring to *In re Trepca Mines Ltd*[34] for the historical antipathy of the common law towards champerty. The court's helpful survey paid particular regard to the then most recent decisions on the subject, including *Trendtex*[35] and *Giles v Thompson*, but it also had regard to statutory intervention as a powerful indication of evolving public policy. Lord Phillips cited the following well known passage in the judgment of Oliver LJ in *Trendtex*:

> There is, I think, a clear requirement of public policy that officers of the court should be inhibited from putting themselves in a position where their own interests may conflict with their duties to the court by agreement, for instance, of so called 'contingency fees'.[36]

---

[33] *Factortame Limited v Secretary of State for the Environment, Transport and the Regions (No. 2)* sub nom. *R (on the application of Factortame and others) v Secretary of State for Transport, Local Government and the Regions* [2002] EWCA Civ 932, [2002] 4 All ER 97, [2003] QB 381.

[34] *Trepca Mines Ltd (No. 2)* [1963] 1 Ch 199, especially the passage in the judgment of Lord Denning MR at pages 219–20:

> The reason why the common law condemns champerty is because of the abuses to which it may give rise. The common law fears that the champertous maintainer might be tempted, for his own personal gain, to inflame the damages, to suppress evidence, or even to suborn witnesses. These fears may be exaggerated; but, be that so or not, the law for centuries has declared champerty to be unlawful, and we cannot do otherwise than enforce the law; and I may observe that it has received statutory support, in the case of solicitors, in section 65 of the Solicitors Act 1957.

[35] *Trendtex Trading v Credit Suisse* [1980] 1 QB 629, CA.

[36] See *Trendtex* at 663.

2.46 However, at paragraph 34 of the judgment in *Factortame*, the court observed of Oliver LJ's remarks:

> The introduction of conditional fees shows that even this requirement of public policy is no longer absolute. This case raises the question of whether the requirement extends to expert witnesses or others in a position to influence the conduct of litigation and, if it does, whether on the facts of the present case the agreements concluded by Grant Thornton can be justified.

2.47 At paragraph 36, the court continued:

> Where the law expressly restricts the circumstances in which agreements in support of litigation are lawful, this provides a powerful indication of the limits of public policy in analogous situations. Where this is not the case, then we believe one must today look at the facts of the particular case and consider whether those facts suggest that the agreement in question might tempt the allegedly champertous maintainer for his personal gain to inflame the damages, to suppress evidence, to suborn witnesses or otherwise to undermine the ends of justice.

2.48 Having referred extensively to *Giles v Thompson*, the court concluded, at paragraph 44, that:

> This decision abundantly supports the proposition that, in any individual case, it is necessary to look at the agreement under attack in order to see whether it tends to conflict with existing public policy that is directed to protecting the due administration of justice with particular regard to the interests of the defendant. This is a question that we have to address. In so doing we revert to the statement of Lord Mustill, at p 153 [in *Giles v Thompson*], that 'the rule, now in the course of attenuation, which forbids a solicitor from accepting payment for professional services calculated as a proportion of the sum recovered from the defendant...survives nowadays, so far as it survives at all, largely as a rule of professional conduct'. With respect, this statement is not correct. The basis of the rule is statutory. It is now necessary to look at the relevant statutory provisions, not merely because Mr Friedman has submitted that they are indicative of public policy which extends beyond the confines of the statutory provisions, but because he has submitted that the most recent statute, which came into force after the events with which we are concerned, would have outlawed the 1998 agreements. If this is correct, it strongly supports his contention that those agreements were in conflict with public policy.

2.49 The court examined s 58 of the Courts and Legal Services Act 1990, in its original and amended form. It was that section which provided for conditional fee agreements in respect of advocacy or litigation services not to be unenforceable, in specified circumstances, and subject to the requirements that might be prescribed by the Lord Chancellor. The court (at paragraph 56) interpreted the section 'as applying to the provision of advocacy and litigation services by those authorised in accordance with the earlier sections to exercise rights of audience or conduct litigation'; there was nothing in the section to suggest that it was intended to apply to the provision of services ancillary to the conduct of litigation by the many different categories of person who have, in the past, been accustomed to assist with the conduct of litigation. The court (at paragraph 57) considered that this conclusion was supported by the regulations made under the section; the Conditional Fee Agreements Regulations 1995; the Conditional Fee Agreements Regulations 2000, and the definition of 'legal representative' contained therein. Whilst recognizing that there was 'good reason' why principles of maintenance and champerty should apply with particular rigour to those conducting litigation or appearing as advocates, the court conclusion (at paragraph 61) was that the section applied only to such persons. The court then stated, at paragraph 62, a recognition of a public policy shift:

> More generally, however, section 58 evidences a radical shift in the attitude of public policy to the practice of conducting litigation on terms that the obligation to pay fees will be contingent upon success. Whereas before this practice was outlawed, it is now permissible—subject to the requirements imposed by the section. These requirements do not appear designed to mitigate the mischief that had led to the banning of contingency fees—the undesirability of the interests of officers of the court conflicting with their duties to the court. Rather the requirements appear designed to protect the litigants concluding conditional fee agreements who, when the section was first enacted, were required to pay any 'uplift' out of their recoveries. Conditional fees are now permitted in order to give effect to another facet of public policy—the desirability of access to justice. Conditional fees are designed to ensure that those who do not have the resources to fund advocacy or litigation services should none the less be able to obtain these in support claims which appear to have merit.

2.50 In light of these conclusions, the court then considered the position of expert witnesses, and at paragraph 73, it stated that an expert giving evidence on a contingency fee basis would have a financial interest in the outcome of the proceedings, which was 'highly undesirable', so that it would be a 'very rare case indeed' in which the court would be prepared to consent to an expert being instructed on such a basis. However, in the following paragraph the court emphasized that Grant Thornton had not performed the role of expert witnesses.

2.51 The court held, at paragraphs 79–82, that public policy was not affronted by the fact that Grant Thornton agreed to act on terms that made their remuneration contingent upon success in the proceedings. The same public policy considerations attaching to access to justice, identified in *Hamilton v Fayed*,[37] mitigated any criticism that there might otherwise have been of the arrangements made on a contingency basis. Further, it was relevant that by the time that the arrangements were concluded, liability had been established, subject to an appeal to the House of Lords, and Grant Thornton would have no role to play in that appeal.

2.52 As for the objection that the arrangements involved 'sharing the spoils', the court was not prepared to accept that the terms agreed were justified merely because they constituted the only way in which the claimants could obtain access to justice.[38]

---

[37] *Hamilton v Al Fayed* [2002] EWCA Civ 665.
[38] Para 83.

However, it considered that the 8 per cent agreed was not extravagant, and the arrangement should have appeared attractive not merely to the claimants, but to the government, who would be liable to pay reasonable costs which would be likely to be assessed on an hourly rate basis, in respect of which 8 per cent would be likely to act as a cap. Furthermore, as to any temptation on the part of Grant Thornton to 'inflame the damages', that firm were 'reputable members of a respectable profession', subject to regulation, so that no reasonable onlooker would suspect that Grant Thornton might be tempted to deviate from performing their duties in an honest manner. Still further, the preparation of the computer model used for undertaking damages calculations was the product of work jointly undertaken by another government department along with Grant Thornton, counsel were heavily involved in the settlement process, and the litigation was conducted by well known and highly experienced commercial solicitors. In the circumstances any suggestion that Grant Thornton might have attempted to procure a settlement at odds with their appreciation of the merits was unrealistic.

2.53 The court had to consider whether the nature of the services provided by Grant Thornton and their agreement to act on a contingency fee basis offended against public policy. They concluded that it did not and that the Costs Judge below had been correct in finding that the retainer agreements were not contrary to public policy under the 'vestigial remnants of the law of champerty'.

6. *Gulf Azov Shipping Co Ltd v Idisi*

2.54 In this case the Court of Appeal[39] considered whether a person who assisted in funding and presenting litigation had stepped beyond the role of 'a pure funder' so that he was exposed to having a costs order made against him under s 51 of the Supreme Court Act 1981. The claimants recovered summary judgment against the first three defendants ('the original defendants') for damages for the unlawful detention of a ship and its crew in Nigeria for a period of nearly two years. The claimants sought costs orders against the fourth and fifth defendants ('D4' and 'D5'), who were joined as parties pursuant to CPR 48.2(1)(a) for that purpose. D4 was a lawyer practising in Nigeria. The deputy judge (Arthur Marriott QC) found that D4 had personally intervened to assist the original defendants, providing, from his own resources, a substantial contribution to their litigation funding. He found also that D4 was closely involved in the conduct of the original defendant's defence, dealing with solicitors, and encouraging his niece to make a witness statement and providing evidence himself. The deputy judge stated that what had taken D4's case out of the category of a 'pure funder' was 'principally his personal participation in the conduct of the litigation at a critical time' for the original defendants. He ordered that D4 (and also D5) should pay the claimants' costs. D4 appealed.

---

[39] [2004] EWCA Civ 292.

The Court of Appeal (Lord Phillips MR, Tuckey and Jacob LJJ) allowed D4's **2.55** appeal. The judgment of the court was delivered by Lord Phillips who, at paragraph 35, referring to *Hamilton* (which it analysed fully) as authority said:

> The approach to making an award of costs against a non-party has had to accommodate the change in public policy which has recognised that access to justice can properly be procured by giving those who provide legal services an interest in the outcome of the litigation.

After a careful review of the facts of the case, the court, at paragraph 51, reached **2.56** the conclusion that 'by far the most significant act performed by Mr Egbe was the provision of the necessary funds. Everything else that he did was merely ancillary to that. It was conduct designed to reassure the court that the funds were being provided.' The court could see no logical basis for finding that the actions taken by D4 designed to ensure that the provision of funds had the desired consequence of enabling the original defendants' case to be heard, 'so transformed the nature of [D4's] involvement as to justify an order that he should pay the costs of the proceedings.' It went on to observe, at paragraph 53 that:

> There is no suggestion that [D4] had any personal interest in the outcome of the litigation, or that his intervention gave him any such interest. In this respect his position contrasts with that of those who provide legal services on a conditional fee basis, yet even they do not expose themselves to risk of being ordered to pay the costs of proceedings that they support in this way.

Referring to counsel's submission that D4's role, insofar as it went beyond that of **2.57** a 'pure funder', was that of a 'pure assister', the Court of Appeal observed at paragraph 54, moving slightly away from the distinction drawn in *Hamilton*,

> We are not sure that the adjective 'pure' assists in the analysis. It is, we believe, designed to draw a distinction between those who assist a litigant without ulterior motive and those who do so because they have a personal interest in the outcome of the litigation. Public policy now recognises that it is desirable, in order to facilitate access to justice, that third parties should provide assistance designed to ensure that those who are involved in litigation have the benefit of legal representation. Intervention to this end will not normally render the intervener liable to pay costs. If the intervener has agreed, or anticipates, some reward for his intervention, this will not necessarily expose him to liability for costs. Whether it does will depend upon what is just, having regard to the facts of the individual case, if the intervention is in bad faith, or for some ulterior motive, then the intervener will be at risk in relation to costs occasioned as a consequence of his intervention.

The Court of Appeal's decision, following the public policy discussed in *Hamilton*, **2.58** recognized that it is desirable, in order to facilitate access to justice, that third parties should be able to provide assistance designed to ensure that those who are involved in litigation have the benefit of legal representation without exposure to personal costs liabilities. The court found that there was no justification for the exceptional costs order made by the judge against D4, who was not a party to the substantive proceedings.

7. Arkin v Borchard Lines Ltd & Ors

2.59 *Arkin*[40] was a landmark decision in which long-awaited and invaluable guidance was given concerning the potential liabilities of commercial funders. The case itself was, in the words of the Court of Appeal, 'a disastrous piece of litigation'. It involved an impecunious claimant, Yeheshkel Arkin, lawyers acting under a CFA, and financial support from professional, commercial, funders. The claimant sought damages against several defendants for alleged breaches of Articles 81 and 82 of the EC Treaties. The claim failed on every front.

2.60 Mr Arkin had commenced his action with the benefit of legal aid which was withdrawn almost immediately after he had issued proceedings. His legal team were thereafter retained under conditional fee agreements. He required funding to instruct experts, and he reached a non-champertous agreement with Managers and Processors of Claims Ltd (MPC) to fund the cost of an expert forensic accountant, in return for a contingent fee representing a percentage of any damages recovered.

2.61 At first instance the judge, Colman J, rejected an application, made under s 51 of the Supreme Court Act 1981, for costs against the funder. Colman J observed that Mr Arkin's claim had been the subject of favourable advice from counsel; he found that if Mr Arkin had not entered into a funding agreement, he could not have pursued his claim. He held that it was highly desirable that impecunious claimants who have reasonably sustainable claims should be enabled to bring them to trial by means of non-party funding, expressing the view that if all professional funders were subject to non-party costs orders, there would be no such funders to provide access to the courts to those who could not otherwise afford it.

2.62 In the Court of Appeal, Lord Phillips, delivering the judgment of the court (Lord Phillips, Brooke and Dyson LJJ), began his review of the authorities, at paragraph 23, by considering the principle of 'costs shifting' under which costs usually follow the event. He continued:

> The main principle that underlies the rule is that if one party *causes* another unreasonably to incur legal costs he ought as a matter of justice to indemnify that party for the costs incurred. A defendant who has wrongfully injured a claimant and who has refused to pay the compensation due should pay the costs that he has *caused* the claimant to incur, so that the claimant receives a full indemnity. A claimant who brings an unjustified claim against a defendant so that the defendant is forced to incur legal costs in resisting that claim should indemnify the defendant in respect of the costs he has *caused* the defendant to incur. Causation is usually a vital factor when considering whether to make an award of costs against a party.
>
> 24 Causation is also often a vital factor in leading a court to make a costs order against a non-party. If the non-party is wholly or partly responsible for the fact that

---

[40] [2005] 1 WLR 3055, CA, [2005] EWCA Civ 655.

litigation has taken place, justice may demand that he indemnify the successful party for the costs that he has incurred....

2.63 Having reviewed the leading authorities, Lord Phillips considered the decision of the Judicial Committee of the Privy Council, on appeal from the Court of Appeal of New Zealand, in *Dymocks Franchise Systems (NSW) Pty Ltd v Todd*,[41] which had not been available to Colman J at the time of his decision. In *Dymocks* the Board held that a costs order should be made against a non-party funder which had advanced funds to the defendant in the litigation secured by a debenture. Lord Brown, delivering the Opinion of the Board said, at paragraph 25:

> (1) Although costs orders against non-parties are to be regarded as 'exceptional', exceptional in this context means no more than outside the ordinary run of cases where parties pursue or defend claims for their own benefit and at their own expense. The ultimate question in any such 'exceptional' case is whether in all the circumstances it is just to make the order. It must be recognised that this is inevitably to some extent a fact-specific jurisdiction and that there will often be a number of different considerations in play, some militating in favour of an order, some against. (2) Generally speaking the discretion will not be exercised against 'pure funders', described in para 40 of *Hamilton v Al Fayed (No 2)* [2003] QB 1175, 1194 as 'those with no personal interest in the litigation, who do not stand to benefit from it, are not funding it as a matter of business, and in no way seek to control its course'. In their case the court's usual approach is to give priority to the public interest in the funded party getting access to justice over that of the successful unfunded party recovering his costs and so not having to bear the expense of vindicating his rights. (3) Where, however, the non-party not merely funds the proceedings but substantially also controls or at any rate is to benefit from them, justice will ordinarily require that, if the proceedings fail, he will pay the successful party's costs. The non-party in these cases is not so much facilitating access to justice by the party funded as himself gaining access to justice for his own purposes. He himself is 'the real party' to the litigation, a concept repeatedly invoked throughout the jurisprudence: see, for example, the judgments of the High Court of Australia in *Knight v FP Special Assets Ltd* (1992) 174 CLR 178 and Millett LJ's judgment in *Metalloy Supplies Ltd v MA (UK) Ltd* [1997] 1 WLR 1613. Consistently with this approach, Phillips LJ described the non-party underwriters in *TGA Chapman Ltd v Christopher* [1998] 1 WLR 12, 22 as 'the defendants in all but name'. Nor, indeed, is it necessary that the non-party be 'the only real party' to the litigation in the sense explained in the Knight case, provided that he is 'a real party in... very important and critical respects': see *Arundel Chiropractic Centre Pty Ltd v Deputy Comr of Taxation* (2001) 179 ALR 406, 414 referred to in the *Kebaro* case [2003] FCAFC 5 at [96], [103] and [111]. Some reflection of this concept of 'the real party' is to be found in CPR r 25.13(2)(f) which allows a security for costs order to be made where 'the claimant is acting as a nominal claimant'. (4) Perhaps the most difficult cases are those in which non-parties fund receivers or liquidators

---

[41] *Dymocks Franchise Systems (NSW) Pty Ltd v Todd* [2004] UKPC 39; [2004] 1 WLR 2807.

(or, indeed, financially insecure companies generally) in litigation designed to advance the funder's own financial interests.

2.64 At paragraph 37 in *Arkin*, Lord Phillips said that if Colman J had had the benefit of the summary of the principles given by Lord Brown in *Dymocks*, the court did not believe that Colman J would have approached the fact that MPC were professional funders in the way that he did. Lord Phillips, having referred extensively to the earlier authorities, including *Dymocks*, said (at paragraph 38) that whilst not disputing 'the importance of helping to ensure access to justice, we consider that the judge was wrong not to give appropriate weight to the rule that costs should normally follow the event'. Lord Phillips explained why the decision in *Factortame*, upon which Colman J had relied heavily was not a case in which there was any need to take into account the balancing factor that costs should normally follow the event:

> In our judgment the existence of this rule, and the reasons given to justify its existence, render it unjust that a funder who purchases a stake in an action for a commercial motive should be protected from all liability for the costs of the opposing party if the funded party fails in the action. Somehow or other a just solution must be devised whereby on the one hand a successful opponent is not denied all his costs while on the other hand commercial funders who provide help to those seeking access to justice which they could not otherwise afford are not deterred by the fear of disproportionate costs consequences if the litigation they are supporting does not succeed.

2.65 The court then went on to set out the approach to be adopted to professional funder's costs liabilities:

> 39 If a professional funder, who is contemplating funding a discrete part of an impecunious claimant's expenses, such as the cost of expert evidence, is to be potentially liable for the entirety of the defendant's costs should the claim fail, no professional funder will be likely to be prepared to provide the necessary funding. The exposure will be too great to render funding on a contingency basis of recovery a viable commercial transaction. Access to justice will be denied. We consider, however, that there is a solution that is practicable, just and that caters for some of the policy considerations that we have considered above.

> 40 The approach that we are about to commend will not be appropriate in the case of a funding agreement that falls foul of the policy considerations that render an agreement champertous. A funder who enters into such an agreement will be likely to render himself liable for the opposing party's costs without limit should the claim fail. The present case has not been shown to fall into that category. Our approach is designed to cater for the commercial funder who is financing part of the costs of the litigation in a manner which facilitates access to justice and which is not otherwise objectionable. Such funding will leave the claimant as the party primarily interested in the result of the litigation and the party in control of the conduct of the litigation.

> 41 We consider that a professional funder, who finances part of a claimant's costs of litigation, should be potentially liable for the costs of the opposing party to the extent of the funding provided. The effect of this will, of course, be that, if the funding is provided on a contingency basis of recovery, the funder will require, as the price of the funding, a greater share of the recovery should

the claim succeed. In the individual case, the net recovery of a successful claimant will be diminished. While this is unfortunate, it seems to us that it is a cost that the impecunious claimant can reasonably be expected to bear. Overall justice will be better served than leaving defendants in a position where they have no right to recover any costs from a professional funder whose intervention has permitted the continuation of a claim which has ultimately proved to be without merit.

42 If the course which we have proposed becomes generally accepted, it is likely to have the following consequences. Professional funders are likely to cap the funds that they provide in order to limit their exposure to a reasonable amount. This should have a salutary effect in keeping costs proportionate. In the present case there was no such cap, and it is at least possible that the costs that MPC had agreed to fund grew to an extent where they ceased to be proportionate. Professional funders will also have to consider with even greater care whether the prospects of the litigation are sufficiently good to justify the support that they are asked to give. This also will be in the public interest.

43 In the present appeal we are concerned only with a professional funder who has contributed a part of a litigant's expenses through a non-champertous agreement in the expectation of reward if the litigant succeeds. We can see no reason in principle, however, why the solution we suggest should not also be applicable where the funder has similarly contributed the greater part, or all, of the expenses of the action. We have not, however, had to explore the ramifications of an extension of the solution we propose beyond the facts of the present case, where the funder merely covered the costs incurred by the claimant in instructing expert witnesses.

44 While we have confined our comments to professional funders, it does not follow that it will never be appropriate to order that those who, for motives other than profit, have contributed to the costs of unsuccessful litigation, should contribute to the successful party's costs on a similar basis.

2.66 Thus, since MPC had contributed £1.3m to the costs of Mr Arkin, it was ordered to pay that sum by way of a contribution to defence costs.

2.67 By its decision in *Arkin*, the Court of Appeal established a framework within which professional funders could operate and understand the extent of the commercial risks which they ran by becoming involved, with a view to profit, in funding the other party's litigation. Generally, unless they had entered into champertous agreements (as discussed in *Dymocks*), where their degree of control of the litigation, or their anticipated reward from it, was outside acceptable limits, funders would not be exposed to unlimited costs liabilities in respect of third parties. The case struck a balance between the competing considerations that, on the one hand, a successful party should recover costs which another party has caused him to incur, and on the other, that it was public policy to help to ensure access to justice. The consequence of capping funders' exposure to another party's costs is, of course, that such other party is left to bear a proportion of its own costs which otherwise it might never have incurred. It is such parties who, in this context and to that extent, pay the price of giving effect to the public policy of enabling access to justice.

8. *London & Regional (St George's Court) Ltd v Ministry of Defence*

2.68 In this case[42] the freeholders of a building leased it to the claimant under a Building Agreement which required the Claimant to carry out refurbishment works. Under a separate Agreement for Lease, the claimant sublet the property to the defendant, but agreed to carry out the refurbishment works, which were carried out under a Building Contract made between the claimant and the builders. Litigation ensued between the claimant and the defendant, the claimant asserting that it had procured the builders to carry out additional works ('the variations') as required by the defendant. Issues arose between the builders and the claimant as to various matters; they reached a Settlement Agreement, which included provision for claims, or potential claims, against the defendant ('the MOD claims'). The claimant warranted to the builder that it had not done anything to prejudice the validity of the MOD claims, and in the future would not do anything to prejudice such claims, and provided that the builders should be entitled to pursue those claims against the defendant in lieu of the claimant, using the claimant's name. Further, the builders were to have full and unfettered control of the conduct of the claims, and to indemnify the claimant in respect of any costs liabilities. The claimant was to be entitled to the first £200,000 of any proceeds of the claims, but thereafter the builders were entitled to any recoveries.

2.69 The defendant objected that the Settlement Agreement was champertous, and that the builders were officious intermeddlers who had complete control of the litigation. One objection taken was that the warranty as to doing nothing to prejudice the MOD claims meant that the claimant's own witnesses would be obliged to give a less than frank account of the claims when giving evidence. Thus, it was suggested, the proceedings had a tendency to corrupt public justice.

2.70 Coulson J referred to the review of authorities, on the law of maintenance and champerty, by Underhill J in *Mansell v Robinson* [2007] EWHC 101 (QB), noting in particular that the rules against champerty 'so far as they have survived, are primarily concerned with the protection of the integrity of the litigation process in this jurisdiction'.[43]

2.71 Coulson J rejected the suggestion that the Settlement Agreement was champertous. He held that the builders had 'an entirely legitimate financial interest in the outcome of the proceedings'; they had provided the cost of the disputed variations and incurred the costs in carrying out the works. The position was, therefore, 'as far from maintenance and champerty as it is possible to get'.[44] Coulson J also found that the Settlement Agreement had no tendency to corrupt public justice, but was designed simply to ensure that a party who had done the work could attempt to obtain reimbursement

---

[42] [2008] EWHC 526 (TCC).
[43] See para 103, and *Papera Traders Co Ltd v Hyundai (Merchant) Marine Co Ltd (No 2)* [2002] 2 Lloyds LR 692.
[44] Para 108.

from the party who had benefited. He found that whilst witnesses might feel a tension between the terms of the warranty and an obligation to tell the truth, it was necessary to be realistic, and that on its proper construction the warranty would not affect the actual giving of evidence under oath, so that it would not affect the reliability of evidence called; had there been any potential threat from the warranty to the public administration of justice, then the relevant provision could have been severed from the rest of the Settlement Agreement.

2.72 Whilst *London and Regional* was not concerned directly with litigation funding, Coulson J's reasoning is significant for the operation of third party funding. In practice funders will require warranties and representations, as to the truth of instructions and alignment of conduct in a fashion supportive of the case, from those who seek their assistance. This is not unreasonable given the very substantial investment that funders must frequently make in order to enable a case to be pursued. The judgment recognizes that such commitments are not sought so as to interfere with the integrity of the proceedings, and should not be construed in that fashion. It is difficult to conceive of a term that would be interpreted as requiring a party to conceal the truth in breach of obligations as to disclosure and to stating the truth. Any term that imported such a requirement would clearly be void for contravening public policy.

9. *Merchantbridge & Co Ltd v Safron General Partner 1 Ltd*

2.73 This case[45] concerned, unusually, liability of non-parties for adverse costs arising from funding a defence rather than a claim. The action concerned a claim for damages or payment of fees arising under an investment advisory agreement which had allegedly been terminated in breach of contract. The claim succeeded. The first defendant was the general partner, and fund manager, of a limited partnership which had operated an investment fund ('the Fund'). The remaining nine defendants ('the non-parties') were said to be investors in the Fund, or to have been involved with the funding of the costs of the defence of the action. The basis of the application for costs by the successful claimants, under s 51 of the Senior Courts Act 1981, was that the non-parties had funded, substantially controlled, and were interested in the defence of the first defendant, and that they were the 'real parties' who had funded or controlled the proceedings for their own benefit and interest. Some of the non-parties accepted that they had contributed to funding but maintained that the vital ingredients of personal benefit and interest were absent. Another group contended that only one of them was a funder, and that it had acted reasonably and in good faith throughout, was a reluctant funder, and did not control the litigation. The first defendant was without funds as it had been closed as an investment vehicle.

2.74 The trial judge, HH Judge Mackie QC, began his judgment by expressing his concern at how what had been intended to be a short, summary exercise for the

---

[45] [2011] EWHC 1524.

determination of non-party costs liabilities had become very expensive and time consuming satellite litigation in which the cost issue was being determined almost five years after judgment had been delivered in the trial. It is to be anticipated that such expensive and time consuming satellite litigation will be a continuing part of the landscape in respect of non-party costs claims, certainly whilst the principles applicable to such matters are still being established. As Judge Mackie observed, the process of costs determination upon non-party costs applications is not straightforward because of the proliferating number of authorities at the appellate level which deal with guidelines, and the appellate guidance is contained in cases which often have unusual facts and give rise to diverse considerations. A further complicating factor which he identified was that the law 'has moved a considerable distance', so that many of the earlier authorities are not as authoritative as they once were.

2.75 The judge recognized that it will generally be relevant whether the non-party is responsible for the litigation taking place and has caused the successful opponent to incur costs that it would not otherwise have done. He noted that the cases demonstrated that the non-party's interest does not have to be financial, and that an order can be made if the non-party has an interest but does not exercise any control. (The latter situation is, of course, very much the case with litigation funders.)

2.76 The judge concluded that the funders had a legitimate interest in the outcome of the proceedings, but he distinguished it from a case of 'pure' litigation funding by disinterested parties as in *Hamilton v Al Fayed*;[46] the non-parties had the benefit and interest of removing what was perceived to be a nuisance. He went on to find that although this was the funding of a defence rather than a claim, the funders did control the litigation, and that when the non-parties decided to fund it, the first defendant participated, and when they decided to stop funding, the first defendant took no part in the case; when they decided that the first defendant should resume conduct of the action and provided funds, it did so. If the defence had not been funded, the claimants would have obtained a default judgment.

2.77 The judge held that the non-parties took rational commercial decisions throughout, and that whilst no moral blame attached to them, they took a decision to fund the case in which they had an interest of their own to protect, controlling all major decisions themselves and leaving only minor ones to their agent. But for their decision to fund, the claimants' costs would have been much less.

2.78 The judge found that several of the non-parties should be liable to pay nothing, because their part had been 'either mechanical or...well above the real fray'. The remaining non-parties were ordered to pay the costs without limit. He distinguished the case from *Arkin*. It had been submitted on behalf of one of the non-parties that

---

[46] *Hamilton v Al Fayed* [2002] EWCA Civ 665.

an order requiring the funder to pay costs which were greater than the amount funded, would be unfair. The judge disagreed. He explained that '*Arkin* was based on a concern that professional funding for a discrete part of an impecunious claimant's expenses would cease to be available if that funder faced potential liability for the whole of the defendants' costs.' The decision in *Arkin* was designed:

> ...to cater for the commercial funder who is financing a part of the costs of the litigation in a manner which facilitates access to justice and which is not otherwise objectionable. Such funding will leave the claimant as the party primarily interested in the result of the litigation and the party in control of the conduct of the litigation.[47]

2.79 The public policy considerations in *Arkin* were found not to apply to the different factual situation in the case being considered. No limit was imposed, in the circumstances, upon the costs orders made.

2.80 It is clear from the concluding passages in the judgment that particularly important factors affecting the result had been the judge's findings as to interest and control.

10. *Sibthorpe and Morris v Southwark London Borough Council*

2.81 Sibthorpe[48] was a Court of Appeal decision on champerty. Two cases, heard together, concerned the extent to which a solicitor is prevented from indemnifying a client against any liability for costs in a piece of litigation, in which they are acting for the client. Both cases were claims against a local housing authority for damages for breach of covenant.

2.82 The solicitors were instructed under conditional fee agreements (CFAs) both of which contained a clause which provided for indemnity to the client in the following terms: 'If you lose, you pay your opponent's charges and disbursements. You may be able to take out an insurance policy against this risk. If you are unable to obtain an insurance policy against this risk, we indemnify you against payment of your opponent's charges at the end of the case if you lose. This means that we will pay those charges.'

2.83 The substantive actions were compromised on terms providing for payment of a sum to the claimants with costs to be subject to detailed assessment unless agreed. The claim for costs was disallowed by the deputy master on the basis that the solicitors were not entitled to costs because the presence of the indemnity in the CFAs made the arrangement champertous. He held that it was unlawful for a solicitor to agree to conduct litigation on terms which gave the solicitor a financial interest in the outcome, save where legislation permits and that since there was no legislation which so permitted the CFAs were invalidated in their entirety.

---

[47] *Arkin v Borchard Lines* at para 40.
[48] [2011] 1 WLR 2111, CA.

2.84 The claimants appealed and Macduff J took a different view from the deputy master.[49] He concluded that whilst the indemnity was not sanctioned by legislation, jurisprudence showed that the law had moved on, and that the question of whether an agreement was void on the grounds of champerty should be decided by reference to the facts and circumstances of the particular case. He decided that there was no public policy reason in these cases for invalidating the CFAs.

2.85 The defendant appealed to the Court of Appeal (Lord Neuberger MR, Lloyd and Gross LJJ). Lord Neuberger delivered the leading judgment; Lloyd LJ delivered a short concurring judgment, adopting Lord Neuberger's reasoning for rejecting the argument that the indemnity was unenforceable as being champertous, and Gross LJ agreed with both judgments. Lord Neuberger MR carried out a careful review of the historic and recent authorities on champerty and maintenance. He distinguished arrangements between those who conduct litigation or provide advocacy services from agreements where the person conducting the litigation is not a party. Where the arrangements are made with lawyers instructed in the litigation, he concluded that they have been treated as a special category or species of champertous agreements, and were subject to stricter rules.[50] (This, of course, was subject to the statutory provision for CFAs under s 58 of the Courts and Legal Services Act 1990, but the indemnity under consideration was not permitted by that provision.) It follows from Lord Neuberger's analysis that the assessment as to the impact of champerty is different in such cases from those concerned with an agreement between a client and a litigation funder.

2.86 It was well established law, when the case concerned was decided, that it would be champertous for a lawyer to take a financial interest in a piece of litigation, save as provided for by legislation. In usual circumstances, the financial interest concerned would be a share in the proceeds of a successful claim. The situation under consideration was different. It consisted of the responsibility to pay the defendant's legal costs if the case was lost. As Lord Neuberger observed at paragraph 42, there was no case in which such an arrangement had been held to be champertous; champerty introduced the notion of a division of spoils, as he noted in the following paragraph. He added, at paragraph 44, that to find the arrangement champertous, the court would have had to extend the law on champerty at a time when, as was apparent from judicial observations in the cases he had reviewed, the scope of champerty was to be curtailed rather than expanded.

2.87 The CFAs were unobjectionable save for the indemnity. In the end, the desire to accommodate access to justice prevailed over rival considerations. Lord Neuberger MR addressed this point directly in the concluding passages of his judgment dealing with the topic:

---

[49] [2010] 4 Costs LR 526.
[50] See paras 37–41.

49 Access to justice is an essential ingredient of a modern civilised society, but it is difficult to achieve for the great majority of citizens, especially with the ever reducing availability of legal aid. This has been accompanied by a shift in legislative policy towards favouring the relaxation of previously tight professional ethical constraints, in order to enable a variety of more flexible funding arrangements (which some applaud and others believe give too much weight to consumerism and involve expensive regulation). In these circumstances, I find it hard to accept that, by shouldering the risk of an adverse order for costs against his client, a solicitor is acting contrary to public policy, which is, of course, the basis for the law of champerty. It is one thing to say, in relation to contracts with those who conduct litigation, that the reach of champerty should not be curtailed by the courts. It is quite another to say that, in relation to such contracts, the law of champerty should be expanded. I bear in mind in this context the observation of Danckwerts LJ in *Hill v Archbold* [1968] 1 QB 686, 697, that the law in this area 'depends upon the question of public policy, and public policy...must be alterable by the passage of time'...

51 In my view, we should accede to the argument that it would be inappropriate in the 21st century to extend the law of champerty. There is some force in the argument that economic logic supports the case for condemning the indemnity as champertous. However, the rule against champerty is not entirely logical in its extent or limits, judicial observations strongly suggest that champerty should be curtailed not expanded, and, given that champerty is based on public policy, it is hard to see how arrangements such as the indemnity, at the very least in connection with litigation such as that in these cases, are against the public interest or undermine justice.

11. *Jennifer Simpson (as assignee of Alan Catchpole) v Norfolk & Norwich University Hospital NHS Trust*

This case[51] demonstrates that despite the considerable inroads which the legal policy of allowing access to justice has made as to the reach of the principles of maintenance and champerty in the modern age, the historic policy considerations which underpinned those torts still have their application in circumstances when access to justice considerations are not in play. The case related to an assignment of an action. **2.88**

Mrs Simpson's late husband had contracted MRSA whilst in hospital. His death was not caused by MRSA, but Mrs Simpson believed that the hospital had failed to implement appropriate infection control procedures. She commenced a damages claim, as her late husband's personal representative, against the defendant in relation to her late husband's suffering due to the infection, but it was compromised without admission of liability. **2.89**

Mr Catchpole, another patient at the same hospital, had issued proceedings for personal injury after contracting MRSA. He later assigned all his rights in his claim to Mrs Simpson for the consideration of £1. Her motive in pursuing the **2.90**

---

[51] [2012] QB 640, CA.

claim appeared to have been to force the hospital to confront its failure to implement adequate infection control procedures.

2.91 The defendant applied to strike out the action as being void for champerty as Mrs Simpson had no legitimate interest in the case.

2.92 The case was struck out by the district judge, whose decision was upheld by the judge on appeal. The Court of Appeal (Maurice Kay, Moore-Bick LJJ, and Dame Janet Smith) upheld the decision of the judge, although it found that he had been wrong to hold that the claim for damages for personal injury was not assignable. The Court of Appeal held that the law does not recognize the assignment of a bare right to litigate unsupported by an interest of a kind sufficient to support the assignee's pursuit of proceedings for his own benefit. An assignment of a cause of action for the purpose of enabling an assignee or a third party to profit from litigation would generally be void as savouring of champerty. Mrs Simpson's motives were not of a kind that the law recognized as sufficient to support an assignment of what would otherwise have been a bare right to litigate an action.

2.93 Moore-Bick LJ, with whose judgment both other members of the court agreed, expressly stated, at paragraph 22, that access to justice was not a consideration in the case because there was no reason to believe that Mr Catchpole could not have pursued his claim as easily as Mrs Simpson, if he had wished to do so.

2.94 At paragraph 24 of his judgment, Moore-Bick LJ highlighted the continuing development of the law in this field (which for the reasons mentioned by HH Judge Mackie QC in *Merchantbridge* will continue to contribute to the delay and complexity of the satellite litigation concerned with application for costs against non-parties), and the policy consideration which militate against permitting the assignment of bare rights to litigate:

> Since the law on maintenance and champerty is open to further development as perceptions of the public interest change, I do not think that it is possible to state in definitive terms what does and does not constitute a sufficient interest to support the assignment of a cause of action in tort for personal injury. However, I do not think that it is in the public interest to encourage litigation whose principal object is not to obtain a remedy for a legal wrong, but to pursue an object of a different kind altogether. If the claimant's real concern had been to ensure that the assignor was able to obtain compensation, she could have taken steps to enable him to pursue the litigation in his own name, but in truth her only interest in the litigation is to pursue a campaign against the hospital. In my view it would be damaging to the administration of justice and unfair to defendants for the law to recognise an interest of that kind as sufficient to support the assignment of a cause of action for personal injury, because the conduct of the proceedings, including aspects such as a willingness to resort to mediation and a readiness to compromise, where appropriate, is entirely in the hands of the assignee and is liable to be distorted by considerations that have little if anything to do with the merits of the claim itself. There is a real risk that to regard a collateral interest of this kind as sufficient to support the

assignment of a cause of action for personal injury would encourage the purchase of such claims by those who wished to make use of them to pursue their own ends.

12. *Cecil & others v Bayat & others*

From the case discussed above, it is apparent that the courts have recognized the part which litigation funding has to play in affording access to justice, and legal policy has been shaped accordingly. However, there are limitations upon the extent to which the need for funding will be accommodated in the procedural aspects of litigation, as well as in the developments of the substantive law, as is well demonstrated by the decision of the Court of Appeal (Rix, Wilson, Stanley Burnton LJJ) in *Cecil & others v Bayat & others*.[52] The case should be considered by any party who is facing a potential limitation problem and who is apprehensive about serving proceedings before funding arrangements are put in place, for as Stanley Burnton LJ said at paragraph 51, limitation defences are, in the context of claims which do not include claims for death or personal injury, blind to the resources of the claimant. **2.95**

The claimants had brought proceedings for damages against the defendants in the USA; those proceedings had been dismissed without determination of the merits, and the claimants' appeal against that decision had been dismissed. The claimants had expended large sums of money in the US proceedings. Consequently, it took them some time to bring proceedings in England. Their claim was issued in May 2008, whilst the limitation period in respect of the claims concerned would have expired in November of that same year. They made an application to the court to extend time for service of the claim form, contending that they had not yet completed their financial arrangements to cover the cost of funding the case; they were in the process of obtaining litigation funding. Various judges at first instance granted extensions of time to the claimants for the service of the claim form, and Hamblen J refused the defendants' application to set aside those orders. The defendants appeal to the Court of Appeal was allowed, and Hamblen J's order was reversed. The court's leading judgment was delivered by Stanley Burnton LJ, with whose judgment both other members of the court agreed, Rix LJ doing so in a concurring judgment. **2.96**

The court held that an application to extend time for service of a claim form, made in circumstances in which a limitation defence might be prejudiced, would only be granted in exceptional circumstances, and if a claimant had taken all reasonable steps to serve the claim form within its period of validity but had been unable to do so. **2.97**

Stanley Burnton LJ held (at paragraph 54) that the balance of hardship had not been considered properly. The primary question was whether, if an extension of time is granted, the defendant will, or may, be deprived of a limitation defence. **2.98**

---

[52] [2011] 1 WLR 3086, CA.

The claimants' loss of their claim was examined but the defendants' loss of their limitation defence was ignored; further (at paragraph 55), he observed that the stronger the claim, the more important is the limitation defence, which should not be circumvented by an extension of time for serving a claim form, save in exceptional circumstances. He held that where limitation is imminent but funding is not in place, the wish on the part of the claimants to put funding in place before serving the claim form was not a good reason to extend time for service, especially where extension might deprive the defendant of a limitation defence. The claimant should have issued and then applied for a stay of the proceedings whilst the funding arrangements were concluded. He explained, at paragraphs 42 and 43, that

> ...it was not for the claimants unilaterally to decide to postpone service of their claim form. They should have served it in the period of its initial validity, and, if they were not in a financial position to proceed immediately with the claim, they should have issued an application seeking a stay, or an extension of the time for procedural steps to be taken. I do not accept that this would necessarily have involved great legal costs. The nature of their application would have been apparent. It would have been for the court to ensure that those costs were kept within acceptable limits, and if necessary an order limiting the claimants' cost exposure in respect of that application could have been sought under CPR r 44.18. The court would, in my view, have been astute to prevent the claimants being unduly prejudiced by any attempt by the defendants to seek to proliferate costs at that very early stage.

2.99 He added that:

> ...any forensic difficulties caused by the financial constraints of the claimants should have been the subject of case management by the court.

2.100 The court's decision was, therefore, that it had been viable for the proceedings to have been issued and served, without funding and costs protection having been in place, and there is a distinction to be drawn between the funds and adverse costs protection required to commence proceedings, from that which is required to take a case to trial.

2.101 The correct manner in which to address the difficulty under consideration is, therefore, to issue and serve, and then, if it is still required, to seek a stay.

13. *Tinseltime Ltd v Eryl Roberts & Ors*

2.102 The application for a non-party costs order in this case[53] raised an issue of general importance, namely whether or not a solicitor who takes on a case for an impecunious claimant under a conditional fee agreement where there is no after the event (ATE) insurance policy in place, and who also agrees to fund the disbursements

---

[53] [2013] PNLR 4, [2012] EWHC 2628 (TCC).

necessary to allow the case to proceed, thereby constitutes himself a non-party funder and renders himself liable to a non-party costs order in the same way as if he were a commercial non-party litigation funder.

This case provides support for the position that solicitors who act on a CFA, and who also provide funding for disbursements, will not generally be liable for adverse costs as a non-party funder. However, the judgment also suggests that future decisions on solicitors' liability might be different in the case of damages based agreements which were introduced in April 2013. **2.103**

The judge, HH Judge Stephen Davies, considered the important much earlier cases of *Tolstoy*,[54] where the solicitors acted *pro bono* and *Hodgson*[55] where immunity from costs was affirmed in relation to solicitors acting upon a CFA. **2.104**

The judge held that it was not appropriate to make a non-party costs order against a solicitor who acted for an impecunious claimant under a conditional fee agreement where there was no ATE policy in place, and who also agreed to fund the disbursements necessary to allow the case to proceed. There was no difference between the position of a solicitor acting under a CFA who had agreed to fund disbursements under the CFA and one who had not, since both arrangements were permitted and were regarded as meeting a recognized legitimate public policy aim. It made no difference, he held, that the solicitor knew that the client was impecunious and that there was no ATE policy in place. **2.105**

The judge concluded (paragraph 56) that the authorities established the following principles: **2.106**

(1) the starting point in any case must be the first principle stated by Lord Brown in *Dymocks*, namely that the ultimate question is whether in all the circumstances it is just to make a non-party costs order, that this is a fact specific enquiry, and that it must be recognized that in a particular case the court may have to balance a number of different considerations, some of them conflicting;
(2) the starting point when considering the position of a solicitor is that it must be shown that he has in some way acted beyond or outside his role as a solicitor conducting litigation for his client to make him liable for a non-party costs order;
(3) the starting point when considering the position of a solicitor acting under a CFA is that the fact that he stands to benefit financially from the success of the litigation, in that otherwise he will not be able to recover his profit costs or his success fee, does not of itself mean that he has acted in some

---

[54] *Tolstoy v Aldington* [1996] 1 WLR 736.
[55] *Hodgson v Imperial Tobacco* [1998] 1 WLR 1056.

way beyond or outside his role as a solicitor conducting litigation for his client; and

(4) the starting point when considering the position of a solicitor acting under a CFA who has agreed to fund disbursements under the CFA should be no different from the case of a solicitor who has not, since both arrangements are permitted and are regarded as meeting a recognized legitimate public policy aim. The position is no different where the solicitor knows that the client is impecunious and that there is no ATE policy in place; that is because acting for clients who are impecunious does not take the solicitor outside his role as such and, indeed, it is consistent with the recognized public policy aim of promoting access to justice, and because there is no obligation on a solicitor acting under a CFA to ensure that ATE insurance cover is in place when his client is impecunious.

2.107 The Judge suggested (at paragraph 57) that whilst it was unrealistic to seek to identify what would, or would not, be sufficient in any individual case to render it just to make a non-party costs order, in the majority of cases there would have to be present something beyond the combination of factors which he identified in the four principles mentioned, such as some financial benefit to the solicitor over and above the benefit which he could expect to receive from the CFA, or some exercise of control of the litigation over and above that which would be expected from a solicitor acting on behalf of a client, or some combination of both.

2.108 The judge's approach in this case seems to have been vindicated by the decision of the Court of Appeal in *Flatman v Germany* considered next.[56]

14. *Flatman v Germany*

2.109 In this case[57] the successful defendants sought orders for disclosure of documents relating to the funding arrangements between unsuccessful claimants and their solicitors. These were personal injury cases and both claimants were represented by the same firm of solicitors. The claimants were impecunious and were without ATE insurance. The county court judge refused the defendants' applications, but on appeal to the High Court, Eady J granted the disclosure orders sought, holding that by funding disbursements a solicitor stepped outside the normal role of a solicitor and thereby became potentially liable to a third party costs order. The Court of Appeal granted permission for a second appeal.

2.110 The Law Society intervened in the second appeal, which resulted in an analysis on the circumstances in which a non-party costs order would be appropriate. The Court of Appeal (Mummery, Richards, and Leveson LJJ) held that Eady J was wrong in holding that a solicitor who funded his clients disbursements was,

---

[56] See in particular para 50 in *Flatman*.
[57] [2013] 1 WLR 2676, CA.

without more, to be treated as the real party to the litigation, so that the basis upon which disclosure had been ordered was not justified. However, the Court of Appeal dismissed the appeals because of further information which had come to light to control the course of the litigation, by pressing on with it without ATE cover contrary to the express instructions of their client in one case. This possibility, the court held, more than justified the disclosure orders.

15. *Harcus Sinclair (a Firm) v Buttonwood Legal Capital Limited & Ors*

2.111 The circumstances in which a litigation funder may terminate a funding arrangement are matters of some importance to solicitors, clients, and funders. This High Court decision[58] is the only reported case on the point known to the author. The funder, Buttonwood Legal Capital Limited (BLC) entered into an agreement to lend money to the clients in order for them to pursue a very substantial and high cost claim. Harcus Sinclair was the firm of solicitors holding the money advanced, and did so as stakeholders; it was not the firm acting for the clients, who were represented by another firm of solicitors ('the solicitors'). Harcus Sinclair brought an interpleader action to determine whether, and if so, to whom it should pay the money.

2.112 BLC was provided with an initial preliminary advice from counsel on the prospects of the claim at the commencement of the funding process. The funding agreement was concluded in the expectation that a more detailed opinion would be provided as the case progressed. The funding agreement contained a clause providing that BLC were entitled to terminate the agreement unilaterally where, in their reasonable opinion, the prospects of success were 60 per cent or less. After significant funds had been drawn down in respect of ongoing costs, BLC required the solicitors to obtain a full opinion from counsel, but several months later it had still not been provided. Consequently, BLC instructed their own, independent counsel to review the merits of the case, based on the information that they had; they had not been provided with a copy of a letter, which they had requested to see, which related to an issue of repudiatory breach in the underlying claim. The opinions from independent counsel assessed the chances of success at less than 60 per cent; he had not had the benefit of seeing a copy of the letter which had been requested, although counsel appeared to have expressed the view that the absence of the letter had not affected his conclusion. BLC's board considered independent counsel's opinions, and took the view that the prospects of success did not cross the 60 per cent threshold. BLC terminated the funding agreement.

2.113 The clients contended that BLC's opinion was produced without sight of relevant material; in particular, potential witness evidence, and the letter that had been requested. They disputed that BLC's opinion on the chances of success for the claim

---

[58] [2013] EWHC 1193 (Ch).

was reasonable, and contested the effectiveness of the termination of the funding agreement. David Donaldson QC, sitting as a Deputy High Court Judge, found that the decision made by BLC to terminate the agreement was reasonable. The deputy judge said that he proceeded on the basis that the reasonableness of the opinion fell to be determined not only by the material which the opinion former chose to consider, but, if wider, the totality of the material which had then been practically available to it. He held that the witness evidence was not available because it had not been released to BLC, and that the letter also had not been made available. The deputy judge rejected a submission that to come to a reasonable opinion BLC would have had to allow the clients to make representations on the merits. This, he said, was founded upon an unstated premise that the clause in the funding agreement that the requirement that the estimate of prospects be a reasonable opinion extended to matters of process. He held that it was a purely substantive question, to be answered by an objective assessment of the available evidence against the background of the relevant legal rules and principles applicable to the claim. If the estimated figure was by that test within the ambit of reasonableness, it mattered not by what route or process it was reached. The deputy judge observed, in passing, that the court had been concerned with a new type of satellite litigation, of which, given recent developments in the funding of large commercial claims, the courts appeared likely to see much more.

2.114 The litigation funding process requires engagement and interaction from the funder, the lawyers retained, and the client. Funding of cases is based upon the information available to the funders to enable them to make their assessment. Clients who enter into funding agreements have obligations to provide information and to cooperate with funders in order that the funder can continue to be satisfied as to the merits of any case. In this case, the obligations to provide further information were clear and the funding was provided subject to the express provision allowing for the funder to review the prospects of success. It must be unlikely that a court would be prepared to find that a funder's opinion as to merits was not reasonable in circumstances where a funder has taken reasonable steps to obtain relevant information, and has based its assessment on the advice of suitably experienced, and properly instructed, independent counsel who appears adequately to have considered the relevant facts and law.

16. *Excalibur Ventures LLC v Texas Keystone Inc.; Gulf Keystone Petroleum Ltd; Gulf Keystone Petroleum International Ltd; Gulf Keystone Petroleum (UK) Ltd*

2.115 This case[59] has been the subject of considerable comment in the context of its implications for the future of the commerciality of litigation funding. It was, however,

---

[59] [2013] EWHC 2767 (Comm); EWHC 4278 (Comm).

a most unusual case in terms of its size, complexity, duration, and costs levels. The trial lasted five months, and the trial bundle ran to 373 volumes.

2.116 Excalibur Ventures LLC had entered into a Collaboration Agreement with Texas Keystone and also, it alleged, Gulf Keystone Petroleum Limited, an AIM-listed oil and gas exploration company which held interests in production sharing contracts for the oilfields in question. Excalibur claimed that the Collaboration Agreement entitled it to an interest in all four of the contracts claiming specific performance, or damages of more than US$1.6 billion. The defendants denied any liability to Excalibur.

2.117 The claims were dismissed. The judge, Christopher Clarke LJ, was significantly critical of the claimants. He said that the case was 'essentially speculative and opportunistic' and that 'it was based on no sound foundation in fact or law and it has met with a resounding, indeed catastrophic defeat.' It was a complete disaster for Excalibur. It lost on every point.

2.118 The case had received the benefit of litigation funding, a fact of which the court was aware as is apparent from the terms of the costs judgment.[60] The fact that it had become public knowledge that litigation funding had been used was something which piqued the interest of legal commentators as it was such a spectacular defeat for the claimant. There were suggestions that the case represented a major blow to commercial litigation funding, not least because of the levels of costs incurred in the case. The judge noted that Gulf's indications of costs exceeded £15m, and that the figure for Texas was said to be in excess of £10m.

2.119 Furthermore, the judge awarded indemnity costs against Excalibur.

2.120 The judge mentioned that security for costs had been previously provided in the sum of £17.5m. He recorded that funders had failed to give any indication that they would pay any of the costs that Excalibur had been ordered to pay, although it appeared that they had so far financed the litigation as far as Excalibur's costs were concerned. Even so, the judge ordered that still further security for costs should be provided within a 14-day period, and directed that if it was not, then the defendants should be at liberty to join the funders. This order, he said, would signal to them that if they did not put Excalibur in funds, they would have to face a claim that they should pay the costs. He was, however, at pains to point out at the conclusion of his costs judgment that nothing which he had decided should be taken to indicate that the court would take any particular course in relation to any one or more of the funders.

2.121 The case underlines that funding, although potentially high return, is also high risk. Whether the result in *Excalibur*, and the very considerable downside for

---

[60] [2013] EWHC 4278 (Comm).

funders which it highlighted, will have the chilling effect on litigation funding that some have feared, and others hoped for, remains to be seen. Its features were, however, very unusual; it was far from what represents a typical case for funding.

2.122 The case may yet be of more interest in terms of adverse costs. Whilst the costs limits described in the decision in *Arkin*[61] have not yet been the subject of reconsideration, it may be that the time for reappraisal will come soon. In *Tinseltime* the court was invited by counsel making the application for costs against the solicitor to reconsider the *Arkin* cap on the exposure of funders, in the light of observations made by Sir Rupert Jackson, in his Final Report reviewing civil justice litigation, but the judge declined to do so, saying that it was not open to him as a first instance judge.

C. Conclusions

2.123 A summary of the state of English law as regards funding, champerty, and maintenance was very helpfully set out in 2008 by Coulson J and was approved by Jackson LJ in his Preliminary Report as follows:

> a) the mere fact that litigation services have been provided in return for a promise in the share of the proceeds is not by itself sufficient to justify that promise being held to be unenforceable: see *R (Factortame) Ltd v Secretary of State for Transport (No 8)* [2003] QB 381;
>
> b) in considering whether an agreement is unlawful on grounds of maintenance or champerty, the question is whether the agreement has a tendency to corrupt public justice and that such a question requires the closest attention to the nature and surrounding circumstance of a particular agreement: see *Giles v Thompson*;
>
> c) the modern authorities demonstrated a flexible approach where courts have generally declined to hold that an agreement under which a party provided assistance with litigation in return for a share of the proceeds was unenforceable: see, for example, *Papera Traders Co Ltd v Hyundai (Merchant) Marine Co Ltd (No.2)* [2002] 2 Lloyd's Rep 692;
>
> d) the rules against champerty, so far as they have survived, are primarily concerned with the protection of the integrity of the litigation process in this jurisdiction: see *Papera*.

2.124 The financing of litigation is not by itself sufficient to constitute maintenance. Additionally, an agreement to finance a piece of litigation in return for a share of the proceeds is not automatically champerty. There would need to be evidence of an improper motive whether it be malicious or vexatious, causing delay or abuse of process or some other form of impropriety.[62] In order to decide if third party

---

[61] *Arkin v Borchard Lines.*
[62] *Buday v Location of Missing Heirs Inc* [1993] 16 OR (3d) at 262.

litigation funding is permissible in any particular matter there has to be an analysis carried out of the facts of that specific case.

2.125 There are, of course, certain differences between funded litigation and other cases. Quite obviously, a fundamental difference is that in a funded case, each month the legal bill raised by the client's solicitors is paid by the funder rather than the client. Some funders deposit the full amount of the facility into the solicitors' client account once the funding agreement is signed; others pay on a monthly or other regular drawdown request. Either way, the whole essence of the arrangement is that the funder pays the legal bills.

2.126 There is quite widespread lack of understanding as to the extent to which the litigation funder can influence the decision making process in a case. This may be attributable to confusion with the rights of insurers to conduct claims on behalf of their insured. As the authorities which have been considered above demonstrate, loss of control of the conduct of a claim by the funded party to the funder is likely to render the funding arrangement susceptible to being held unenforceable as champertous. Funders will be conscious of this, and will not wish to risk have their funding agreements declared unenforceable, with the concurrent risk that they could be held liable to a third party for all of the costs of the litigation without an 'Arkin cap'. This danger was expressly recognized in Sir Rupert Jackson's Preliminary Report, at paragraph 15.3.2.

2.127 Litigation funding has a long history, from the ancient Greeks and medieval England via twentieth-century Australia. However, its use in modern day litigation in England and Wales is tolerated as it provides 'access to justice'. The evolution of the law in the recent past has largely been a response to accommodate this need. There can be no doubt that the impetus for change in judicial attitudes was much reinforced by the introduction, in the Courts and Legal Services Act 1990, of arrangements making conditional fee agreements permissible. Initially such arrangements were to be permitted in respect of the types of claim which had commonly been funded with the benefit of legal aid, but with the passing of the Access to Justice Act 1999, the scope for alternative funding of claims was much widened, and the development of legal policy in the field has continued apace. It shows little sign of slowing down, and no doubt the additional raft of changes introduced in April 2013 following the Jackson Review will spawn further changes in the development of legal policy.

2.128 As explained above, whilst the historic ancient crimes and torts of maintenance and champerty have been abolished, the public policy which lay behind them, and which continues to inform the law, has survived though in an ever developing form. A third party litigation funder cannot impose their will on a client. They cannot have the final decision making authority which remains with the client. The relationship between the solicitor and the client does not change, although under the terms of a funding agreement, the client's solicitors will usually be required to report regularly on developments and progress to the funder. Some funders will take a keen interest in such matters, which is to be expected since the funder is often making a substantial investment in the litigation.

2.129 In Australia, litigation funders' scope for influence on the client and the case was considered in *Fostif*,[63] a case discussed in Chapter 3. However, for now, it suffices to say that the decision allows funders in Australia to exercise far more control and influence over a case than would ever be allowed, currently, in England.

2.130 The author's experience, personal and anecdotal, is that in most funded cases the solicitors and clients are happy to allow the funder to be involved in the regular client updates on the case. Similar experience is that many clients and their legal advisers welcome the contribution made by a funder's representatives who can sometimes introduce additional experience, perceptions, knowledge, and assessments. The client will be bound by the funding agreement to cooperate fully with the funder's requests for information. Additionally, the agreement usually allows the funder to be notified of all offers received and to have the choice of whether to be present at any appropriate meetings, for example, consultations with leading counsel, strategy discussions, or mediations.

2.131 The law on maintenance and champerty has developed considerably in the last 50 years and litigation funding (clearly a practice which falls within the historic definitions of champerty and maintenance) is now thought to be acceptable as a matter of public policy, as long as the funder does not start to control the litigation, or exert too much influence or control. Equally, both the reality of who is actually the party to litigation and for whose benefit the litigation is being brought are also relevant. There is a point at which the real party ceases to be the named party and becomes the party with the most to gain, in other words the agreement over the division of the proceeds of the case is also a relevant factor—particularly if the funder is to receive more than half of the proceeds.

2.132 As Lord Phillips MR said, when giving the judgment of the Court of Appeal in *Factortame*,[64] although no longer a crime, 'champerty survives as a rule of public policy capable of rendering a contract unenforceable'. To assess this it is necessary to look at the arrangement or agreement in the round—does it undermine the purity of justice? Each decision is, and will be, made on a case by case basis. Whilst it is inevitable that the law will develop on this basis, absent statutory intervention, this carries with it the inevitable disadvantage to all involved in funded litigation that there is real uncertainty as to the limits of

---

[63] *Campbells Cash & Carry Pty Ltd v Fostif Pty Ltd* [2006] HCA 41.
[64] *R (Factortame Ltd) v Secretary of State for Transport, Local Government and the Regions (No 8)* [2002] EWCA Civ 932, [2003] QB 381, at 399, para 31.

what is, and is not, permissible, and as to the extent of adverse costs exposure. It does not serve the interests of those involved in funded litigation that the uncertainties which arise have to be resolved in complex and expensive satellite litigation, as was recognized in the judgment of HH Judge Mackie QC in *Merchantbridge*. It is, therefore, to be hoped that a statutory backed code for funding will ultimately clarify the law in this field; this is something considered further later in this book.

3

USE OF FUNDING

A. Use of Funding	3.01	4. Alternative business structures	3.90
B. Why is Funding Used?	3.06	F. International Landscape	3.92
C. Which Cases?	3.20	1. United States	3.95
1. Subject matter	3.33	2. Australia	3.112
2. Client	3.37	3. New Zealand	3.124
3. Merits	3.40	4. South Africa	3.126
4. Value	3.43	5. Canada	3.129
5. Forum/venue/jurisdiction/		6. France	3.132
applicable law	3.49	7. Germany	3.133
6. Enforceability	3.51	8. Caribbean	3.135
D. Lower Value Cases	3.54	9. Channel Islands	3.139
E. Alternative Methods	3.70	10. Dubai and Qatar	3.141
1. Portfolio funding	3.72	11. Ireland	3.143
2. Basket of cases	3.83	12. Hong Kong	3.144
3. Hybrid DBA funding	3.86	13. Singapore	3.148

A. Use of Funding

3.01 There are many different ways to make use of litigation funding, which 'umbrella' term covers all litigation related finance. It has generally conjured up the image of a one-off arrangement whereby a single, very high value case is funded on the claimant side. Whilst that is the traditional use of third party litigation funding, it is by no means the full extent of the entire funding universe.

3.02 This chapter is concerned with the various ways of using litigation funding, and why a choice might be made to use it. In the market, even as it has developed today, different funders offer differing approaches and structures. They have varying degrees of flexibility, and their respective structures allow them to approach funding services in a number of alternative ways. The review considers funder methods and schemes, as well as the types and value of cases. This chapter also deals with what it is that funders look for, and what funding costs.

3.03 Some funders will be interested only in the traditional third party funding model of high value cases. Others, however, see a necessity to consider alternative opportunities. The litigation funding market in England throws up a finite number of cases each year which fit the traditional model. Funders need to maintain a range of investments across their portfolio in order to spread their risks. As a result, in order to do this, they may look to differing types of arrangements with law firms and with clients.

3.04 Cases differ in many ways and the litigation funding market's appetite for certain cases varies from funder to funder. The full range of applications of funding will be covered, along with the way funding may or may not be appropriate, or available. These considerations will include all of the following and more: forum, venue, value, nature of case, and applicable law. In short, a very good starting point for considering if a funder will like a case is to consider if it would appeal as an attractive risk to an ATE insurer.

3.05 A further but extremely important factor in the availability and structure of litigation funding is the jurisdiction. A review of the international landscape and a number of jurisdictions is carried out later in this chapter.

B. Why is Funding Used?

3.06 It is well known to any litigator who has had some exposure to the world of third party litigation funding that there are certain cases which are deemed to be suitable for such funding.

3.07 The increased discussion over third party litigation funding is hardly surprising. The concerns following the Jackson reforms, and their implementation, coupled with a recession in which the cash flow of many law firms has been adversely affected, have caused many commercially minded managing partners to search for methods of expanding their respective firms' work bases and means of accelerating the payment of fees.

3.08 Litigators are having to be innovative to survive, and to gain work from their competitors. In the current environment there are many factors that have tended to exert a downward pressure on fees. The economic climate since the 'Great Recession' which began in around 2008 has caused many, even traditional institutional clients, to look for ways to reduce their legal fees, along with other business costs. Client driven pressures have not merely affected hourly rates, but have extended to agreements for capping, fixed fees, and the use (at least until the reforms which came into effect in April 2013) of CFAs. In addition, court 'costs management', more widespread use of costs capping, and other case management techniques likely to be introduced as a result of the current Chancery Modernization Review, are also likely to limit the levels of costs that can be earned from litigation. The litigation world has changed, and still more change is contemplated. For many litigation lawyers, by no means all of this change is to their disadvantage. Litigation funding, constrained or precluded, as it was, by the rules of maintenance and champerty, has enabled many cases to be brought which only a decade or so ago could not have been. A significant amount of work in the High Court today is taken up with funded cases. This should mean that legal practitioners who can adapt and offer alternatives to standard retainers will survive better.

3.09 Several options are available. The immediate and obvious solution is to use someone else's money, hence the heightened discussion over and assessment of third party funders. *Litigation Funding Magazine* lists several funders. Many listed would more accurately be described as brokers; the *Magazine* now identifies the status of each of the entrants. It is unclear how much business is actually undertaken by many of those listed.

3.10 A significant check on the volume of business for funders is undoubtedly the lack of awareness of the facility, and understanding of its operation in the legal marketplace. The same scepticism that surrounded the use of conditional fees by solicitors (and especially counsel) in high value commercial disputes, remains evident in the use of funding. The legal profession generally has been slow to adapt and to embrace a scheme that could help its members to expand their practices or even just to survive the economic downturn and pressures mentioned above. The changes to recoverability of success fees, brought about by LASPO[1] have not assisted with that.

3.11 Funders could provide the perfect solution. The use of funding offers the client the ability to minimize risk, does not have any negative effect on their cash flow, and ensures payment of lawyers. When clients are being very careful how they spend, or even if they spend, their legal budget, the dispute resolution teams need to consider the use of all the options available them. CFAs are good for the clients' cash flow, they are not so good for the law firms'. Everyone has overheads to cover so the use of a discounted rate CFA has grown. The lawyers receive something as the case goes along and the client will appreciate that the legal team is, to some extent at least, sharing in the 'financial pain' in the sense that some part of their remuneration is likely to be conditional and deferred.

3.12 Although different funders have different methods of operation, the usual requirement is that the lawyers operate on some form of discounted CFA with ATE insurance at the very least, for opponent's costs. Some funders will require 'both sides' cover, so even if they lose they are reimbursed their outlay. That is less commonplace. One of the biggest issues faced by funders is the lawyers' ability to estimate fees accurately. So the use of a case funding limit, or facility level based on a pre-agreed 'full rate' budget, is employed to address the problem, in most cases. Costs budgeting has become a feature of litigation only in very recent times. However, since the changes to the Rules of Court introduced in April 2013, costs budgeting is a feature of civil litigation, and therefore it is something which legal teams have

---

[1] Legal Aid, Sentencing & Punishment of Offenders Act 2012 Part 2.

had to embrace. The task of estimating fees to funders is, however, a more onerous one, than in connection with costs budgeting for costs management purposes. This is because whereas necessary, but not reasonably anticipated, additional costs incurred in the litigation are likely to be the subject of a revised budget for court costs management considerations, a funder will not always be so willing to revise a budget. Its interest will be to limit, as tightly as possible in advance, its exposure. Costs contingencies therefore need to be carefully considered.

3.13 However, with the competing interests of clients, legal teams and funders, a model consisting of funding, a discounted CFA, and after the event insurance, is a useful one.

3.14 Taking the real life practical example of a mid-sized company deciding whether to embark on a piece of litigation, or not, the realities of the decision making for that client are clear. They had been wronged, three years ago, by a much larger competitor. They have a claim with good prospects of success worth, if they are successful, around £7m. Their legal fees to bring the claim will be £1m. On a traditional basis, if they lose they will have spent £1m on their own lawyers and will be looking at paying out another £1m to their opponent's lawyers. They have survived the recession, with some cuts and some downsizing, but they are in good shape. However, they do not have the cash flow to risk £1m on legal fees with the risk of another £1m if they lose. Should they put it down to experience and move on, or is there an alternative? Their lawyers believe in the case, but cannot take it on at full risk. It may be a long and hard battle and they need to be paid as they go along, at least in part.

3.15 A third party litigation funder can offer the prospective claimant the ability to fund the litigation so there is no cash flow burden to the client. The funder will insure against the prospect of an adverse costs order—alleviating that burden and risk for the client and the client will pay (usually) to the funder between 15 per cent and 40 per cent of their damages if successful (or a multiple of three times the legal spend (whichever is the greater)), in return. The positive for the client is that they win and receive approximately 60 per cent of the damages recovered. They have spent nothing, they have had no cash flow burden whatsoever, and have had no risk. The downside is their time and effort (which may be considerable, but would be the same in any litigation), and the loss of the portion of the award which is payable to the funder, but they have had no financial risk. They have been insulated against unknown potential financial exposure.

3.16 It may be that the largest firms of solicitors can still demand standard fee paying retainers, but not all dispute resolution departments can rely upon that luxury. That said, even such firms have clients with cases that fit the profile of the traditional litigation funders. These clients, who operate in the harsh commercial world of overheads and cash flow restraints, are where the funders have found their regular customers.

3.17 Both lawyers and clients have an opportunity, in appropriate cases, to consider the alternative of litigation funding and its benefits. Funding has now become something that should be discussed between lawyer and potential client at the very first opportunity, not least to satisfy the professional obligations of the litigation lawyer, in making clients aware of all the options available to finance the litigation. This would be the case even where the solicitors giving advice were not themselves prepared to accept cases on a funded basis, and the client might need to be referred elsewhere. Increasingly, it is an option being taken by commercial claimants, and one taken regularly by choice rather than necessity. The financial outlay in litigation can be prohibitive, but many businesses do not make a decision to litigate on the basis of direct legal cost alone. They consider many other factors, not least the reputational risks and other indirect costs.

3.18 One factor considered in deciding on whether to engage with funders emanates from the same area of concern. It is extremely important for claimants, and especially those who can afford to fund the litigation themselves, to be sure that they are in control of their own case, that they will give the instructions to their lawyers, and that they have the final decision making authority. As is evident from Chapter 2, the intermeddling in someone else's litigation in England may no longer be a criminal offence, but it could be very relevant to the issue of whether a particular funding arrangement is champertous and therefore void, an outcome that any funder would wish to avoid. In England and Wales, it is, therefore, important, for the reasons considered in Chapter 2, that the control of the litigation and the ultimate decision making lies with the client, just as it would in a case which was not funded.

3.19 The caveat to that is that in Australia, as is explained later in this chapter, the position is not entirely the same and funders are permitted to become more heavily involved in the litigation process than here, as the rules of champerty and maintenance have been further eroded than is the case in England.

C. Which Cases?

3.20 In a litigation funder's ideal world there would be many cases worth hundreds of millions of pounds, that require minimal funding, with limited factual material to prove on the basis of readily available evidence, and which could be decided by a swift and decisive preliminary issue. In reality, those cases do not need funding very often, and those that do are few in number.

3.21 Whilst that may be the ideal case for anyone to run or to fund, there are certain key areas that a litigation funder will focus upon and there are basic necessary requirements and factors that are key to a funder's decision to fund.

3.22 The use of litigation funding by defendants is extremely rare. Quite naturally, the usual use of funding is by a claimant as they are bringing the claim and expect that, if successful, they will receive an award of damages. It is from this award that the funder is repaid.

Use of Funding

3.23 Other than where there is a counterclaim, so that the position of the defendant is not dissimilar to that of a claimant, the options for defendants are very limited given the nature of what they are seeking to do, namely, to defeat the claim against them. The usual issue for defendants is that their likely success in a case is avoiding having to pay money. Consequently, the usual arrangement, in claimant cases, whereby funds are expected to be received on success, does not apply.

3.24 One possibility is for the defendant to define what 'success', in terms of the defence of the case, would be and then to agree with a funder what they would receive in return for funding the defence and on what basis.

3.25 For example, if there were a situation where two parties were in dispute as to a payment from one to the other, ordinarily the claimant alone would be likely to seek funding. However, where a large sum of money had been either frozen subject to court order or paid into court, then the issue of money being available at the end of the case might be satisfied and the ability to fund the defendant would become a possibility.

3.26 In this scenario, the defendant might dispute that any of the funds are due to the claimant and take that stance publicly and in its pleaded case. However, privately the defendant may accept that there is a figure which, if recovered, would be deemed to be a success, rather than the total loss of all of the funds, which would be an absolute defeat.

3.27 If the defendant wanted to seek funding it would be able to offer something to a litigation funder, on success, which might enable them to provide funding. Using real figures, let us say that in a dispute over the sales commission due to an intermediary, a proportion of the proceeds of sale of an asset were ordered to be frozen and then paid into court during the currency of proceedings to decide how much, if any, sales commission was due to the intermediary. The sum frozen is £50m.

3.28 The defendant believes a 'success' would be to pay only £10m. If that were the result then it would have saved some £40m from the claimed amount all of which is at risk in the event that for whatever reason the defendant could fund its defence of the litigation against it. That would be the sum 'won'.

3.29 The defendant's lawyers' budget is, for this example, £2m. A funder might want to receive a return of a multiple of that investment (say three times) or a percentage of the sum 'won' (say 30 per cent), whichever is the greater. The defendant and the funder agree that the definition of 'success' in the proceedings is any award to the claimant of less than £30m. If the claimant wins less than £30m the funder would receive a return of a minimum of three times its investment, possibly more.

3.30 In that scenario, if the claimant is awarded £15m, the defendant is left with £25m. The amount 'won' is the difference between the award and £30m, namely £10m. The funder would receive £7.5m. The defendant would be left with £17.5m.

3.31 The scenario is not an everyday occurrence in commercial litigation, but it does happen. The example is borrowed, with considerable adjustment in detail and figures, from a real funding proposal. Equally the method suggested for the funding of defendants is one considered by a number of funders. Without the sums being frozen or readily available, the prospects for defendant funding are not high unless the defendant is an individual or entity of some financial wherewithal. If the defendant can demonstrate the ability to pay the funder, then the returns from a source other than the case itself then the funding is much more feasible.

3.32 The decision to make use of litigation funding is not always driven by financial interest and many cases are funded by choice as opposed to necessity. If a large corporate entity with significant financial resources were to choose to use litigation funding to defend a case then as long as the definition of 'success' can be agreed between funder and defendant funding would be entirely possible.

1. Subject matter

3.33 Each funder will have its own specific criteria. Although most litigation funders are generally keen to invest across a range of differing types of cases to spread their risk, some keep entirely to one kind of case, such as intellectual property and patent cases. Additionally there are funders who work only in the field of matrimonial law, and others in the area of insolvency.

3.34 The majority of funders work across the entire commercial spectrum and avoid specialisms. However, within these broad commercial areas they will have their preferences. Given the range of criteria that will be applied by most litigation funders there are certain sorts of case that are attractive to a funder.

3.35 By way of example, arbitration cases are very often a popular choice with litigation funders. Depending upon the funder's preference as to forum, a suitable venue and applicable law, arbitrations often meet the necessary requirements. The budgets in these kinds of cases tend to be quite high and the values in dispute are equally large.

3.36 Given the need to spend significant sums on bringing these actions, clients in these maters will very frequently consider litigation funding to alleviate some of the financial burden. The high values in dispute in these cases are attractive to funders as well as the relative ease of enforcement of arbitral awards and low likelihood of appeals. It should be added that not all funders share this view of arbitral proceedings, especially those with an international element where there may be issues as to enforceability of an award in a particular jurisdiction.

2. Client

3.37 When deciding whether or not to invest in a particular case, a funder will consider with some care the client that is presenting the case to them. Any investor in any venture would consider who their proposed partners are, how they might react in certain situations, and particularly what their motivation is for bringing the litigation.

3.38 The funder is not entitled to control the decision making or force a funded client to do or not do something. Accordingly, a funder needs to be satisfied as to what the client will decide to do in certain situations and, most importantly, what the client wants out of the litigation. Once the funding is agreed and the case starts there is little or nothing that the funder can do if the client decides to have a day in court rather than take a sensible commercial offer.

3.39 Equally, the funder will consider the legal team and their experience in the particular area in question. Whilst it has happened, no funder should advise a client that they would fund their case but for the current legal team, but the quality and experience of the team will undoubtedly feature in the decision making process.

3. Merits

3.40 It is almost so obvious that it does not require a section specifically to state that in order for a case to be considered for litigation funding it should have good prospects of success on the merits. Although occasionally, the detractors from funding have suggested that funders may encourage the pursuit of frivolous litigation or fund cases that lack merit, the reality is that this is not true. No commercial funder will wish to risk money on a plainly unmeritorious case.

3.41 Admittedly, there are some cases that divide opinion as regards the merits of the case. These are also unlikely to be backed by a litigation funder. Funders do not wish to blaze a trail or make new law. They do not like cases which rely simply upon one person's word against another's. (As to this, there can be no hard and fast rule, because the circumstances might be such that one person's account is inherently implausible.) Cases which rely on the law rather than witnesses will be preferred, but obviously the majority of cases require some of both.

3.42 There seems to be a general view in the litigation world that funders require cases to have prospects of success of at least 60 per cent. In fact most professional funders will rely upon their own assessment of the case rather than someone else's. That said, it is a useful starting point if counsel has already given a view on the merits in writing. It is most likely that the reference to a 60 per cent threshold comes from the ATE industry rather than the funding world, although there are significant similarities in case review and criteria.

4. Value

3.43 The value of the likely recovery in a case is a basic and obvious factor of huge importance. Put simply, if the case is not likely to be of sufficient size then the chances of it being accepted by a funder are remote—subject of course to how much is required by way of funding.

3.44 There is usually a minimum value of case below which funders will not consider funding. With the mainstream of funders in England that threshold is around the £3m to £5m figure. The reason for this is the ratio between likely damages awarded and the amount of the budget. Many funders work on a minimum ratio of 4 to 1. Others require 10 to 1.

3.45 On a 4 to 1 ratio, a case with a £3m value could have a maximum budget of £750k. If the funder required a 10 to 1 ratio then the budget could only be £300k. The funders that require the higher ratios tend to have a higher minimum value for this reason.

3.46 The theory behind the ratios is simple. In the experience of many funders, in most cases the budget increases and the quantum assessment decreases. If the funder has anticipated that possibility by insisting on funding a ratio of 10 to 1, then when these things happen, there should still be enough money available at the end of the case to ensure the funder and the client receive what they expected.

3.47 When a funder considers the value of a case it will be looking to ensure that the value can provide the required return on capital invested from the damages. This depends upon the size of the budget, the size of the damages, and also the pricing demanded from the funder.

3.48 The more the funder wants the higher the damages need to be. The pricing is dictated by a number of factors. There will be a minimum return on capital that a funder needs. Added to this will be variables including the length of the case and the likely term for which the money will be at risk as well as the perceived risk of losing the investment.

5. Forum/venue/jurisdiction/applicable law

3.49 A key factor for funders is the jurisdiction of a case and the law to be applied; they will want to operate in a jurisdiction in which they feel comfortable. Outside England, most funders are happy in the common law jurisdictions of Australia, the USA, and generally the Caribbean courts, with Cayman and the British Virgin Islands fairly regular areas of operation for funders. The Channel Islands are a newer, but popular, venue.

3.50 The Dubai International Financial Centre (DIFC) and the Qatar Financial Centre (QFC) are regimes that funders will be reasonably comfortable in but by contrast the local courts of both countries would most likely be jurisdictions that a funder would not consider. In the arbitration world funders will have their preference as to forum, venue, and applicable law. Those may not be decisive as regards funding but will be taken into account.

6. Enforceability

3.51 The subject of enforceability is extremely important for a litigation funder. There is little point in funding a case to a successful outcome if ultimately there is no obvious route to obtaining the proceeds of the litigation and the return on your investment. Accordingly, whilst the merits of a case are vital, of equal importance is the ability to recover the damages.

Funders will consider carefully the prospects of recovery and enforcement and will conduct extensive due diligence to ensure they are satisfied. Where there is a professional liability insurance policy indemnifying the defendant, the issue is easier to resolve, hence the attraction of professional negligence cases to funders. **3.52**

The ease of enforcement is one attraction of arbitration awards to litigation funders. The New York Convention,[2] which provides recognition and enforcement of foreign arbitral awards by the contracting states, is beneficial to funders when considering and assessing the potential enforcement of cases subject to arbitration. **3.53**

D. Lower Value Cases

Third party funding is an area of high risk and high reward. In order to apply the traditional third party funding model a claim has to have three key elements. First, it has to be high in value; secondly, it must have good prospects of success; and thirdly, it must have a defendant who can afford to pay. **3.54**

The very high returns that can be made in litigation funding are more likely to be found in the world of hedge funds and given the rewards it is no surprise that this is an area of fast growth in the UK. As a result there has been a substantial increase in the number of firms offering to fund cases in the last 12 months. However, nearly all of these organizations have a threshold for claim value that is in excess of £1m. Most will say that £5m is the lowest value they will consider. The reason for this is simple mathematics. These funders seek a high return for their high risk investment. Litigation is not a science and it can be unpredictable so funders will be looking for a minimum of their money back plus three times their investment as a return. Others will look for a straight percentage of the proceeds of the case and that may work out to be far more. **3.55**

Many funders, would consider funding matters of that value (£5m) if the mathematics suggested the arrangement would be viable. In fact, many have funded one-off cases of that level. There are of course specialist funders who operate in the field of low value clams in England, albeit very few. There is no substantial well-developed market at the moment for funding lower value claims but that may change given the huge size of that market and the demand, compared to the traditionally sized very substantial cases. **3.56**

---

[2] The Convention on the Recognition and Enforcement of Foreign Arbitral Awards 1958.

3.57 Historically, there were various methods of funding which were open to solicitors. Some have fallen by the wayside, others have simply been too risky or too expensive for one side or the other.

3.58 Of the historic methods, one of the first financing models used a consumer credit agreement (CCA). A client would borrow money from a finance house on a term of three years or less. An ATE insurance policy was used to insure the loan. The money was drawn to pay solicitors' disbursements, with the lawyers working on a full CFA. This model had very high interest rates and was used at the consumer end of the market, primarily in personal injury cases. It went out of favour when some claims companies that were inextricably linked to these kinds of financing packages ran into financial difficulties, exposing insurers who insured the loans to very substantial losses.

3.59 Another, a simpler model that followed after the CCA schemes became unpopular (with clients and the Solicitors Regulation Authority (SRA)) was the direct lending route. Solicitors took on the associated debt themselves. Following the huge losses that some insurers suffered after agreeing to pay back the balances on the consumer credit loans, they decided they would no longer insure the debt. The result was that the only way for lawyers to obtain finance was to borrow the money themselves, or at least underwrite their clients' borrowings. This allowed solicitors working on a CFA to use the borrowing to pay disbursements.

3.60 Whilst historically there have been ways to fund low value cases, more recently those methods have been less than attractive to lawyers and clients. The advent of the reforms being put into place by LASPO and pursuant to the Jackson Report mean that methods for funding and running lower value cases have to change. ATE policies are necessary in lower value civil and commercial disputes; until the reforms introduced in April 2013 came into effect, any solicitor that did not recommend one, or at least discuss the desirability of putting one in place and the risks of not doing so, might be held to be negligent and could even be in breach of the SRA's conduct rules. However, premiums for such policies, with very limited exceptions, are no longer going to be recoverable for cases subject to the rules which came into effect in April 2013. This presents a problem. If premiums are not to be recoverable, then there is no reason for insurers to make them contingent and to defer the payment of them. They will therefore need to be paid by someone. Law firms doing volume work with an insurer, and with a good track record of success, may well be able to reach accommodating terms with insurers. Those that do not have such relationships will struggle to insure one-off cases other than with a premium payable up front.

3.61 In the coming years, the funding of lower value claims may be achieved in a number of ways. The advent of alternative business structures (ABSs) could provide an answer. Already law firms are being considered for investment from private equity. It is an easy step for those investors to extend their facilities so that law firms can offer terms to clients that are attractive to them and to the firm. The additional opportunities that law firms offer to investors under the ABS umbrella are endless, and funding cases is just one of the potential money making opportunities. ABSs may interest some investors but not all.

3.62 Funders work on a portfolio approach to their investments. They like to have a range of cases in value and term. The wider they spread their risk the less likely that one individual failure will cause them a real financial problem in the long run. Insurers have managed to pick winning cases in around 80 per cent of cases during the period that the ATE market has been running, so realistically there is no reason why funders should not operate with the same sort of success rate, if they apply similar principles. If that is what they do then they will make significant money and that will continue to provide a popular asset class for investors at the high value end.

3.63 But many investors are used to receiving a minimum of 20 per cent per annum as a return and like a regular return on their investment. High value litigation funding cannot be relied upon to satisfy such a requirement but lower value higher volume funding might. This is not a suggestion of a return to the models that featured in the early part of the century and the mass personal injury funding. However, a well managed (and insurance backed) scheme with a law firm receiving a regular amount of money per case for disbursements and work in progress across a range of cases could work well for funders, lawyers, and investors. These schemes are already being launched.

3.64 A figure of around 20 per cent per annum is not an unrealistic rate of return for specialized unsecured lending against cases. It is still a high risk investment opportunity but with reasonably good returns. There will be no shortage of potential investors.

3.65 One thing is obvious. The method used for traditional third party funding does not work for all lower value cases. The budgets for these cases are large and capital adequacy requirements brought in by the Code of Conduct and set down by the Association of Litigation Funders means that significant sums of capital are tied up, potentially, for a long period of time with no return. Funders are used to waiting for their returns but they expect them to be large. That does not work in the lower value market. As the lower value funded claim market develops, this position might well change.

3.66 With the increase in popularity of litigation funding in the UK, traditional funders may find that the increased competition drives down their returns. The author's view is that currently this is less likely than some commentators predict because experience shows that there remain far more cases available for funding than there is capital to fund those cases. However, as the market develops, there is good reason to suppose that as more funders join it, competition will increase with consequent pressure to drive down returns.

3.67 But, what is more likely is that funders will realize that the key to dominating the funding market, when it is a competitive one, is ensuring that when the best cases are available, they are offered to them first. Clearly, relationships with lawyers and clients, a good reputation, and competitive pricing will be keys to that, but having a range of products which includes a facility for lower value cases can only help. Put simply, a funder who funds a law firm's lower value cases, is more likely to benefit from reciprocation. It is claims capture that is the key to success and funding high and low value cases will assist with that. Speed of decision making, consistency in approach, and not raising expectations of funding, only later to dash them, are all likely to be important to lawyers when recommending funders.

3.68 Traditional funders are likely soon to perceive that there are potential opportunities for them at the lower levels of quantum. The portfolio acquired by providing a facility to a law firm to run lower value claims at a good rate of steady return is a significant asset for a funding company and its investors.

3.69 However, traditional funding remains high risk. Whilst investors from the venture capital world are used to risks, the portfolio approach to providing facilities to lawyers to fund lower value cases is a much lower risk. The investment itself will be insured, but the returns are regular and higher than other asset classes.

E. Alternative Methods

3.70 Traditional third party litigation funding is what most litigators would describe when asked how litigation funding works. That is not the only method of litigation finance. There are no set rules as to how a funding product should be designed, save that it has to work within the confines of the law and pubic policy of the jurisdiction in which it operates.

3.71 Some litigation funders have become very flexible and innovative in their offerings. The funding of one-off large cases remains the high end funders' core business, but the ability to offer schemes that work generally for the law firms is an ideal way for funders to capture business and build relationships.

1. Portfolio funding

3.72 Often funders use the term 'portfolio'. It usually means the set of cases that they, as a fund, have invested in. It is the portfolio approach that provides the funders with the ability to take losses on cases, which inevitably there are in litigation.

3.73 The theory, and indeed practice, has shown that the losses can be offset by the wins across the board and as long as the value of the winning cases is greater than the amount expended on a losing case, the funder will make a profit. The longest running funders have demonstrated this approach successfully.

The need for funders to maintain a portfolio of cases is well known. One way of extending this approach is for a funder to work with a law firm to fund its portfolio of cases. The experience of companies in the legal expenses insurance industry is that the closer their relationship with a particular law firm, the more likely it is that they will continue to receive all of their work rather than the one-off cases. This is a protection against what the insurance industry refers to as 'adverse selection'. The principle is not quite the same in the funding world given that not all cases need funding, nor would they all fit the criteria. **3.74**

There are a number of reasons why a portfolio based lending approach is beneficial and attractive to law firms. Law firms manage the number of cases they have at any one time. They are constrained by the level of contingent work in progress that they have at any one time and the need to apply resources to cash generating business as well as contingent revenue. **3.75**

Litigation funders can assist with this problem. The methods adopted can be divided into two distinct bases. One, lending to the law firm itself, the other lending to clients. **3.76**

In order to assist a law firm with freeing up some of its contingent work in progress a litigation funder can agree to fund some of the work in progress across the portfolio of the firm's cases. This may be done on the basis of a percentage of all the cases in the portfolio and a pre-agreed level, for example of 30 to 50 per cent of the time recorded. The law firm and the funder would agree in advance the criteria for what type of case and what values of case would be acceptable. **3.77**

The returns to the funder would be based on either an annual interest rate of drawn funds or a percentage of the uplift claimed under the firm's CFA. There would undoubtedly be a minimum set return to the funder. The method of remuneration to the fund would be dictated by whether it was a recourse or a non-recourse scheme. If the fund were to be repaid in any event, then an annual interest rate would be payable, and it is likely that the funder would have insured its capital investment against loss. This reduces the price paid for the money, as the risk is reduced. **3.78**

If the scheme were non-recourse then the returns to the funder would be higher but the risk to the firm lower and the returns would be based upon the uplift charged by the law firm in each case or aggregated across the portfolio. The key issue here is to remember that funding can be flexible and as long as the risk is understood by the funder and there is an ability to obtain a sensible return for that risk then it will consider a scheme of this nature, whether it be akin to one of the examples in paragraphs 3.75, 3.76, and 3.77 or a combination of them. **3.79**

The advent of the Jackson reforms and the arrival of damages based agreements ('DBAs') has improved the prospects of a firm being able to lay off some of its contingent risk with a funder. Whilst the arguments continue regarding hybrid DBAs **3.80** and the interpretation of Regulation 4,[3] the use of a full DBA has not been commonplace. In the scenario in paragraph 3.76 where the funder decides that it wants to adopt a more traditional non-recourse method of investment, the returns need to correlate with the risk involved. If the portfolio of cases is a CFA based caseload then post-Jackson the uplift is limited to what is recovered from the clients' damages and is limited to 100 per cent of the fees, at best, and realistically will be lower than that in most cases that do not reach trial.[4]

3.81 With a DBA based caseload the available returns are likely to be higher and therefore more conducive to a portfolio based funding arrangement for the lawyers. The principle of lending on a non-recourse basis as against work in progress across a portfolio of cases remains the same, but the returns can be higher as the fees due to the law firm are going to be higher, subject to accurate quantum assessments, than in a CFA case.

3.82 For example, a law firm may wish to limit itself to a capped total amount of work in progress at risk at any one time. It could increase the amount of work it takes on if it agreed with a funder that they would provide an advance as against a half or one-third of the work at any one time. With a £6m limit on contingent based fees the firm could increase its capacity to £9m or £12m without increasing its risk or exposure. That would allow the law firm to take on more work, to expand, or simply to improve its cash flow. The funder's remuneration would be recovered from the law firm's entitlement to a share of the damages of successful cases.

2. Basket of cases

3.83 A variation on the theme of portfolio based lending is for a funder to fund the litigation in a basket of cases. The difference here is that the lending across a portfolio has to be to the law firm as the cases will have a number of different claimants. In a 'basket' based approach, the client would be the same entity with a number of different claims.

3.84 This arrangement is particularly popular with in-house or general counsel of corporations who are looking for ways to increase their legal budget without increasing their legal spending. It allows the client to pursue litigation that it might not have been able to previously but it also has a further effect of enabling the funding of cases which may not have individually been eligible for litigation funding, but by combining that case with others which are larger, the combination of the likely fees and returns allows a funder to become involved.

---

[3] DBA Regulations [SI 2013/609], Regulation 4.
[4] There are some exceptions to this, most notably in insolvency cases. See the Legal Aid, Sentencing and Punishment of Offenders Act 2012 (Commencement No. 5 and Saving Provision) Order 2013, Article 4.

3.85 These schemes can also be used in the insolvency world where an office holder may have multiple claims against different defendants arising from the same insolvency, and where each case is not individually large enough to warrant litigation funding.

3. Hybrid DBA funding

3.86 DBAs continue to divide opinion in the litigation world. It seems that the prospect of a hybrid DBA is something that would appeal to most litigators. The chance to receive a monthly fee for a proportion of the work carried out and the prospect of a significant payment at the end of the case can be an attractive proposition for a law firm. The hybrid element allowing payment as the case goes along alleviates the cash flow burden of a full DBA.

3.87 With the current ongoing uncertainty over the ability to work on a hybrid DBA retainer and no immediate prospect of that changing, litigation funders have developed products to create the benefits of a hybrid DBA whilst the law firm operates with an acceptable and uncontroversial retainer. The key to these schemes lies in the use of litigation funding in the USA. Contingency fees have always been an acceptable form of retainer for American lawyers in litigation matters. They receive a payment from the proceeds if they win. Historically, legal practice in the USA has not been controlled by the 'indemnity principle' in the way that the English legal system has; nor have the principles of maintenance and champerty prevented the development of contingent fee agreements.

3.88 It is normal practice in the USA for a law firm to be retained on a contingency fee and for lawyers then to seek non-recourse funding from a litigation funder in order to provide cash flow. The law firm will then 'sell' part of its percentage in the recoveries to the funder. The client may or may not be aware of this relationship. The funder is likely to insist that the client is aware and is in some way bound into the arrangement in order to protect them against the client and to safeguard their investment.

3.89 In these roots lies the concept of hybrid DBA funding. There are two ways to achieve the result. In one situation the client and the funder enter into a standard litigation funding agreement to pay certain legal fees in return for a percentage of the proceeds upon success. The lawyers are paid a percentage of their hourly rate for their fees as the case progresses. Additionally there is an agreement between the funder and law firm to split the proceeds received by the funder in a pre-agreed manner. The second method is for the lawyer to enter into a standard DBA with its client and then seek separate funding, in the manner described in paragraph 3.87 in the USA based situation.

4. Alternative business structures

3.90 Alternative business structures were introduced by the Legal Services Act 2007. The changes allowed non-lawyers to invest in and to own law firms in England

and Wales. This has led to the suggestion that law firms may consider stock market flotation, although to date only one law firm operating in England is listed and that is an Australian entity.[5]

3.91 The changes allow the prospect of external investment in law firms and that provides a further avenue for litigation funders to consider. The potential for change in the litigation market and legal landscape generally is considered in Chapter 10 but the most complete way for a litigation funder to invest in a law firm's litigation department or to provide funding for its entire portfolio is by direct investment in the firm as an ABS. This may have already occurred, although the author does not know whether this is the case.

F. International Landscape

3.92 This chapter also provides an overview of the international funding market, paying particular attention to the United States and the birthplace of litigation funding—Australia.

3.93 The English marketplace may have seen huge growth in funding with a number of new funders entering the market in recent years, but there are other jurisdictions that have seen a similar increase in awareness and a general acceptance of third party litigation funding.

3.94 The main jurisdictions that have witnessed this increased activity are England and Wales, the United States, and Australia.

1. United States

3.95 In the USA, litigation funding is not as well developed, and there is no, or mostly only a very rare use of the adverse costs regime. Contingency fees are used in many cases. Additionally, damages awards, almost invariably made by a jury, are very much higher than in England or Australia. This means that lawyers can afford to run meritorious cases by taking a significant proportion of the proceeds.

3.96 Funding is becoming established in the USA, but it is still a relatively new concept and it is certainly not prevalent in high value commercial matters.

3.97 However, the financial constraints on corporations and the tightening of legal budgets are the same in the USA as is the case everywhere else. The use of third party funding is on the increase. Lawyers who have taken on cases on a fully contingent basis for 40 or 50 per cent of the proceeds are usually required to meet all payments throughout the case—experts and other disbursements. The need to improve cash

---

[5] Slater & Gordon, listed on the ASX. There are however law firms which form part of a listed group of service companies such as the Quindell Plc.

flow, cover the overheads, and increase liquidity means that many contingency fee solicitors are 'selling' their contingent interests to litigation funders. This is only likely to increase in the short term.

3.98 Litigation funding continues its advance in the United States, albeit that it is viewed with more caution than it is in the UK or Australia. The main reason for a slower uptake is the widespread use of contingency fees in the United States, which had remained impermissible in the England (pre-LASPO) and still are in Australia.

3.99 There has been more interest recently, given worldwide cash flow restraints, in funding in the USA and, anecdotally, funders report a growth in approaches from contingency fee lawyers to provide facilities in return for a share of their own contingency fee. The slower growth in the US commercial litigation market is not mirrored in the international arbitration world, where the use of funding by US law firms is much more commonplace.

3.100 The concerns with funding in the US are mainly at the consumer end with a historic growth of very expensive loans to plaintiffs payable out of their awards. There are also concerns in commercial cases over the potential abuses and the control funders can exert. Additionally, the state system has led to a slower breakdown of the rules on maintenance and champerty with a wide range of views in individual state courts across the USA.

3.101 Increasing discussion on the subject led the New York Bar Association to issue a formal opinion[6] in February 2011 confirming that representing clients in non-recourse litigation funding arrangements was not unethical, but there were waiver of privilege issues to overcome. The American Bar Association issued their own White Paper[7] to guide attorneys through the conduct issues of litigation financing in 2011. The waiver of privilege issue remains a problem for funders in the USA. The Delaware case of *Leader Technologies Inc*[8] confirmed that the release of privileged information from attorney to funder amounted to a waiver of privilege and made the documentation discoverable. However, in the Eastern District of Texas, the decision in *Mondis Technologies*[9] was that this did not amount to a waiver of privilege and the documents were protected by the work-product doctrine.

3.102 The judgment in *Quick Cash Inc*[10] should give funders in the US some confidence. The court held that a funding agreement was not usurious even though the annual

---

[6] <http://www.nycbar.org/ethics/ethics-opinions-local/2011-opinions/1159-formal-opinion-2011-02>.
[7] <http://www.americanbar.org/content/dam/aba/administrative/ethics_2020/20111019_draft_alf_white_paper_posting.authcheckdam.pdf>.
[8] *Leader Technologies, Inc v Facebook, Inc* 719 F Supp 2d 373, 376 (D Del 2010).
[9] *Mondis Technology Ltd v L G Electronics Inc* No 2:07-cv-565, 2011 WL 1714304, at *3 (ED Tex 4 May 2011).
[10] *Kelly, Grossman & Flanagan LLP v Quick Cash, Inc*, No 04283-2011, 2012 WL 1087341 (Suffolk Co 2012).

interest compounded to some 40 per cent. The advances were non-recourse and it was the lawyers who borrowed the money. The New York Supreme Court did however suggest that the outcome might have been different if the borrowers had been less sophisticated.

3.103 At the beginning of 2014 there were further key developments in the USA. The funding world received a fillip in a case involving a British company heard in Chicago, Illinois.[11] The company, Miller UK Limited, was found by a federal magistrate not to have breached state law in turning to third party litigation funders. It did so as it pursued a trade secrets case against Caterpillar, the heavy equipment specialists. In a pre-trial hearing, the judge rejected claims from Caterpillar to see details of the litigation funding arrangement.

3.104 The argument deployed by Caterpillar's lawyers was one of the usual ones—namely, that the arrangement was not covered by client confidentiality, and was in breach of the principles concerning the meddling with other people's lawsuits. In short, they tried to use the funding arrangement as a mode of attack, which failed.

3.105 The importance of the case in Illinois shows that this arrangement is protected by the court. This decision follows the trend that is being set across most of the USA where funding is becoming an acceptable method of financing litigation.

3.106 Those with vested interests in preventing litigation are always going to be averse to the practice of litigation funding. Indeed, critics such as the Institute for Legal Reform (and the author believes Caterpillar is a member of Institute's parent body, the US Chamber of Commerce) have been vocal in their attacks on the funding industry. Their 2009 report entitled *Selling Lawsuits*[12] argues that third party litigation financing:

(i) Encourages frivolous and abusive litigation
(ii) Raises ethical concerns
(iii) Is a recipe for concern in class and mass actions.

3.107 It is one thing to be critical of frivolous and spurious litigation, it is quite another to use that as a blanket excuse of protecting members by seeking to prevent perfectly legitimate actions being brought against them. In many cases the sheer size and resources of the defendant and its likely litigation tactics are a threat to the very financial existence of a plaintiff. The ability to make use of litigation financing can help those with legitimate grievances to have their case heard and to receive the appropriate compensation.

---

[11] *Miller UK Ltd v Caterpillar, Inc*, ND Ill, No 10 C 3770, 1/6/14.
[12] J Beisner, J Miller, and S Rubin, *Selling Lawsuits, Buying Trouble* (US Chamber Institute for Legal Reform, 2009).

It should also be noted that around the same time as the Illinois decision, a survey[13] of lawyers (admittedly carried out by a litigation finance firm) in the USA on their attitudes to third party funding was released. Of the many findings there were a few which stood out. One was the statistic from lawyers at private law firms, showing 65 per cent of them believe TPF levelled the playing field. It also showed 64 per cent of them believed litigation funding meant good cases could be brought whereas before they might not have been pursued.   **3.108**

That is a stark contrast in attitudes from those of the detractors, although some would say the arguments are obvious, they are no less compelling. But another finding uncovered was that corporate leaders are increasingly receptive to the idea, with 50 per cent of financial executives saying law firms should explain third party funding as a payment option at the outset of a case.   **3.109**

With the USA being a federal system, attitudes differ from state to state but generally there is a rise in the use of litigation funding and a growing acceptance of its use.   **3.110**

The American jury based system for damages awards, in which juries are often free to treat damages as being at large, without the constraints, applicable in England, of establishing damages by reference to particular proved loss (save in exceptional cases, such as in libel actions, where general damages can be awarded), does enable the costs of funding, at least to some extent, to be absorbed in the award of damages. Thus what, on an English measure of loss, might be recovered in full by a plaintiff, could stand a chance of being recovered, without being eroded by funding costs. There is no prospect of this result in England, where, in the light of the Jackson reforms, in cases beginning after March 2013, not even ATE premiums will be recoverable from the defendant.   **3.111**

2. Australia

The third party litigation funding market in Australia is very mature in comparison with England and Wales. It market developed in the 1990s to fund insolvency litigation. Australia has a similar legal system to England and Wales in that it does not allow contingency fees and has an adverse costs regime.   **3.112**

A study into the effect of third party litigation funding in Australia conducted by David L Chen and David S Abrams[14] concluded that third party funders had made a significant impact on the Australian legal system. The study used data from the Australian courts and from a leading funder to consider the effect of funding on court management, volume of litigation, establishment of precedent, and development of the law.   **3.113**

---

[13] <http://www.burfordcapital.com/wp-content/uploads/2014/01/2013-SURVEY-REPORT-FINAL-2014-01-14.pdf>.
[14] 'A Market for Justice: A First Empirical Look at Third Party Litigation Funding', *University of Pennsylvania Journal of Business Law*, 15 (2013), 1075.

3.114 In areas where funding was greatest, the court system experienced greater activity. The study covered the passage of cases that accepted funding and those that were rejected, but were brought without funding.

3.115 In short, the empirical data collected from real funding experiences in Australia show that whilst more cases were brought and settlement times were longer in funded cases, the expectation was that once defendants recognized the increased appetite for litigation on behalf of funded claimants and their greater resources, they were more likely to settle.

3.116 At least for the present, litigation funding has continued to go from strength to strength in the jurisdiction where it started (allowing for the fact that traditionally it had limited application in England from the later nineteenth century as the review of cases in Chapter 2 demonstrates). Since the historic decisions in *Fostif*[15] and then *Trendlen*[16] effectively abolished the common law rules on champerty and maintenance, litigation funding has been widespread and commonplace in the Australian court system.

3.117 Litigation funding in Australia received support from the Law Council of Australia and the Law Institute of Victoria.[17] Although the commentary on litigation funding has not always been positive and occasionally the judiciary[18] has been critical, *Fostif*[19] changed the landscape for litigation funding in Australia and the jurisdiction has not looked back since. It has a thriving market with a number of well known funders.

3.118 The evolution of the situation in Australia is described very helpfully by Hodges, Peysner, and Nurse[20] in their January 2012 review of litigation funding:

> The revolutionary change in policy occurred when challenges to litigation funding based on common law prohibitions of maintenance and champerty were resolved by the High Court of Australia in 2006 in the Fostif case in favour of legitimising the role of funding.[1] The High Court listed the following arguments in favour of this change:
>
> a. 'the social utility of funded proceedings';[2]
> b. its potential to foster the aims of Australian class action legislation;[3]
> c. 'inject a welcome element of commercial objectivity into the way in which [litigation] budgets are framed';[4] and
> d. increase the efficiency with which litigation is conducted.[5]

---

[15] *Campbells Cash & Carry Pty Ltd v Fostif Pty Ltd* [2006] HCA 41.
[16] *Mobil Oil Australia Pty Limited v Trendlen Pty Limited* [2006] HCA 42.
[17] See Law Council of Australia, 'Submission to Standing Committee of Attorneys-General', 14 September 2006; J North, 'Litigation Funding: Much to be Achieved with the Right Approach' (2005) 43 *Law Society Journal* 66, 69.
[18] J Eyers, 'Regulate litigation funders, judge urges', *Australian Financial Review*, 24 January 2011, 3, quoting Chief Justice Keane of the Federal Court; also Keane JA, Judge of the Queensland Court of Appeal, in Access to Justice and Other Shibboleths, speech on 10 October 2009, available at <http://www.jca.asn.au/attachments/2009AccesstoJustice.pdf>.
[19] *Campbells Cash & Carry Pty Ltd v Fostif Pty Ltd* [2006] HCA 41.
[20] Christopher Hodges, John Peysner, and Angus Nurse, *Litigation Funding: Status and Issues*, January 2012.

e. The High Court considered that existing doctrines of abuse of process and the courts' ability to protect their processes would be sufficient to deal with a funder conducting themselves in a manner 'inimical to the due administration of justice'.[6]
f. 'In jurisdictions which had abolished maintenance and champerty as crimes and torts, New South Wales, Victoria, South Australia and the Australian Capital Territory, there were no public policy questions beyond those that would be relevant when considering the enforceability of the agreement for maintenance of the proceedings as between the parties to the agreement. [7] In other words, once the legislature abolished the crimes and the torts of maintenance, these concepts cannot be used to found a challenge to proceedings which are being maintained. Their only relevance is in a dispute between plaintiff and funder about the enforceability of the agreement.'[8]

[1] Campbells Cash and Carry v Fostif [2006] HCA 41.
[2] Fostif v Campbells Cash and Carry [2005] 63 NSWLR 203. Upheld Campbells Cash and Carry Pty Ltd v Fostif Pty Ltd (2006) 229 CLR 386.
[3] Kirby v Centro [2008] FCA 1505.
[4] QPSX Limited v Ericsson Australia Pty Ltd [2005] FCA 933, at [54].
[5] QPSX Limited v Ericsson Australia Pty Ltd [2005] FCA 933, at [54].
[6] Campbells Cash and Carry Pty Ltd v Fostif Pty Ltd (2006) 229 CLR 386 at [93]. See also Jeffery & Katauskas Pty Limited v SST Consulting Pty Ltd (2009) 239 CLR 75 at [26], [29]–[30].
[7] Campbells Cash and Carry Pty Ltd v Fostif Pty Ltd (2006) 229 CLR 386 at [84]–[86].
[8] M Legg, L Travers, E Park and N Turner, 'Litigation Funding in Australia' paper at the Law Society of New South Wales Young Lawyers' 2010 Annual Civil Litigation One Day Seminar, 13 March 2010.'

3.119 As discussed already, Australia, like England, has an adverse costs regime. Whilst in England, the recommendation is that funders should be responsible for the losing party's legal fees, in Australia the 2009 decision in *Jeffrey & Katauskas Pty Limited*[21] decided the opposite—although in practice most clients would expect the funder to provide such an indemnity as part of the funding package.

3.120 In 2009 in *Brookfield Multiplex*[22] the full Federal Court held that the funding arrangements created an unregistered 'managed investment scheme' which would have required the funders to hold a Financial Investment Service licence to be eligible to fund the case. In 2010 the government announced that it would exempt litigation funding from full licensing, given the importance of litigation funding for access to justice.

3.121 In the 2011 *Chameleon*[23] case, the litigation funding agreement was initially held to be unenforceable as it was a financial product, dealt with without a Financial

---

[21] *Jeffery & Katauskas Pty Limited v SST Consulting Pty Ltd* (2009) 239 CLR 75.
[22] *Brookfield Multiplex Limited v International Litigation Funding Partners Pte Ltd (No 2)* [2009] FCAFC.
[23] *International Litigation Partners Pte Ltd v Chameleon Mining NL (Receivers and Managers Appointed)* [2012] HCA 45.

Services Licence. The decision was overturned on appeal. But, given the consequential exemption provided to funders in Australia by the Australian Securities and Investment Commission, it seems unlikely to change things much.

3.122 The Law Council of Australia shares this view. The Corporations Amendment Regulation 2012 (No 6) exempted litigation funders from the need to apply for and hold an Australian Financial Services Licence.[24] The High Court's decision in *International Litigation Partners Pte Ltd v Chameleon Mining NL*[25] has the effect that litigation funders will not be required to hold a Financial Services Licence.

3.123 Following the *Fostif* decision, the legitimacy of the involvement of funders in fundamental decisions and their influence and control over the case was established. The largest difference between the Australian funding regime and those in England and the USA is the extent to which the funder can control the decision making process and exert influence.

3. New Zealand

3.124 Whist the growth of litigation funding in New Zealand has been slower than in other jurisdictions, it is now a market available to litigation funders.

3.125 The decision in *Saunders v Houghton*[26] (known as the 'Feltex' decision as it relates to the IPO of Feltex Carpets) recognized the need for New Zealand to follow the general trend in common law jurisdictions, to allow the use of litigation funding.

4. South Africa

3.126 In 2013, in South Africa the spotlight was drawn to a litigation funder's success in the National Potato Cooperative's victory in its claim against PWC.[27] This is the same case which nearly a decade earlier had changed the legal landscape by affirming the process of litigation funding and diminishing the rules of champerty and maintenance.

3.127 In the 2004 decision the Supreme Court had concluded that once the Contingency Fees Act 66 of 1997 had made speculative fee arrangements permissible, then the need for champerty and maintenance had diminished, if not disappeared, and funding arrangements were acceptable.

3.128 The market is receptive to litigation funding and continues to grow.

---

[24] In relation to schemes mentioned in para 5C.11.01(1)(b) or (c) of the regulations.
[25] *International Litigation Partners Pte Ltd v Chameleon Mining NL (Receivers and Managers Appointed)* [2012] HCA 45.
[26] *Saunders v Houghton* [2010] 3 NZLR 331.
[27] *PriceWaterHouse Coopers Inc and Others v National Potato Co-operative Ltd* [2004] (6) SA 66 (SCA).

5. Canada

3.129 Canada has the same approach to adverse costs as in England and Wales. This jurisdiction has seen more litigation funding activity recently. Historically it has not been an attractive market for funders due to the lower level of legal fees and level of damages awards along with a lack of judicial endorsement.

3.130 However, the *Manulife*[28] decision in 2011 is widely thought to have been the catalyst for an increase in funder interest. The judge held that the funding agreement in that case did not violate rules on champerty and maintenance and was beneficial to access to justice.

3.131 In the recent case of *E. Eddy Bayens and others v Kinross Gold Corporation and others*[29] the Canadian High Court approved an English based funder's litigation funding agreement in a class action noting that they were regulated by the Association of Litigation Funders of England and Wales, which has provisions to ensure (i) non-interference in litigation; (ii) confidentiality; and (iii) capital adequacy of litigation funders.

6. France

3.132 France operates under a civil, codified system. There is no provision against the use of litigation funding in France. Whilst there may be concerns raised by lawyers and the judiciary, it is likely that public policy would allow funding on the basis of access to justice and allow the use of a commercial funder with a legitimate interest. There is little opinion on the subject primarily because of the relatively low level of legal fees in France. As such, the market in France is very small and not seen as an area where growth is expected in the near future, albeit there is some interest in the process.

7. Germany

3.133 In Germany there is no common law doctrine of champerty or maintenance. Germany, and also the Netherlands, have become a favourite jurisdiction for cartel actions where often the claims are assigned to a special purpose vehicle, formed for bringing the case, which receives the funding. There is an active funding market in Germany which is well established.

3.134 The costs regime is such that whilst there is an adverse costs system, the level of fees is much lower than England and Wales, on average some 10 to 20 per cent only of the equivalent costs in England. The funding market continues to thrive, with particular emphasis on cartel damages cases.

---

[28] *Dugal v Manulife Financial Corporation* [2011] ONSC 1785 (SCJ).
[29] *E. Eddy Bayens and others v Kinross Gold Corporation and others* (2013) ONSC 4974.

8. Caribbean

3.135 In the various jurisdictions across the Caribbean, the general tenor of the response to litigation funding has been cautious but positive. In the Bahamas, while there is no reported case directly on funding, in *Massai Aviation Services v Attorney General*[30] the court noted the diminishing relevance of the rules of champerty and maintenance.

3.136 The Bermudan legal system has had the benefit of considering a litigation funding agreement and its validity. The case of *Stiftung Salle Modulable and Rutli Stiftung v Butterfield Trust (Bermuda) Limited*[31] decided that a litigation funding agreement was permitted.

3.137 In the British Virgin Islands, another Crown dependency, the legal system bears significant resemblance to the English system. The case of *Hugh Brown & Associates (Pty) Ltd v Kermas Limited*[32] came before Mr Justice Bannister. He demonstrated a willingness to accept litigation funding, and whilst he noted that he was not addressed on the lawfulness of the arrangement, he was willing to accept that it was correct that there nothing wrong with the arrangement.

3.138 The Cayman Islands, with a system almost identical to that of the British Virgin Islands, has indicated its belief that the doctrines of champerty and maintenance do not serve any current social purpose.

9. Channel Islands

3.139 In Jersey, the litigation funding market was given a boost when the Jersey courts expressly approved the use of funding in the *Valetta Trust*[33] case. Jersey is very much a jurisdiction where litigation funding is accepted.

3.140 Guernsey does not yet have any decided case on the point but it is widely understood that the Guernsey courts will take the same approach as the Jersey courts.

10. Dubai and Qatar

3.141 These are not two jurisdictions that one would immediately suggest as possible venues for commercial litigation and litigation funding. However, the establishment of primarily English based legal systems in the Qatar Financial Centre and the Dubai International Financial Centre has changed things a little. The domestic courts remain unattractive to funders.

---

[30] *(1) Massai Aviation Services (2) Aerostar Limited v (1) Attorney General (2) Bahamasair Holdings Limited* [2007] UKPC 12.
[31] *Stiftung Salle Modulable and Rutli Stiftung v Butterfield Trust (Bermuda) Limited* [2014] Bda LR 13.
[32] *Hugh Brown & Associates (Pty) Ltd v Kermas Limited* [2011] (BVIHCV(COM)).
[33] *In re Valetta Trust* [2011] JRC 227, 2012 (1) JLR 1.

11. Ireland

Ireland is a difficult jurisdiction for litigation funders. The rules of champerty and maintenance still prevail. In the case of *Thema International Fund plc v HSBC Institutional Trust Services (Ireland) Limited*[34] the court saw nothing wrong in a shareholder with an interest in the litigation funding the same. However, it went on to affirm that the position of a professional funder with no interest in the outcome of the case, other than commercial, would be champertous.

3.143

12. Hong Kong

Hong Kong is where the solicitor Winnie Lo[35] was jailed for 15 months for conspiracy to maintain an action in 2009. There is hope for the funding market though. Her conviction was recently overturned on appeal where the Court of Final Appeal recommended that reform of this area of the law should be considered.

3.144

Whilst recent case law suggests an increase in the recognition and the legitimacy of litigation funding in the local courts for the purpose of providing access to justice, this is still a jurisdiction that funders are wary of, for now.

3.145

In the 2012 case of *Re Po Yuen (To's) Machine Factory Limited*,[36] Mr Justice Harris clarified the court's expectations of the standards and professionalism required of a litigation funder. He confirmed that the liquidators of a company in liquidation could enter into a funding arrangement with a third party and that the funding may come in the form of a contingency fee arrangement with the third party.

3.146

Mr Justice Harris's endorsement and more liberal approach demonstrates the developing body of case law in Hong Kong, which recognizes litigation funding for liquidators as a lawful exception.

3.147

13. Singapore

Singapore has historically been a jurisdiction that has enforced the rules of maintenance and champerty with some vigour. More recently it has wished to be seen as somewhere which is amenable to commercial litigation. The courts take guidance from Australia and England but have been reluctant to go as far as those courts in stepping back from the strict regimes of historic days. Singapore is looking to

3.148

---

[34] *Thema International Fund plc v HSBC Institutional Trust Services (Ireland) Limited* [2011] IEHC 357.
[35] *Winnie Lo v HKSAR* [2011] FACC 2/2011.
[36] *Re Po Yuen (To's) Machine Factory Limited* [2012] HKCU 816.

promote itself as a litigation and arbitration hub and is working very hard to show the world that it is ready for that role. In doing so there is likely to be a review of its system and an acceptance of funding commercial litigation matters; the external pressures upon any jurisdiction wishing to develop itself as a major litigation centre are likely to become irresistible. The same observation must apply to Hong Kong.

3.149 Litigation funding is certainly on the rise in other jurisdictions and around the globe generally. The world of litigation funding continues to expand. It is difficult to conclude other than that litigation funding is very much here to stay and will continue to develop. It is now established across most of the world's leading litigation centres as a worldwide tool for litigators and their clients, and in the other jurisdictions which wish to be perceived as significant for international litigation, present indications, at least, suggest that they will have little prospect of resisting the tide.

4

FUNDER MODELS

A. Funder Models	4.01	F. Publicly Listed	4.57
B. 'Case by Case' Funding	4.09	G. Case Study: Burford Capital	4.64
1. 'One-off' funders	4.10	H. Case Study: Therium Capital	
2. 'Fund raiser' funders	4.21	Management Limited	4.73
C. Family Office	4.33	I. Case Study: Vannin	
D. Private Equity	4.43	Capital	4.82
E. Investment Fund	4.48	J. Conclusion	4.89

A. Funder Models

4.01 Each of the litigation funders in England and Wales is different. At the time of writing, the Association of Litigation Funders (ALF) has seven funder members. To anyone who had little or no experience of litigation funding, there would be no reason to expect that there would be any significant difference between those seven funders but, in fact, save for the basic features, they are all structured differently and operate differently. Whilst a few have similar structures they span the range of models that have so far been used to create and run litigation funding entities.

4.02 This chapter will review some of the funding structures and it will detail the characteristics of the funder models and discuss the potential advantages and disadvantages of each. The chapter concludes with a case study of three different types of funder structure.

4.03 The different funders in the market source their funds from a variety of backgrounds and use differing structures. These include the mainstream professional funders, one-off or one-time funders, case by case funders, hedge funds, private equity, investment funds, listed funds, and family offices. Some have disparate investors, some have only one.

4.04 There are common features among the various structures as there are some basic and fundamental elements to being a litigation funder. The mainstream professional funders in England and Wales have applied for and been approved as members of the Association of Litigation Funders of England and Wales. The ALF is the body responsible for regulating the litigation funding industry in England and Wales and has published a Code of Conduct for Litigation Funders operating in that jurisdiction. The Code sets out criteria for membership and provides rules covering capital adequacy and certain requirements as to how a funder may terminate a funding agreement. There is a more detailed analysis of the ALF, its requirements, and function, in Chapter 9.

4.05 Quite clearly, in order to be a litigation funder, one basic requirement is access to a significant amount of capital. That is the case even in relation to those funders who fund on a one-off basis and are not involved in the industry as a professional and mainstream participant.

4.06 As well as significant capital, a litigation funder needs to have considered and developed investment criteria. The criteria may be different from one funder to the next, but each will have a strategy. That may be simply to invest in cases on a one-off basis having been seduced by the potential for very lucrative returns (and possibly very significant losses). It may be, as is the case with the mainstream funders, a carefully planned approach ensuring that there is a varied spread of types and size of case throughout the funder's portfolio in order to protect as much as possible against the inevitable losses which will occur, it being well accepted in the litigation world, and more importantly in the litigation funding world, that losses are inevitable.

4.07 Some funders will choose a range of broadly similar cases, others will invest in many different sorts of cases across varied jurisdictions. Other funders will choose a specific subject matter such as intellectual property and patents and invest solely in those areas as a specialist funder.

4.08 Whilst all litigation funders will have some basic similar features they will also vary significantly in other ways which will distinguish them from each other. For example, some funders will operate a portfolio of investments in cases, others will adopt a single case strategy.

B. 'Case by Case' Funding

4.09 There are two categories of this type of funding. The first is a more traditional method of funding particular cases as and when the need to do so arises: 'one-off' funders. The second is akin to being a litigation funding broker where the funder raises money for a specific case on a case by case basis. It has been suggested that this is a method by which alleged litigation funders, with little or no money of their own, masquerade as real or mainstream litigation funders. These funders are also distinct from the professional funding brokers who have a legitimate place in the market. There are five such broker[1] organizations who now have 'broker' membership of the ALF. There is a clear distinction between these professional and well regarded brokers who describe themselves as such, and the organizations which claim to be funders, but have no funds.

1. 'One-off' funders

In the earlier years of the litigation funding industry, this type of 'one-off' funder was fairly commonplace. Litigation funding satisfies a financial need. Litigation is expensive. There are many occurrences of the basic litigation funding scenario, namely that an entity, insolvency office holder, or individual has a claim which may recoup a significant sum of money if successful. But, the missing ingredient, being the most vital, is the ability to fund the litigation to a conclusion. For many years in insolvency situations cases were brought using a combination of conditional fees for lawyers and either one or a number of wealthy creditors were asked to fund litigation. This is an example of one-off funding. **4.10**

Often the funder in this situation would be a creditor bank or financial institution. This process began to grow and spread in popularity as it became a tried and tested method of recovering assets and safeguarding the value in a liquidation or other insolvency regime. This method provided a return for the funder and enabled the litigation to be brought for the benefit of the creditors as a whole. The individual funder not only recovered some of its original entitlement as a creditor but also made a healthy return on its investment in the litigation. This is, in effect, the root of most of the litigation funding that now takes place. **4.11**

From these sorts of situations, it became more and more commonplace for cases to be funded on an individual basis. Inevitably, with the growth in the knowledge of these sorts of arrangement the number of 'funders' prepared to make an investment in litigation grew. **4.12**

The returns that could be achieved started to attract the attention of hedge funds who have regularly been involved in funding one-off cases. Additionally, the legal disciplines, types of case, and jurisdictions in which these individual placements could be made began to widen. No longer were they specific to the insolvency world and no longer were these isolated situations. The use of one-off litigation funding remains reasonably widespread, particularly in the USA and Caribbean jurisdictions, and remains popular in the insolvency world. It is less prevalent in England and Wales. **4.13**

This sort of funding does not feature in the mainstream of the litigation funding world, particularly in England, because of the nature of the arrangement. The funder in these cases is not a professional or mainstream funder. It is involved in a **4.14**

---

[1] Arthur J. Gallagher & Co., Claimtrading Limited, QLP Legal, The Judge Limited, and Universal Legal Protection Limited.

case for specific reasons related to the case (ie as a creditor) or it is making an individual one-off investment. The investors may be a high net worth individual or a hedge fund looking for a different sort of risk profile and returns.

4.15 In some situations a one-off funder can be the ideal litigation funding partner. The funder may be a creditor, particularly a creditor which is a financial institution. It will often have some knowledge of the case or the area already and should be able to act reasonably swiftly.

4.16 Depending upon the arrangement and the experience of the particular funder, the terms may be more or less competitive than what is offered by some in the mainstream funding market. A pre-existing creditor may be willing to provide funds on attractive terms. However this very much depends upon the specific funder and the circumstances. For example, a hedge fund which has not been involved previously may have a different approach and its pricing may be very expensive.

4.17 One of the disadvantages of using a one-off funder is often the pricing. By definition, if a funder is making the investment on a one-off basis, they will not have the benefit of a portfolio of cases. That is likely to mean that the price for the investment is high as the funder cannot recoup any potential losses across the portfolio. The disadvantage to the funder of course is obvious.

4.18 In a situation where a creditor is also the funder, there is potential for conflict. The funder's interests may be aligned with the claimant and the creditors but not always. There may be situations where this may be an issue, particularly when it comes to receiving offers and deciding upon acceptance. Additionally, there can be difficulties where advice is received that the case is not going as well as anticipated. At this point issues such who has control over the litigation may come into play.

4.19 It is for these reasons that lawyers and litigants are usually best advised to use funder members of the ALF. A one-off funder will not be such a member, however trustworthy and financially sound it may be. Without ALF membership there is no independent assessment of the individual funder's capital adequacy or ability to fund the case to a conclusion. The worst case scenario for any litigant is to find that their funding source has been exhausted. Of course, there are ways to protect against that, for example insisting on the full budget being deposited with the lawyers and independent audit of the funder's finances.

4.20 Additionally, the one-off funder will not have subscribed to the ALF Code of Conduct (i) governing termination of any funding agreement, (ii) providing for what happens if there is a dispute with the funder, and (iii) providing for a guarantee that the funder will not interfere in the decision making in a case.

2. 'Fund raiser' funders

4.21 It would be expected that one basic necessity for a litigation funder is that the funder has significant capital resources. That is the case with all of the mainstream funders in England and Wales that have become members of the ALF. If they did not, then they would not have been able to satisfy the membership criteria, most particularly as regards capital adequacy. Accordingly, there is no representative of this 'fund raiser' type of funder in the ALF or in the mainstream of the industry any more. Historically, however, that was not the case and there are still some of these 'fund raiser' funders in the market undertaking business. However, it seems likely that the creation of the ALF has placed the continued existence of this sort of funder in some danger, or at least under some pressure.

4.22 There is nothing inherently wrong with the basic idea of a 'fund raiser' funder. It is a simple concept which can, in some circumstances, fulfil a very useful function. The model is essentially that the funder needs to find someone with a viable legal case which needs litigation funding in order for it to be pursued. Then having secured an exclusivity period from the client, the funder goes about seeking investment in the particular case. The longer the exclusivity period, the better for the funder, as that is the time limit available to the funder to go out and raise the necessary money from investors.

4.23 Some of these funders are more ambitious. They will seek to agree terms across a portfolio of cases and then look to obtain investment across the entire range. That is possibly more attractive to investors given the likelihood of an overall success across the portfolio rather than a one-off investment. It is of course more difficult to achieve success with this route. It is difficult enough to find one case and negotiate sufficiently lengthy exclusivity terms with the client who needs funding. To do that with a larger number of clients is extremely hard.

4.24 Whilst there is nothing wrong with the concept, the most regular objection to this method of litigation funding is the lack of transparency and misleading nature of what is being done. Funders who operate using this process need to explain to the other parties involved in the process that they do not have funds and will not be using their own resources. Lawyers and the clients must not be led to believe that the 'fund raisers' are using their own funds when in fact during an exclusivity period they are looking to raise the necessary capital by pitching the case or cases to investors. If this occurs, valuable time and resources on the part of clients and lawyers might be wasted.

4.25 One way that 'fund raisers' are able to attract capital in the short time period available is to offer a capital guarantee to investors. Most litigation funders operate their portfolios on the basis that the losses are very much outweighed by the wins. Funding only one case at a time precludes such a basis of operation. To counter this, and to make the offering more attractive to investors, such 'fund raisers' offer to insure the capital invested so that the investor will never do any worse as a result of the transaction than receiving their capital back. The fund raisers achieve this by purchasing an 'own sides costs and disbursements' ATE policy. The investment money received is to be used to pay for solicitors' fees and disbursements during the litigation. If there is an own side's policy of insurance in force, then in the event that the case is unsuccessful the insurance policy will pay back the fees and disbursements paid out. These can then be returned to the investor, thus restoring their capital position.

4.26 In conception such schemes can be attractive, but they face practical difficulties. First, most clients involved in litigation are under some time pressure to finalize their funding arrangements and proceed with the case. For this reason they do not want to be tied into a long period of exclusivity. That is a problem in this scenario as the funder requires a reasonable amount of time to agree an arrangement with an investor or investors. That process can take a long time since the investment is likely to be a significant sum of money.

4.27 Secondly, ATE policies for own sides costs are not very easy to place in the legal expenses market, particularly when they are for large limits of indemnity to cover the substantial sums invested in a case. Even if the policy can be obtained it is likely to be for a high priced premium. Additionally, because of the funding model, namely the capital guarantee, the premium would also have to be either contingent or insured and repayable—although this scheme could allow for a premium to be paid up front rather than deferred to the end of the case.

4.28 Thirdly, there is the difficulty in arranging such fund raising activities within the time scale of an exclusivity arrangement. There are some funders who seek 90 days exclusivity. Most ask for less as realistically no commercially aware client is prepared to wait that length of time only to find that funding has been declined or that the funds cannot be raised (albeit from the client's perspective the result is the same, that is to say that there is no funding for the case).

4.29 The last issue with 'fund raising' funders is that of pricing. As discussed earlier, the majority of these funders rely on a capital guarantee to obtain investment which is likely to increase the cost to the client. Even in the pre-Jackson era, the premium paid in relation to own side's costs was not recoverable. If the premium is paid in advance then that amount is added to the funding required together with the return on that funding, usually a multiple of the funded amount. Unsurprisingly, the capital guarantee that provides certainty for the investor is unlikely to reduce the price to the client of the litigation finance. There is a tension between ensuring the security of capital, and the cost of finance.

4.30 In the author's view, in order for the litigation funding market to work efficiently and well for the benefit of clients who are seeking to make use of it, it is very important that funders' prospective clients have a full understanding from the outset of the implications of entering into arrangements with any particular funder. Clients need to know that a decision as to funding will be made within a defined, and relatively short, timescale. They also need to know the likely cost to them of entering into a funding arrangement, however the funding arrangements may be structured.

It is also likely to be relevant to a client that the proposed funder may have to raise capital from an external source in order to fund a case, because this may raise the prospect that the funder's ability to raise finance, as distinct from the merits of the case, may affect whether funding becomes available. **4.31**

If there is to be regulation of litigation funding, then provisions for ensuring that such matters have to be addressed as preliminary information to be provided to prospective clients would be welcome. At the time of writing, s 58B of the Courts and Legal Services Act 1990 (as inserted by s 28 of the Access to Justice Act 1999) has still not been brought into force. Section 58B(3)(a) enables the Secretary of State to prescribe that a funder is a person of a particular description. Under s 58 B(4) regulations can be made so that a funder must be approved by the Secretary of State or by an approved person. The section also permits regulations to be made requiring prescribed information to be provided to a litigant before an agreement is made. Given the speed at which the funding market is developing, it is be hoped that these provisions will be brought into force and used to address the problems described above in conjunction with the work of the ALF. **4.32**

C. Family Office

The family offices of ultra high net worth families invest in many and varied asset classes. It should therefore be no surprise to anyone that litigation funding is an asset class in which family offices have taken a keen interest. Litigation funding has no correlation with the financial markets, and in fact it is suggested that it is counter-cyclical as litigation tends to increase during an economic downturn. **4.33**

Of the (current) seven funder members of the ALF in England and Wales, at least two litigation funders have direct links to the family office world. Others may well do so through their varied investor base. **4.34**

The models adopted by family offices are effective and professional. From outside they appear to behave in the same way as all other funders. As discussed previously, all of the litigation funders, regardless of structure, will have adopted investment processes and procedures which are in many ways similar. There will be similar due diligence undertaken by all of the funders. The differences will be in the investment criteria. **4.35**

For example, it could be that, for reasons of speed of return, certain funders will not wish to be involved in international arbitration matters. Some will shun group actions for fear of managing a disparate group of clients and others will avoid patent and IP litigation due to its inherent difficulty and the need for specialist expertise. **4.36**

The distinguishing features of a single or 'club deal' family office backed litigation funder are that the funder is privately owned and subject to the control of the **4.37** family office or offices. Invariably the litigation funder will be a wholly owned or majority owned subsidiary of the family's group of companies.

4.38 Usually this type of litigation funder is well capitalized and structured. It tends to be organized with a team of industry professionals to advise on investments. Such a team would normally include lawyers and financial professionals providing a useful combination of legal and investment experience to review cases and decide upon which pieces of litigation to invest in. Ultimately though, and obviously this is wholly dependent on the structure, the final decision making could be that of the family office itself or even a family member.

4.39 One of the benefits of such a litigation funder is undoubtedly the financial resources that it can apply. Membership of the ALF is an important part of operating in the litigation funding market in England and Wales and satisfying the necessary capital adequacy requirements of the ALF is easy for these well funded entities. That allows the litigant and the lawyers in a case to be confident that the funder is going to want to fund and to be able to fund their case to a conclusion, subject to the merits remaining good. Additionally, if they sign up to the Code of Conduct of the ALF they project themselves as transparent, mainstream, and professional litigation funders. Whilst non-ALF funders may share in all of these qualities, membership of the ALF represents a commitment to a set of common and objective standards.

4.40 The nature of the structure of the family office under consideration also assists in their ability to fund unusual cases. They are able to fund in a flexible and innovative way if necessary. They do not have set rules other than those defined by the family office. It may be that they are conservative in their investments but that is their choice; they do not have to be so.

4.41 One of the issues that family office advisers sometimes encounter in general, but also in the litigation funding world, is the potential for there to be a lack of detachment from those who hold the money from those who invest it on their behalf. This is very much the case if a family member has a role in the decision making process. Whether or not the family member has a veto on any decision—and that is not unheard of—the mere fact that the advisers are investing the money of someone who sits and discusses the case with them in an investment committee can cause difficulties. Tensions are unlikely to be high whilst cases are running successfully and when they win, but no experienced funder would predict a perfect track record, nor expect one. However, once the first defeat is encountered it is important to ensure that the decision making process does not change for the worse.

4.42 This lack of detachment, of those who are the real investors in the project from the actual investment process, can be an issue. It is not one which is encountered in some of the other structures used in litigation funding. That said it is not always a bar to being a successful litigation funder and the observation is not necessarily a criticism.

D. Private Equity

4.43 An alternative method used by a number of litigation funders is to seek their investment from the field of private equity. In a similar fashion to the family office world, the attraction of litigation funding to private equity is its lack of market correlation and the ability to make large profits. A private equity investor would provide either a rolling facility upon agreed terms or make an investment in the business for a combination of equity and debt positions.

4.44 Invariably a funder will have approached the private equity investor with a proposed structure and taken one of the routes outlined in this chapter. If the private equity investor is providing debt and equity then the structure of the entity is going be important to them. They may appoint one or more positions on the board and will often control the company. They will also want to be involved in the decision making process to ensure that the investment decisions are made with regard to the agreed investment criteria, and will therefore most probably want to sit on the investment committee also.

4.45 It is not uncommon in these situations for there to be key milestones which it is for the business to reach over certain time periods which would then allow the funder to unlock further capital for funding. In other words, once the business model is proved, then the funding facility may be increased or the pricing reduced.

4.46 One potential difficulty for a litigation funder structured in this manner is again the lack of detachment, at least at the outset, from the source of funding. In the same way that it may be difficult for a family office backed funder to avoid the influence of the main investor, the same applies to the private equity investor as the investment comes primarily from one source. The potential for intervention from investor appointed board members may not be a difficulty in all scenarios, but it is a possibility. There would be an agreed investment strategy dealing with the types of cases, size, and the jurisdictions that the funder proposes to invest in. On the face of it, as long as these criteria are kept to, then there should be no tension. Indeed, as the model is proved and the business progresses and becomes more mature with a track record of sound investment, these difficulties may recede entirely.

4.47 There are several successful private equity backed funders in the marketplace in England and Wales.

E. Investment Fund

4.48 Several of the major players in the litigation funding market worldwide and particularly in England and Wales are structured as investment funds. This is a popular and effective way of obtaining investment and then deploying the capital.

4.49 Usually the investment vehicle will be based in an offshore jurisdiction such as the Channel Islands where the fund structure will be subject to local regulatory laws and the financial service compliance regime of the jurisdiction. So if the fund is based in Guernsey it will be subject to regulation by the Guernsey Financial Services Commission. All the investments will go into the offshore fund and the investors may be a mix of institutions, pension funds, and other forms of investor including family offices and high net worth individuals.

4.50 The named litigation funding entity acts as the investment adviser to the fund and is usually based onshore in England. It may well also be regulated for its investment advisory activity by the Financial Conduct Authority.

4.51 In order to raise the investment into the fund there will be a prospectus prepared which provides details of what the fund proposes to do, how it will do it, and what returns are anticipated from its investment activities. Obviously there are no guarantees with any investment into a fund. The investor or the investor's professional advisers will rely upon the track record, background, and sector performance of the investment adviser before deciding to invest. If the fund raising activities are a second or third fund of the same sort of company, and more capital is being raised to continue the investment activities then previous performance of such a fund is a fairly basic assessment of abilities of the investment advisers or fund managers.

4.52 The basis upon which the fund has published its proposed investment strategy to the investors creates the parameters for the investment committee of the investment adviser to the fund—that is, the litigation funder. Investors will be relying upon the investment adviser to manage the fund in the way they represented. Accordingly whilst the funds are further removed from the investors than in a family office or private equity backed regime, there are still restrictions upon the fund and how the funds are invested. This is not necessarily a bad thing and the discipline of keeping to a tried and tested method and not looking to invest outside specific case types or jurisdictions has created solid and successful funders. What it does not allow is the innovation or flexibility that may be possible with more freedom from other structures.

4.53 The litigation funder in this scenario fulfils an advisory role and advises the fund. It has a similar structure to other funders in that there will be an advisory committee of experienced legal and financial personnel and it will have a strict regime and process for receiving, reviewing, and assessing and ultimately investing in new cases, which it would also have set out in its offering literature.

4.54 An advantage of this structure is the detachment of the funders from the investors themselves. Whilst the fund has to be managed to the expected regime, there is no direct investor input into the decision making process and within the necessary confines the funders are able to invest in whatever cases they like. Funders operating in these circumstances should benefit from an absence of the potentially emotional involvement of the investors.

One key element of a fund structure is that, once the fund has completed its fund raising and the fund is fully operational, then there is no question as to the capital adequacy of the funder and there can be no issue with its ability to fund a case to its conclusion. ALF membership and capital adequacy certification are not problems for this type of litigation funder. **4.55**

Further, the additional regulation and scrutiny to which this kind of litigation funder is subjected to can only add to the funder's credibility. **4.56**

F. Publicly Listed

The listed litigation funders are unsurprisingly some of the largest funding providers in the world market. Currently only one, Burford Capital, listed on the AIM in London, operates full time in the jurisdiction of England and Wales. **4.57**

The money that is invested in litigation funding by a listed funder is raised from the sale and acquisition of its shares on whichever market it is listed. A prospectus is prepared setting out the way the company proposes to do business. It will cover the management of the organization, the investment criteria, and process. It will also cover what the company is trying to achieve, namely what it expects to deliver. It will set out the likely returns to investors in both capital growth by way of share value and income from dividends. **4.58**

The structure of the funder and its advisers can vary but the basic principle remains that the capital is raised and deployed by decisions of the management team and directors. The decision as to whether an investment should be made or not sits with the investment committee and then the board of directors implements the decision. **4.59**

There are some obvious advantages to being a publicly listed litigation funder. The first is the transparency of its capital. The amount of capital available to invest and the ease with which a listed funder's financial position can be verified should provide most litigants and lawyers with any amount of comfort they may need as to the funder's financial credentials. There is obviously a downside to that transparency: if for whatever reason things are not going to plan then that is also in the public domain and easily checked. **4.60**

One very key difference between this structure and the other forms of litigation funder is the very real detachment from investors. The board and management will remain accountable for their decisions and will be required to make investments based upon what they represented to the market when offering the shares. But, once they have the money they are allowed to make decisions that they deem appropriate to produce the suggested return on capital deployed. This structure is further removed from the source of the capital than a traditional fund structure. The decisions made are almost entirely driven by ensuring the investment produces the best returns available. **4.61**

4.62 The size of the funder and available capital is clearly an advantage to a listed litigation funder. The financial might of such a funder is clear. Within sensible boundaries there are unlikely to be many investments in cases which are too large for a funder of this size.

4.63 A difficulty that any listed organization can face is the perception, and in many cases the reality, of the effect on speed, flexibility, and responsiveness. In comparison to the smaller funders, the decision making process can appear to be cumbersome and seem slower than competitors, although that is not always the situation in relation to listed funders, who in fact can be both fast and extremely flexible in their approach. That said, the disadvantages of this structure are that the management have to report results regularly in public—this creates pressure for regular news flow to show that progress is being made and returns achieved which sits in tension with the longer term nature of the investments. The public reporting also is in tension with the confidential nature of the funding activity.

G. Case Study: Burford Capital

4.64 Burford Capital ('Burford') has kindly agreed to assist in a case study to explain its structure and approach to litigation finance. Burford is the world's largest provider of investment capital and risk solutions for litigation and is publicly traded in London. Its management team is one of the most experienced in the industry, responsible for managing a diversified portfolio of investments. Burford has a market capital approaching $500 million. Since inception, 26 investments have generated $173.9 million in gross investment recoveries and $67 million net of invested capital, producing a 63% net return on invested capital. Burford's investments are wholly focused on litigation finance. Accordingly, the company's success is not correlated to common market fluctuations. This has made Burford appealing to large institutional investors, who have bought and held the vast majority of the shares since the company was formed.

4.65 Burford's founders had distinguished careers prior to the company's launch. Its Chief Executive Officer, Christopher Bogart, was formerly the General Counsel of Time Warner Inc., then one of the world's largest media companies; was Chief Executive Officer of Churchill Ventures Limited; and was trained as a litigator at Cravath, Swaine & Moore. Burford's Chief Investment Officer, Jonathan Molot, is a Professor of Law at Georgetown University Law Center in Washington, DC, having started his legal career as a law clerk to Justice Stephen Breyer on the US Supreme Court. The Chairman of Burford, Sir Peter Middleton, serves as Chairman of Marsh & McLennan Companies and served as Group Chairman of Barclays Bank PLC.

4.66 The company is a Guernsey corporation, and as such has to comply with various national regulators, including the Guernsey Financial Services Commission and the UK's Financial Conduct Authority. Due to its public listing the company reports as required with detailed financial updates as well as specifics on its investments and operations. Such reports not only provide transparency to investors, but also offer law firms and potential clients an excellent view into the company's significant capital holdings and professional operations. Burford has offices in the UK and US.

4.67 In addition to offering funding and ATE insurance on single cases, Burford has developed a number of innovative financing models. It has provided funding to law firms for single cases and portfolios of cases (allowing them to de-risk CFAs), capital financing to clients (where litigation provides the collateral for cash flow to a company), the financing of insurance policies, and it was the first in the UK market to introduce a funding vehicle for so-called hybrid DBAs. Burford is more than a simple case funder; it is a full-service provider of litigation finance—meaning that it is open to a myriad of financing structures that treat litigation as a financial asset.

4.68 Burford considers investment opportunities anywhere in the world, with a particular focus on the US, the UK, and international arbitration matters. The company's investment policy emphasizes a diversity of investments across a broad range of variables, including duration, geography, law firm, size of investment, and type of litigation. Burford invests in all kinds of commercial matters—with an emphasis on contract, securities, fraud, and competition matters. It also has a deep interest in insolvency litigation, and has entered into a partnership and equity investment with Manolete Partners, an expert funder in UK insolvency matters.

4.69 Virtually all of Burford's underwriting is handled in-house by an experienced team of former commercial litigators with vast and deep experience. Burford's underwriters undertake a rigorous and disciplined case assessment that ensures that good cases move quickly through its pipeline of opportunities. The process is simple but effective. Any new case received into the pipeline will be reviewed critically at a 'triage' stage, where an underwriter will test basic threshold requirements of a case, including a first pass on the merits, jurisdiction, quantum, counsel, and size of budget. If the case is one which, on its face, should be considered for funding then the case will pass through this stage quickly and receive a fuller review.

4.70 The second level review will include a deeper dive on key aspects of the case and identify specific risks to be considered. This more detailed analysis of the facts and legal issues is similar to the review that a lawyer considering a contingency arrangement would undertake before going forward on a new matter. This is likely to include further discussion and meetings with the lawyers and clients involved in the case. These discussions will involve a more detailed assessment of the legal analysis behind the lawyer's assumptions, a review of the evidence, an assessment of the proposed budgetary, and ultimately, pricing terms for funding.

4.71 As part of the underwriting process, a case will typically be presented to Burford's investment committee twice, first at initial intake and again for final approval.

4.72 The Burford investment process benefits both from a team of experienced underwriters as well as the insight of an investment committee that engages in rigorous debate and discussion about the matters it considers. Because the entire process is in-house, Burford is able to be nimble and responsive to time pressures often associated with the need for litigation funding and can be flexible in designing a funding structure that meets the specific needs of each client. Moreover, its permanent capital structure means that clients in need of funding can be assured that capital and ATE insurance will be available when they need it.

H. Case Study: Therium Capital Management Limited

4.73 Therium Capital Management ('Therium') has kindly agreed to assist in a case study to explain how they are structured and how they are funded. As far as the writer is aware, Therium is a unique structure in the litigation funding market, drawn on the investment fund model.

4.74 Therium was launched by its principals, Neil Purslow and John Byrne, at the beginning of 2009 and is one of the longest established funders of commercial litigation and international arbitration. Therium is a long term supporter, and founding, funder member, of the ALF and has been actively involved in the development of the Code of Conduct since prior to its adoption. Neil Purslow is also a director of the ALF.

4.75 Therium is a hybrid structure; cases are funded by Therium itself with backing from a series of funds, each individually advised by Therium. The investor base is diverse and new funds are launched regularly from a range of private and institutional investors. Once raised, each new fund is committed alongside the existing funds by Therium as it takes on new case commitments until that fund is fully deployed into investments. Each fund has its own corporate governance structure and investment mandate appropriate to the investors in that fund and decisions on whether to invest in a particular case are taken by each fund on advice from Therium. The funds are set up to manage the significant risks involved in litigation funding with Therium ensuring that each invests across a diversified pool of cases and observes strict investment parameters.

4.76 An advantage of the hybrid structure is that Therium has a high degree of control over the investment activity whilst benefiting from a broad and diverse investor base and these together provide a stable platform for Therium's ongoing funding activity. Therium is therefore insulated from the vagaries of individual investor sentiment and ups and downs in investment activity from deploying a single fund or investing on behalf of a single family office or private equity house. The model has enabled Therium to deliver funding to its clients consistently and yet remain flexible to adapt to market needs. The multiple fund approach also means that Therium has been able to return capital to investors and move into profit more rapidly than it could have done with a more unwieldy funding structure.

4.77 Therium's investment strategy focuses exclusively on commercial litigation, international arbitration, and complex disputes, principally in the UK but also internationally. Therium has investments in the UK, continental Europe, North America, Australasia, and in offshore jurisdictions. Typical cases would involve shareholder disputes, professional negligence claims, international arbitration, group actions, and financial services matters as well as general contractual disputes. Therium does not fund individual consumer related cases such as divorce, personal injury cases, clinical negligence, or wills and probate although some of these areas are funded on a different model through its sister company, Novitas Loans.

4.78 Because of the flexibility which its hybrid funding structure permits, Therium has been able to meet the needs of clients, funding across a wide range of case types and sizes from the largest cases in the market to making smaller investments where required.

4.79 Therium is typically approached for funding by the lawyers acting on a case or by a broker, or in exceptional cases, by the clients themselves direct. Cases may be taken on for funding at any point from prior to issue of proceedings up to shortly before trial of the action. The due diligence on the case is undertaken by Therium itself internally using information and analysis provided by the legal team and client, culminating in a recommendation to fund by Therium to the investment committees of the individual funds which will fund the case. Because the due diligence and analysis, the negotiation of funding terms, the documentation of funding, and the ongoing management of each investment are undertaken by Therium centrally on behalf of all the funds it advises, the style and approach are consistent across funds and throughout the life of the cases. The close involvement of the principals in the selection, structuring, and monitoring of the investments and particularly in the decision to fund, allows for a flexible and pragmatic yet disciplined approach at all levels of the operation.

4.80 As a funder member of the ALF, Therium's funding model in England and Wales complies with the ALF Code of Conduct. In particular, Therium does not seek to control settlement of the cases it funds nor dictate the strategy. Funding may however also be provided on alternative models, for instance by providing funding through law firms acting on contingency fees or into portfolios of cases through one firm.

4.81 Therium has been an important part of the funding market in England and Wales for some years. It is a mature and well known funder with a strong track record as well as being run by an experienced and credible management team.

I. Case Study: Vannin Capital

4.82 Vannin Capital ('Vannin') has kindly agreed to provide details of its structure and processes. Vannin was formed at the end of 2010 by three lawyers and a highly successful entrepreneur using a private equity house based on the Isle of Man. The litigation funding world was relatively unknown even then, although Vannin played a very large part in raising the industry's profile over the next few years.

4.83 The Vannin story is an example of how good capitalization and a sensible investment process can generate success in the litigation funding world. The capital which Vannin deploys in its investments comes from Bramden Investments, an Isle of Man based private equity house. Bramden makes a range of investments and litigation funding is one it was convinced to entertain due to the potentially high returns.

4.84 The structure that was created is an Isle of Man protected cell company. Each cell is independent from other cells within the structure and so theoretically the failure of any one cell would be isolated financially from the rest of the corporate entity, including its core and the remaining cells. Vannin creates a new independent cell for each new investment. It then capitalizes that cell using funding from its facility with Bramden.

4.85 The investment criteria that are applied to the analysis of cases covers very much the same approach as with any funder. The cases must be of good merit. Quantum must be significant, usually over £5m, at least covering the requisite budget by a factor of 10 to 1 and there should be no issues of recoverability. Vannin is one of the larger funders with a facility of over £100m to call upon so large budgets and big cases do not trouble them.

4.86 Experience over the time they have been in existence has allowed the development of their investment criteria and the process. There is an investment committee which includes the founders of the business. Their usual procedure is to carry out an initial review of cases and offer indicative terms subject to due diligence which is carried out during a 28-day exclusivity period. As with some funders, Vannin has a varied and wide spread of cases across a large portfolio of investments and makes strategic decisions as to certain types of case and the number they should invest in at any one time.

4.87 This structure and processes give Vannin certain advantages over other funders. Their investment decisions are fast, given the constituency of their investment committee. The structure also allows them to be flexible in terms of what they do, how they do it and, importantly, how they price it.

Funder Models

4.88 This funder has risen from a new entrant to a cornerstone of the litigation funding world, in a short period of time. This, in itself, tends to confirm how rapidly the funding market is developing.

J. Conclusion

4.89 Litigation funders have chosen a number of varied schemes and different methods to provide a structure and platform to use for the purposes of investing in litigation. They all have their advantages and disadvantages. Some are better for one kind of litigation and clients and others for different types. No one litigation funder is better than the other based solely upon their structure.

5

THE FUNDING PROCESS

A. The Funding Process	5.01	3. Section Four—'Changes to Project Plan'	5.99
B. Brokers or Direct Approach to Funders?	5.11	4. Section Five—'Excluded Costs and Liabilities'	5.101
C. Key Areas	5.25	5. Section Six—'Conditions Precedent and Warranties'	5.102
1. Merits and quantum	5.28	6. Section Seven—'Payment of Reasonable Costs'	5.104
2. Budget	5.36	7. Section Eight—'Adverse Costs'	5.105
3. Strategy	5.42	8. Section Nine—'Claimant's Obligations'	5.106
D. Intake Review and Assessment	5.44	9. Section Twelve—'Security for Costs'	5.108
E. Indicative Terms	5.50	10. Section Thirteen—'Treatment of Claim Proceeds'	5.110
F. Negotiation	5.52	11. Section Fourteen—'Confidentiality'	5.112
G. Term Sheet	5.57	12. Section Fifteen—'Termination'	5.114
H. Exclusivity	5.60	13. Section Twenty-Five—'Dispute Resolution'	5.118
I. Due Diligence Assessment	5.65	14. 'Schedule'	5.120
J. Pricing	5.74	15. Appendix 1—'Project Plan'	5.121
K. Retainers	5.87	16. Appendix 2—'Reliance Letter'	5.122
L. ATE	5.90	17. Appendix 3—'Priorities Agreement'	5.123
M. The Litigation Funding Agreement	5.91	N. Conclusion	5.128
1. Section Two—'Agreement to Fund'	5.95		
2. Section Three—'Payment Terms and Interest'	5.98		

A. The Funding Process

5.01 The aim of this chapter is to provide an explanation of the stages to the process of a typical litigation funding application. The areas that are covered include the process itself as well as an explanation of what the litigation funder will be looking for in the application or request.

5.02 Each litigation funder will have a similar process although the detail may differ from one to another. The process described in paragraphs 5.03 to 5.08 is a combination of the varying procedures used by the main litigation funders operating in England and Wales. It may not be accurate as regards the specifics of a particular funder, but this description will assist in the understanding of the funding process generally.

5.03 The process begins with the submission of key documents about the case which will include an assessment from the solicitors, or more likely from counsel. The assessment will cover the merits and deal with liability and quantum. Thereafter each funder's process may differ slightly but essentially it will involve a detailed review of the case and the client, with particular reference to whether the proposed defendant has the means to meet a judgment of the size anticipated.

5.04 This stage will include internal risk assessment and the views of external counsel may be obtained. If the initial review of the case is positive as to the merits and the funder wishes to make an indicative offer of funding the next steps vary slightly between funders.

5.05 The issue of detailed due diligence and the requirements for exclusivity depend on the specific procedures of each of the funders. In most situations where a funder is going to spend money on external counsel they will want to have secured an exclusive arrangement with the client before doing so, although not always. It is at this stage that, having made an indicative and non-binding offer of terms, the funder and the client would negotiate the initial terms, but they are subject to further detailed due diligence. The terms may be renegotiated after that process. This does not always happen and does so only if there is a reason to justify the change, namely something which has been identified in the process which changes the funder's or the client's view. Some funders will deal with this part of the process by taking an option to invest on these indicative terms, others will agree non-binding commercial terms subject to the due diligence process. Other funders do not ask for exclusivity in the normal course of events as they will deal with all of the due diligence process internally.

5.06 Following a successful due diligence review, which can take from one month to three months depending upon the litigation funder, the next step is to finalize the terms of the litigation funding agreement itself. The process would invariably start during the due diligence period to ensure that matters do not take any longer than absolutely necessary.

5.07 This step includes a review of the proposed retainer arrangements with the solicitors and with counsel and a discussion over the final budget, which will have been discussed in some detail already. Some funders will insist on counsel and solicitors working at a discounted rate, under hybrid or partial CFA. They will want the lawyers to 'buy into' the case and the fact that the legal team is working at a discount in return for an uplift on success may give the funder some comfort. Other funders take the view that it is for them to assess the case, and that the nature of the retainer with the lawyers should not, and does not, make any difference to the lawyers' performance.

5.08 Whilst the budget is an estimate, and subject to the assumptions made, it will invariably be incorporated into the funding agreement. The amount of the funding facility required needs to be defined and that comes from the budget. The lawyers will be asked to agree the budget and the funding agreement will have provisions for the way in which the budget can be increased. There will be provisions for the budget to be decreased but, in the author's experience, that is never required. With the due diligence completed, retainers in place, an agreed budget, and a final version of the litigation funding agreement, the process is complete.

5.09 Additionally, by way of practical example, at the end of this chapter there is an analysis of the litigation funding agreement used by the established and well known English litigation funder, Therium Capital.

5.10 This chapter concludes with a review of the process and an assessment of what is needed to enhance the prospects of a litigation funding application resulting in a successful offer of finance from the litigation funder.

B. Brokers or Direct Approach to Funders?

5.11 The first question for any lawyer considering an application for litigation funding is whether to approach the funder directly or to engage the services of a litigation funding broker. A litigation funding broker works with the lawyer and the client to prepare the funding application and will approach appropriate funders with the request for litigation funding.

5.12 The broker will then continue to be involved in the process until the funding arrangement has been completed. They will attend meetings with the parties and assist in the discussions and negotiations. Most lawyers will have negotiated only a few, if any, litigation funding agreements—although this is changing as funding has become more commonplace. Most clients will go through the process only once, hopefully.

5.13 A good litigation funding broker will have the benefit of seeing many different funding applications and understanding the differences and nuances between the various litigation funders. The litigation funders in the market will at different times prefer different types or size of case. The brokers keep abreast of those preferences and idiosyncrasies and are therefore able to target the most appropriate funders for a particular case at any time. By understanding which funder is likely to take on a particular case and focusing on them as much or even more than offering a comprehensive search of the market, a good broker may add value to the process.

5.14 The market in England and Wales is unique in this respect. Whilst there are funding brokers in other jurisdictions, the concept of using a litigation funding broker outside England and Wales is relatively unusual. In the United States brokers are virtually unheard of and the practice of using them is rare. Equally, that is the case in Australia.

5.15 It is likely that there are two main reasons for this. First, the size of the market and the number of litigation funders operating in it. In the United States and in Australia, the number of funders is relatively low in comparison to England and

Wales. The market is larger than here and so there is much less competition. It is very unusual, if not unheard of, for a litigation funder to have to compete for a particular case: there are no 'beauty parades' before the client and lawyers to persuade them to use one funder over another.

5.16 The second reason is the origin of litigation funding brokers. The litigation funding brokers in England did not all start life as funding brokers. The majority of them began life as legal expenses insurance brokers (primarily ATE insurance) and adapted their business models to include the litigation funding offering. It is a sensible and obvious step in the English marketplace. Australia, and particularly the USA, do not have a market for ATE insurance and so there has been no equivalent broker transition.

5.17 The decision as to whether to use a funding broker or not is entirely one of personal preference for the lawyers and clients seeking litigation funding. If the lawyer running a case is familiar with the funding process and aware of the litigation funding market and the funders available then the use of brokers may not assist greatly. Equally, if a legal team has pre-existing relationships with certain litigation funders then the need for a broker may diminish. However, whilst most funders operate on terms which are broadly similar, often the clients will want to see what each of the funders' terms will say before making a final decision.

5.18 In order to facilitate that process the lawyers will have to present the case to the different funders to whom they have made an application. There is a school of thought that this process can be done more efficiently and more cheaply in terms of lawyer time, with the use of a broker.

5.19 One further reason why lawyers in England and Wales have considered the use of funding brokers is the same reason that has been given for the previous rise of ATE insurance brokers in recent history. Very often the lawyers in the case believe their skills are best utilized being lawyers rather than assessing the funding market and making the most appropriate approach to a litigation funder or funders. In the early years of ATE insurance lawyers were concerned that they were required to advise on the best ATE policy for the client. In fact that was not their role, and they were never required to be insurance brokers. However, to avoid criticism, or worse, lawyers often used an ATE broker to obtain the best policy for their client.

5.20 The same considerations seem to apply to the litigation funding market. Whilst lawyers have a duty to advise their clients on the various methods available to them they do not have to be experts in litigation funding. However, a lack of knowledge of the funding process, and of the various litigation funders, makes some litigators wary of delving into the market unaided and so, in this situation, the brokers have continued to provide a useful service.

5.21 The obvious difference between using a broker or not doing so is the fact that a broker will require payment for their time and efforts. Most of the fee arrangements are based on a percentage of the returns received by the litigation funder and payable by the funder. This is not always the case and the fee may be passed on to the clients, directly or indirectly—a fairly common practice in the finance world where arrangement fees are paid by the borrower. Occasionally the author has seen fee agreements which provide for a payment from the client and the funder.

5.22 Some brokers require an upfront payment, some are paid solely on a contingent basis, namely if the case wins. Some brokers are paid a fee in any event, others use a combination of arrangements. The majority of litigation funding brokers are paid a percentage of the profits which the funders makes on the case, as and when there is a successful outcome. Additionally, some litigation funding brokers may also be able to assist with the provision of ATE insurance, and obviously where this happens there will also be a commission due to the broker for placing the insurance. This will be payable by the ATE insurer and will be an agreed percentage of the premium paid for the policy. If the premium is deferred or contingent, then the commission will be payable as and when the premium is in fact paid.

5.23 From a litigation funder's perspective each approach also has its merits. Dealing with a broker can occasionally be easier than dealing with a law firm directly, due to their relative experience in dealing with funding and litigation funders. However, it is important for the funder to engage directly with the client and the lawyers to understand the case and the clients properly. On occasions this can be more difficult with a funding broker involved. That is not always the case and the better brokers are alive to the need for that engagement. Obviously the use of a broker can be more expensive for the client, but given the sums involved in cases which require funding, the amount the broker takes may be deemed worthwhile.

5.24 There are many litigators who do not see the need to use a litigation funding broker. There is no right or wrong way to approach the subject of seeking litigation funding for a client. Each approach has its advantages and disadvantages to the client. Ultimately, the use, or non-use, of a broker is a matter for the lawyer and their client.

C. Key Areas

5.25 The key documents that a litigation funder wishes to see in order to assess the merits of a particular case are fairly universal amongst funders. As the funder's process of review and investigation continues there may be different aspects of the case which are of more interest to one funder rather than another and where they require more detail or documentation. But, the basic starting point is the same for most cases and most funders.

5.26 Any litigation lawyer who has made an application for ATE insurance will be familiar with the kind of process that ensues. An application for litigation funding is very similar to that process. Some funders will have an application form, in the same way that some ATE insurers do. Most of the litigation funding brokers have their own forms for the application.

The key areas to focus on are liability and quantum, but with careful reference to the issue of recoverability and whether the defendant has the means to pay the award. **5.27**

1. Merits and quantum

The litigation funder needs to be provided with enough information to allow them to be able to assess the basic legal merits of the particular case in three areas, namely liability, quantum, and recoverability. The funder also needs to understand how much is needed to run the case—the budget. **5.28**

In most cases a litigation funder will want to see the following documentation to start with: key correspondence, counsel's opinion, and any documents upon which the case is based, for example, any contractual documentation plus any pleadings if the proceedings have been issued. **5.29**

If proceedings have not been issued then any letter of claim and response is important. A litigation funder will want to know what the other side is saying about the case and why. The reaction and response from the defendant is crucial information, if it is available. Obviously, if proceedings have been issued then those papers are crucial. All the pleadings that are available should be provided. **5.30**

The key for any litigation funder at the very start of this process is to be able to ascertain whether on the face of it a particular case fits the funder's requirements as to type of case, and size of case. The headline information must explain this to the funder. **5.31**

Litigation funders look at many cases and many clients and lawyers think that their case is watertight as regards the issue of liability and that damages will be recovered at the top range of that pleaded. When reviewing a case a funder wishes to be pointed to the basic proposition of what happened, why it is a good case, and how much is a realistic estimate of quantum. **5.32**

Then, prior to reviewing the case in any detail the litigation funder will look to the issue of recoverability. Regardless of how good the case is on liability and how large the likely quantum is, neither is relevant if there is not a very good prospect of recovering the award. That is the area that a funder will focus upon initially and in the most detail. **5.33**

If the case is a claim against a professional with an indemnity insurance policy, then that is a good starting point. The basic assumption is that the insurance will cover the damages. Claims against high value financial institutions and large corporate defendants are equally positive from a recoverability perspective. The same applies to the funding of cases in the arbitration world. **5.34**

5.35 A litigation funder is rarely going to be interested in a case that requires several offshore trusts to be broken open before payment can be claimed. Even if the funds are possibly there to be claimed or the award can be enforced, the more difficult or elongated the enforcement process, the less likely that a funder will be interested. In the same way a claim against an obviously impecunious defendant will not be of interest either.

2. Budget

5.36 One of the most important documents in any application for litigation funding is the budget. The budget is a key document from the mathematical perspective of assessing any claim. If a case has good merits and has very good prospects of recovering a damages award, the case may still not be suitable for funding if the ratio of costs to likely damages is not within a ratio that the funder is comfortable with. Some funders will be comfortable with a ratio of likely damages to costs of 4 to 1, others require a minimum of 10 to 1.

5.37 There are several reasons behind any litigation funder's cautious approach. In the experience of most funders there is a serious likelihood that the initial figures for budget and for quantum will change. The general funder's view is that in relation to the budget, the figure invariably increases and in relation to quantum, the figure invariably reduces. Whether or not this assessment is accurate, it is sensible for any funder to follow the rule of thumb. If the budget does require an increase, then it is much better for the funder to be able to accommodate the increase if it is justified rather than be forced into a difficult position where a budget increase is needed for the proper prosecution of the claim but the figures for proposed returns do not justify such an increase.

5.38 Despite criticisms from certain quarters, the litigation funding industry is extremely keen to fund cases where everybody involved in the claim can benefit from the success. It is extremely unwise for a litigation funder to fund a case where the client has no benefit in making a positive contribution and working hard toward a successful outcome. If there is no financial incentive for the client then that is a serious concern for viability of the case. For this reason all funders wish to ensure that the client will receive a sufficient proportion of the potential award that they remain motivated.

5.39 For this reason, the arithmetic that a funder carries out in its initial assessment needs to have sufficient room for manoeuvre and amendment should things change for the worse as regards the budget and quantum.

5.40 There is little point in submitting an application with a budget which is inaccurate or understated. A funder will carry out a critical review and assessment of the case and what is needed to run the case and win it. Without exception, the mainstream professional litigation funders have lawyers within their teams who have handled many complex and significant pieces of litigation with very large budgets. When the funders review the budget they will know very quickly if the budget is not realistic or does not adequately allow for all eventualities.

The key when submitting a budget for a proposed case is to ensure that all aspects of the strategy have been considered and that the assumptions on which the case is based are reasonable. A funder will be as concerned about an inadequate budget as an overly generous one. **5.41**

3. Strategy

A sensible and coherent strategy is essential. It is also a very good way of ensuring that a litigation funder has confidence in the legal team to demonstrate that the strategy is clear and well thought out. The assumptions on which the strategy is based are very important, particularly in providing an accurate budget. The case strategy drives the budget calculation. It is very difficult to complete an accurate budget without first having considered what the strategy is for giving the case the best opportunity to be successful. Any litigation funder considering a case will be extremely interested in understanding what the key issues are in the case, what needs to be proved, and how it is proposed that will be done. **5.42**

Whilst a litigation funder should be careful not to offend any lawyer or law firm, they will be assessing the lawyers as well as the case. It is important to the funder that the investment they are making is well protected and that the legal team running the case is experienced in the right areas. Whilst it is not for the litigation funder to pick and choose the law firm and the lawyer with conduct, given their inability to interfere in a case, they are permitted to consider whether their investment is being protected and the case is in safe hands. Although a litigation funder should never seek to move a case away from the existing firm (unless they are content to have that reputation and prepared for the mistrust from lawyers that will ensue), the funder may decline the opportunity to invest in a piece of litigation if they are not comfortable with the team. However, a thorough assessment of the case with a well conceived and practical strategy will be useful in persuading a funder to accept a case for funding. **5.43**

D. Intake Review and Assessment

The first step for any application funding is the consideration of the application by the litigation funder. Each of the litigation funders in the market adopts a similar approach to the case review and assessment process. As has been discussed, the procedure is very similar to that of an ATE insurer's underwriting process. The facts of the case must be understood and the legal merits considered. Thereafter there is a consideration of the evidence available, or not available, and the likelihood of the **5.44** needed evidence being obtained is reviewed. Proving liability is obviously essential but an accurate assessment of quantum and recoverability is key. That is no different from the position in the post-Jackson world of the ATE insurer, with the recoverability of ATE premiums no longer available (except in historic cases, and for a limited time in some insolvency matters) and payment coming from damages actually received.

5.45 All funders will carry out an initial review, an early case assessment or intake assessment. This is a first review of the paperwork on the case and the law firm providing it. It records the basic details of the claim. The funder will assess early whether it is a case which fits that funder's basic criteria. There are many applications made for litigation funding each month and in the same way that lawyers have to filter out the enquiries they receive from clients, particularly via internet enquiries, litigation funders have to conduct the same filtering exercise.

5.46 The type of case, jurisdiction, and applicable law will be relevant as well as the likely quantum and proposed budget. Litigation funders prefer to operate in jurisdictions in which they have experience and in which they are satisfied there is a consistency of decision making. The English based funders will fund cases in a number of jurisdictions but prefer common law systems. They have little appetite for obscure jurisdictions and applicable law.

5.47 Additional considerations include whether the case fits the litigation funder's usual funding criteria from the perspective of possible returns and if there is going to be a liquid settlement or award at the conclusion of the case. Most litigation funders will have no interest in holding the recovered asset or assets from a case or trying to sell them to realize their return. If the case is unlikely to produce a monetary judgment then the funder is unlikely to be interested in funding that case.

5.48 The funder will consider whether there are any obvious concerns on recoverability, on the strategy or on the economics of the case.

5.49 If the case passes the early assessment and fits the basic criteria then it is likely that a funder will consider offering some indicative commercial terms for the client to consider.

E. Indicative Terms

5.50 As and when the funder has completed the initial case review they will reach a conclusion as to whether the case is one that fits with their basic funding criteria and one which, subject to detailed further due diligence, they would be prepared to fund. If they decide that the case is one for further consideration then the next step is usually to offer some indicative commercial terms. Each of the mainstream funders operates in a different way but the basic approach is similar. The reason that indicative terms are given early in the process is to ensure that the clients and the lawyers understand what the likely terms will be before the transaction proceeds too far. If the terms are unacceptable by some distance then all parties can extract themselves before too much work is done. In the author's experience, whilst in most cases the lawyers have given the clients a basic background on litigation funding prior to the application and they have been primed as to the likely costs of the funding, there have been some situations where clients are simply unaware of the standard pricing used in non-recourse litigation funding transactions. Those clients who are expecting an annual interest rate to be charged are shocked when they are told they may have to pay three times the facility or more, on a successful outcome.

5.51 Some funders will issue indicative commercial terms, subject to further detailed due diligence. Others will ask for an option to fund the case, at the funder's election on agreed terms, within a finite timescale. In both cases the effect is the same ultimately. In the first scenario, the indicative terms are followed by a period of negotiation, usually, as to what terms can be agreed between the parties, how large the facility is, and what the litigation funder receives for their investment and when. If those indicative terms can be agreed then the funder will wish to enter into an exclusivity period of between one month and three months, albeit it can be shorter (rarely longer) depending upon the circumstances and the need for an expedited decision. The option in the second scenario creates exclusivity in any event, but the negotiation process may well be similar. Some funders decide that they do not need exclusivity.

F. Negotiation

5.52 Once the indicative terms have been provided by the litigation funder the client is aware of the cost of the proposed funding package. The offer is strictly conditional and subject to much more detailed consideration of the case and to agreeing the terms of the litigation funding agreement.

5.53 At this stage the client is able to commence the negotiation of the commercial terms. On occasions this is conducted through the lawyers, but often they step out of the process and the funder deals with the client directly. If there is a broker involved, then they will also be party to this process, or even facilitate the negotiations as the middle man. Whichever route is followed the client needs to consent to the terms at this stage to allow matters to proceed further.

5.54 There is little opportunity for the client to discuss the terms again before the completion of the transaction. That is not to say that the client cannot raise objections or change their mind at any stage throughout the process up until the funding agreement has been signed. However, no funder will react well to a renegotiation just before completion—just as any counterparty in a transaction would object to a late change in terms.

5.55 It is possible that the litigation funder may seek to amend the terms or change the budget after the next level of due diligence, though. If there is something which changes the position on the merits of the case or its suitability then the funder may seek to increase the pricing or to amend the structure of the deal. The indicative terms are always subject to due diligence and final contractual completion.

5.56 As and when the parties have agreed that the initial terms are acceptable then the transaction will move forward and the litigation funder will be able to issue a term sheet for acceptance.

G. Term Sheet

5.57 The timing of the production of a term sheet by the litigation funder, setting out the terms upon which they would be prepared to fund a case, may vary from funder to funder. Usually it would be at the completion of the negotiation process and before the final due diligence assessment begins. The wording, and timing, of the formal offer of a facility will be specific to each of the funders but the effect is the same. Once the initial assessment has been carried out and initial terms have been offered and negotiated or accepted then there is likely to be a formal offer issued by the litigation funder to the client. As regards timing, it may be that the formal offer of terms follows the final due diligence review and the offer is stated to be subject to final due diligence and the funding contract.

5.58 The term sheet or formal offer will set out the details of the facility to be offered for the purposes of funding the specific piece of litigation. It will include the amount to be offered as well as any restrictions on its use and any key milestones or triggers for the release of funds.

5.59 The document will record the returns required by the funder and the structure of the arrangement. It will set out how the returns are calculated. Lastly, the term sheet will set out the period for which the offer may be open for acceptance and any conditions required to be satisfied. Usually this will include satisfactory due diligence and possibly the placement of an ATE policy acceptable to, or compatible with, the litigation funder, in terms of policy wording, premium, and extent of cover.

H. Exclusivity

5.60 In order for the litigation funder to complete their due diligence they will usually require that the client accepts the terms offered and agrees to enter into a period of exclusivity to match the duration of the due diligence period needed. There are exceptions to this and there are funders who have decided not to insist on exclusivity but generally it is required.

5.61 Whilst some funders will be content to use their own internal resources for the assessment of cases, in some situations the funder will need to instruct external counsel or other adviser, to review the case. Other funders will do so as a matter of course as part of their standard investment process. This can be a relatively expensive exercise and the commitment to spend tens of thousands of pounds to investigate the merits of a case is not a step that a funder would want to take without an agreement that the client was not in discussions with another funder. Whilst no funder wishes to miss out on a good investment opportunity, and will undoubtedly be unhappy when another funder signs a case in their place, that situation is exacerbated when the funder missing out has spent money on the assessment process.

5.62 Exclusivity periods can vary from a very short period of 14 days to as long as three months. There are funders who insist on exclusivity from the outset of discussions—this is not popular with lawyers or clients but it is impossible for a litigation funding broker to work with. Three months is a long period of time for any client to be bound into dealing with one funder only. Whilst the funder needs time to examine the case in detail and to be satisfied as to the prospects, that can usually be done in significantly less time. The risk to the client is that the litigation funder takes that period of time but concludes at the end of the period that it does not wish to continue with the case. The client has lost three months and is back where they started. Such setbacks will represent a major problem for a client seeking to raise funding in the late stages of the limitation period. This is something which clients and legal advisers need to keep very much in mind. Since it may be necessary to approach several funders before an acceptable arrangement is concluded, a very generous period should be allowed, by way of margin, before the limitation period is set to expire.

5.63 A 14-day period is extremely short, and most unusual. However, there are situations where a funder has to move quickly. It may be that the client needs to reach agreement in a short period of time because, as mentioned earlier, there are impending time limits such as limitation, or court deadlines. There are ways in which this very short time period could be accommodated but invariably a funder would be unhappy about such a timescale and alternative arrangements would usually need to be made to extend the period whilst protecting against the expiration of any relevant deadline.

5.64 The exclusivity period is of more benefit to the litigation funder than to the client and is a standard part of the process of providing litigation funding. The length of the period is negotiable in most circumstances in order to accommodate the needs of both parties giving the protection that a funder needs and avoiding the funding process becoming excessively lengthy for the client.

I. Due Diligence Assessment

5.65 From the litigation funder's perspective the most important part of the funding process is the detailed due diligence. This is the stage of the process where the funder will dive down into the detail of the case. The initial stages of review look at the law and the merits of an action on the basis that everything they have been told is accurate. During this due diligence stage, the litigation funder will test all of the assumptions presented and, to the extent it is possible, the evidence.

5.66 This will involve a thorough examination of the facts presented. The funder will want to meet the lawyers to discuss the case and to meet with the clients and any key witnesses to assess for themselves the strength of any proposed evidence.

5.67 The funders will also want to meet with the instructed leading and junior counsel to discuss their views on the case and the strategy to be employed.

5.68 All of the information placed before the funder in the application will be tested and verified. However, the process will include investigation into wider areas. There will be some background checks carried out on the clients to ensure that they have the authority to enter into the agreements—the funders will want to have sight of the usual 'know your client' information provided to the lawyers. The funder will also want to know what is driving the client and what the client wants from the litigation. Funders have no interest in clients that are out for revenge or trying to create new law. The funder needs to be content that the client will make a commercial decision at the appropriate time, given that the funder will not be able to influence any of the decisions.

5.69 Importantly the funders will also look into the proposed defendants to the extent that they can. They will want to assess the ability of the defendants to meet any judgment. They may carry out research into the litigation that has been faced by the defendants previously and how they have behaved, who they have instructed, and their approach generally.

5.70 If the case is an international arbitration, for example a bilateral investment treaty case, then the funder may examine the historic dealings of the particular country and their history of payment of such awards.

5.71 Ultimately, having examined and tested the information available and completed any possible research, the litigation funder will decide whether they are comfortable with the case and the lawyers and prepared to enter into a business relationship with the clients. If they are uncertain on any of these points then they may not fund the case.

5.72 The due diligence process is a condensed version of what litigation funding is all about. Funders must examine the case and the stakeholders in the case to identify and highlight the risks involved. They must then consider the likelihood of those risks coming to pass and the effect of them if they do so.

When that has been considered there will be further discussion with the lawyers and client to find ways to mitigate or insulate against the risks. If the conclusion is that it is not possible to protect adequately against the risks and the funder cannot become comfortable, then they will not continue with their involvement and the funding process will end.

J. Pricing

It is appropriate when looking at the funding process to consider some of the variables which will affect the pricing of a litigation funding arrangement.

Most litigation funders will require returns based upon a multiple of their investment or a percentage of the damages awarded in the particular case. That is a well known formula. Usually the arrangement would be that the return is based upon whichever is the greater of a percentage of the award or the multiple. Occasionally clients will try to persuade a funder to use the 'spent' funds rather than 'whole' facility as the multiplicand. Almost invariably the response from the funder is that they will not do that as they are required to tie up all of the necessary capital to cover the entire facility for the duration of the case. Some funders will deposit the facility in full in any event.

Any mainstream funder will rely upon the fact that the client will want to be reassured that the funder has sufficient funds to be able to finance the case for its entirety, as well as any other cases the funder has in its portfolio. The seven current funder members of the ALF will have had to meet the ongoing capital adequacy requirements of the organization and adhere to the Code of Conduct. They would say that it is not reasonable on the one hand for the funder to be required to tie up the necessary funds to meet the capital adequacy requirements and on the other hand receive no return for that money.

As with all aspects of litigation funding, different funders have different approaches. The proposed multiple of facility, or percentage structure, is rarely the end point of any commercial discussions between funder and client.

The returns that a funder will be looking for will be dependent on many factors, including the basic cost of the money to the funder, their overheads, or other specific matters depending upon the funder's structure, for example the proposed returns they have committed to pay their investors.

It is sometimes the case that funding for a particular matter will be divided up in tranches or stages, particularly if the value of the case is at the lower level of the usual financial limits of litigation funding. This process is used by some litigation funders to improve the ratio of costs to damages. This form of staging allows the funder to commit the funding to the case in tranches which are fixed to either key stages in the proceedings or the length of time that the case takes. The milestones may be effluxion of time, so 6, 12, or 18 months, although they may be key stages in the case or simply on exhaustion of the funds from the previous tranche. Often the stages will mirror those used in a staged ATE policy, for example, pre-issue, exchange of witness evidence, and 90 days before trial.

5.80 The benefit to the client of the funding being committed in tranches is that the returns will also be linked to those stages. For example, the returns to the funder may be based on a multiple of the cumulative facility made available. If the facility is divided into three stages then the cost to the client may be the multiple based on the cumulative stage facilities rather than the entire budget for the case. Accordingly the cost of the facility is reduced, unless of course the case runs to trial.

5.81 The pricing structures that a funder can offer are not set in stone albeit there are fairly standard starting points for each of the mainstream organizations. The pricing offered will reflect the funder's views on the likely duration of the investment, the perceived risk, the value, the size of the budget, the perception of the client, and control.

5.82 The duration of the case is relevant for two reasons. First, the longer the money is out, the higher the risk and consequently the return that the funder will want. Secondly, the longer the case goes on, the more likely it is that the case will go to trial. At trial the risk to the funder increases. The perceived risk will take into account the chances of losing, the chances of winning less than anticipated, and the chances of the case going to trial. Additionally, the earlier in the evolution of the case that a client applies for funding the less is known about the defendant's likely reaction. The later in the proceedings, the more mature the case has become and the more information, documentation, and evidence there is available for the funder to assess. This makes it very much easier for the funder to assess the merits. However, if the case is too close to trial, the window to settle the case is shorter, the risk increases, and the investment starts to become less attractive to the funder.

5.83 There is always a concern that a case remains strong on liability but that the level of quantum diminishes as the defendants chip away at the expert evidence and the various heads of damage claimed. The funder will take into account a victory at a much lower level than the way the case is put either by settlement, or by judgment with potential costs consequences.

5.84 The size of the budget is a relevant variable in pricing the case. The effect of a large loss on the portfolio is not good. Where it is possible to see large returns then the funder will do so. A large budget will only be funded if the case is large enough on a cost to damages ratio to justify the funding needed. In those situations a funder will want to obtain the highest possible returns.

5.85 The client is also a factor. A litigation funder cannot exert control on the litigation or on the client's decisions in the litigation. They can exert influence using the contractual arrangements between the funder and the client. For example, if there is a case which has good merits for settlement, but may be less attractive if it were to go to trial, then a funder may create a financial arrangement which would suit the client better financially if they were to settle earlier rather than press on with a view to achieving a higher award, at greater risk, at trial. The returns can be geared towards a lower return to the funder if the case settles early; inevitably many clients believe that their cases will settle early.

If the funder cannot be sure of what the client really wants from the litigation or what decision they will make in certain circumstances then the contractual arrangements can seek to corral the client. Of course, if a funder is so concerned about a client's likely reaction to different scenarios, they would more likely decline the investment. **5.86**

K. Retainers

As part of the due diligence process the funder will be finalizing the proposed budget with the client and the lawyers. Part of that process is agreeing the terms of the retainer with solicitors and counsel. Frequently, a litigation funder requires solicitors and very often counsel to have some of their fees discounted and to be paid in full with a success fee, on a successful conclusion to the case. This has two effects. It can reduce the budget and also supposedly incentivizes the lawyers. From the author's perspective, whilst the concept is comprehensible, the likelihood that any good lawyer would operate differently in the two fee paying scenarios seems wholly unrealistic. However, it seems to be a common requirement in funded cases. Other funders operate on a capped fee basis which seems a sensible alternative. In this scenario the lawyers would agree to work to a fixed or capped budget for the case. In the event that the budget proves to be inadequate, for whatever reason, and the case requires further work to be done, in excess of the budget and above the fee ceiling, then the lawyers must carry out that work at their own risk on a contingent basis to be paid only upon a successful outcome to the case. **5.87**

However, the hybrid, discounted, or partial CFA remains the retainer of choice for litigation funders when dealing with solicitors or counsel. The only difficulty with that arrangement in the post-Jackson era of English litigation is that the success fees are not recoverable from the losing defendant in most cases. **5.88**

This presents a further negotiation between client and funder over who should pay the success fee. The debate covers whether it should be the client, from their share of the damages, the funder from theirs, or a combination in accordance with their respective share of the proceeds. **5.89**

L. ATE

Most litigation funding agreements will be conditional upon there being adequate ATE insurance in place. The level of cover will have been stipulated or agreed **5.90** previously. The basic reason for this is the *Arkin*[1] decision, considered in detail in Chapter 2, which provided that a funder would be responsible for adverse costs up to the extent of its funding if the case was lost. Lord Justice Jackson suggested that this cap should be removed.[2] Any professional funder would either arrange or insist upon ATE cover for a sensible limit of indemnity, and given that the law is developing quite rapidly in this area, it is eminently foreseeable that the Court of Appeal might respond to this call in the Jackson Report by revisiting the general liability limit established in *Arkin*. Funders need to factor this additional exposure into their case assessments. Clients and their lawyers also need to be alert to the point; depending upon the contractual terms applicable between funder and client, the client may have a liability to indemnify the funder in respect of any costs liability. If the ATE policy simply matches the limit of the investment of the funder, this could readily prove to be inadequate if other parties to the litigation have incurred a higher level of costs. Furthermore, clients and their lawyers need to take into account that whilst a costs order can be made against a funder under s 51 of the Senior Courts Act 1981, primary liability for adverse costs will fall upon the client. Ensuring adequacy of insurance cover is therefore an important consideration for all concerned in pursuing a claim.

M. The Litigation Funding Agreement

5.91 The agreement governs the relationship between the funder, the client, and often also the lawyers. An example of a litigation funding agreement and priorities agreement used by the well known London based funder Therium can be found in Appendix 1. An explanation of the key sections follows in paragraphs 5.95 to 5.119. This agreement has been approved by the ALF as compliant with the ALF Code of Conduct.

5.92 This particular set of documents has a separate agreement relating to the priorities of payment rather than a 'Waterfall' or priority of payments clause contained in the main funding agreement which deals with who is paid in what priority, particularly when there is not enough money recovered to be able to pay everyone in full. Some funders will incorporate all of this into one funding document and require the lawyers to be a party to that; others will have a separate Deed of Priorities and Litigation Funding Agreement. Often the arrangements over priorities will require the input of an ATE insurer, particularly if there is a deferred or contingent element to the ATE insurance premium payable on a successful conclusion to the case.

5.93 This agreement is based upon the solicitors working under a form of CFA and the funding being provided in up to four tranches. These are set out in the project plan agreed between the lawyers, the client, and the funder.

---

[1] *Arkin v Borchard Lines Ltd & Ors* [2005] 1 WLR 3055, CA, [2005] EWCA Civ 655.
[2] Rupert Jackson LJ, *Review of Civil Litigation Costs: Final Report*, 9 December 2009, Ch 11.

5.94 The opening sections of the agreement deal with the usual matters of operative provisions and definitions.

1. Section Two—'Agreement to Fund'

5.95 This creates the agreement that the funder will pay the legal costs of the action in return for payment of their money back plus a fee for doing so, if the client is successful in obtaining money or money's worth from the case.

5.96 In this agreement the funder agrees only to fund the costs on the first tranche of funding. This will be a particular part of the case as defined in the Project Plan appended to the agreement. This may cover, for example, pre-issue, the commencement and service of proceedings, the defence and reply, if any.

5.97 Under this agreement, if the funder remains content with the merits of the case at the end of this, then they have the right to elect to continue to fund into the next stage. This agreement allows the funder the ability to exit the arrangement at the end of each stage. It also provides that if the funder elects to continue into the next stage then they must confirm that they have sufficient funds to meet the financial obligation of doing so.

2. Section Three—'Payment Terms and Interest'

5.98 The amount of the payment to the funder is defined here. The funder receives back their investment, the 'Reasonable Costs Sum', being the amount paid out by the funder. The 'Contingency Fee' is the funder's return on the investment. If the payment to the funder by the client is late under the terms of the agreement then interest is payable.

3. Section Four—'Changes to Project Plan'

5.99 The 'Project Plan' is attached to the funding agreement. It defines the stages of the proceedings and the work being done in each of the 'tranches'. It also sets out the budget for the case divided into stages.

5.100 The agreement is predicated upon there being no counterclaim involved in the case. Equally, the funding agreement as drafted does not envisage the funding covering an appeal. Clearly there may be situations where a fund and client will want to extend the arrangement. This section provides the mechanism for doing so.

4. Section Five—'Excluded Costs and Liabilities'

5.101 The items that will not be paid by the funder are defined in this section, for example any costs over and above those deemed 'reasonable' and any costs incurred by the client's default or failure to comply with a time limit.

5. Section Six—'Conditions Precedent and Warranties'

5.102 It is not unusual to have conditions precedent to the funding agreement coming into force. In this agreement the funder requires that an appropriate ATE policy has been incepted and that the agreement dealing with the priority of payments is executed.

5.103 In addition there are certain warranties given. In particular that the client has taken legal advice and that they also acknowledge that the funder's decision to fund the case is based upon the information supplied by the client and that there has been full disclosure of the material facts and information.

6. Section Seven—'Payment of Reasonable Costs'

5.104 The funder agrees to pay the fees incurred by the legal team as long as they are reasonable in amount and are incurred in accordance with the 'project plan'. The funder has the opportunity to challenge the fees if they think that they are in any way unreasonable, by serving a notice to challenge the amount.

7. Section Eight—'Adverse Costs'

5.105 A condition to this funding agreement was that there should be an ATE policy in force. This section excludes the funder's liability to pay adverse costs and provides an indemnity to the funder from the client in respect of any such costs. The client has the benefit of the ATE policy rather than the funder.

8. Section Nine—'Claimant's Obligations'

5.106 Within this section the client agrees to cooperate fully throughout the case and to give prompt instructions to the legal team. The client is also obliged to ensure that they comply with the terms of the ATE policy.

5.107 In addition it is here that the funder ensures that the client is obliged to allow the funder to be kept up to date by the lawyers, to attend any meetings thought appropriate, and to receive a monthly update. Some funders would go further and require the client to instruct their lawyers to permit the funders to carry out a more rigorous monitoring assessment of the case at regular intervals.

9. Section Twelve—'Security for Costs'

5.108 In every case the funder will have discussed security for costs with the lawyers and the issue will have been included in the 'project plan' as something to be paid either by the funder or by way of deed or bond from an ATE insurer.

5.109 The ATE policy is for the benefit of the client and under this section the funder seeks to ensure that the ATE provider is aware of the funder's involvement, albeit it is unlikely that they would not know, and that the client holds the proceeds payable under the policy for the benefit of the funder so that the funder is reimbursed if there is a need to pay out security or any adverse costs.

10. Section Thirteen—'Treatment of Claim Proceeds'

5.110 Aside from the fact that the funder will want the client to recover any proceeds of the case as swiftly as possible (clause 11), there needs to be a clear understanding of how the proceeds of the litigation are treated. First, the proceeds are held on trust for the funder, so far as the funder has an entitlement. This agreement provides that the proceeds are paid into the solicitor's client account, as would be normal practice.

5.111 What follows then is the drawing of an account of who is due what and the money is released in a timely fashion.

11. Section Fourteen—'Confidentiality'

5.112 The parties agree to keep the details of the agreement confidential. Funders prefer matters to be kept confidential and never discuss the terms of any financial arrangement they have entered into. Occasionally, it is beneficial for a case to be brought into the public eye and for the defendant to be made aware that a funder is backing the litigation. (In some cases, such as ones involving Group Litigation Orders, it is almost inevitable that the involvement of funders will become public knowledge. This is because such cases will often involve promoting the case publicly, and the availability of funding will need to be explained in the material circulated.) The defendant, if well advised, is likely then to appreciate that a funder and an ATE provider have examined the merits in some detail as have their external advisers. It may have no effect on the case but occasionally it can focus a defendant's mind to the benefit of the claimant.

5.113 Additionally, it may bring a defendant to realize that a war of attrition and the expense of heavy legal bills will not be a concern for the client.

12. Section Fifteen—'Termination'

5.114 The termination provisions are extremely important. The understanding of when the client or the funder can withdraw from the arrangement and what happens in each of those circumstances is vital.

5.115 In this agreement if, at some point during the case, the funder believes that the merits no longer justify funding, then they can withdraw on five business days' notice. If that occurs then the funder is entitled to nothing, unless the case goes on to be successful and make a recovery. Then they are entitled only to the reimbursement of their outlay, plus accrued interest.

5.116 If the funder terminates because it is believed that the client has committed a material breach of the agreement then the funder is entitled to their money back, and interest, in any event, regardless of whether the case wins. However, if the case wins then the funder is also entitled to the return it would have received if it had continued.

5.117 If the funder commits a material breach leading to termination by the client then the funder forfeits any right to its returns from recoveries but remains entitled to repayment of its outlay.

13. Section Twenty-Five—'Dispute Resolution'

5.118 Any funder which has joined the ALF will be required to ensure that its agreements meet the criteria of the Code of Conduct, particularly with reference to the dispute resolution procedures.

5.119 The parties agree that if they cannot resolve a dispute between them as regards a proposal for settlement of the case or the terminate of the agreement then the issue will be resolved by an independent Queen's Counsel. The opinion of that Queen's Counsel is binding upon the parties.

14. 'Schedule'

5.120 The Schedule to this agreement formalizes the details of the case and the lawyers involved. It also sets out the budgeted amounts for each of the proposed stages and the agreed percentage of recoveries that the funder is entitled to on success.

15. Appendix 1—'Project Plan'

5.121 The 'project plan' is a key document in relation to this funding agreement. It records the strategy and the amounts to be spent at each stage of the case. It also sets out what work is to be carried out in each stage by the lawyers. It incorporates the budget and the case plan.

16. Appendix 2—'Reliance Letter'

5.122 The 'reliance letter' is a letter in which the instructed lawyers accept a tortious duty of care to the funder so that the funder can consider action against them if they cause the funder to lose money as a result of their negligence, for instance because they miss a limitation period or are struck out for non-compliance with an order. The lawyers act for the client and not for the funder and this direct acceptance and acknowledgement provides confirmation that they are aware of the reliance on them as lawyers by the funder and their duty to the funders.

17. Appendix 3—'Priorities Agreement'

5.123 The 'priorities agreement' is only really needed where the recoveries are not as large as everybody expected them to be and there is not enough money to pay everyone in full.

In some cases this agreement is included in the litigation funding agreement itself. Here it is a separate deed with the lawyers, client, funder, and any ATE insurer as parties. Recital 'E' to the agreement sets out exactly the purpose of the document.

5.124

The way this document records the priorities is to ensure first that the solicitors receive their basic costs, the funder is reimbursed their outlay, and the insurer is paid back any adverse costs outlay. If there are insufficient funds then the solicitor, funder, and insurer are paid *pari passu*. Next if funds permit, the insurer, funder, and solicitors receive their returns or uplift. Finally, the client receives anything that is left.

5.125

This may look as though the client is the only one who is unlikely to benefit. However, the funder, solicitor, and insurer have all taken a risk, deferred their financial entitlements and paid out significant resources by this point.

5.126

In reality, unless this stage has been reached by a judgment which is lower than had been hoped, the decision to take a low settlement is likely to be done on a consensus between, client, lawyers, and funder. If on acceptance of what may be the best possible negotiated outcome, the client has no financial entitlement under the strict interpretation of the agreement, then the client is going to have no interest in settlement and may elect to press ahead to trial to see if a judge can be persuaded. The client would have nothing to lose. In that situation it must be likely that a funder would take a commercial view and seek to agree something which gives all parties an incentive to avoid the risk of trial and accept the sensible offer.

5.127

N. Conclusion

Whilst the funding process is broadly the same when dealing with every professional and mainstream litigation funder in England and Wales, there are some differences.

5.128

Funders differ in their flexibility, their understanding of litigation, the speed of response and case assessment, and their flexibility over pricing. Other than that there is very little to choose between them. Some litigation funders add value to the litigation process but are not overly intrusive. Others add little or nothing to the litigation process yet may wish to be involved, by way of update, in the minute detail.

5.129

The key for any client is to find a litigation funder that they can work with. During the application process the clients and the lawyer will come into contact with the funders and see how they perform and how they operate.

5.130

Clients should be alive to agreeing a period of exclusivity much over one month. The reality is that it should not generally take any longer than that to assess a case. If the funder suggests it does, that may be an indication either of their lack of

5.131

5.132 It is important when seeking funding that the key documents are provided, preferably including a recent opinion from a QC, recording good prospects of success, and assessing quantum. Funding should not be sought too early, although discussions and a dialogue with a funder from an early stage are a good thing to ensure that the documentation being produced will fit that funder's application criteria. Additionally, these discussions can set the parameters of what is needed from the client and the lawyers in order to obtain a positive response from a funder. Depending on the stage at which funding is sought, it is important to explain the reasons for applying at that point. If early in the case, or late in the day, then the client must provide an honest explanation. Of equal importance is for the client to demonstrate any funds already spent, if they have done so. Funders will always need to be able to understand what has been invested by the clients already, even if they are not disposed to reimburse them.

5.133 One last area worthy of mention is that of appeals. Most litigation funding arrangements do not cover or anticipate the prospect of an appeal. It is prudent for clients and lawyers to raise the question of an appeal. The most likely response from a funder in most cases would be to wait and see what happens with the case. If the case is successful then both the funder and the client have an incentive to resist an appeal from the losing opponent. If the case is lost, then it may be the funder can be persuaded to spend further fees in the hope of recouping a loss. It may be of course that the funder may view it as throwing good money after bad and decide to cut its losses.

resources or an inability to operate at the necessary pace. Either way it is an indication of what may be in store for the client in the future and should be avoided.

6

COSTS AND INSURANCE

A. Costs and Insurance	6.01	D. Security for Costs	6.39
B. ATE Insurance	6.07	E. Costs of Setting up Funding and ATE	6.56
C. Payment of the Insurance Premium	6.14	F. Funders' Costs Risk	6.57
1. Payment in full on inception	6.18	G. *Excalibur*	6.62
2. Deposit premium	6.27	H. Conclusion	6.67
3. Fully deferred premium	6.30		

A. Costs and Insurance

6.01 There is always the thorny issue of adverse costs in litigation. It is the filter that protects the English legal system from some of the more surprising cases that have been brought in jurisdictions where there is no standard rule on costs shifting, such as the United States.

6.02 A man in the United States called Ernie Chambers once filed a court action against God. His claim against the Almighty was for 'widespread death, destruction and terrorisation of millions upon millions of the Earth's inhabitants'. Chambers had been a long-serving Senator in Nebraska when he filed his claim. He did it, it is reported, to expose how the court system was open to abuse of frivolous claims being brought and is quoted as saying: 'The Constitution requires that the courthouse doors be open, so you cannot prohibit the filing of suits, anyone can sue anyone they choose, even God.'

6.03 In another similarly strange episode, a judge, Roy Pearson, filed a claim against a dry cleaner for ruining the trousers of his suit. The suit cost $700, but the damages figure in the law suit filed by Mr Pearson was nearly $50 million. Pearson was a judge in the District of Columbia when he filed what is commonly known as the 'pants lawsuit'.

6.04 In England, it has been said for a long time that there is a growing culture of litigation. But there are deeply concerned voices saying we are in danger of moving towards a culture of unmeritorious, frivolous, and false claims which are more commonplace in the United States. The claims mentioned in paragraphs 6.01 and 6.02, and other examples which are similar, make for great press headlines. They are just two cases which highlight how English courts, without the protection of an adverse costs regime, could change.

6.05 However, whilst the adverse costs regime in this country serves to protect our court system from cases of the nature described in paragraphs 6.01 and 6.02, it does present an issue for any client involved in a piece of litigation. It is also something at the forefront of any litigation funder's mind when preparing to fund a client's litigation.

6.06 The financial risk to clients and to litigation funders, of an adverse costs order is one that must be considered and provided for. This chapter deals with the options available in respect of ATE insurance when combined with litigation funding, and important matters of which to be aware, and includes a review of the insurance premium options and the issue of security for costs. In addition the chapter deals with who may be responsible for the adverse costs which may be incurred either by way of court order or contractually, and how a litigation funder will want to ensure that the client and the funder are protected against them.

B. ATE Insurance

6.07 The issue of adverse costs can usually be dealt with by the purchase of an after the event legal expenses insurance policy ('an ATE insurance policy') to insure the client against the risk of having to pay an opponent's costs up to a maximum limit of indemnity and subject to certain policy terms and conditions. It is not a perfect solution for every circumstance but is very close.

6.08 The advantages of taking out an ATE insurance policy are obvious from the client's perspective. In the event that things do not go to plan and the case is lost then there is a way to pay the adverse costs which are due to be paid to the opponent. If the policy does not cover the liability in full it should (depending upon the advice received by the client as to the necessary limit of indemnity) mitigate substantially against such a payment.

6.09 The benefits of buying such insurance are therefore self-evident. However, some clients still decide that they do not want to pay for such a policy. For most lawyers who understand the inherent risk in litigation and particularly the risks involved in taking a matter to trial, the decision as to whether to purchase ATE insurance or not is a fairly easy one. At least, this was the case before the Jackson reforms precluded recovery of the cost of premiums from the losing party; the decision is now a more difficult one. Some clients believe their cases are very strong. ATE policies can cost as much as 50 per cent or 60 per cent of the limit of indemnity. In a case where a client is firmly of the belief that they have a good case and will win, they may see it as difficult for them to justify paying out a large sum. However, many seasoned litigators would no doubt agree that the risk of losing is worth insuring against, however good one thinks one's case is.

6.10 There are risks in taking out the ATE insurance, although they are minor concerns in comparison to having to pay all of an opponent's legal costs without any insurance. An ATE policy has specific reporting requirements, which are rarely onerous, but do require some interaction with the insurer. This can increase the client's costs minimally. The costs of liaising with the insurer and setting up the ATE policy and assisting the insurer with their due diligence are not recoverable from a losing opponent. This is in much the same way that the costs of setting up a funding arrangement and dealing with the third party litigation funder are not recoverable *inter partes*.

6.11 Although the usual practice in litigation is to use ATE, in arbitration it is less well known. There is not always the same presumption as regards adverse costs. Costs shifting is not necessarily the starting point, so whilst there are arbitration regimes in which costs shifting is adopted as the norm there is sometimes less of a costs risk from the client's perspective. In this case the client may decide not to insure.

6.12 In any case where solicitors are instructed in England and Wales the professional obligation is to advise on the availability of ATE insurance for adverse costs. These obligations are examined in more detail in Chapter 9.

6.13 Whilst there are professional obligations upon solicitors to advise clients about the availability of ATE, any litigation funder will be thinking about it at the outset of budgetary discussions on any case. The need for ATE insurance on a funded case in England and Wales is paramount from the funder's perspective. When a case that has been financed by a litigation fund is lost, and an adverse costs order is made, the funder is liable to pay the adverse costs up to the level of the amount of their funding.[1] For this reason any professional litigation funder will require either an ATE policy governing adverse costs to be purchased on the legal expenses market or for some other provision to be made with the funder. That may include the lodgement of cash by the funder for use if an order is made, or for an indemnity to be provided by the funder. In both of these scenarios the litigation funder will expect a healthy return for the capital being risked either as part of the budget facility provided for costs in running the litigation or as an extra amount with a separate basis of return to the funder.

C. Payment of the Insurance Premium

6.14 Under s 29 of the Access to Justice Act 1999, provision was made for the recovery of ATE policy premiums by way of costs. This provision came into effect on

---

[1] *Arkin v Borchard Lines* [2005] EWCA Civ 655.

1 April 2000. Since March 2013, and the advent of the Jackson reforms, the position as to recovery has been effectively reversed. The Legal Aid, Sentencing and Punishment of Offenders Act 2012, and the regulations made under it, have very seriously restricted the recoverability of ATE policy premiums. Section 58C(1) of the 2012 Act excludes recovery unless permitted by regulations made under s 58C(2). Transitional provisions were included in the Act, but going forward from April 2013, pursuant to the regulations made thereunder, it is only in clinical negligence cases that the cost of premiums may be recoverable as costs, and then only to a limited extent. Almost all litigation which has traditionally been the subject of commercial litigation funding will consequently fall outside the scope of ATE policy premium recovery, with the result that the costs of insurance will be borne by clients, or funders, to the extent that funders cannot pass on costs to their clients. This change in the rules on recovery of a reasonable ATE premium from a losing opponent by way of adverse costs has caused the insurance markets, solicitors, and litigation funders to reconsider the position as to costs protection carefully. Invariably, litigation funders are dealing with the high value end of the litigation market, in other words the cases they fund are very high value. There is a school of thought that due to the size of these disputes, and the potentially huge recoveries that are made, the insurance premium pales into insignificance and its recovery, or the lack of it, has little impact on the figures involved.

6.15 There are, of course, cases where that is true. But, in the majority of cases, funded or otherwise, it has had an impact. It is possible to draw comparisons between the English market today (post-March 2013) and the Australian market where, although there is no mature or very active ATE market, there is a growing awareness of the ability to buy ATE. In Australia, as with the Caribbean jurisdictions, it has never been possible to recover such premiums. This has resulted in the use of ATE insurance never really becoming commonplace in those jurisdictions, although it is used on occasions.

6.16 The situation in England and Wales is that the market saw huge growth in the use of ATE from 1 April 2000[2] and the implementation of section 29, Access to Justice Act 1999, allowing for the recovery of ATE policy premiums. Now, with the changes introduced by the Jackson reforms, the use of ATE has very much reduced, particularly in lower value claims where the premium would have a significant effect on the amount left for the client after deduction of premium. There can be little doubt that the non-recoverability of premiums will serve as a significant inhibition from arranging ATE cover in many cases. This may have the effect of reducing overall litigation costs, but it may also have the effect that some meritorious claims are not litigated because litigation without ATE policy cover is

---

[2] Access to Justice Act 1999 s 29, in force 1 April 2000.

not acceptable to a client or a funder, and the cost of cover tilts the balance against the financial viability of a claim.

In funded cases, a potential litigant will, in reality, have little choice, because funders will in practice require ATE cover (in some form) to be arranged. Although the premium can have a significant impact in some cases, the use of ATE has continued with few exceptions because of the funder's need to insulate against adverse costs. If a funder loses a case that is quite obviously a financial loss. But then to compound the loss by having to pay out further sums in adverse costs to the winning opponent adds insult to the injury of defeat. Litigation funders in this jurisdiction will always take advantage of ATE insurance or other provision for adverse costs. Accordingly, given that ATE is a necessity for the funders, the only area of negotiation is the amount and the timing of the premium to be paid for the ATE policy. **6.17**

1. Payment in full on inception

In an ideal world, judged from their perspective, every ATE insurer would request and receive payment in full for the entire amount of the premium for the policy on inception. This would be very much like other classes of insurance business, where clients seek insurance and then pay a premium to put the policy on risk. **6.18**

The ATE market is unusual in that it must be one of the few classes of insurance where a risk is taken on by the insurer yet nothing is paid by the insured at the time by way of premium in most cases. Following the Jackson reforms, several commentators predicted that this method of operation would change. Indeed certain ATE insurers attempted to implement such a change by seeking upfront premium payments in funded cases at the very least. Other insurers have attempted to increase their premiums on cases by seeking a share of the damages paid—a 'damages based premium'. This remains unusual but in the author's experience certain ATE providers are keen to make higher rewards for the risks they take, given the level of returns that they believe funders receive. An upfront premium is not yet the usual method of paying for a premium. **6.19**

However, there are benefits to the insured, the client, of such an arrangement. When ATE insurers are assessing the risks across their portfolio and the returns they need by way by premium in order to cover losses and make the required level of profits, it is very difficult for them to charge a premium much less than 60 per cent of the limit of indemnity needed, if the premium is to be deferred. On a case where the premium is paid upfront then the insurer has at least the premium to mitigate any payment out. With a deferred premium the insurer may have to make a payment out under the policy but has not received any premium at all. **6.20**

The reality of the ATE market is that with premiums being paid upfront, the amount of premium should reduce. An ATE insurer may be able to bring the rates down to somewhere near or below 20 per cent of the level of indemnity—a marked difference when compared with 'trial' premium rates on a deferred premium basis. **6.21**

6.22 The benefit to the client of paying a premium on inception is that the amount paid across the course of the case for ATE insurance will be lower. The downside is that the sum is paid rather than not paid. It may be paid in stages throughout the case, but the more that is paid upfront the lower the rate applied by the ATE insurer.

6.23 From the perspective of the funder, the issue of fully paid premiums as opposed to deferred premiums is really a matter of ethos and structure. Those funders who operate more akin to an insurer—the family office or private equity structures, usually prefer to keep a careful eye on cash flow. They pay, but they pay when they have to so as to reduce the amount they have drawn on the facility they have been provided with. The less they draw the less they pay for the facility. This makes perfect financial sense.

6.24 A funder operating under this regime will wish to defer payment of the premium if at all possible. If they have to pay it at the end of the case then that will only be on success and when the returns are due in—even though the ultimate outlay may be higher.

6.25 Some funders will be happy to pay a premium, as they are keen to advance funds. The structure of certain funders means that they (or their investment advisers) are remunerated by reference to funds deployed. In these situations an upfront premium is preferable to the funder. Additionally, the funder will then make a return, on success, on the payment. Whilst it is possible that from the client's perspective the position may be neutral, it is unlikely. If the premium is paid on inception then the rate is lower, but the client is likely to be paying a multiple on the funds advanced by the funder to pay that lower premium. So whilst the price of the insurance may be lower, the real cost to the client is likely to be higher, on a successful case.

6.26 As a result of the price differential between deferred and paid premiums and the encouragement of the insurance providers, there is now a market for premium funding from litigation funders. The cases need to be large enough to justify the payment of a return to the funder on the amount paid by the funder and the premium has to be of a size to be of interest to a funder, but there are cases which fit the criteria.

2. Deposit premium

6.27 One way of reducing the premium rate on an ATE policy, and an alternative to paying the full premium upfront or in stages, is to pay a deposit premium, with the balance of the premium deferred to the end of the case. The balance of the premium is usually only payable on success and is therefore contingent rather than deferred. Strictly speaking if the premium is deferred then the payment of it is simply delayed. If the premium is contingent then it is payable only upon the occurrence of a defined set of circumstances which in practice will be that the case was successful.

6.28 A deposit premium is also a useful compromise for a litigation funder. The majority of funders will not wish to deposit with the lawyers an amount equivalent to the likely adverse costs payable to cover the costs in the event of defeat (unless the client is prepared to give the funder a healthy return on those funds as if they were part of the budget), so ATE insurance is a much more financially efficient option. The funder is also reducing the cost of the insurance.

6.29 From the ATE insurer's perspective, a deposit premium is also a useful compromise. The insurer receives some money, usually non-refundable, to mitigate against the potential outlay they may face. Accordingly the rate charged for the policy will be reduced in comparison with a fully deferred premium. The funder will not need to incur such a large outlay of funds as they would in a fully upfront premium yet the funder will still be able to make a healthy return on the amount paid out for the deposit, and with a lower sum being paid the figures will work much better as regards the overall ratio of outlay to damages.

3. Fully deferred premium

6.30 For most clients the prospect of paying for adverse costs protection only in the event of winning the case is a difficult concept to comprehend. Once understood it is an attractive method of buying insurance coverage. If the case is lost, then the insurer pays out for the amount of the costs awarded against the client (subject to the limit of indemnity), yet has received no benefit for making such a commitment, save the promise of payment if the case is successful.

6.31 This is the scenario if the premium is deferred and contingent, which is the case with most deferred premiums in ATE insurance. If the premium is simply deferred then it is payable, regardless of result, at the end of the case. The effect of this deferred and contingent premium arrangement is that the price of the insurance is consequently higher than a premium paid on day one as we have already considered.

6.32 This may be more expensive, but the mindset of most clients in this situation is that they prefer to pay only on success, albeit at a higher rate.

6.33 From a funder's perspective this may not make much difference to them. If they want to commit funds to a case then the prospect of an upfront payment for the premium may be more attractive, as are the potential additional returns on the extra outlay, but some litigation funders would be content with a deferred and contingent premium, subject to two matters. The first is the issue of where the deduction is made for the premium and second is the issue of the waterfall or priority of payments.

6.34 In relation to the first matter, the premium payment will invariably be deducted from the proceeds of the case before any division of the funds is made. In some situations the client will be required to pay for the premium from their share. Rarely, if ever would it come out of the litigation funder's share.

6.35 The second issue is the priority of payments in the event that the case is successful and therefore the condition activating the requirement to pay the full ATE premium is met. This is no issue when the case is won and the damages awarded and paid are sufficient to meet all the calls on the money. However, when the damages are lower than anticipated or a deal is struck with the defendant which is less lucrative than had been planned at the outset of the litigation then the waterfall clause comes into effect.

6.36 In this situation the ATE insurer will always insist upon sitting high up the ladder. The insurer takes the view that had the premium payment been made in full at the start of the case then they would not need to be troubled with the waterfall clause as they would not have become involved in issues as to priority of payment. The ATE insurer, quite justifiably, expects to be paid first. After all they have taken the risk of covering the adverse costs, without any payment of premium. The funder will often respond in that situation that they too have taken a significant risk, without payment, in fact the opposite—they have paid out large sums of money, so at the very least there should be an equal recognition of the risks taken when the priorities are considered. It is at this point that funders are reminded by insurers that the reward for the funder's risk is significantly higher than that of the insurer—unless there is some form of damages based premium.

6.37 One of the changes that has occurred in the litigation funding marketplace is the realization on the part of funders that the ATE process is one that they can control themselves. Historically one of the areas of the funding process that has slowed the process was the ATE application and this part of the process was not something that the funder could influence.

6.38 If the funder can control, or influence, the ATE aspect of the process then they are able to move matters through their procedures at a faster pace. There are litigation funders who own their own ATE insurer—this is the ultimate in a seamless process. However other funders have created arrangements with either one or a syndicate of insurers in order to be able to provide ATE cover on cases that they decide to fund. No doubt the next stage, if it has not already been reached, is for the funder to set up their own captives, or for insurers to consider entering the funding market.

D. Security for Costs

6.39 The financial profile of the applicants for litigation finance has changed over recent years. In the early days of the industry, most clients seeking litigation funding were doing so as a matter of necessity. Without exception every professional mainstream funder in England and Wales would confirm now that there is an approximately equal division between clients that are looking for litigation funding by choice and clients who are funding because they are unable to pay their legal fees themselves.

6.40 Despite this recent change in the financial strength of many litigation funders' clients, there remains a regular need for those clients to receive assistance in dealing with requests for security for costs from defendants. Obviously the trigger for security for costs being granted is not solely the financial position of the claimant, although it is very much the main reason for any such application by a defendant. Many cases which are funded within this jurisdiction and issued in London involve foreign claimants and therefore the issue of their domicile can be key, particularly if they have no permanent base within the jurisdiction.

6.41 For this reason, one of the first things that any litigation funder will consider is whether or not security for costs is likely to be requested by the other side. The funder will include this issue as part of the due diligence discussions with the client and the lawyers when discussing the budget.

6.42 A funder can deal with security for costs in three ways. First, they can ask the client to put up the money. Secondly, the funder can add the necessary amount to the budget facility in order to meet any application security by depositing funds, and thirdly the funder can use the benefit of having already purchased an ATE policy, if they have, and purchase a bond or deed which would be acceptable to the court and the defendant as a cash equivalent.

6.43 The first of these options is unlikely to find favour with the client. The fact that they are subject to a security for costs request is usually indicative of their financial position. As has just been discussed, it is not always the case but those clients who have chosen funding and have a choice whether to use their own money are unlikely to want to risk the capital involved in lodging security with the court.

6.44 The second option is that the funder puts up the money and deposits the cash in court to satisfy the request for security. This will suit many funders as it is a further additional sum which is added to the budget. From the client's perspective it may not be the most efficient method of dealing with the security request. The funder will be seeking a minimum return on the funds and given the likely minimum return for any funder is going to be around three times their investment, the extra facility provided could prove very expensive to the client. It could also have a significant impact on the ratio of damages to budget which may in itself increase the price to the client.

6.45 If there is no other option then the client has no choice and their only way to mitigate against such costs is to seek security to be deposited in tranches, which is a fairly usual method adopted by the courts.

6.46 One thing that funders do not want to do is allow the defendant to turn the security for costs application into a distraction and for it to become a major tactical battle in the case or an early examination of the merits. As any litigator knows defendants often use security for costs applications to test the claimant's mettle. The litigation funder will want to diffuse the issue and agree the principle of security at an early stage if that is appropriate. The effort can then be applied to the assessment of what the amount of the security should be and the stages that the agreed amounts are paid.

6.47 The third option as regards meeting any security requires there to be an ATE policy in place with an ATE provider that has the ability to write a bond or deed of indemnity. Most of the ATE providers are able to do this themselves or work with an organization that will take the ATE provider's policy and produce a bond on the strength of it.

6.48 The issue that many defendants have with an ATE policy is that the insurer has the ability to void the policy or avoid payment under the policy in the event that the client, the insured, has done anything in breach of the policy terms, or has failed to effect necessary disclosure. Defendants facing funded claims have deployed this concern to suggest that an ATE policy alone is not enough to protect a successful defendant and ensure that they receive their costs if they are successful. The number of occasions where an ATE insurer has voided the terms of a policy and not paid out by way of adverse costs is, anecdotally only, a very small figure.

6.49 In recent cases the courts have been more amenable to the suggestion that an adequate ATE policy may in some circumstances be adequate security—without more. This point was considered by Akenhead J in *Michael Phillips Architects Limited v Rilkin*.[3] He held that the ATE policy was not sufficient to resist a security for costs application and found that 'it is necessary where reliance is placed by a claimant on an ATE insurance policy to resist or limit a security for costs application for it to be demonstrated that it actually does provide some security. Put another way, there must not be terms pursuant to which or circumstances in which the insurers can readily but legitimately and contractually avoid liability to pay out for the defendant's costs.' In that case, however, the insurers were entitled to determine cover if they concluded that there were no reasonable prospects of recovering damages. Thus should they form an unfavourable view of the case at any stage, they could terminate cover, and leave the defendant with no protection from the policy.

6.50 However, in the more recent decision of *Geophysical Service Centre Co v Dowell Schlumberger (ME) Inc*[4] the fact that a claimant had ATE insurance cover which could be terminated by insurers was not regarded as negating the security which it afforded to a defendant in respect of costs. Stuart-Smith J held that it was necessary to form a view of the likelihood of circumstances arising which might enable the policy to be avoided. He considered that there was no material which raised more than a theoretical chance that the policy would be avoided. The court concluded

---

[3] *Michael Phillips Architects Ltd v Riklin & Riklin* [2010] EWHC 834 (TCC).
[4] *Geophysical Service Centre Co v Dowell Schlumberger (ME) Inc* [2013] EWHC 147 (TCC), HT-12-168.

that even though there were provisions within the policy which would allow the ATE insurer to cancel the policy, there would still be a liability on the part of the ATE insurer to provide cover the date of cancellation. The court also took into account the strength of the relationship between the insured's solicitor and the insurers, and the defendant's having a potential remedy against the insurer under the Third Party (Rights Against Insurers) Act 1930 in respect of any liabilities. The application for security for costs was refused.

6.51 These cases demonstrate that the exact terms of the policy in question are extremely important. Whilst it is possible to use an ATE policy as security without more, many defendants will continue to argue, where possible, that the policy is not adequate. It is therefore very important that those advising a client, as to arranging an ATE policy, pay close attention to the degree of protection that the policy affords to the other party, or parties; close attention needs to be given to the insurers' rights to cancel, and to provisions as to liabilities to third parties that may have accrued before any cancellation. ATE policies are expensive to arrange, and a significant part of their attraction is that they should be capable of being relied upon to defeat an application for security for costs. For a client to incur, directly or indirectly, the costs of an ATE policy, only then to have to arrange, at further cost, provision by way of security for an opponent's costs, is to be avoided if at all possible.

6.52 Against the background considered above funders will consider the issue of security at the outset and make necessary provision. One of the most effective ways to deal with the potential pitfalls of the ATE policy is to use a bond or deed of indemnity. The objections raised by defendants against the use of an ATE policy as adequate security is the fact that there are provisions within the policy that allow the insurer to step away from the obligation to pay out in certain circumstances, fraud being the principal one: but material misrepresentation or material non-disclosure on the part of the insured may also afford grounds for the insurer to avoid liability to indemnify. As considered above, an insurer may be able to terminate cover by virtue of a reassessment of merits, depending upon policy wording.

6.53 A deed of indemnity or bond from an ATE insurer, or from somebody on their behalf, may deal with this issue. The bond does not contain the exclusions or waivers that are found in the policy wording of the ATE policy. The bond is a promise to pay. It will provide that the ATE insurer will pay, without question, an amount towards adverse costs ordered up to the policy indemnity limit. The way most ATE insurers work is that they will allow their policy to be bonded or a deed to be written in place of a proportion of the indemnity they would provide under the ATE policy. So, for example, an ATE policy has a limit of £1m and security for costs is needed in four stages of £250k up to £1m. As the ATE insurer issues a bond for each £250k, they reduce the limit of indemnity of the ATE policy by that amount.

The bond stands as a pledge to pay without the ability to avoid payment or cancel the policy.

6.54 To obtain such a deed or bond from the ATE insurer, the client and lawyers will have to convince the insurer that the case continues to enjoy sufficient prospects of success. They may need to do so at each stage that further security is put up, namely each tranche of security by way of further bond. In order to issue the bond, the insurer will require further payment, on top of the premium for the ATE policy. Usually the fee for this is between 8 per cent and 12 per cent of the face value of the security being provided.

6.55 The only other route available to the client, aside from the deed or bond, is to address the issue of the restrictions or cancellation clauses in the ATE policy itself at the outset of the case with the ATE insurer. Most ATE insurers will work from a standard policy wording and be very reluctant to amend the wording. But some insurers will be prepared to consider a bespoke policy wording with few restrictions and specifically in anticipation of the application for security for costs. This is more of an option than ever before following the *Geophysical Service Centre Co*[5] decision.

E. Costs of Setting up Funding and ATE

6.56 There is a distinction between the costs of litigation and the costs of setting up the funding for litigation. Put simply, the costs of setting up the funding arrangements that a client may have and the costs of preparation of the application for funding are not recoverable from a losing opponent.[6] The work done by the legal team in seeking protection against adverse costs and negotiation with providers of insurance and funding are costs to the client as they are for the client's benefit. However, that does not mean that they cannot be included as part of the funding provided by the litigation funder. The ATE policy is of benefit to the fund and, as discussed in paragraph 6.12, the funder will want to have an ATE policy in force. It is also to the funder's benefit to have the lawyer and the client produce such information as the funder needs and in a timely fashion to allow the due diligence and assessment process to be done swiftly. If that requires confirmation from the funder that they will meet the costs incurred in dealing with the application for funding, then most funders will oblige. However, the most likely scenario is that the costs incurred by the lawyers in dealing with the funding application, the negotiations, the budget assessment and review, and the litigation funding agreement will be added to the budget facility.

---

[5] *Geophysical Service Centre Co v Dowell Schlumberger (ME) Inc* [2013] EWHC 147 (TCC), HT-12-168.
[6] *Motto v Trafigura Limited* [2011] EWCA Civ 1150.

F. Funders' Costs Risk

6.57 There is a significant risk of adverse costs for any litigation funder. The case law on the subject is clear and if a litigation funder finances a piece of litigation which is unsuccessful then they are prima facie liable to pay some of the adverse costs to the winning opponent, should a costs order be made.

6.58 Although costs orders are not made in every case, the starting point remains that costs follow the event and the loser pays. For funders, the starting point is the case of *Arkin*.[7] The case has been examined in detail in Chapter 2. The basic principle is that a funder is liable to pay adverse costs to the winning opponent up to a limit of the extent of their funding. In other words, if a funder invests £1m in a case then in the event that it loses they may be liable to pay a further £1m, depending upon the level of the opponent's costs.

6.59 The final report prepared by Lord Justice Rupert Jackson on civil litigation costs[8] endorsed third party litigation funding. On the issue of adverse costs he examined the current position and the case of *Arkin* in Chapter 11. Reference is made to the position in Australia and the case of *Katauskas*.[9] In that case the funder was held not to be liable for adverse costs. However, in this jurisdiction the situation prevails and Lord Justice Jackson concluded that 'it is wrong in principle that a litigation funder, which stands to recover a share of damages in the event of success, should be able to escape part of the liability for costs in the event of defeat. This is unjust not only to the opposing party (who may be left with unrecovered costs) but also to the client (who may be exposed to costs liabilities which it cannot meet).'[10]

6.60 He suggested that funders should be liable for the full amount of the averse costs of the winning party to the litigation in a funded case saying unequivocally, 'The funder's potential liability should not be limited by the extent of its investment in the case.'[11]

6.61 The current position by reference to case law in England and Wales is that *Arkin* remains unchallenged so far. The case of *Merchantbridge*[12] dealt with similar issues to *Arkin*. But, in *Merchantbridge*, *Arkin* was distinguished as the funders were not professional funders and the public policy considerations applied in *Arkin* did not apply in *Merchantbridge*.

---

[7] *Arkin v Borchard Lines* [2005] EWCA Civ 655.
[8] Rupert Jackson LJ, *Review of Civil Litigation Costs: Final Report*, 9 December 2009.
[9] *Jeffery & Katauskas Pty Ltd v SST Consulting Pty Ltd* [2009] HCA 43.
[10] Jackson, *Review of Civil Litigation Costs*, Ch 11 para 4.6.
[11] Jackson, *Review of Civil Litigation Costs*, Ch 11 para 4.7.
[12] *Merchantbridge v Safron* [2011] EWHC 1524.

G. *Excalibur*

6.62 A chapter discussing the issue of adverse costs and ATE insurance in the area of third party litigation funding cannot ignore the case of *Gulf Keystone* or *Excalibur*.[13] The case has received a large amount of public review. The main decision and the costs judgment was critical of the claimant's case and the manner in which it was pursued. The case has been identified as one justifying removing the limits in the *Arkin* decision as to the scope of a funder's liability.

6.63 The case has been reviewed in detail in Chapter 2. The third party litigation funders in the marketplace in England and Wales did not fund the case. The funders were not professional litigation funders, save possibly for one United States based entity which acted as a funder and as a broker of funding, mainly in the US market. The other funders involved appear to be a hedge fund and the family office of a high net worth family.

6.64 None of those funders is or was active in the professional litigation funding world in England and Wales. The one party that had some experience of litigation funding operated mainly in the United States where there are very rare examples of adverse costs. It appears that there was no ATE policy acquired as insurance to cover the eventuality of meeting the defendants' costs in the event that the case lost. The case did lose and costs orders followed.

6.65 The issue of security for costs did arise in the case. The claimants were required to lodge significant sums by way of cash deposit to satisfy the defendants' requests and the security ordered by the court. By the conclusion of the trial some £17.5m was lodged. In the costs judgment further sums were ordered to take the total to £23.1m. This was following the decision to award costs on an indemnity basis and having considered that the defendants would recover 85 per cent of their claimed costs. The order providing for the further security to be lodged allowed 14 days for such payment, failing which permission was granted to join the funders as parties to the action.

6.66 The question of whether the *Arkin* cap on liability will need to be considered will depend upon what amount of costs was actually paid by the funders. The adverse costs are going to be around the £23m figure as that was the figure used as security for the costs and the costs of assessment. It seems unlikely that the costs awarded will exceed the funding advanced by the funders, but it is possible as the award of adverse costs has been made on an indemnity basis.

---

[13] *Excalibur Ventures LLC v Texas Keystone Inc.; Gulf Keystone Petroleum Ltd; Gulf Keystone Petroleum International Ltd; Gulf Keystone Petroleum (UK) Ltd* [2013] EWHC 2767 (Comm); EWHC 4278 (Comm).

H. Conclusion

Adverse costs and security for costs issues go hand in hand. Professional litigation funders will consider those issues at the outset of a case and review their options with the clients in some detail. Any professional litigation funder which has experience of operating in England and Wales will ensure that there is adequate protection against adverse costs before committing to funding, it will be a condition needing satisfaction before completion of the litigation funding agreement. They will also have addressed the need for security for costs and either dealt with it by way of agreeing to add funds to the budget to cover such security, or will make provision by way of bond or deed using the ATE insurer. **6.67**

Often funders have their own arrangements for ATE and the ability to bind insurers up to certain pre-agreed and delegated limits. Other funders have their ATE providers. This can speed up the funding process significantly. **6.68**

As for the costs of setting up these arrangements and the funding agreement, the legal fees incurred are not recoverable from the losing side by way of adverse costs. However, most funders will consider adding them to the facility to be drawn on completion of the agreement. **6.69**

7

GROUP LITIGATION

| A. Group Litigation | 7.01 | C. Issues for Litigation Funders | 7.26 |
| B. England and Wales | 7.05 | D. Conclusion | 7.44 |

A. Group Litigation

7.01 Historically, the legal climate in England and Wales has not been as favourable to group or class action litigation as it is in other European jurisdictions. Whilst the concept of group actions is still relatively new across the whole of Europe, legislation has been introduced in Italy, Sweden, and Poland. Additionally, in the Netherlands the introduction of the Collective Settlement of Mass Claims Act 2005 has assisted this type of litigation and the legal regime provides the equivalent of an 'opt-out' system for claimants.

7.02 Across Europe, outside England and Wales, the use of third party litigation funding in class actions has been much more commonplace. One area where funding has been used regularly is in cartel actions. There are a number of funders who specialize in these sorts of actions.

7.03 The legal framework outside England and Wales is significantly more conducive to funding these cartel actions. In England, the adverse costs exposure is some three or four times greater than in the Netherlands, for example, where there is little or no need to purchase ATE insurance cover, thus reducing the cost of the litigation there.

7.04 The method used in the Netherlands and Germany in these sorts of cases involves the assignment or sale of the rights in the litigation to a special purpose company created solely for the case, which then pursues the litigation on behalf of the class. This makes the funding arrangements significantly easier. Cartel damages claims are actions in tort. In the Netherlands there are no regulatory issues over this method of assignment. While the assignment of tortious rights is not permitted in England it is acceptable in the Netherlands and Germany.

B. England and Wales

7.05 For the reasons already discussed, the use of third party litigation funding in class actions has been more prevalent in Germany and the Netherlands than anywhere else. However, there are changes on the horizon in England, with the use of litigation funding featuring in one of the largest pieces of banking litigation that the Commercial Court has seen, namely the shareholder actions against the Royal Bank of Scotland.[1] There is a general increase in the awareness of litigation funding and its benefits. This has meant that a number of group actions that are in their formative stages are looking at litigation funding as a way to bring them to life and to cover the legal costs of the action.

7.06 The government has now introduced a proposed Consumer Rights Bill to Parliament. This draft legislation includes provision for a new collective action for competition claims, together with other proposals for reforming the regime for competition law private actions in England and Wales.

7.07 If this bill is enacted it will create a new 'opt-out' collective action for competition law actions on behalf of consumers and businesses in the Competition Appeal Tribunal (CAT). The policy objective behind this proposal is the hope that it will allow small businesses into new markets by facilitating their means of redress against large and dominant corporations who have acted in an anti-competitive manner. The legislation is also intended to deter conduct such as the practice of price fixing through cartels.

7.08 The CAT will have to certify whether an action should proceed on an 'opt-in' or 'opt-out' basis. Under the 'opt-in' route, as the name suggests, claimants must 'opt in' to the litigation if they wish to benefit from the claim.

7.09 In contrast, when the claim is deemed to be an 'opt-out action', the proceedings are brought on behalf of a defined group, without the need to identify individual group members. This means that all those who fall within the defined group will be bound by the result, including any settlement, unless they elect to 'opt out' of the case.

7.10 In terms of who will be able to act as a representative to bring an opt-out collective action, this includes any claimants (individuals or businesses) who have suffered a loss, as well as genuinely representative bodies such as trade associations. However, a person may only be authorized to act as a representative in proceedings if the CAT considers it 'just and reasonable' for that person to do so—even if they are a class member. In the draft legislation the 'just and reasonable' requirement applies only if the proposed representative was not a class member.

---

[1] *Greenwood & Ors v Goodwin & Ors* [2014] EWHC 227 (Ch).

7.11 The bill also includes a new 'opt-out' collective settlement regime, similar to the Dutch mass settlements regime under the Collective Settlement of Mass Claims Act 2005. This will allow parties to ask the CAT to approve an agreed settlement on an opt-out basis without the need for proceedings to be brought. The bill was presented to Parliament in January 2014 and at the time of writing is making its way through the House of Commons.

7.12 This regime may present a difficulty in obtaining litigation funding for such cases. For litigation funders one of the key issues is the certainty of the numbers in a class or group. An 'opt-out' arrangement does not work for funders. Critical mass is important and the size of any group and the potential returns to the funders are calculations made at an early stage. There will be a level of membership in the group that makes the action sustainable or not from the litigation funder's perspective.

7.13 The current position in England and Wales is that the law has developed to allow two alternative forms of what might be called a class action in other jurisdictions namely representative actions and group litigation orders. In this chapter the focus is on group litigation and group litigation orders (GLOs). The GLO is a relatively new facility for the conduct of multi-party claims, being introduced only with effect from 2 May 2000.[2]

7.14 GLOs may be made, under CPR 19.11, 'to provide for the case management of claims which give rise to common or related issues of fact or law', referred to as GLO issues.[3] CPR Part 19.10–19.15 deals with the circumstances in which GLOs can be made, their effect, their case management, application by a party to a claim for it to be removed from the register, and test cases. The rules are supplemented by Practice Direction 19B which deals with Group Litigation.

7.15 An application for a GLO may be made by either the claimant or the defendant and must be made in accordance with CPR Part 23. It can be made at 'any time before or after any relevant claims have been issued'.[4] Alternatively, the court may make a GLO of its own initiative; however, the making of a GLO is subject to tight judicial control, requiring the consent in the case of the Queen's Bench Division, of the President of that Division, and in the case of the Chancery Division, of the Chancellor.[5] An application for a GLO is made to the Senior Master in the Queen's Bench Division, or the Chief Chancery Master in the Chancery Division.[6]

---

[2] Part III of CPR 19, dealing with Group Litigation, was introduced by the Civil Procedure (Amendment) Rules 2000 (SI 2000/221), coming into effect on 2 May 2000. The new rule was a response to recommendations contained in Chapter 17 of the Final Access to Justice Report (July 1996).
[3] CPR 19.10.
[4] 19BPD 3.1.
[5] 19BPD 3.3.
[6] 19BPD 3.5; outside of London, pursuant to BPD 3.6, the application is to be made to a Presiding Judge or a Chancery Supervising Judge for the Circuit in which the District Registry which has issued the application notice is situated.

7.16 When a GLO is made, the action is assigned to a judge with responsibility for managing the action. The judge is often assisted by a master to hear procedural matters and sometimes by a costs judge. The GLO is made under an 'opt-in' regime.

7.17 A register is established to record the claims and claimants which are to be subject to a GLO. CPR 19.11(2) requires that a GLO must specify the GLO issues which will identify the claims to be managed as a group under the GLO, and specify the management court which will manage the claims on the group register. The GLO may, pursuant to CPR 19.11(3), in relation to claims which raise one or more of the GLO issues, direct claims to be transferred to the management court, order them to be stayed until further order, and direct them to be entered on the group register.[7] Directions for publicizing the GLO may also be given. The Senior and Chief Masters of the Queen's Bench and Chancery Divisions respectively arrange for particulars of GLOs to be published on the website for the Courts and Tribunals Service. 19BPD 2.1 provides that before applying for a GLO the solicitor acting for the proposed applicant should consult the Law Society's Multi Party Action Information Service in order to obtain information about other cases giving rise to the proposed GLO issues. The management court may specify a cut-off date after which no claim may be added to the Group Register unless the court gives permission: 19BPD 13.

Where a judgment or order is given or made in the case on the register which relates to an issue which is covered by the GLO then that judgment or order is binding on the parties to all the other registered claims on the group register at that time, unless the court orders otherwise. However, it is not binding on claimants who, although they raise similar or identical issues, have not been included on the register.

7.18 One recent example of a case where a GLO was made are the various claims brought against the Royal Bank of Scotland in the Commercial Court in London.[8] One of the defined issues stated in the GLO is as follows: 'Whether there were relevant untrue and misleading statements in the Prospectus, within Section 90(1)(b)(i) of FSMA, and if so what they were.' Other main common issues relate to whether loss was suffered, causation, and potential defences under Schedule 10 of the Financial Services and Markets Act 2000 ('FSMA').

7.19 One of the issues that Hildyard J had to address and decide was the matter of the apportionment of adverse costs in the case. CPR 46.6 makes special provision for costs in the case of GLOs. The claimants in the case concerned were in four distinct groups. Two large groups were represented by Bird and Bird, the lead solicitors, and Stewarts Law. There were two other groups of potential claimants before the court;

---

[7] CPR 19.12(1).
[8] [2014] EWHC 227 (Ch).

a shareholder group of some 8,200 members represented by Leon Kaye; and a further group, of institutional investors represented by Quinn Emmanuel Urquhart & Sullivan. The judge referred to the groups respectively as the BB Action Group, the SL Group, the LK Group, and the QE Group.

7.20 The background to the judge's decision is that there is a combination of small consumer shareholders, some 20,000, who made relatively small losses and 170 large institutional shareholders who suffered enormous losses. The total value of the potential claims runs into billions of pounds.

7.21 At the time that the court was asked to consider the issue of costs apportionment the parties suggested their estimates of costs. The Bird and Bird group suggested their fees would be £10–12m, Stewarts Law £8.5m, and the defendants some £41.5m.

7.22 The costs issue before the court was described clearly by Hildyard J in his judgment as follows:

> 23. That primary question must be sub-divided:
> (1) one sub-issue is how the potential liability of all claimants for the Defendants' common costs is to be borne/shared: this is the question of 'adverse costs allocation';
> (2) a second sub-issue is how costs of the Claimants should be borne/shared: this is the question as to
>
> 'Claimants' costs sharing';
> (3) a third sub-issue is how costs incurred are actually to be paid: this is the question of 'actual payment';
> (4) a fourth sub-issue, given the need for certainty of exposure for people deciding whether or not to litigate, is whether, and if so in what circumstances, any directions or orders in respect of the above matters should be capable of being reviewed and altered or revoked: that may be referred to as the question of 'reviewability'.
>
> Adverse costs allocation
>
> 24. The general rule or default position, where the court has made a GLO, is that:
> (3) 'any order for common costs against group litigants imposes on each group litigant several liability for an equal proportion of those common costs': CPR 46.6(3);
> (4) where a 'group litigant' is the paying party, 'he will, in addition to any costs he is liable to pay to the receiving party, be liable for—
>   a) the individual costs of his claim; and
>   b) an equal proportion, together with all the other group litigants, of the common costs': CPR 46.6(4).
> 25. CPR 46.6(2) provides definitions of these phrases:
>   c) 'individual costs' means costs incurred in relation to an individual claim on the group register
>   d) 'common costs' means—
>   costs incurred in relation to the GLO issues;
>   individual costs incurred in a claim while it is proceeding as a test claim; and

costs incurred by the lead solicitor in administering the group litigation; and

e) 'group litigant' means a claimant or defendant, as the case may be, whose claim is entered on the group register.

26. These default and general rules are the starting point: but the Court of Appeal has (albeit in a different context of a multiplicity of claims for industrial injury) encouraged the devising and development of new procedures and techniques adapted to the circumstances of particular group litigation: see Horrocks v Ford Motor Company Ltd, The Times February 15, 1990, and White Book (2013) at 48.6A.2 (page 1542).

27. As suggested by Sir Thomas Bingham MR in Ward v Guinness Mahon Plc [1996] 1 WLR 894 at 900G–H, the court has considerable latitude and the broad question is: what, in the particular situation, does fairness demand, having regard to the objectives of the procedure for a GLO, the nature of the claim, and the positions of the claimants?

28. Where there is, as there is in this case, a very considerable disparity between the values of the claims of different parties, if they are all unsuccessful the default rule is unlikely to meet the requirement of fairness. It is not fair or equitable that an institutional investor with millions, in some cases hundreds of millions, at stake should pay an equal contribution as an individual claimant with claims in the hundreds, or even hundreds of thousands. Adoption of the default rule would tend to negate a primary purpose of GLOs.

29. None of those represented before me, on either side of the dispute, actively contended that the default rule is appropriate in this case. The two competing alternative measures for sharing of any potential liability for the Defendants' common costs were as follows:

(5) several liability for each Claimant in proportion to acquisition cost (as proposed by the LK Group and supported by the SL Group, with some sideline support also from the Defendants); or

(6) several liability for an equal share for each lead Claimant Group, so that (in other words) the adverse costs would be split equally per Claimant Group, with all members of that group then being divided equally or as stipulated by agreement within that group (as proposed by the BB Action Group).

7.23 Bird and Bird advanced the argument that the costs should be split equally between the claimant groups. That would of course give the group with numerically the most clients an advantage.

7.24 The alternative proposition was that the costs should be split with a several liability for each claimant in proportion to acquisition cost that each claimant paid for the shares. This view prevailed with Hildyard J on the basis it was the fairest solution and the one which departed least from the starting point in the CPR. He said:

33. In my judgment, the fairest solution as regards adverse costs liability is that proposed by the LK Group and supported by the SL Group: that is also the solution that seems to me to result in the least departure from the starting point in the Rules, which reflects equality. As it seems to me:

(1) there is neither logic nor fairness in taking as the relevant unit each Claimant Group: the Court should not easily or usually depart from the

starting point (and legal fact) that proceedings are brought by individuals and legal entities (such as bodies corporate) and not by groups (which are self-assembled agglomerations without other legal standing), and that each individual or entity should bear a fair share of the risk in seeking its own reward;

(2) the discrepancy to which I have referred in paragraphs 14 and 15 above between the total number of members in the BB Action Group and the number of those members who are parties to issued claims further undermines the logic and fairness of what the BB Action Group proposes;

(3) whilst for the reasons I have already adumbrated, the starting point of equality of risk for every litigant must, where there is such a disparity in the value of claims, yield to some fairer relationship between risk and reward, the objective should be a fair alignment of risk and reward by reference to the position of each claimant, the group they have chosen to join being of little, if any, legal or logical relevance;

(4) further, the Court should seldom allocate liability to a 'unit' against which no enforcement process can lie: risk should be personal, and personally enforceable;

(5) I have taken into account, and indeed when the matter of costs sharing was first ventilated in July 2013 was much swayed by, the dangers of any allocation which in effect enables persons to litigate at minimal risk individually (which is the mathematical result in the case of persons with small claims, however measured): I have concluded that the advantages outweigh the risk, and it is after all to enable claims where the reward hugely outweighs the risk that the rules have provided for several liability in the context of GLOs. Further, and as Mr Lazarus on behalf of the LK Group stressed, the effect of cost sharing is that even those with large claims face a comparatively small costs exposure: the risk is very much diluted for all.

(6) any weighting or other allocation by reference to the extent of control exercised by the paying party or 'unit' is likely to be (and in my judgment in this case is) too difficult a task: personal responsibility is the better and fairer approach.

34. A further question to be considered, if adverse cost liability is to be imposed on each Claimant, is how the value of each claim is to be measured: that is also relevant to the next sub-issue as to the allocation of Claimants' own common costs. Two principal candidates were discussed:

a) pro-rating by the acquisition cost of each Claimant's shares (most of which had the same subscription price of 200p, although some were subscribed at 230p); or

b) pro-rating by the amount of compensation claimed or recovered.

35. The LK Group and the SL Group propose (a), primarily on grounds of practicality, given the obvious difficulties of precise quantification on any other basis. The other candidate was (b), given (as the BB Action Group pointed out primarily as part of its argument that neither (a) nor (b) was satisfactory) that there may be considerable variations as to actual loss, according to whether, when and for what price a subscriber sold its shares (taking loss as subscription price less sale proceeds).

36. In my judgment, (a) is the most practical result and should be adopted, even though (b) more closely matches the underlying rationale of pro-rating. In summary, my reasons are:

(1) potential reward may in some cases not be easy to measure, and indeed in most cases may depend on which amongst many possible measures is eventually preferred and selected: the objective should be to select a measure that can be applied across the board without material unfairness;
(2) the evidence so far available is thin, but does not suggest support for the hypothetical example suggested by the BB Action Group to illustrate unfairness in solution (b) (which was to contrast a claimant who sold at 180p with one who sold at 40p): so far as the evidence goes, the average loss across all BB members, calculated as subscription cost less sale proceeds, is 80% of the amounts subscribed;
(3) further, on the basis of the SL Group's preferred measure of loss, of subscription cost less true value at the date of acquisition, there is no difference between the damages claimed per share as between different claimants, except in the case of subscribers who paid a 15% premium to acquire shares in a post Rights Issue Placement;
(4) no measurement is fixed and appropriate in every case: there is much to be said for a pragmatic approach: in this case, the measure of subscription price is a fair proxy as an 'across the board' measure of potential reward.

37. That deals with the basis of liability for adverse costs. It remains only in that context for me to confirm, for the avoidance of doubt, that the basis of liability for adverse costs should, in my judgment, apply to all claimants, whether existing or in the future (subject only to the provision for variation, as to which see below).

7.25 This judgment is to be welcomed. It can be taken as guidance as to how courts in future cases, faced with very high value claims, distributed amongst many claimants, some of whom are modestly placed individuals with correspondingly modest claims and others of whom are very large institutions with extremely substantial claims, are likely to deal with such costs questions. It should enable all potentially involved in group litigation, claimants and defendants, legal advisers, insurers and funders, to appreciate the principles upon which costs exposure is likely to be approached.

C. Issues for Litigation Funders

7.26 Group actions are not easy cases for litigation funders in England and Wales. Elsewhere in Europe and in the United States the prospect of funding a group action is more likely. That said these sorts of claims are becoming more popular in England and Wales with the rise of actions brought against financial institutions or in relation to financial mis-selling.

7.27 The initial problem for litigation funders is that of 'seed capital'. Litigation funders, despite the criticism from some quarters, are not venture capital funds. Litigation funders invest on the back of serious and thorough research and having considered the detailed legal merits of an action. In a group action scenario there is the difficulty of surpassing the initial hurdle of engaging with enough clients who qualify for inclusion into the group or class.

7.28 Publicity is a major factor but how does an organization seek publicity without the certainty that once clients engage, the group has the financial resources to launch a claim. Often a litigation funder will be consulted at the very outset of a group's genesis. That is useful from the funder's perspective but not always fruitful.

7.29 Litigation funders may be prepared to engage with a group at an early stage and work with them to publicize the action and rally support and clients for the group action. That is not always the case. Whilst in continental Europe and in other jurisdictions the process of 'book building' is one that litigation funders are familiar with, it is very much a new thing in this jurisdiction. However, this may change with the advent of more high profile cases such as the RBS case mentioned above.

7.30 It is more usual in England and Wales for the group to have to expend some of their own money to prove that there is a significant class available for the litigation before approaching a funder. However, that does seem to be changing and there is a more receptive attitude on the part of funders to provide early, risk, or seed capital to grow the group action book in cases. However that comes with an increased risk to the funder, and therefore a consequential rise in the price of the funding. The earlier that a litigation funder engages with a group and assists in testing the class, the higher the risk to the funder, as they do not know at that stage what the risks are or indeed the extent of the claimant pool.

7.31 Certainty of size of the claimant pool is a very important factor for any litigation funder. No funder will commit to funding an action without knowing what the extent of the universe of the total claims may extend to. That is not unreasonable. The conclusion may be good or bad from a funding perspective. In cases such as these a litigation funder will have to invest a significant amount of time and potentially real money to ascertain whether a case is worthy of consideration. At that point the funder knows only that the claims are potentially of sufficient merit for them to consider investigating further.

7.32 The difficulty comes down to basic mathematics. If the size of the pool is extremely large, such as in the RBS claims mentioned earlier, then there are few problems. However, at the outset of a new potential group action the size of the case is very fluid. The sooner the extent of the potential quantum, at best, can be established, the better. Most funds will be keen to be involved as early as possible and to assist with the case management and potential book build if the case is large enough and they can be convinced over the potential for returns. Other funders make these sorts of cases their lifeblood and operate only in these matters.

7.33 When a funder is invited into a potential action early on, the first need for funding is over the way in which the group of clients can be extended, grown, and developed. If a litigation funder is happy with the concept then the issue of publicity and marketing—seed capital—is discussed. If that can be agreed then the group can proceed to market itself with a view to maximizing the percentage of claimants in the class that actually sign up for the case—on the basis that most of these sorts of cases are 'opt-in' claims.

7.34 Once the funder is convinced of the viability of the case and the publicity drive to attract potential claimants is up and running the next question is whether the group has reached a critical mass. In all cases of this nature a litigation funder will insist upon a minimum level of sign-up from clients. The simple reason for this is that there is a minimum figure of clients which provides a minimum figure of quantum that works from the funder's perspective. As with any case, and as discussed in detail in Chapter 5, a litigation funder has to be convinced that their ratio of funds invested to likely damages is within the range that they are comfortable with. That may be four to one, it may be ten to one, it very much depends upon the funder and the case.

7.35 The funder will set minimum targets and milestones. If they can be met then the funding will continue. The marketing and client acquisition plan will have been discussed in detail and agreed with the funder and the initial 'steering committee' of the group and the lawyers, at a very early stage.

7.36 Once the critical mass has been achieved and a sufficient number of the clients are signed up there are fresh issues to address for the funder. In usual circumstances these matters may have been addressed at the outset. The management of the case, the decision making procedures, and the control and flow of information to all of the clients is important. In most cases of this nature it will be usual for a management committee or a board of directors to be appointed to make decisions on behalf of the group. This board or committee, depending upon the structure of the claimant group, will have delegated authority on behalf the entire group.

7.37 The management decisions, and the decision making as regards such matters as the issue of proceedings and any interim decisions plus of course the important decision of settlement authority, will also be delegated to the committee or board of directors. It would be impossible and impractical to seek the views of every group member in a large and diverse group. Part of the process of joining the group would have been to acknowledge and accept the delegated basis of allowing the board or committee to make decisions for the entire class of claimants.

7.38 The next issue of importance in group actions, both for third party litigation funders and for members of the group, is the issue of adverse costs. As discussed earlier in this chapter the issue of adverse costs can cause some difficulties and the starting point is that each client is liable for adverse costs. The RBS case[9] referred to in paragraph 7.18 is a case where the debate on the adverse costs was examined in full.

---

[9] [2014] EWHC 227 (Ch).

7.39 The complication in that case is the fact that the claimant group is divided into four camps. If the claimants were represented by one set of lawyers then the matter would have been slightly less complicated and boiled down to whether each client was liable on a several basis for the amount of the defendant's costs or whether each client was liable with reference to the value of their shareholding. The debate arises because some shareholders had significantly more share and therefore value than others. If the adverse costs division was on the basis of value then that is significantly different from cost being allocated on the basis of a distribution between each shareholder regardless of how many shares they had.

7.40 Hildyard J concluded in the RBS case that costs should be apportioned by individual claimant by reference to acquisition cost rather than by the amount of shares that they held. This approach was adopted in relation to the claimants' common costs as well as adverse costs. He adopted the principles set out in CPR 46.6(3) and 46.6(4).

7.41 The issue for a litigation funder is less difficult when the funder is the only funder dealing with the case in question. As is evident from the evidence filed during the preliminary skirmishes in the RBS case there is more than one funder involved in the litigation on the claimant side.

7.42 The litigation funders will have had to consider, unsurprisingly, where their liabilities may lie. In that case the defendants have indicated that the likely adverse costs incurred will be in excess of £40m. That is a sum which would be very difficult to place in the English ATE market, as there is simply not enough capacity available to insure that risk.

7.43 A funder would want to ensure, with an eye to *Arkin* and to the potential for the public policy points in that case to be extended in the light of Chapter 11 of Lord Justice Jackson's *Review of Civil Litigation Costs*, that they have adequate ATE cover. It is one thing investing in a case and losing, it is quite another for a funder to lose their investment and then be saddled with the insult of having to pay very large adverse costs in addition.

D. Conclusion

7.44 Group actions are potentially very lucrative cases for litigation funders and there is significant interest in this sort of case in the litigation funding world.

7.45 The issues that funders share with these cases are the ability to achieve a critical mass within a reasonable time frame. Litigation funders will be prepared to fund the building of the claimant book in a case with solid merits but there is a threshold which has to be achieved for the litigation funder to continue with their support. The threshold will be governed by what is a feasible number of claimants to achieve the necessary value in terms of quantum that allows the funder to invest in the case. As has been discussed in previous chapters the issue is one of ratios between the budget that is to be spent on the case and the likely damages award.

7.46 The issue of control and management of the case is easily delegated to a committee or a board of directors in these cases. Additionally, the board or committee will need to have decision making authority on behalf of the entire group to ensure that the lawyers and the funder do not have difficulty with a disparate set of views on settlement figures or other fundamental decisions and instructions to lawyers during the case.

7.47 Lastly, the third party litigation funder will always need to be protected from adverse costs or at least provision made within the funding arrangements for such costs to be dealt with.

7.48 The apportionment of adverse costs is not usually a contentious issue with the CPR setting out the basic rules. However in some cases the usual proposition is challenged such as in the recent case against RBS which came before Hildyard J. In the main each client is severally liable for the cost of their own action and for a proportion of the joint or common costs along with each of the other claimants.

7.49 In these usual circumstances a third party litigation funder can adequately protect themselves and the members of the group from adverse costs by ensuring that there is adequate ATE insurance in place to deal with any potential award of costs in the defendant's favour.

7.50 Costs budgeting and management, now of very widespread application, pursuant to CPR Part 3.12–3.19, should greatly assist all involved in litigation to ascertain at a much earlier stage than was the case prior to April 2013 the likely extent of their, or their clients', costs exposure from becoming, or remaining, involved in a claim. This greater degree of confidence as to the extent of financial implications of litigation involvement should enable many who were previously far more apprehensive about becoming involved to commit themselves to joining the process of group litigation.

8

JACKSON AND DBAs

A. Jackson and Damages Based Agreements	8.01	C. Damages Based Agreements	8.77
		1. The DBA Regulations	8.90
B. Outline of the Changes	8.10	2. Practicalities	8.99
1. Conditional fee agreements	8.11	D. The Effect of Jackson on Third Party Litigation Funding	8.111
2. ATE insurance premium recoverability	8.12		
3. Increase in general damages	8.13	1. Lawyers' costs immunity, DBAs, and third party funding	8.113
4. *Simmons v Castle*	8.15		
5. Increased sanctions under Part 36	8.25	2. Hodgson immunity	8.114
6. Proportionality	8.31	3. Alternative business structures	8.122
7. Costs management orders	8.50	E. Conclusion	8.125

A. Jackson and Damages Based Agreements

8.01 The regime of civil litigation funding and costs was reformed in 2013 with the intention of removing unnecessary costs and restoring balance to the system.

8.02 The reforms followed on from the *Review of Civil Litigation Costs* published by Lord Justice Jackson,[1] a Court of Appeal judge, who carried out a year-long review of the subject. After full consultation, the government published its response on 29 March 2011 indicating the CFA reforms and other related measures, including the introduction of damages based agreements ('DBAs') would be implemented. This was done by Part 2 of the Legal Aid, Sentencing and Punishment of Offenders Act ('LASPO') and associated orders, regulations and changes to the Civil Procedure Rules. The legislation was enacted by parliament on 1 May 2012 and came into force on 1 April 2013.

8.03 The background and motivation to the changes is that the previous conditional fee agreement (CFA) regime could create a situation where a losing defendant might be responsible for paying almost double the costs they would if the claimant's lawyers were not acting on a CFA.

---

[1] Rupert Jackson LJ, *Review of Civil Litigation Costs: Final Report*, 9 December 2009.

CFAs became legitimate in 1995, when section 58 of the Courts and Legal Services **8.04**
Act 1990 (CLSA) took effect. They could be used in personal injury, insolvency, and
certain human rights cases. This was intended to provide access to justice for those
who did not qualify for legal aid, but did not have the resources to pay for legal services.

In 1998, CFAs were extended to all types of proceedings except family and crim- **8.05**
inal. Under these types of agreements, both the success fee and any after the event
(ATE) insurance policy premium (which was purchased to protect the client
against an adverse costs order) were payable by the solicitor's own client and were
not recoverable from the other side. Inevitably, this meant that the client had to pay
these out of any damages received.

In 2000, the regime changed when section 58 CLSA 1990 (as amended by s 27 **8.06**
Access to Justice Act 1999) sanctioned the Conditional Fee Agreements Regulations
2000 (SI 2000/692) (the 2000 Regulations). These Regulations, along with the
Conditional Fee Agreements Order 2000 (SI 2000/823), came into effect on 1
April 2000, and set out the requirements of an enforceable CFA.

The 2000 regime introduced recoverability of the success fee and ATE insurance pre- **8.07**
mium which meant that as the losing party in the matter was liable to pay these 'additional liabilities', they now had an interest in how much was being charged for them.[2]

The regime prior to LASPO coming into force, with recoverable success fees and **8.08**
ATE premiums, allowed claims to be pursued with no real financial risk to the
claimant but with the threat of excessive costs to the defendant. The government
believed that access to justice for all parties depended upon costs being proportionate and unnecessary cases being deterred.

This chapter will examine the detail of some of the Jackson reforms and their **8.09**
impact on the world of third party litigation funding and provide a detailed review
of damages based agreements (DBAs).

B. Outline of the Changes

The key proposals relevant in the field of commercial litigation, implemented by **8.10**
this legislation are discussed below.

1. Conditional fee agreements

The changes brought about by the Jackson reforms and LASPO confirmed the aboli- **8.11**
tion of the general recoverability[3] of the (CFA) success fee and ATE premium from

---

[2] Section 29 Access to Justice Act 1999.
[3] The provisions for abolition of success fees and recoverability of insurance premiums in insolvency cases will not take effect until April 2015.

the losing side, in relation to CFAs that were entered into after 1 April 2013. CFAs remain a popular retainer and are still available post-LASPO, but clients now have to pay their success fees themselves from their damages. The maximum success fee under a CFA will remain at 100 per cent of base costs in commercial litigation cases.[4]

2. ATE insurance premium recoverability

8.12 The changes introduced by the Jackson Reforms provide that there will be no ability to recover the ATE premium from the losing defendant if the ATE policy was incepted post-March 2013.[5]

3. Increase in general damages

8.13 It is proposed that there should be an increase of 10 per cent in non-pecuniary general damages such as pain, suffering, and loss of amenity in tort cases, for all claimants. This was a source of minor controversy since the decision and appeal in the case of *Simmons*.[6] The theory behind the increase in general damages awards is very simple. The abolition of the recovery of success fees from opponents will have an impact on the amount of damages any successful claimant will be left with at the conclusion of their case.

8.14 This is a provision of the Jackson recommendations which did not require legislation and does not form part of LASPO. This aspect of the reforms is being taken forward by the judiciary. This has already happened, albeit that it took two attempts.

4. *Simmons v Castle*

8.15 This was a case in which the claimant sought damages from the defendant for personal injuries which had been suffered when the claimant had been knocked off his motorcycle when it was in collision with a motor car driven by the defendant. The trial judge assessed general damages at £20,000, against which assessment the claimant appealed. The parties reached terms by way of compromise of the appeal, and therefore the consent of the Court of Appeal was required for a variation of the terms of the order made below. The court (Lord Judge CJ, Lord Neuberger MR, and Maurice Kay LJ) took the opportunity to announce an increase in general damages in most tort actions with effect from 1 April 2013. At paragraph 7 of the court's judgment (handed down on 26 July 2012), it specifically referred to the reforms which were to come into effect the following April pursuant to LASPO,

---

[4] In personal injury matters the maximum success fee will be 25 per cent: Article 3 Conditional Fee Agreements Order 2013.
[5] The provisions for abolition of success fees and recoverability of insurance premiums in insolvency cases will not take effect until April 2015.
[6] *Simmons v Castle* [2012] EWCA Civ 1039; *Simmons v Castle* [2012] EWCA Civ 1288.

and to the recommendation by Sir Rupert Jackson that general damages should rise by 10 per cent. Lord Judge CJ, with the unanimous support of the Judicial Executive Board, had previously announced the judiciary's support for the package of reforms, and the judgment recorded that LASPO had been enacted on the basis that the judiciary would give effect to the suggested increase in damages.

8.16 Having explained this background, the judgment continued at paragraphs 19 and 20:

> 19 The only remaining question is precisely how the increase should be applied. We have concluded that it should apply to all cases where judgment is given after 1 April 2013. It seems to us that, while it can be said that this conclusion does not achieve perfect justice in every case, the same thing can be said about any other answer to the question, particularly in the light of a number of the forthcoming changes being made to the costs regime pursuant to Sir Rupert's recommendations. Our conclusion has the great merits of (i) providing a simplicity and clarity, which are both so important in litigation, and (ii) according with the recommendation of Sir Rupert, which is consistent with much of the rationale of the 10% increase in general damages.
>
> 20. Accordingly, we take this opportunity to declare that, with effect from 1 April 2013, the proper level of general damages for (i) pain, suffering and loss of amenity in respect of personal injury, (ii) nuisance, (iii) defamation and (iv) all other torts which cause suffering, inconvenience or distress to individuals, will be 10% higher than previously. It therefore follows that, if the action now under appeal had been the subject of a judgment after 1 April 2013, the proper award of general damages would be 10% higher than that agreed in this case, namely £22,000 rather than £20,000.

8.17 The judgment in July 2012 in the case of *Simmons v Castle* [2012] EWCA Civ 1039, [2013] 1 WLR 1239, was heavily criticized in many quarters, particularly on the basis that it provided some Claimants with a windfall. Whilst the judgment had been used as an opportunity to state the position of the increased damages regime that would be in place post-April 2103 it applied to Claimants generally and not only to those who would suffer from the changes that had initiated the damages increase, namely those being unable to recover the lawyer's success fee from the paying party.

8.18 This was, unsurprisingly, unpalatable to the Association of British Insurers (ABI)—with good reason. They chose, a month after the judgment was handed down, to apply to the Court of Appeal to invite it to reconsider its judgment. Its application was referred to the Court of Appeal for a full hearing. The Association of Personal Injury Lawyers, and the Personal Injuries Bar Association appeared as interested parties at the hearing before the court (Lord Judge CJ, Lord Neuberger PSC, and Maurice Kay LJ). The court recognized that pursuant to s 44(6) of LASPO the amendments to legislation prohibiting the recovery of success fees from a defendant would not apply to cases in which arrangements providing for success fees for advocacy or litigation services had been made before April 2013.

8.19 At the hearing there were also submissions from the Association of Personal Injury Lawyers and the Personal Injury Bar Association.

8.20 The ABI's primary argument was the windfall argument; as the judgment put it at paragraph 31, it would be wrong to permit CFA claimants who were entitled to recover their success fee to benefit from the 10 per cent increase because 'such claimants would have the penny and the bun'.

8.21 At paragraphs 25 and 26 the court set out the reasons given by Sir Rupert Jackson for his recommendation for the 10 per cent increase explained in his Tenth Implementation Lecture; it was a quid pro quo for losing the recoverability of success fees and ATE premiums. It was also noted, at paragraph 27, that Sir Rupert Jackson had observed that the level of general damages was generally on the low side; however, the court explained that this point had been made by Sir Rupert to meet the argument that the 10 per cent increase in damages could be said to represent something of a windfall.

a. Revised judgment

8.22 In October 2012, having considered the various submissions, their Lordships reconsidered their judgment, and concluded at paragraph 50 of their revised judgment:

> 50 In these circumstances, we would, as it were, delete para 19 from our earlier judgment and replace para 20 with the following paragraph: 'Accordingly, we take this opportunity to declare that, with effect from 1 April 2013, the proper level of general damages in all civil claims for (i) pain and suffering, (ii) loss of amenity, (iii) physical inconvenience and discomfort, (iv) social discredit, or (v) mental distress, will be 10% higher than previously, unless the claimant falls within section 44(6) of LASPO. It therefore follows that, if the action now under appeal had been the subject of a judgment after 1 April 2013, then (unless the claimant had entered into a CFA before that date) the proper award of general damages would be 10% higher than that agreed in this case, namely £22,000 rather than £20,000'.

8.23 The amended judgment thus operates so as to ensure that anyone who falls within section 44(6) of LASPO does not benefit from an increase in general damages of 10 per cent and therefore does not receive the windfall of recoverable success fee, ATE premium, and the increased award.

8.24 The court acknowledged, at paragraphs 26–8, that the Jackson reforms had always been intended to be a package (with the inevitable consequence that there would be some respects in which some would benefit and others would suffer, for example, claimants who instructed their lawyers on a standard retainer pre-April 2013 would benefit in a post-April judgment from an increased reward). However, not surprisingly, the court observed that it could not conceivably have been Sir Rupert's expectation, or even intention, that every single one of his recommendations be implemented without any variation.

5. Increased sanctions under Part 36

8.25 Part 36 of the Civil Procedure Rules (offers to settle) has been amended with the intention of equalizing the incentives between claimants and defendants to make and accept reasonable offers.

8.26 The recommendation by Sir Rupert Jackson in his Final Report that there should be a 10 per cent uplift for Claimants who matched or beat their own Part 36 offer has become section 55 of LASPO. The combination of section 55 of LASPO and the Offers to Settle in Civil Proceedings Order 2013 is to increase the incentives to settle a claim, and to deter the rejection of sensible offers of compromise. The intention is to encourage early settlement.

8.27 An additional amount will be payable by the defendant who does not accept a claimant's offer to settle where the court gives judgment for the claimant that is at least as advantageous as the offer. This sanction is to be calculated as:

a. In monetary/damages cases—10 per cent of the award;
b. In mixed (damages & non-damages) cases—10 per cent of the damages award;
c. In non-damages cases—10 per cent of costs awarded.

8.28 The sanction is subject to a tapering system for claims over £500,000 so that the maximum sanction is £75,000. There is only one sanction for split trials. There were no transitional provisions, so these sanctions took effect from 1 April 2013 as regards all awards made thereafter, and offers to settle made before 1 April 2013.

a. 'More advantageous'

8.29 The new Rule 36.14(1A) was one of the first of Lord Justice Jackson's proposals that was implemented. The rule came into effect on 1 October 2011 by way of the 57th Update to the CPR. It stated, 'For the purposes of paragraph (1), in relation to any money claim or money element of a claim, "more advantageous" means better in money terms by any amount, however small, and "at least as advantageous" shall be construed accordingly.'

8.30 It therefore follows (in a departure from *Carver v BAA*[7] and *Gibbon v Manchester City Council*[8]) that any assessment will be based on the provision. The amendments to the CPR 36.14(3) do not exactly follow the 2013 Order, as discussed at paragraph 36.14.1 of Volume 1 of *Civil Procedure 2014* where it is suggested that the words 'up to £1,000,000' in the CPR 'would appear to be unnecessary and may cause confusion'. The author observes that the CPR was amended at CPR 36.14(3)

---

[7] *Carver v BAA* [2008] EWCA Civ 412.
[8] *Gibbon v Manchester City Council* [2010] 1 WLR 2081.

by inserting only one table and applying the cap of £75,000 across all claims, whereas the Order, in respect of an award above £1m provides for a prescribed percentage of 7.5 per cent of the first £1m, and 0.001 per cent of the amount awarded above that figure.

6. Proportionality

8.31 A new test of proportionality in costs assessment has been introduced.

8.32 The concept of proportionality has been familiar since the report by Lord Woolf, which led to the overhaul of civil litigation in the form of the Civil Procedure Act 1997. Sir Rupert Jackson addressed it in his Report, at Chapter 3. His view was that the effect of *Lownds v Home Office*[9] was to insert the test of necessity into the modern concept of proportionality.

8.33 In *Home Office v Lownds*[10] in the Court of Appeal (Lord Woolf CJ, Laws and Dyson LJJ) the court looked at how to apply proportionality and approved the approach in *Jefferson v National Freight Carriers Ltd*.[11] The court introduced a two-stage approach—the global approach and an item by item approach.

8.34 There had to be a global approach which would indicate whether the total sum claimed is or appears to be disproportionate having particular regard to the considerations set out in CPR Part 44.5(3). If the costs as a whole were proportionate according to the test then all that was normally required was that each item should have been reasonably incurred and the cost for that item should be reasonable.

8.35 If the costs as a whole appear disproportionate then the court would need to satisfy itself that the work in relation to each item was necessary, and, if necessary, that the cost of the item was reasonable. Therefore once a decision was reached as to proportionality of the costs as a whole the costs judge would be able to proceed to consider the costs, item by item, applying the appropriate test to each.

8.36 The court was keen to emphasize that a sensible standard of necessity has to be adopted and warned of the danger of setting too high a standard with the benefit of hindsight.

> While the threshold required to meet necessity is higher than that of reasonableness, it is still a standard that a competent practitioner should be able to achieve without undue difficulty.

8.37 It is important to remember that costs may be recoverable from the client but not from the paying party—'When a practitioner incurs expenses which are reasonable but not necessary, he may be able to recover his fees and disbursements from

---

[9] *Lownds v Home Office* [2002] 1 WLR 2450.
[10] *Home Office v Lownds* [2002] EWCA Civ 365.
[11] *Jefferson v National Freight Carriers Ltd* [2002] EWCA Civ 365.

his client, but extra expense which results from conducting litigation in a disproportionate manner cannot be recovered from the other party.'[12]

8.38 The court went on to say[13] that whether the costs incurred were proportionate should be decided having regard to what was reasonable for the party in question to believe might be recovered. Therefore a claimant should be allowed to incur costs necessary to pursue a reasonable claim but not allowed to recover costs increased or incurred by putting forward an exaggerated claim.

8.39 Sir Rupert Jackson found the guidance in *Lownds* unsatisfactory. He recommended the reversal of *Lownds* and stated that the CPR should provide that the fact that the costs have been necessarily incurred does not make them proportionate, so as to reverse explicitly the effect of *Lownds*.

8.40 He further recommended that the CPR should be amended to include a definition of 'proportionate costs' along the following lines:

> Costs are proportionate if, and only if, the costs incurred bear a reasonable relationship to:
> a) the sums in issue in the proceedings;
> b) the value of any non-monetary relief in issue in the proceedings;
> c) the complexity of the litigation;
> d) any additional work generated by the conduct of the paying party; and
> e) any wider factors involved in the proceedings, such as reputation or public importance.

8.41 In his Fifteenth Lecture of the Implementation Programme, Lord Justice Neuberger MR[14] addressed the issue of Proportionate Costs. He began by stating that there had been a failure to implement proportionality as a test in respect of costs assessment. He suggested that Sir Rupert Jackson had identified correctly that the fault lay with 'the old approach of allowing costs which were considered to be reasonable and necessary to the litigation, with reasonableness and necessity being considered on a narrow basis, largely without regard to the ultimate value of what was at stake in the proceedings'. This was the approach followed in *Lownds*. Lord Justice Neuberger felt that this approach should be reversed.

8.42 He went on, 'In this way, as Sir Rupert said, disproportionate costs, whether necessarily or reasonably incurred, should not be recoverable from the paying party. To put the point quite simply: necessity does not render costs proportionate.'

8.43 He felt that the problem with retaining a test of necessity was that it would be misleading as it might be misleading to say that proportionality takes precedence over necessity in an assessment.

---

[12] *Home Office v Lownds* [2002] EWCA Civ 365 at para 37.
[13] At para 39.
[14] Lord Justice Neuberger MR, Fifteenth Lecture of the Implementation Programme, 30 May 2012.

8.44 The better approach, in his view, was to remove reference to necessity and only refer to reasonableness. He hoped that the courts would develop the law as Sir Rupert Jackson had described it:

> …in an assessment of costs on the standard basis, proportionality should prevail over reasonableness and the proportionality test should be applied on a global basis. The court should first make an assessment of reasonable costs, having regard to the individual items in the bill, the time reasonably spent on those items and the other factors listed in CPR rule 44.5(3). The court should then stand back and consider whether the total figure is proportionate. If the total figure is not proportionate, the court should make an appropriate reduction. There is already a precedent for this approach in relation to the assessment of legal aid costs in criminal proceedings: see R v Supreme Court Taxing Office ex p John Singh and Co [1997] 1 Costs LR 49.

8.45 Accordingly a new CPR Rule 44.3 and rule 44.4(1) was introduced and there is a new test of proportionality embodied in the rules. Additionally, an amendment was to be made to CPR 1.1 so that it read as follows:

> 1.1
> (1) These Rules are a new procedural code with the overriding objective of enabling the court to deal with cases justly.
> (2) Dealing with a case justly and at proportionate cost includes, so far as is practicable—
>   (a) ensuring that the parties are on an equal footing;
>   (b) saving expense;
>   (c) dealing with the case in ways which are proportionate—
>   (i) to the amount of money involved;
>   (ii) to the importance of the case;
>   (iii) to the complexity of the issues; and
>   (iv) to the financial position of each party;
>   (d) ensuring that it is dealt with expeditiously and fairly;
>   (e) allotting to it an appropriate share of the court's resources, while taking into account the need to allot resources to other cases and
>   (f) enforcing compliance with rules, practice directions and orders.

8.46 It is intended that the new rule will introduce into general conduct in civil matters the fundamental element of the Woolf and Jackson Reforms. Sir Rupert Jackson explained in his Report:

> The policy which underlies the proposed new rule is that cost benefit analysis has a part to play, even in the realm of civil justice. If parties wish to pursue claims or defences at disproportionate cost, they must do so, at least in part, at their own expense.[15]

8.47 Lord Neuberger was keen to emphasize that the new proportionate costs rule should operate throughout the life of a case rather than just on the assessment of costs: 'the forthcoming new approach to proportionate costs, as implemented through the

---

[15] Jackson, *Review of Civil Litigation Costs*, at 3.5.17.

new costs rule, will operate before the issue of the claim form, throughout the life of proceedings, and then at the end of proceedings when costs come to be assessed…'[16]

8.48 However, Lord Neuberger did not develop further his definition of proportionality or how it is to be assessed:

> While the change in culture should reduce the scope of costs assessments at the conclusion of proceedings, it will not obviate the need for a robust approach to such assessments. Again the decision as to whether an item was proportionately incurred is case-sensitive, and there may be a period of slight uncertainty as the case law is developed.
>
> That is why I have not dealt with what precisely constitutes proportionality and how it is to be assessed. It would be positively dangerous for me to seek to give any sort of specific or detailed guidance in a lecture before the new rule has come into force and been applied. Any question relating to proportionality and any question relating to costs is each very case-sensitive, and when the two questions come together, that is all the more true. The law on proportionate costs will have to be developed on a case by case basis. This may mean a degree of satellite litigation while the courts work out the law, but we should be ready for that, and I hope it will involve relatively few cases.[17]

8.49 Most cases are not of public importance, and it should be relatively easy to state what level of costs would be proportionate to spend to recover sums of £50,000, £100,000, or £250,000. It seems we shall have to wait and see what the 'satellite litigation' brings.

7. Costs management orders

8.50 Sir Rupert Jackson's Final Report identified the need for the court to take on the important role of costs management as a necessary part of case management. He felt it was no longer acceptable for questions of costs to be left to the end of litigation when the costs had been spent and that some control on the expenditure of costs should be implemented as part of the case management process. That control will now be provided by costs management, which is being introduced by rules changes as part of the implementation of the recommendations in the Final Report.

8.51 Costs capping, one part of the costs management process, was introduced into the CPR in April 2009 following the Court of Appeal's comments in the case of *Willis v Nicholson*.[18] The rules were originally introduced at CPR Part 44.18–44.20 but are now to be found at CPR Part 3.19–3.21. They are supplemented by Practice Direction 3F—Costs Capping. The rules largely reflect the parameters that had previously been established by the case law, and they essentially codify the test outlined in *Smart v East Cheshire NHS Trust*,[19] namely that a costs capping order will only be made if there is a substantial risk that without such an order costs will be

---

[16] Neuberger, Fifteenth Lecture of the Implementation Programme.
[17] Neuberger, Fifteenth Lecture of the Implementation Programme.
[18] *Willis v Nicholson* [2007] EWCA Civ 199.
[19] *Smart v East Cheshire NHS Trust* [2003] EWHC 2806.

disproportionately incurred. Previously there was no specific reference in the Civil Procedure Rules to the court's power to impose a costs cap.

8.52 Any cost cap will apply only to future costs, in other words those costs incurred after the costs capping order has been made. It does not apply to any success fee or ATE insurance premium. A costs capping order can be made in respect of the whole litigation or just a part of it, for example the costs of providing disclosure. With the introduction of costs management, the need for control of costs by means of capping orders should be much reduced.

a. Essential elements of costs management

8.53 Sir Rupert Jackson set out four essential elements of costs management:[20]

    a. The parties prepare and exchange litigation budgets or (as the case proceeds) amended budgets.
    b. The court states the extent to which those budgets are approved.
    c. So far as possible, the court manages the case so that it proceeds within the approved budgets.
    d. At the end of the litigation, the recoverable costs of the winning party are assessed in accordance with the approved budget.

8.54 The need for costs management was generally supported during the consultation exercise. In order to test costs management a number of pilot schemes were set up, initially in the Birmingham Mercantile and TCC courts and in defamation cases in London and Manchester. The pilot schemes assisted in formulating the rules which have now been made by the Civil Procedure Rule Committee and came into force on 1 April 2013.

b. The new rules

8.55 These are CPR 3.12 to 3.18 and PD 3E and a new form of precedent H for producing costs budgets.

8.56 The outline of the scheme of costs management is as follows. First, it applies generally to all multitrack cases commenced on or after 1 April 2013 in a county court, the Chancery, or Queen's Bench Division (except the Admiralty and Commercial Courts) unless the court otherwise orders and to any other proceedings where the court so orders. Pursuant to their powers under CPR 3.12(1)(b) and (c) the Chancellor and the President of the Queen's Bench Division directed respectively that in the Chancery Division and the TCC and Mercantile Courts the costs management provisions of the CPR should not apply to cases of over £2m in value. For cases commenced on or after 22 April 2014, pursuant to CPR 3.12 the costs management provisions applied to all cases where the amount of money claimed was £10m or more, except where the court orders otherwise.[21]

---

[20] Jackson, *Review of Civil Litigation Costs*, 4.1.4.
[21] The 72nd Update to the CPR came into force on 22 April 2014. This limited the costs budgeting provisions to Part 7 Multi-track claims except where the claim is valued at £10m or more. In

8.57 Secondly, unless the court otherwise orders, all parties except litigants in person must exchange cost budgets in the form of precedent H, by the date specified in the notice served under rule 26.3(1) (the notice of proposed allocation), or if no such date is specified, seven days before the first case management conference.[22] In default the budget will only comprise applicable court fees.[23] This sanction will apply to parties who fail to file a budget on time, and relief from the sanction will not normally be granted unless either the breach concerned was trivial or there was a good reason for it; see the decision of the Court of Appeal in *Mitchell v News Group Newspapers Ltd* [2014] 1 WLR 795.[24]

8.58 The court may then manage the costs and make a costs management order. However, whether or not it has made a costs management order, in making any case management decision, the court will have regard to any available budgets of the parties and will take into account the costs involved in each procedural step.

8.59 A costs management order will, pursuant to Rule 3.15, record the extent to which the budgets are agreed between the parties and, where not agreed, record the court's approval after making appropriate revisions. When a budget has been revised, the party has to refile the approved budget with recast figures. Where a costs management order has been made, the court will then control the parties' budgets in respect of recoverable costs. The court may set a timetable or give other directions for future reviews of budgets, and may, for instance, consider a revised budget by convening a costs management conference, conducted where practicable by telephone or in writing.[25]

8.60 The exercise of producing a costs budget and of dealing with and approving costs budgets must be kept under control. There are limits on the costs which can be recovered for preparing a costs budget and in carrying out the budgeting and costs management process, where a costs management order is made.

8.61 The parties are encouraged to seek to agree costs budgets, in whole or in part after they have been exchanged and the court will record any such agreed budget. Insofar as budgets are not agreed, the court has to review, make any appropriate revisions, and approve the costs budgets. The Practice Direction contains guidance which is aimed at limiting the scope of argument which might otherwise occur where costs budgets are not agreed.

---

other types of case the court will have the discretion to implement costs management and parties will be able to apply for costs management if it is deemed appropriate by the circumstances of the individual case.

[22] Rule 3.13.
[23] Rule 3.14.
[24] See, however, the more recent decision of the Court of Appeal in Denton v T H White & others [2014] EWCA Civ 906 in which the Court of Appeal revisited the approach to be taken to the failure to comply with rules, practice, directions and orders. Denton suggests that henceforth relief from sanctions will be available unless a breach has been serious, and even then an important consideration will be the interests of justice.
[25] Rule 3.16.

8.62 In summary:

(i) The court's approval relates only to the total figures for each phase of the proceedings, although in the course of the review the court may have regard to the constituent elements of each total figure.
(ii) The court will not undertake a detailed assessment in advance but rather will consider whether the budgeted costs fall within the range of reasonable and proportionate costs.
(iii) The court does not approve costs that have been incurred before the date of any budget. It may however record its comments on those costs and take those costs into account when considering whether the subsequent costs are reasonable and proportionate.

8.63 During the course of litigation a party is required to revise its costs budget if significant developments in the litigation warrant a revision. The revised budget is then sent to the other party to seek agreement. If there is not agreement the revised budget is sent to the court with reasons for the change and the objections of the other party. The court may then approve, vary, or disapprove the revisions, having regard to the developments. If interim applications are made which, reasonably, were not included in the budget, then the costs of those applications shall be treated as additional to the approved budget.

8.64 Where there is a costs management order, it then has an impact on the assessment of costs. When assessing costs on a standard basis the court will have regard to the receiving party's last approved or agreed budget for each phase of the proceedings.

c. Practical aspects

8.65 Many large firms of solicitors already have sophisticated costs systems which are used to record costs and most litigation teams have cost budgeting systems. However, the pilot schemes have shown that the production of costs budgets requires a new discipline for all involved in the process—solicitors, counsel, counsel's clerks, and judges. Summary assessment of costs has shown that the courts can make interim decisions on the quantum of costs but the ability to assess the reasonableness and proportionality of costs in advance is a different discipline that needs new skills.

8.66 There are two particular aspects that are important now costs management has been introduced. First, the court will have to apply a new proportionality test to the costs budget. As stated in the Final Report,[26] the judge carrying out costs management will not only scrutinize the reasonableness of each party's budget, but also stand back and consider whether the total sums on each side are 'proportionate' in accordance with the new definition. If the total figures are not proportionate, then the judge will only approve budget figures for each party which are proportionate. Thereafter if the parties choose to press on and incur costs in excess of the budget,

---

[26] Jackson, *Review of Civil Litigation Costs*.

they will be litigating in part at their own expense. It will be important for judges to apply the test consistently and for parties and their lawyers to be aware of the impact on recoverable costs.

Secondly, the court, in deciding what directions to give, will have to consider the cost impact of those steps. A good example is disclosure where, particularly with electronic disclosure, costs can soon become disproportionate. The court will have to question whether, for instance, it is proportionate to have standard disclosure or whether the costs of more limited disclosure is a proportionate way of proceeding in a particular case. **8.67**

Other examples of cases where the court will have to consider the impact of costs include expert evidence and witness statements. **8.68**

d. Making a costs management order

By Rule 3.15, the court is given discretion as to whether to make a costs management order. In the Final Report[27] it was accepted that in complex high value commercial litigation, such as that in the Commercial Court, it might not be appropriate to make a costs management order. There may also be circumstances where, for instance, a mediation is going to take place within the near future and it might not be appropriate to make a costs management order or to make one prior to the mediation. **8.69**

However, subject to particular cases where it might not be appropriate to make a costs management order or where the timing of the costs management order might be deferred, the courts are likely to make costs management orders both in the cases which are defined in CPR 3.12(1) and in other proceedings outside the defined class. **8.70**

As costs management is necessary for proper case management and the furtherance of the overriding objective there will, in most cases, be a presumption in favour of making a costs management order. **8.71**

e. Costs budgets

The court will encourage the parties to discuss and agree costs budgets and it is hoped that, over time, the scope for disagreement will become less as those involved in the process become more familiar with the costs budgeting process. There will however be some cases where the court will need to decide on contested items within the costs budget before the budget can be approved. Guidance is given in Practice Direction 3E on the approach of the courts. The focus will be both on the total costs and the overall costs for each stage of the proceedings. **8.72**

Whilst the court will consider the underlying time estimate and applicable rate in reviewing the overall cost of a stage, the court is not embarking on a detailed **8.73**

---

[27] Jackson, *Review of Civil Litigation Costs*.

assessment. This is to discourage a detailed 'line item' approach which can lead, in itself, to increased costs and satellite issues. Rather, there is encouragement for a lighter approach which considers whether the total budgeted costs of each stage are reasonable and proportionate costs for the particular case.

8.74 As far as changes to the budget are concerned, the onus is on the parties to put forward revised costs budgets if significant developments in the litigation warrant such revisions. Those are then provided to the other party or parties for agreement and, if agreed, the agreement of the revised costs budget will be notified to the court. The court will only become involved in that process if there is disagreement, in which case the party seeking to revise the costs budget will send the court that revised budget, the reasons for the revisions, and the objections raised by the other party or parties.

8.75 The court may then hold a costs management conference that, it is thought, will generally be dealt with by telephone or in writing, leading to approval, with or without variations, or disapproval of the revised budget.

8.76 As regards the detailed assessment of costs, the costs budgets will form a central part of any costs assessment. On standard assessment the court will not depart from the approved or agreed budget unless satisfied that there is good reason to do so; this is likely to reduce the area of dispute. Equally the fact that a party has seen and considered the other party's budget from an early stage is likely to lead to fewer disputes at the end of the process.

C. Damages Based Agreements

8.77 One of the long awaited and eagerly anticipated reforms suggested by Lord Justice Jackson was the introduction of a damages based agreement basis of paying fees to lawyers in litigation.

8.78 Damages based agreements is the statutory term, under s 58AA of the Courts and Legal Services Act 1990, for agreements sometimes known as contingency fees. However, 'contingency fee' is a broad term which technically covers all private legal funding arrangements between representatives and claimants in which the payment of a fee to the representative is contingent on the successful outcome of the case, including CFAs.

8.79 DBAs are therefore a type of 'no win no fee' arrangement, like CFAs, as the representative is only paid if the case is successful and does not receive any payment if the case is lost. However, DBAs differ from CFAs in that the payment which the representative receives is calculated by reference to the damages awarded to the client, rather than an uplift on the representative's base costs.

8.80 DBAs allow representatives to claim a proportion of their clients' award of damages as their fee and are therefore suitable mainly for use in cases where the claimant receives a sum by way of damages.

8.81 Prior to April 2013 legal representatives were not permitted to act under DBAs in civil litigation. However, solicitors were permitted to act under DBAs in 'non-contentious' business, including cases before tribunals. The use of DBAs has developed in tribunals over the past few decades and they are now commonly used in the Employment Tribunal in particular, but also in some tax tribunals and in pre-issue stages of other types of litigious matters.

8.82 In his *Review of Civil Litigation Costs*, Lord Justice Jackson stated, at page 135:

> 4.1 Having weighed up the conflicting arguments, I conclude that both solicitors and counsel should be permitted to enter into contingency fee agreements with their clients on the Ontario model. In other words, costs shifting is effected on a conventional basis and in so far as the contingency fee exceeds what would be chargeable under a normal fee agreement, that is borne by the successful litigant.
>
> 4.2 In my view the arguments in favour of contingency fees set out in PR paragraph 20.3.2 outweigh the arguments against, as set out in PR paragraph 20.3.3. Furthermore, it is desirable that as many funding methods as possible should be available to litigants. This will be particularly important if my earlier recommendations are accepted, that CFA success fees and ATE insurance premiums should become irrecoverable.

8.83 He recommended the introduction of contingency fee agreements using the 'Ontario model'. Additionally he commented that the conventional basis of costs shifting should apply, namely, loser pays or costs follow the event.

8.84 The government's response was set out in the 'Consultation Paper Reforming Civil Litigation Funding and Costs in England and Wales—Implementation of Lord Justice Jacksons Recommendations', at paragraph 13:

> Damages-based agreements (DBAs/contingency fees) will be allowed to be used in civil litigation. DBAs are another type of 'no win no fee' agreement, but the lawyer's fee is related to the damages awarded, rather than the work done by the lawyer. The Government will lift the restriction on their use in civil litigation. DBAs will provide a useful additional form of funding for claimants, for example in commercial claims. Successful claimants will recover their base costs (the lawyer's hourly rate fee and disbursements) from defendants as for claims, whether funded under a CFA or otherwise, but in the case of a DBA, the costs recovered from the losing side would be set off against the DBA fee, reducing the amount payable by the claimant to any shortfall between the costs recovered and the DBA fee. DBAs will be subject to similar requirements for parties to the agreement as for CFAs. For example, the amount of the payment that lawyers can take from the damages in personal injury cases will be capped (at 25% of damages excluding for future care and loss). However, the Government is not persuaded that there should be a requirement for a claimant to obtain independent legal advice in respect of a DBA.

8.85 The government broadly agreed with Lord Justice Jackson's proposal and the result was section 45 of LASPO:

> 45 Damages-based agreements
> (1) Section 58AA of the Courts and Legal Services Act 1990 (damages-based agreements) is amended as follows.
> (2) In subsection (1) omit 'relates to an employment matter and'.
> (3) In subsection (2)—
>   (a) after 'But' insert '(subject to subsection (9))', and
>   (b) omit 'relates to an employment matter and'.
> (4) Omit subsection (3)(b).
> (5) After subsection (4)(a) insert—
>   '(aa) must not relate to proceedings which by virtue of section 58A(1) and (2) cannot be the subject of an enforceable conditional fee agreement or to proceedings of a description prescribed by the Lord Chancellor;'.
> (6) In subsection (4)(b), at the beginning insert 'if regulations so provide,'.
> (7) In subsection (4)(d) for 'has provided prescribed information' substitute 'has complied with such requirements (if any) as may be prescribed as to the provision of information'.
> (8) After subsection (6) insert—
>   '(6A) Rules of court may make provision with respect to the assessment of costs in proceedings where a party in whose favour a costs order is made has entered into a damages-based agreement in connection with the proceedings.'
> (9) After subsection (7) insert—
>   '(7A) In this section (and in the definitions of 'advocacy services' and 'litigation services' as they apply for the purposes of this section) 'proceedings' includes any sort of proceedings for resolving disputes (and not just proceedings in a court), whether commenced or contemplated.'
> (10) After subsection (8) insert—
>   '(9) Where section 57 of the Solicitors Act 1974 (non-contentious business agreements between solicitor and client) applies to a damages-based agreement other than one relating to an employment matter, subsections (1) and (2) of this section do not make it unenforceable.
>   (10) For the purposes of subsection (9) a damages-based agreement relates to an employment matter if the matter in relation to which the services are provided is a matter that is, or could become, the subject of proceedings before an employment tribunal.'
> (11) In the heading of that section omit 'relating to employment matters'.
> (12) In section 120(4) of that Act (regulations and orders subject to parliamentary approval) for '58AA' substitute '58AA(4)'.
> (13) The amendments made by subsections (1) to (11) do not apply in relation to an agreement entered into before this section comes into force.

8.86 The section makes provision for DBAs, for assessment of costs where a client has entered into a DBA, and relies for detail on the proposed DBA Regulations: The Damages Based Agreements Regulations 2013.

These regulations came into force on 1 April 2013 and DBAs became permissible 8.87
in all civil litigation with effect from that date. The regulations provide outline
rules, provisions, the framework, and the detail of how DBAs are to work. The
DBA model adopted is the 'Ontario' model, based upon the contingency fee model
in Ontario, Canada. This system has a provision for costs recovery from the losing
party, as regards a sum equivalent to base costs and disbursements.

The essential provisions are as follows: 8.88

- In personal injury cases there is a 25 per cent cap on the amount of damages that can be taken as the lawyer's fee under a DBA and this can only be taken from sums recovered in respect of general damages for pain, suffering, and loss of amenity, and damages for pecuniary loss other than future pecuniary loss.
- There is a pre-existing cap in any event of 35 per cent in employment tribunal matters;
- There will be a cap of 50 per cent of damages for all other cases.

All sums concerned include VAT.

Lawyers acting under a DBA are required to comply with the indemnity principle; 8.89
see CPR rule 44.18(2). This means their fee will be restricted to what is due under
the DBA. If their DBA 'payment', or fee, is less than the amount they would otherwise have been entitled to by way of recoverable base costs from a losing defendant,
then the DBA fee would be paid by the defendant.

1. The DBA Regulations

The two key regulations are Regulation 3 and Regulation 4. 8.90

> Regulation 3
>
> Requirements of an agreement in respect of all damages-based agreements
>
> 3. The requirements prescribed for the purposes of section 58AA(4)(c) of the Act are that the terms and conditions of a damages-based agreement must specify—
>   (a) the claim or proceedings or parts of them to which the agreement relates;
>   (b) the circumstances in which the representative's payment, expenses and costs, or part of them, are payable; and
>   (c) the reason for setting the amount of the payment at the level agreed, which, in an employment matter, shall include having regard to, where appropriate, whether the claim or proceedings is one of several similar claims or proceedings.

This deals with the essential requirements of all DBAs. These essentials include 8.91
the details of the claim, or which parts of the claim are covered by the DBA, the
circumstances in which the fee is payable, and the reason for fixing the percentage
at the level agreed. This is a similar provision to the need for explanation of the

level of success fee in a CFA and will require a similar risk assessment explanation. The explanation is believed to be necessary as there is no requirement for a client to be advised to seek independent advice before signing up to a DBA with their lawyer. The issue of independent advice was considered by the government but it was concluded that it would not be required as a necessary protection. Despite the absence of such a requirement as a legal condition of the validity of a DBA, it would be sensible for legal advisers to consider, in each case, whether a client should be advised to seek, or to consider seeking, independent advice concerning entering into a DBA. This is because it is inherent in the negotiation of DBA terms that the interests of the client and the lawyer are in conflict, with the lawyer's interests being to secure the maximum share of any award for himself, and the client's interests being to minimize the lawyer's share. It might be said that this is true of any commercial negotiation, but the relationship between lawyer and client is not a purely commercial one; the lawyer owes fiduciary duties to the client, which entitle the client to the single-minded loyalty of the lawyer; see the discussion of the nature and duties incidental to fiduciary relationships in the judgment of Millett LJ, as he then was, in *Bristol & West BS v Mothew* [1998] Ch 1, at pages 16–22, and especially at page 18. It would not seem to be an answer to this concern that the relationship of lawyer and client does not exist at the stage of negotiating the DBA, because in many cases, well before such negotiation has begun, the lawyer will have been retained to advise in relation to the prospects of the case, and to undertake preliminary work, so that he will already have undertaken to act for the client in circumstances which have given rise to a relationship of trust and confidence. No doubt it will be said that when negotiating the terms of a DBA, the lawyer is not acting as a fiduciary but as a principal. Whilst as a matter of legal analysis it may be possible to divide aspects of the lawyer and client relationship in this fashion, in practice it may be difficult to segregate them satisfactorily. The client will look to the lawyer, as a legal adviser safeguarding the client's interests, for guidance as to the merits and risks of the case; yet those same matters will be highly relevant to the negotiation between lawyer and client when it comes to setting the amount of the payment that the lawyer is to receive. The risk for the lawyer is that in negotiating the terms of a DBA by reference to the matters upon which the lawyer is also advising the client (merits and risk), the lawyer will be said to be dealing with his client. Where a fiduciary deals with his client he is required to prove that the transaction is fair and that full disclosure of all facts material to it were disclosed; even inadvertent failure to make disclosure entitles the client to rescind the transaction; see *per* Millett LJ in *Mothew* at page 18D–E. To minimize the risk of an attack on the validity of the DBA, and the lawyer's entitlement thereunder, for the client to seek independent advice might well be thought worthwhile, although cost will inevitably be incurred in taking that step. These same considerations did not arise in relation to CFAs prior to April 2013, because the lawyer's success fee was recovered from another party, and therefore its recovery did not conflict with the client's interests.

Regulation 4 provides: **8.92**

Payment in respect of claims or proceedings other than an employment matter

4 .—
(1) In respect of any claim or proceedings, other than an employment matter, to which these Regulations apply, a damages-based agreement must not require an amount to be paid by the client other than—
   (a) the payment, net of—
      (i) any costs (including fixed costs under Part 45 of the Civil Procedure Rules 1998); and
      (ii) where relevant, any sum in respect of disbursements incurred by the representative in respect of counsel's fees, that have been paid or are payable by another party to the proceedings by agreement or order; and
   (b) any expenses incurred by the representative, net of any amount which has been paid or is payable by another party to the proceedings by agreement or order.
(2) In a claim for personal injuries—
   (b) the only sums recovered by the client from which the payment shall be met are—
      (i) general damages for pain, suffering and loss of amenity; and (ii) damages for pecuniary loss other than future pecuniary loss, net of any sums recoverable by the Compensation Recovery Unit of the Department for Work and Pensions; and
   (b) subject to paragraph (4), a damages-based agreement must not provide for a payment above an amount which, including VAT, is equal to 25% of the combined sums in paragraph (2)(a)(i) and (ii) which are ultimately recovered by the client.
(3) Subject to paragraph (4), in any other claim or proceedings to which this regulation applies, a damages-based agreement must not provide for a payment above an amount which, including VAT, is equal to 50% of the sums ultimately recovered by the client.
(4) The amounts prescribed in paragraphs (2)(b) and (3) shall only apply to claims or proceedings at first instance.

This particular regulation has attracted some attention since the release of the DBA **8.93** Regulations. 'Payment' is defined in Regulation 1 as follows:

'Payment' means that part of the sum recovered in respect of the claim or damages awarded that the client agrees to pay the representative, and excludes expenses but includes, in respect of any claim or proceedings to which these regulations apply other than an employment matter, any disbursements incurred by the representative in respect of counsel's fees.

It is the amount due to the lawyer on success out of the damages recovered. **8.94** Regulation 4 says that this is the only payment allowed under the Regulations. This suggests that there is no provision or authority for a hybrid DBA with a payment of base costs as the case progresses, as has commonly been the case under CFAs. Opinion is divided on whether this interpretation is correct, and at present there is no judicial authority on the issue. Any lawyer today purporting to enter into a hybrid DBA therefore runs the risk that it may later be declared to be invalid.

8.95 This definition of the 'Payment' includes any amount due to counsel, so counsel would have to be paid out of the success fee. It does not, however, include other disbursements.

8.96 Regulations 4(2), (3) and (4) set out the detail of the caps that can be applied to the 'payment' or the fee due on success out of recoveries.

8.97 As stated in paragraph 8.87 the cap is 25 per cent in personal injury cases and 50 per cent in other civil litigation. These amounts include VAT. The caps only apply to first instance cases (Regulation 4(4)) and consequently there is no cap on appeals so lawyers are free to charge a higher percentage in appeal matters, possibly to reflect the increased risk if for example seeking to overturn a decision.

8.98 Counsel's fees are also included in the amount of the Payment and will therefore be deducted from the solicitor's entitlement.

2. Practicalities

8.99 The Ontario model of DBAs works on the basis that base legal costs are recoverable from the losing party in the usual costs shifting manner. These costs are calculated on the normal hourly rate that prevails *inter partes* for the particular case.

8.100 The amount which is recovered from the losing party is then set off against the amount of damages due to be paid to the lawyer under the DBA, thus reducing the amount to be deducted from damages.

8.101 There is a significant question mark on the likely use of DBAs in lower value claims when there is an opportunity to earn base costs plus an uplift in a CFA. The client will obviously fair better under DBAs at the lower levels though.

8.102 The way in which this legislation is expected to work in practice is demonstrated in the following example.

8.103 A client approaches a solicitor to seek advice regarding a breach of contract. The potential damages have been assessed at £1m and the client and solicitor consider that the claim could be run under a DBA. The solicitor conducts due diligence into the assets of the defendant, constructing an informed opinion as to whether it is worth pursuing the claim under such an agreement. After careful consideration, the solicitor and the client enter into a DBA under which they agree for the solicitor to receive 30 per cent of the claimant's damages award as payment for remuneration, expenses, and VAT.

8.104 The DBA is signed by the client and the solicitor and specifies the nature of the proceedings as the recovery of damages by the client resulting from a breach of contract. It also specifies the reasons as to why these amounts have been agreed, such as the risk assumed by the representative by taking on the client's claim.

8.105 The court awards the claimant £1m in damages and £100,000 in costs from the defendant resulting in the recovery of £1.1m by the claimant. Under the DBA, the solicitor receives £300,000, namely 30 per cent of the total damages. The base costs and disbursements are calculated using the standard hourly rate a solicitor charges and are recovered from the other party to the litigation. The solicitor is then paid £100,000 in costs by the defendant and is additionally paid £200,000 by their client to equal the total amount agreed.

8.106 If in the same scenario the figures were slightly different then this will illustrate the part that the indemnity principle may play in these cases, particularly in lower value awards.

8.107 Assuming the same DBA arrangement between client and solicitor, and consider the position if the court had awarded £1m in damages but the base costs claimed by the solicitors are £350k for running the case to trial. The solicitor will receive, as in the other example, 30 per cent of the award in costs, namely £300,000. However when it comes to claiming back the base costs the solicitors will be limited to £300,000. The reason for this is the indemnity principle.

8.108 Sir Rupert Jackson made reference to the Indemnity Principle in his Preliminary Report:[28]

> 4.13 The recovery of costs between the parties is subject to the indemnity principle (not to be confused with the indemnity basis of assessment—see below). While the successful party is unlikely to recover all of its costs, a party can never recover more than its costs (i.e. a party cannot profit from the recovery of its costs). The case of Harold v Smith[29] initially recorded this principle as follows:
>
> Costs as between party and party are given by the law as an indemnity to the person entitled to them: they are not imposed as a punishment on the party who pays them, nor given as a bonus to the party who receives them. Therefore, if the extent of the damnification can be found out, the extent to which costs ought to be allowed is also ascertained.

8.109 In his Final Report Sir Rupert Jackson states succinctly of the indemnity principle at paragraph 5.1.1, 'In essence the principle prevents a party recovering more by way of costs from an opponent than it is obliged to pay to its own lawyers.'

8.110 Accordingly, in the example in paragraph 8.106 above, if the solicitors' fee under the DBA is £300k, then that is the maximum amount that can be recovered by way of costs from the other side as it is the maximum amount that the client has a liability to pay their solicitor, namely £300k. The benefit here falls to the losing

---

[28] Jackson, *Review of Civil Litigation Costs*, para 3.4.13.
[29] (1860) 5 H & N 381; 157 ER 1229.

opponent. Under a standard fee arrangement where the client was paying an hourly rate to the solicitor and the base costs were £350k, then the losing opponent would be facing a potential adverse costs payment of £350k rather than an amount limited to £300k.

D. The Effect of Jackson on Third Party Litigation Funding

8.111 The issue of DBAs has raised concerns with some litigation funders.[30] They have expressed concern over the CJC proposals concerning DBAs and the lack of clarity generally, but particularly on the issue of adverse costs. It is possible that the history of costs in this area means that solicitors who fund litigation could face similar adverse costs exposure to that of litigation funders.

8.112 It is certainly worth looking at the history of the case law and then analysing the new proposals and comparing them with the Code of Conduct for litigation funders.

1. Lawyers' costs immunity, DBAs, and third party funding

8.113 The Civil Justice Council (CJC) Working Party on Damages Based Agreements reported in July 2012 and produced their recommended draft for the regulations on DBAs. This prompted some debate in the litigation funding world. Third party litigation funders were concerned that the implementation of the recommendations and proposed draft Damages Based Agreement Regulations 2012 ('DBA Regulations') set out by the CJC would leave them at a disadvantage and create an uneven playing field when it comes to them competing for business with solicitors proposing to fund cases under a DBA.

2. Hodgson immunity

8.114 The current immunity from adverse costs orders afforded to solicitors acting under conditional fee agreements (CFAs) is derived from two cases. The first is *Tolstoy-Milslavsky v Aldington*,[31] which was then followed by the well known decision in *Hodgson v Imperial Tobacco Limited*.[32] The relevance of the Tolstoy decision, which related to a solicitor acting *pro bono*, is that the leading judgment from Rose LJ recognized that there was no ground to award costs against a solicitor merely for acting for no fee as this was in the public interest and provided access to justice.

8.115 The Hodgson decision made it clear that there was no difference between a lawyer acting under a CFA and a lawyer not acting under a CFA as regards their liability

---

[30] <http://www.cdr-news.com/categories/third-party-funding/a-question-of-contingency>.
[31] *Tolstoy-Milslavsky v Aldington* [1996] 1 WLR 736.
[32] *Hodgson v Imperial Tobacco Limited* [1998] 1 WLR 1056.

for the other side's costs. Lord Woolf MR said that, 'The existence of a CFA should make a legal adviser's position as a matter of law no worse, so far as being ordered to pay costs is concerned, than it would be if there was no CFA.' Thereby the court extended to those acting on CFA, the principle that legal advisers acting *pro bono* should be protected from adverse costs exposure and thus set up what became known as 'Hodgson immunity'. That remains the position today.

The question of whether a solicitor has crossed the line from providing access to justice as opposed to 'funding' a case is a subject which has been considered in a number of cases since the Hodgson decision. The issue of when a non-party would be liable for adverse costs was considered in *Symphony Group Plc v Hodgson*. The bar for such an order was set high by Balcombe LJ as 'exceptional'. *Dymocks Franchise Systems (NSW) Pty Ltd v Todd (Costs)*[33] clarified the position that 'exceptional' meant no more than outside the ordinary run of cases and went on to reopen the distinction between commercially motivated funders and 'pure funders' which had been discussed in *Hamilton v Al-Fayed*.[34] 'Pure funders' are, as defined in *Hamilton* at paragraph 40, 'those with no personal interest in the litigation, who do not stand to benefit from it, are not funding it as a matter of business, and in no way seek to control its course'. **8.116**

Lord Brown stated that generally speaking the discretion would not be exercised to award costs against a 'pure funder'. However, where the funder is not a 'pure funder' in the terms set out in paragraph 8.115 and does in fact control or benefit from the proceedings things would be different. He continued at paragraph 25, 'The non-party in these cases is not so much facilitating access to justice by the party funded as himself gaining access to justice for his own purposes. He himself is "the real party" to the litigation.' **8.117**

This theme continues throughout the cases which have followed. The real test is whether the lawyers are 'the real party' to the proceedings. The next significant case on the issue was *Myatt v National Coal Board*.[35] The defendants, in this case, alleged that the claimants' solicitors were acting under unenforceable CFAs, and succeeded on the point before the costs judge. The matter was pursued to the Court of Appeal where the claimant's solicitors again failed. The Court of Appeal decided that the overriding reason that the appeal was launched was for the benefit of the solicitors as they were set to lose out on significant fee income if they were unable to enforce their CFAs. The relative benefit to each of the individual claimants was minimal. This suggested that the lawyers were the real party to the appeal, and acting outside the role of solicitor and they were ordered to pay half of the costs of the appeal. **8.118**

---

[33] *Dymocks Franchise Systems (NSW) Pty Ltd v Todd* [2004] UKPC 39.
[34] *Hamilton v Al-Fayed* [2002] CA Civ 665.
[35] *Myatt v National Coal Board* [2007] EWCA Civ 307.

8.119 So, the starting point is that a solicitor acting under a CFA enjoys protection from the decision in Hodgson as regards adverse costs, despite having an interest in the outcome of the proceedings. But, if the solicitors go further and exercise control or run the case for their own benefit, they are likely to suffer financially. This is in stark contrast to the current position as regards third party litigation funders and their responsibility to pay adverse costs in a case which loses. The decision in *Arkin v Borchard Lines*[36] provided that a professional third party litigation funder would be responsible for the winning opponent's costs to the extent of their funding.

8.120 The Report of the Working Party on Damages Based Agreements covers eight terms of reference. These include a review of whether, and if so in what circumstances, a lawyer acting under a DBA should be liable for adverse costs. Unsurprisingly, they begin by considering the solicitors' position when acting under a CFA and cite *Hodgson v Imperial Tobacco Limited*. The Working Party recommended that 'some appropriate mechanism (possibly the CPR) is adopted to extend "Hodgson immunity" or such protection as the Court of Appeal has held exists, from adverse costs to lawyers acting on a DBA'. The reasoning behind this was that, in their view, there was little difference between a solicitor acting under a DBA and a CFA, and that the existing case law allowed costs orders to be made against solicitors who step over the boundary between solicitor and funder by their actions. However, the assessment suggests that in the Working Party's view the 'Hodgson immunity' does not presently extend to lawyers acting under a DBA, and that would appear to be a correct analysis in the light of existing case law. It would be rash for any lawyer considering acting under a DBA to assume that he would fall within the umbrella of the Hodgson immunity, or that a court would be prepared to extend the immunity beyond its present limits.

8.121 Also, the Working Party considered whether a third party litigation funder should be liable for only limited adverse costs in a DBA case, under the *Arkin* principle which concerned a CFA. They considered that consistency of approach as between DBAs and CFAs was desirable, and they proceeded to recommend that 'some appropriate mechanism (possibly the CPR) is adopted to make it clear that the *Arkin* principle also applies to a [litigation funder] who provides commercial finance in a DBA case'. This suggests that the Working Party's view is that at present a funder in a DBA case may not have the benefit of the cap on liability introduced by *Arkin*, or at the very least that this is not clear. It would, therefore, be prudent for funders to assume in DBA cases that they may not be held to enjoy the benefit of the *Arkin* cap on liability, pending any change in the CPR or some other 'appropriate mechanism', or a judicial decision extending the application of *Arkin* to such cases.

---

[36] *Arkin v Borchard Lines* [2005] EWCA Civ 655.

3. Alternative business structures

8.122 Additionally, the Working Party referred to speculation about the effect of alternative business structures ('ABSs') on the liability of funders for adverse costs where the funder has an ownership share in the ABS. They decided that this was not a matter that could presently be the subject of rules or regulation and that this was a matter best left for the courts to resolve if and when a question arises in a particular case. This acknowledges the possibility that the courts will determine that despite funding litigation through the medium of an ABS, a funder could still be held to have a liability for adverse costs. To date the point has not been considered, but it is possible to envisage that it will be held that such an ABS is no more than an agent for the funder whose liability should not be affected by use.

8.123 Since the suggestion that contingency fees would be legitimized using the Ontario model of DBAs when LASPO became law, third party litigation funders have been concerned that lawyers acting under a DBA may present a significant threat to them, if the adverse costs regime was not similar for both lawyers and traditional funders. Specifically their concern is that if the Hodgson immunity is extended to DBAs, then lawyers would have an unfair advantage. Funders argue that there is little or no difference between a third party funder and a lawyer acting on a DBA. Both are funding the case for a division of the proceeds on success. They are both responsible for the litigation taking place, which was the main thrust of the reasoning behind the funder being held responsible for part of the adverse costs in *Arkin*.

8.124 The litigation funding community also suggests that the principle of immunity set out in 'Hodgson' for CFAs should not simply be transposed on to the use of DBAs. The argument is that the returns available to a lawyer under CFA are significantly different from those available under a DBA and that this changes things to the extent that the existing principles cannot be applied. In light of the principles described in *Dymocks* and *Myatt*, there is some force in the argument that acting under a DBA pushes the solicitors closer to being a funder and 'the real party' to the proceedings.

E. Conclusion

8.125 The DBA Regulations make no reference to adverse costs or whose liability they are. Neither do they refer to any of the other issues which third party funders are required to deal with in the Code of Conduct for Litigation Funders ('Code'), for example, the matter of independent advice to the client or capital adequacy and financial strength of the funder.

8.126 Sir Rupert Jackson concluded in his Final Report:[37]

> 4.7 Potential liability for adverse costs. There is one important difference between tribunal proceedings (in which contingency fee agreements are currently used) and litigation, namely the potential liability for adverse costs. Agreement must be reached at the outset as to how any adverse order for costs will be met. If it is agreed that the solicitors will meet any such order (as quite often happens in Canada), then this additional risk should be reflected in the percentage recovery to which the solicitors will be entitled in the event of success.

8.127 Evidently it was anticipated by Sir Rupert Jackson that solicitors acting under a DBA may decide to cover the client's adverse costs for a higher return from the damages. Such an arrangement would render irrelevant the *Hodgson* question.

8.128 However, one may question whether any of this really makes any difference in practical terms. The argument from the litigation funders is that the playing field should as between funders and lawyers should be a level one. The funders feel that absent similar controls and measures to those of the Code being put in place for DBAs and the law firms which run them, then funders will be at a disadvantage when competing against lawyers for business. Additionally the suggestion has been made that some funders, in the event that there is no adverse costs liability imposed on lawyers acting under a DBA, may decide to change their methods and operate through some form of ABS, with a view to escaping the liability for adverse costs.

8.129 Both of these outcomes may occur to a lesser extent. It seems unlikely that the mainstream funders will look to change their models any more than they were doing in any event. It would also be surprising if a phalanx of law firms suddenly decided to take a far larger risk based case load than previously, merely because the returns in some cases might now be better. (It must be remembered that except in some very large cases, the rewards under a DBA could well be less for lawyers than remuneration by way of traditional costs.) Solicitors are relatively risk averse and whilst the upside in a DBA could in some cases be a better proposition than in a CFA case, the risks remain.

8.130 It seems highly likely that in fact what will happen is that funders will continue to fund base costs and that lawyers acting under a DBA and third party litigation funders will work together as they do under the existing CFA and discounted CFA regime. Obviously this is subject to a clarification of the DBA regulations or use of the 'hybrid' DBA funding schemes that have been originated by some funders.[38] In fact funding may increase even more than it has in the last few years, once clients have become used to the concept of sharing the proceeds of litigation, something which is still currently alien in the English system. A likely scenario is that there will be no great change in things. Much of the discussion over who will be better

---

[37] Per para 4.7.
[38] Buford Capital's Hybrid DBA scheme.

placed and whether funders or lawyers on a DBA will be at an advantage is likely to prove to be academic.

8.131 In short, whilst the landscape has changed to some degree and things look, at least superficially, to be different, in practice business will be conducted much as usual. Lawyers still have the same professional obligations through the SRA Code of Conduct and they will continue to owe the same duties to their clients that they always have done. Solicitors are still obliged to advise their clients about the funding of litigation and their potential liability to adverse costs, even if the solicitors were not to have a personal liability for costs because of an extension of the Hodgson immunity.[39] Additionally, solicitors who fail to advise their clients properly in respect of the potential liability for adverse costs and those who do not take steps to protect their clients by way of after the event legal expenses cover, will be held to have been negligent.[40]

8.132 Realistically, these professional obligations do level the playing field. If a client is faced with the choice between instructing a solicitor on a DBA with no costs cover, or using a litigation funder who has a liability for costs and both are looking to share in the proceeds of the case, then it seems highly unlikely that the client will take up the option which involves having no adverse costs protection.

---

[39] IB 1.13 and IB 1.16 SRA Code of Conduct 2011.
[40] *Adris and others v RBS* [2010] Costs LR 598.

9

PROFESSIONAL OBLIGATIONS

A. Introduction	9.01	C. Solicitors	9.43
B. The Association of Litigation Funders	9.02	1. Conduct rules	9.49
1. Membership	9.05	2. Solicitors' duties	9.58
2. Code of conduct	9.08	D. Conclusion	9.92

A. Introduction

9.01 In third party litigation funding transactions there are professional obligations to consider for the lawyers and also for the litigation funders. All of the aspects of a solicitor's professional regulatory obligations are considered in this chapter. This chapter also addresses the areas in which litigation funders must adhere to their own self-imposed regime of regulation.

B. The Association of Litigation Funders

9.02 In June 2007 the Civil Justice Council (CJC), a body established under section 6 of the Civil Procedure Act 1997, amongst other things to make proposal to the Lord Chancellor for the development of the civil justice system, published advice to the Lord Chancellor in a paper entitled 'Improved Access to Justice Funding Options and Proportionate Costs—The Future Funding of Litigation, Alternative Funding Structures'. The third recommendation in that paper related to the proper regulation of the third party funding industry. The CJC formed a high-level working party that included senior lawyers, academics, and business managers to consider this issue further. A draft Code of Conduct for Third Party Funding was produced by the working party. In 2010 Sir Rupert Jackson's *Review of Civil Litigation Costs: Final Report* was published. This recommended self-regulation for the litigation funding industry, by way of a voluntary code of conduct. Following this the draft Code of Conduct was revised. In July 2010 the CJC opened a consultation on the Self Regulatory Code for Third Party Funding which closed in December 2010. A summary of responses was published in June 2011.

The Code of Conduct for Litigation Funders was published by the Civil Justice **9.03**
Council Working Group on Third Party Funding in November 2011, and the
Association of Litigation Funders (ALF) was formed and charged with administering self-regulation of the industry in line with the Code. The Code sets out the
standards by which all full funder members of the ALF must abide, and meets each
of the key concerns set out by Lord Justice Jackson in his Civil Litigation Costs
Review.

The ALF is an independent body that has been charged by the Ministry of Justice, **9.04**
through the CJC, with delivering self-regulation of litigation funding in England
and Wales. The ALF was founded in November 2011, and its creation coincided
with the launch of the Code of Conduct. The creation of the ALF and the Code
of Conduct were approved by the CJC, the Master of the Rolls Lord Neuberger of
Abbotsbury, and Lord Justice Jackson.

1. Membership

The ALF has two types of member, the full membership of being a 'funder' member, **9.05**
and associate members. In order to be a funder member an applicant must be
doing business as a litigation funder within the jurisdiction of England and Wales.
Currently there are seven funder members of the ALF. In addition to the funder
members there are seven associate members. These members are funding brokers,
an overseas funder, a law firm, and academics.

An application for membership, or for associate membership, begins with the completion **9.06**
of a standard application form and the payment of a subscription and a
membership fee. There are some additional requirements for prospective funder
members to meet. In addition to the completed application form, those applicants
must also provide a copy of written evidence from a third party that they have
access to funds, and certify that they will maintain capital adequacy in line with
the provisions of the Code of Conduct.

Additionally, a prospective funder member is expected to provide a copy of their **9.07**
litigation funding agreement (LFA) to a barrister instructed by the ALF for the purposes
of review and consideration. That copy of the LFA remains confidential and is
not be disclosed to the members of the ALF board or anyone else. The barrister then
assesses independently whether the prospective funder member's LFA complies with
the requirements of the Code of Conduct and whether the applicant is suitable for
membership. The directors and board of the ALF do not intervene in that process.

2. Code of conduct

The original Code of Conduct ('Code') was published in November 2011. A revised **9.08**
version of the Code was published in January 2014 with a tightening of the ongoing
capital adequacy provisions and introduction of a complaints procedure.

a. Formalities

9.09 The first three clauses of the Code state the purpose of the Code, identify whom it governs, and provide the definition, for the purposes of the Code, of a litigation funder:

1. This code (the Code) sets out standards of practice and behaviour to be observed by Funders (as defined in clause 2 below) who are Members of The Association of Litigation Funders of England & Wales (the Association) in respect of funding the resolution of disputes within England and Wales.
2. A litigation funder:
   2.1 has access to funds immediately within its control, including within a corporate parent or subsidiary (Funder's Subsidiary); or
   2.2 acts as the exclusive investment advisor to an entity or entities having access to funds immediately within its or their control, including within a corporate parent or subsidiary (Associated Entity), (a Funder) in each case:
   2.3 to fund the resolution of disputes within England and Wales; and
   2.4 where the funds are invested pursuant to a Litigation Funding Agreement (LFA) to enable a party to a dispute (the Funded Party) to meet the costs (including pre-action costs) of resolving disputes by litigation, arbitration or other dispute resolution procedures.
   In return the Funder, Funder's Subsidiary or Associated Entity:
   2.5 receives a share of the proceeds if the claim is successful (as defined in the LFA); and
   2.6 does not seek any payment from the Funded Party in excess of the amount of the proceeds of the dispute that is being funded, unless the Funded Party is in material breach of the provisions of the LFA.
3. A Funder shall be deemed to have adopted the Code in respect of funding the resolution of disputes within England and Wales.

9.10 Thus the Code makes provision in respect of the conduct and practice of funder members of the ALF in England and Wales. A funder must have access to funds or be an adviser to an entity that does have access to funds for the purposes of investing in litigation and the resolution of disputes. The investment must be governed by way of a litigation funding agreement (an LFA) and such funds should be invested to meet the legal fees. Additionally, all funder members are deemed to have adopted the Code in relation to their funding of litigation in England and Wales.

9.11 An important safeguard is set out in clause 2.6 where it is made clear that unless a client has acted in material breach of the LFA then a litigation funder is not permitted to seek any payment from the client in excess of the proceeds of the dispute. In other words, a client who acts in accordance with the LFA should never end up in a situation where they owe money to the funder.

b. Subsidiaries and associated entities

9.12 There are some funders who operate their investment arrangements and structures so as to ensure that associated or subsidiary vehicles are used for certain investments. Some funders set up a special purpose vehicle for each investment they make. Whilst these funding vehicles are usually wholly owned (although not always) by a funder member of the ALF, the vehicle itself will not be a member. In a co-funding scenario where two or more funders jointly fund a piece of litigation it is possible that they may decide to use a specially incorporated entity to use for investing in the litigation, capitalized by their respective agreed investment. This vehicle would then contract with the client under the LFA and receive the proceeds of the litigation on its successful conclusion. Clauses 4 and 5 of the Code provide as follows:

> 4. A Funder shall accept responsibility to the Association for compliance with the Code by a Funder's Subsidiary or Associated Entity. By so doing a Funder shall not accept legal responsibility to a Funded Party, which shall be a matter governed, if at all, by the provisions of the LFA.
> 5. A Funder shall inform a Funded Party as soon as possible and prior to execution of an LFA:
>   5.1 if the Funder is acting for and/or on behalf of a Funder's Subsidiary or an Associated Entity in respect of funding the resolution of disputes within England & Wales; and
>   5.2 whether the LFA will be entered into by the Funder, a Funder's Subsidiary or an Associated Entity.

9.13 It is possible, depending upon the specific funder's structure, that the funder member of the ALF never actually invests in litigation; for example with a fund structure the investment adviser may be the funder member and the fund itself may not.

9.14 Clauses 4 and 5 deal with these situations so as to ensure that the client is aware of the arrangements, and in particular clause 4 means that the funder member of the ALF is expressly responsible for any subsidiaries or associates for the purposes of the ALF and the Code, but not as regards the provisions of the LFA—that will be a matter of contract between the client and the funder.

9.15 The funder member is required to advise clients whether the LFA is to be between the client, a funder, or an associated or subsidiary entity. Additionally, the funder member must advise the client if they are acting on behalf of the associated or subsidiary entity. Clarity of the arrangement is key for the ALF and the client. One very simple reason for this is that complaints to the ALF can be made only in relation to the ALF's members. But for clauses 4 and 5 a funder may have been able to avoid any complaint by using a subsidiary structure.

9.16 Clause 14 provides that any breach by an associated entity or subsidiary of the funder member will be deemed to be a breach of the Code by the funder member themselves.

c. Conduct and control

9.17 Under the Code, funder members are prevented from exerting control over the litigation or from settlement negotiations and from causing the client's lawyers to act in breach of their professional duties. This is in line with the practice, in England & Wales, of keeping the roles of funders, litigants, and their lawyers separate. Because of their interest in the litigation, funders will wish to be kept informed of the progress of the case. Most litigation funders will also have considerable litigation experience. The interaction of the funders with the lawyers and the clients is often a benefit to the client and the legal team.

9.18 The first part of clause 9 deals with the issue of taking independent legal advice. Funder members are required to take reasonable steps to ensure that the clients they are funding have done so.

9.19 Clause 9.2 requires funders to ensure that they do nothing which may cause a client's lawyers to do anything which may breach their conduct rules, and additionally clause 9.3 requires that a funder will not seek to influence a member of the client's legal team to 'cede control' of the conduct of the case to the funder. Clauses 9.1–9.3 of the Code are in the following terms:

> 9. A Funder will:
> 9.1 take reasonable steps to ensure that the Funded Party shall have received independent advice on the terms of the LFA prior to its execution, which obligation shall be satisfied if the Funded Party confirms in writing to the Funder that the Funded Party has taken advice from the solicitor or barrister instructed in the dispute;
> 9.2 not take any steps that cause or are likely to cause the Funded Party's solicitor or barrister to act in breach of their professional duties;
> 9.3 not seek to influence the Funded Party's solicitor or barrister to cede control or conduct of the dispute to the Funder...

d. Capital adequacy of funders

9.20 Clause 9.4 of the Code deals with the issue of capital adequacy and requires funders to maintain adequate financial resources at all times in order to meet their obligations to fund all of the cases they have agreed to invest in. Additionally, funders are required to maintain an ongoing review of their ability to be able to cover their aggregate funding liabilities under all of their funding agreements for a minimum period of 36 months and to maintain access to a minimum of £2m of capital.

> A funder will:
> 9.4 Maintain at all times access to adequate financial resources to meet the obligations of the Funder, its Funder Subsidiaries and Associated Entities to fund all the disputes that they have agreed to fund and in particular will;
> 9.4.1 ensure that the Funder, its Funder Subsidiaries and Associated Entities maintain the capacity;
> 9.4.1.1. to pay all debts when they become due and payable; and
> 9.4.1.2. to cover aggregate funding liabilities under all of their LFAs for a minimum period of 36 months.
> 9.4.2 maintain access to a minimum of £2m of capital or such other amount as stipulated by the Association;
> 9.4.3 accept a continuous disclosure obligation in respect of its capital adequacy, including a specific obligation to notify timeously the

Association and the Funded Party if the Funder reasonably believes that its representations in respect of capital adequacy under the Code are no longer valid because of changed circumstances;

9.4.4 undertake that it will be audited annually by a recognised national or international audit firm and shall provide the Association with:

9.4.4.1. a copy of the audit opinion given by the audit firm on the Funder's or Funder's Subsidiary's most recent annual financial statements (but not the underlying financial statements), or in the case of Funders who are investment advisors to an Associated Entity, the audit opinion given by the audit firm in respect of the Associated Entity (but not the underlying financial statements), within one month of receipt of the opinion and in any case within six months of each fiscal year end. If the audit opinion provided is qualified (except as to any emphasis of matters relating to the uncertainty of valuing relevant litigation funding investments) or expresses any question as to the ability of the firm to continue as a going concern, the Association shall be entitled to enquire further into the qualification expressed and take any further action it deems appropriate; and

9.4.4.2. reasonable evidence from a qualified third party (preferably from an auditor, but alternatively from a third party administrator or bank) that the Funder or Funder's Subsidiary or Associated Entity satisfies the minimum capital requirement prevailing at the time of annual subscription.

9.5 comply with the Rules of the Association as to capital adequacy as amended from time to time.

9.21 Funders are required to maintain an ongoing review of their ability to be able to cover their aggregate funding liabilities under all of their funding agreements for a minimum period of 36 months and to maintain access to a minimum of £2m of capital. The Code deals with a need for and general provision as regards solvency at clause 9.4.1. This is obviously a fundamental point for any litigation funder. Any lack of funds is a serious and basic problem. Clause 9.4.2 stipulates the need to have access to a minimum of £2m. That is not a large sum in the litigation funding world when the majority of the funder member litigation funders operate with capital of more than £30m under management. However, it is a large enough figure to ensure that those litigation funders who join the ALF are serious and well capitalized litigation funders. It will no doubt increase over time.

9.22 Additionally there is a requirement for the funder to be able to cover any liabilities under the terms upon which the funder has invested in any case or where they have undertaken to provide financial assistance, for a period of 36 months. This is a rolling period of 36 months as is evident from other requirements of capital adequacy referred to later in the Code; in other words funders must always be able to meet their aggregate funding liabilities for a future period of 36 months rather than a once a year snapshot confirmation of the position which might allow a funder to be compliant at the time of confirmation but not continuously throughout the year.

9.23 By clause 9.4.3 the funder is required to accept an ongoing duty of disclosure in relation to the capital adequacy provisions of the Code. This represents a change from provisions of the initial Code having been included in the revised version of January 2014. This change is designed to emphasize that it is not sufficient for a funder merely to comply with the capital adequacy provisions at any point in the year on an annual basis, but not throughout the year. There is a specific obligation on funders to make a swift notification to the ALF if their financial position changes to prevent certification of capital adequacy for whatever reason.

9.24 Clause 9.4.4 is extremely important for funders and the ALF from the perspective of transparency and credibility. It is the requirement on the part of the funders to ensure they are audited annually by a recognized national audit firm and that evidence is provided by a third party as to the £2m minimum capital requirement.

e. Other costs

9.25 The funder member must provide clarity as to what is being paid for and what is not:

> 10. The LFA shall state whether (and if so to what extent) the Funder or Funder's Subsidiary or Associated Party is liable to the Funded Party to:
> 10.1 meet any liability for adverse costs;
> 10.2 pay any premium (including insurance premium tax) to obtain costs insurance;
> 10.3 provide security for costs; and
> 10.4 meet any other financial liability

Clause 10 requires an express reference in an LFA as to whether the funder is meeting adverse costs or any ATE premium and to what extent if so. The funder is also required to confirm if they are providing security for costs or any other financial liability.

f. Termination and approval of settlements

9.26 Provision for the funder's termination and approval of settlements is contained in clauses 11 to 13 of the Code:

> 11. The LFA shall state whether (and if so how) the Funder or Funder's Subsidiary or Associated Entity may:
> 11.1 provide input to the Funder Party's decisions in relation to settlements;
> 11.2 terminate the LFA in the event that the Funder or Funder's Subsidiary or Associated Entity:
> 11.2.1 reasonably ceases to be satisfied about the merits of the dispute;
> 11.2.2 reasonably believes that the dispute is no longer commercially viable; or
> 11.2.3 reasonably believes that there has been a material breach of the LFA by the Funded Party.
> 12. The LFA shall not establish a discretionary right for a Funder or Funder's Subsidiary or Associated Party to terminate a LFA in the absence of the circumstances described in clause 11.2.

13. If the LFA does give the Funder or Funder's Subsidiary or Associated Entity any of the rights described in clause 11, the LFA shall provide that:
   13.1 if the Funder or Funder's Subsidiary or Associated Entity terminates the LFA, the Funder or Funder's Subsidiary or Associated Entity shall remain liable for all funding obligations accrued to the date of termination unless the termination is due to a material breach under clause 11.2.3.

9.27 The Code provides that funders must behave reasonably and may only withdraw from funding in specific circumstances. The funder member's LFA may only allow provision for withdrawal in those situations. The reason behind this is that it is very important for a client to know that subject to their case retaining the good prospects of success that persuaded the funder to enter into the LFA, the case will remain funded through to its conclusion.

9.28 The three bases for termination are set out in clause 11.2. The first is where, reasonably, the funder ceases to remain satisfied over the merits of the case. In other words the case has deteriorated as it has continued. The number of reasons for such a possibility are without limit. They will include many familiar circumstances that will arise in the course of litigation: experts' reports do not achieve what had been expected; evidence that was anticipated to be available is not in fact forthcoming; a major witness upon whom much reliance had been placed is shown to be unreliable; documents which undermine the case are revealed by another party upon disclosure. In these circumstances a reassessment of the merits of the case results in a conclusion that it does not have sufficient prospects of success to justify continuing with it. For a case in which the problem of unfavourable reassessment was considered, see the discussion of *Harcus Sinclair v Buttonwood Legal Capital* in Chapter 2.[1]

9.29 The second situation in which the Code permits a right of termination to a funder is where the funder reasonably believes that the dispute is no longer commercially viable. A funder might wish the provision to be interpreted to mean that no reasonable person in the funder's position would continue to spend money on the litigation. This will occur where the anticipated quantum of an anticipated award, or the prospect of its being successfully enforced, has reduced substantially to the point that a funder would not judge that any potential reward, or prospect of it, to merit increasing capital exposure. The difficulty for a funder in this situation is that whilst it might not be commercially attractive for a funder to continue in some circumstances, it does not necessarily mean that a client who was privately paying would refrain from funding the case further. Of course, this is one reason for the dispute resolution provision in clause 13—it may be that this is the most likely area for disagreement. The inclusion of the dispute resolution mechanism does not, however, resolve the difficult question of the perspective from which commercial

---

[1] *Harcus Sinclair (a Firm) v Buttonwood Legal Capital Limited & Ors* [2013] EWHC 1193 (Ch).

viability is to be judged. That question is a matter of law. The author's view is that commercial viability is to be judged from the point of view of a reasonable and prudent person, with adequate resources to pursue the claim, standing in the shoes of the litigant. This is because it is the litigant's case that is being funded, and the purpose of the LFA is to fund that case. Business and financial considerations that might be peculiar to the funder, and which are extraneous to the case itself, should not affect the assessment. Any other interpretation might enable a funder to introduce as a relevant consideration, for example, a change in its circumstances. It is, however, necessary to introduce an objective yardstick for judging commercial viability, hence the suggested attribution to the litigant of the qualities of reasonableness and prudence.

9.30 The third basis for termination is where the funder reasonably believes that the client has committed a material breach of the LFA. This provision is less stringent, from the funder's perspective, than that applicable in most commercial contracts in which the 'innocent' party can terminate upon the other's repudiatory breach, generally understood to be a breach which has the effect of depriving the 'innocent' party of substantially the whole benefit which it was the intention of the parties that he should obtain from the contract.[2] 'Material breach' suggests something less fundamental than this. On the other hand, from the litigant's perspective, the provision is less rigorous than that in most insurance contracts, where an insurer is entitled to avoid a policy for the insured's non-disclosure of any matter which might have influenced the judgment of a prudent insurer in accepting the risk or fixing the premium.[3]

9.31 In the cases of all termination rights, however, it is to be noted that the funder's right is subject to his establishing a view, or belief, which is reasonable, whether as to a change in the merits, commercial viability, or breach. This gives rise to several observations. First, in relation to matters of a reasonable state of mind, views may differ among reasonable people. Thus the fact that not every funder would form the same pessimistic view of a case, does not mean that a particular funder's view is unreasonable. Secondly, the burden of proof will be upon the funder to demonstrate that there are objectively reasonable grounds for the state of mind relied upon. It will not suffice for the funder to demonstrate that he has complete conviction in his reassessment of the case, or the lack of commercial viability, unless he can also establish that there are grounds which reasonably cause that state of mind to exist. He will also need to demonstrate that he genuinely does have that state of mind; the mere presence of reasonable grounds for such a state of mind will not suffice if the funder does not genuinely share that view. Thirdly, as to termination for a material breach, the issue is whether the funder reasonably

---

[2] See *Photo Production Ltd v Securicor Transport Ltd* [1980] AC 827, HL, especially *per* Lord Diplock at page 849DE–.
[3] See the discussion in *Colinvaux's Law of Insurance*, 9th edition, chapter 6.

believes that there has been such a breach. Thus if the funder has on such grounds formed that view, he is entitled to terminate, even if the litigant has not, in fact, committed such a breach.

Clause 12 provides that an LFA cannot give the funder any discretionary right to terminate the LFA save for the three scenarios described. Clause 13 sets out the obligations on termination in the three situations. If the funder terminates the agreement then they remain liable for all funding obligations to that point, unless the termination is in consequence of a material breach by the client. **9.32**

In relation to settlements, clause 11.1 says that a funder must state in the LFA whether they are able to provide input into the settlement decision making. In practice whilst many funders would want to be involved in and be able to influence the settlement discussions, the reality is that the clients will always want to retain ultimate control and decision making. This area is a very sensitive subject for the lawyers, the clients, and the funders. **9.33**

The settlement discussions will often include input from the ATE insurer, if there is one. It would be most unusual if the ATE policy did not require that settlement offers be notified to the ATE provider. Often the ATE insurer will be represented at settlement meetings or mediation. At the very least they will be available by telephone. **9.34**

The result is that once a settlement offer is made at a sensible level, the decision to continue with a case or not and accept the offer can be heavily influenced by the ATE insurers' appetite for continuing to cover the risk. They will be guided by the lawyers but will of course have their own independent view of things, and their own contractual rights in respect of termination. **9.35**

g. Dispute resolution

Where there is a dispute about termination or settlement, a binding opinion must be obtained from an independent QC, who has been either instructed jointly or appointed by the Bar Council. Clause 13.2 makes this provision. **9.36**

> 13.2 if there is a dispute between the Funder, Funder's Subsidiary or Associated Entity and the Funded Party about settlement or about termination of the LFA, a binding opinion shall be obtained from a Queen's Counsel who shall be instructed jointly or nominated by the Chairman of the Bar Council.

The independent opinion may be on the prospects or the commercial viability of funding or material breach by the litigant. However, it may be that there is a significant difference of opinion as to whether a case should be settled or not. The client and the funder may have different views and the independent opinion may be needed to decide upon a course of action. Of course, there are limits to the help that this opinion could provide if the decision must be made quickly. **9.37**

h. Complaints

9.38 A new addition to the Code[4] is the complaints procedure.

> 15. The Association shall maintain a complaints procedure. A Funder consents to the complaints procedure as it may be varied from time to time in respect of any relevant act or omission by the Funder, Funder's Subsidiary or Associated Entity.

9.39 As stated earlier one of the reasons to ensure that the client knows whether or not a funder is acting on behalf of a subsidiary and ensuring that the funder is responsible to the ALF for the actions of a subsidiary or associate is so that a complaint can be made against the funder using the ALF complaints procedure.

9.40 The full complaints procedure is set out in Appendix 3. The initial complaint is reviewed by the ALF General Counsel to ensure it is a complaint that complies with the terms of reference of the ALF complaints procedure; for example, obviously, that the complaint relates to a member of the ALF. The complaint is then reviewed to assess if it discloses a potential breach of the Code by a member. If so a preliminary report is prepared for the board of directors of the ALF.

9.41 If the preliminary report fails to disclose a breach or potential breach by the member then it can be summarily dismissed. If it does disclose grounds for investigation then General Counsel will seek a formal response from the funder member. Ultimately the matter may be referred to an outside independent counsel for investigation and determination.

9.42 The sanctions available to the ALF if a complaint against a member is upheld are:

(i) a private warning (including where appropriate recommendations as to future practice);
(ii) a public warning (including where appropriate recommendations as to future practice);
(iii) publication of the Opinion (subject to any redactions which Independent Legal Counsel shall identify in order to ensure that no matter confidential to the parties is disclosed);
(iv) suspension of membership of the ALF for any identified period of time;
(v) expulsion from membership of the ALF;
(vi) the imposition of a fine payable by the Member to the ALF, up to a limit of £500;
(vii) the payment of all or any of the costs of determining the Complaint.

C. Solicitors

9.43 Although litigation funding is a relatively new industry, the relevant obligations upon solicitors are not at all new. Solicitors' duties in relation to the funding of litigation

---

[4] Updated January 2014.

and the explanation of the options available have been well known for many years. However, the practice of giving such advice has been very much improved over the last few years, particularly since the more regular use of ATE insurance and as the legal profession has become more aware that there are a number of options and retainers available for clients.

9.44 Solicitors need to be aware of the risks that they face. There are many parallels to be drawn as to what is required of solicitors in relation to ATE and litigation funding. In Chapter 5 when the process of litigation funding was examined, the rise of the litigation funding broker from the ashes of the post-Jackson volume ATE world was discussed. One of the suggested explanations for the rise of the use of litigation funding brokers is the concern on the part of solicitors that they do not know enough about the litigation funding market to be able to give good advice on matters including which funder to use, the benefits of using a funder who is a member of the ALF, and usual or appropriate terms for a particular litigation funding arrangement.

9.45 Quite properly, some solicitors do not feel it appropriate for them to advise on such matters as they do not have the necessary market knowledge and information. They use a broker who is well versed in the process and up to date with what each of the professional and mainstream funders is looking for at that particular time. Other solicitors are themselves experienced in litigation funding and quite prepared to give the necessary advice to clients.

9.46 The key difference, as it is in the ATE environment, is that the broker is giving advice and making an 'advised sale', thus taking on the responsibility to give the most appropriate and best advice to the client where possible. This was the same scenario some years ago when solicitors were faced with a new set of issues in having to advise clients over which ATE policy they should purchase. The brokers took away the difficulty for a solicitor by conducting the whole process and giving the necessary advice.

9.47 In reality, in the same way that solicitors did not act as insurance brokers after the changes brought about by the Access to Justice Act,[5] (with regard to recovery of ATE premiums) they do not need to be funding brokers, fund managers, or investment bankers in the litigation funding era. They do not need to understand the mechanisms behind the pricing of a litigation funding deal or to be familiar with every funder in the marketplace, although to do so would make their position very much easier. They simply have to advise on the availability of funding and, when offered, what the effect of the terms is, especially where they might be obviously outrageous or lacking in commerciality. The commercial bargain is for the clients to agree. Equally, as is evident from the professional obligation placed upon litigation funders by the Code, funders are not allowed to do anything which would cause a solicitor to breach any professional obligation. During the case the funders,

---

[5] Access to Justice Act 1999.

clients, and solicitors are on the same side, though there may be differences of view as to extensions of budgets, or the wisdom of settlement. The difficult time in the relationship is when the terms are being negotiated.

9.48 In all relationships there are situations where there is potential for conflict. This part of the chapter considers what solicitors should advise upon at the outset of a piece of litigation, and the need for full disclosure of the details of the case, good and bad. The client must be advised about all of their options, they should also be given advice upon the terms of the LFA and their effect. Additionally there are issues that have arisen over the years since the use of ATE insurance began and there may be lessons to learn from the mistakes made in dealing with an application for ATE insurance.

1. Conduct rules

9.49 In 2007, the Solicitors' Code of Conduct made reference to a number of matters which it was incumbent upon a solicitor to discuss with their client when advising them before they embarked upon a piece of litigation.

9.50 Rule 2.03 covered the areas of costs information that should be given to a client. The basic information required to be provided was much as is to be anticipated and would have formed the basis of what prior to that would have been called a 'Client Care' or 'Rule 15'[6] letter.

9.51 The new element introduced in the 2007 Code of Conduct is the necessity to advise a client about the potential for adverse costs being incurred and the possibility that someone other than the client might pay their fees. The funding of the case is something specifically mentioned at Rule 2.03(d)(ii). Whilst in 2007 third party litigation funding was very much a niche area with little or no profile in the litigation market, the need to advise of the availability of alternative funding was a conduct issue.

9.52 However, Rule 2.03 (g) was the more obvious rule to consider. From 1999 there was a significant rise in the use of ATE. By 2007 it was most unusual for a litigator not to discuss the use of ATE insurance with a client. This rule made any lack of discussion and a failure to advise a conduct issue for solicitors:

> 2.03 Information about the cost
>
>> (1) You must give your client the best information possible about the likely overall cost of a matter both at the outset and, when appropriate, as the matter progresses. In particular you must:
>> (a) advise the client of the basis and terms of your charges;
>> (b) advise the client if charging rates are to be increased;

---

[6] Referring to the previous incarnation of the conduct rules, being the Guide to Professional Conduct of Solicitors last printed in 1999. Rule 15 dealt with client care and costs information.

(c) advise the client of likely payments which you or your client may need to make to others;
(d) discuss with the client how the client will pay, in particular:
   (i) whether the client may be eligible and should apply for public funding; and
   (ii) whether the client's own costs are covered by insurance or may be paid by someone else such as an employer or trade union;
(e) advise the client that there are circumstances where you may be entitled to exercise a lien for unpaid costs;
(f) advise the client of their potential liability for any other party's costs; and
(g) discuss with the client whether their liability for another party's costs may be covered by existing insurance or whether specially purchased insurance may be obtained.

9.53 In the SRA Code of Conduct 2011, there is a change in the composition of the way that the rules are explained with a shift to 'indicative behaviours' which show supposedly that the solicitor has achieved the necessary outcomes and therefore complied with the Principles[7] of the SRA Handbook. The SRA Code, '*forms part of the Handbook, in which the 10 mandatory Principles are all-pervasive*'.[8]

9.54 The outcomes that seem the most relevant to the issue of fees and litigation funding are O(1.12) and O(1.13). The solicitor must achieve these outcomes:

O(1.12) clients are in a position to make informed decisions about the services they need, how their matter will be handled and the options available to them;

O(1.13) clients receive the best possible information, both at the time of engagement and when appropriate as their matter progresses, about the likely overall cost of their matter...

---

[7] SRA Code of Coduct 2011:
The Principles
You must:
1. uphold the rule of law and the proper administration of justice;
2. act with integrity;
3. not allow your independence to be compromised;
4. act in the best interests of each client;
5. provide a proper standard of service to your clients;
6. behave in a way that maintains the trust the public places in you and in the provision of legal services;
7. comply with your legal and regulatory obligations and deal with your regulators and ombudsmen in an open, timely and co-operative manner;
8. run your business or carry out your role in the business effectively and in accordance with proper governance and sound financial and risk management principles;
9. run your business or carry out your role in the business in a way that encourages equality of opportunity and respect for diversity; and
10. protect client money and assets.

[8] SRA Code of Conduct 2011, Introduction to the SRA Code of Conduct.

9.55 For a solicitor to show that these are the outcomes that they have achieved their indicative behaviour is appropriately set out in IB(1.13) and IB(1.16).

> IB(1.13) discussing whether the potential outcomes of the client's matter are likely to justify the expense or risk involved, including any risk of having to pay someone else's legal fees;
>
> IB(1.16) discussing how the client will pay, including whether public funding may be available, whether the client has insurance that might cover the fees, and whether the fees may be paid by someone else such as a trade union...

9.56 These indicative behaviours show a significant resemblance to the 2007 Code of Conduct. In order for a client to make informed decisions they need to have all of the information available to them about their case and the proposed steps to be taken, along with the likely costs involved. The client then needs to understand what the risks are including whether there is a chance that they might have to pay the opponent's costs and how that risk might be mitigated with some form of ATE.

9.57 The wording may be slightly different as is the newer SRA approach to the Code of Conduct, but the message is still clear. Solicitors are required to advise clients as to the availability of ATE insurance and litigation funding, and any other alternative method of funding their litigation. This means that it is a matter of professional conduct for any solicitor who does not advise their client as to the availability of litigation funding.

2. Solicitors' duties

9.58 Solicitors' duties to clients, under their contractual retainer, regarding the clients' funding options seem to fall into three categories. First, there is the duty to advise on the various funding options that may be available to fund the client's particular piece of litigation. This includes the use of litigation funding and the use of ATE insurance and is clearly set out in the previous section dealing with the obligation under the SRA Code of Conduct.

9.59 This duty does not necessarily extend to the giving of advice on the most appropriate method of funding a particular case, namely the recommendation of one funder over another, or the best available terms for funding and ATE insurance. But it would extend to providing the client with all of the information, at least as to their existence, on those options for them to be able to make their own decision.

9.60 This might go so far as to ensure that a client was aware of the ALF Code of Conduct and the benefits to a client of working with a funder member and recommending the necessity for research into a litigation funder's credentials and capital adequacy; if, with that solicitor, the instruction proceeds to the point where funding is considered, the duty would, it is the author's view, extend as far as mentioned.

9.61 It must, however, be remembered that a solicitor, though under a duty to mention options, has no duty to hold himself out as willing to undertake work on the basis of anything other than an entirely traditional retainer. Some solicitors will not wish to work with funders, or on even partial CFAs, for the perfectly good reason that they may not be willing to accept the constraints of funder's budgets, or rates, or payment timeframes. A solicitor is entitled to explain briefly that funding might be available for the case, but if the client wishes to pursue that possibility, then it would not be available with that solicitor. Clearly, if the client wishes to pursue funding options, in those circumstances, any retainer, if already in existence, is likely to come to an end, so any further duties will not arise thereunder. The remaining duties discussed below will arise on the assumption that the client proceeds, and together with the solicitor considers funding options.

9.62 Secondly, there is general duty on the part of the solicitor to give advice to ensure that the client understands the terms of the retainer, the obligations on the client, and what those obligations mean and their effect.

9.63 Lastly, there is a duty to ensure the client appreciates the terms of the other funding arrangements they have decided to use. For example, the deduction of a deferred or contingent ATE premium from damages in a successful case and the effect of any LFA at particular levels of settlement value so the client understands the net recovery that they are likely to receive in those different scenarios.

9.64 Potentially, there are separate duties which solicitors should consider and those are to the funder or the ATE insurer rather than the client. Whilst ATE insurers and litigation funders use their own methods for assessment of the merits of a particular case, they can work only with the information provided to them in most circumstances. The principle of '*uberrimai fidei*' applies to insurance and the contractual arrangements with a litigation funder will require a warranty that the client and their lawyers have provided all of the relevant material for review.

9.65 A solicitor will need to explain to his client that a funder is likely to want to be able to speak frankly to the solicitor about the case as it develops, so that the client will need to accept that the solicitor can do so freely from time to time. This should be recorded in writing.

a. Funding options

9.66 Since the use of CFAs and ATE insurance became a regular method of funding litigation there has been a detailed examination of solicitors' duties to their clients as regards funding options. The majority of these cases relate to the early challenges and skirmishes of the so-called 'costs war' of the size of a reasonable ATE premium and the compliance by solicitors with the then CFA regulations.

9.67 The case of *Sarwar v Alam*[9] concerned the issue of 'before the event' (BTE) insurance and what advice should be given by solicitors at the outset of a case. It set out the 'proper modern practice'[10] in this regard when solicitors are advising about funding possibilities. This was then considered in the appeals heard together in *Myatt* and *Garrett*.[11] Both cases were personal injury matters run by solicitors under a CFA with ATE insurance policies.

9.68 The appeals related to the enforceability of CFAs entered into prior to November 2005. A less prescriptive approach was described in *Myatt* as regards the checklist of matters to be considered by solicitors in advising clients prior to entering into a CFA and taking out ATE insurance, although the court declined to set down rigid guidelines suggesting solicitors should do what is 'reasonable' in the circumstances, which will include the nature of the client.

9.69 In *Garrett*, the issue related to the allegation of non-disclosure by the acting solicitors of their interest in the purchase of a particular ATE policy by the client. The solicitors received referrals of personal injury work by virtue of their being on the panel of a particular claims management company (CMC). As a condition of panel membership, the solicitors were required to use a particular ATE policy sold by the CMC, for the cases referred. Whilst the solicitors did not receive a commission from the sale to the client of the ATE policy from the CMC, the court held them to have an interest in the policy as their continued panel membership relied upon their using that policy. This was not disclosed to the client. It was also noted that under the Solicitors' Financial Services (Conduct of Business) Rules 2001[12] the solicitor should have advised the client that he was contractually obliged to recommend the particular ATE policy.

9.70 Appendix 1 of the Rules[13] provides as follows:

> (b) Where a firm recommends a contract of insurance (other than a life policy) to a client, the firm must inform the client whether the firm has given advice on the basis of a fair analysis of a sufficiently large number of insurance contracts available on the market to enable the firm to make a recommendation in accordance with professional criteria regarding which contract of insurance would be adequate to meet the client's needs.
> (c) If the firm does not conduct a fair analysis of the market, the firm must:
>   (i) advise the client whether the firm is contractually obliged to conduct insurance mediation activities in this way;
>   (ii) advise the client that the client can request details of the insurance undertakings with which the firm conducts business; and provide the client with such details on request.

---

[9] *Sarwar v Alam* [2002] 1WLR.
[10] See *Sarwar* at [45–6].
[11] *Garrett v Holton Borough Council; Myatt v National Coal Board* [2007] 1 WLR 554.
[12] Now the SRA Financial Services (Conduct of Business) Rules 2001.
[13] SRA Financial Services (Conduct of Business) Rules 2001.

Professional Obligations

Whilst *Myatt* and *Garrett* are cases that were more relevant some years ago due to the nature of the specific retainer based arguments, *Garrett* in particular demonstrates the pitfalls that solicitors may encounter but also it demonstrates exactly why some solicitors are concerned about the prospect of recommending an ATE policy to their client. Whilst solicitors do not need to be experts in ATE insurance they do need to have done more than simply recommend the first policy they come across. Hence, why many solicitors use an ATE broker or obtain several quotes for ATE to protect themselves.

9.71

There is an important parallel to be drawn between ATE and litigation funding generally through these cases and the general duties owed by solicitors across these areas. What is clear from the case law and from the SRA Code of Conduct is the solicitors' general duty to advise on the availability of the ATE and litigation funding.

9.72

Solicitors who fail to advise clients on the availability of ATE insurance may undoubtedly face allegations of negligence. The lack of advice on ATE and the failure to procure an ATE policy was considered in two recent cases. In *Adris*,[14] the failure of the solicitors to obtain ATE insurance (significantly despite the solicitors' literature suggesting that insurance would be arranged) was found to amount to a gross breach of their duty to the clients and rendered the solicitors liable to a non-party costs order. In *Heron*,[15] the solicitors' failure did not.

9.73

In *Adris*, a non-party costs order was made against the solicitors firm who had been acting for the claimants in consumer credit claims. The cases had been referred by a claims management company. The solicitors had received substantial funding from the claims management company to run the cases on a CFA for the clients. The clients were not advised about ATE and it was not put in place, despite the literature which suggested that it would be. The failure to advise on the absence of ATE and the lack of ATE cover itself rendered the solicitors liable for the adverse costs. The key was that the litigation would not have commenced had the clients been aware of their potential liability for the defendant's adverse costs or had they been advised that the failure to place an ATE policy on risk would leave the clients with that potential costs exposure. As a result of the solicitors' negligence, costs were incurred by the defendant in fighting the case.

9.74

In *Heron*, the appeal by the insurers of a defendant in a personal injury action was dismissed by the Court of Appeal and the insurers' application for a non-party costs order against the solicitors acting for the claimant failed. The solicitors' alleged failure to act properly for the claimant, in failing to ensure that ATE was

9.75

---

[14] *Adris and others v RBS and others* [2010] EWHC 941.
[15] *Heron v TNT (UK) Limited* [2013] EWCA Civ 469.

obtained, had not demonstrated that the solicitors had become the 'real party' to the litigation so as to justify the order sought. If that was the case, then every act of negligence by a solicitor in the conduct of litigation which meant that an opposing party incurred costs which might not otherwise have been incurred would be sufficient for a non-party costs order.

9.76 The case of *Adris* was distinguished. In that case the judge had considered that the clients would not have proceeded with the litigation without ATE. That was not the case here. Leveson LJ distinguished *Adris* by reference to the solicitors' literature in that case suggesting that insurance would be in place, and said that this was a 'fact-sensitive jurisdiction'. Accordingly, a solicitor's failure to obtain ATE cover would not have impact on the other side's costs unless it were shown that the costs would not have been incurred.

9.77 It was concluded that a professional negligence claim (rather than an application for a non-party costs order) brought by the client would be the appropriate forum to determine the extent to which the solicitors were liable to compensate the client in relation to any costs that may have to be paid to the defendant.

b. Terms and effect of the retainer

9.78 The duty upon a solicitor to explain the nature of the retainer and its effect before entering into the arrangement with the client is set out in the Australian case of *McNamara*.[16] This case raised the issue of whether or not there is a duty upon a solicitor to explain to a prospective client the meaning and practical effect of the proposed retainer that has been offered by the solicitor and if there was such a duty, the extent of that duty. It was decided that the fiduciary duty owed by a solicitor to a client does not commence when the retainer is signed but when the negotiations over the retainer begin. A solicitor has an affirmative duty of disclosure to the client over matters which are relevant to the retainer.

9.79 This case concerned the provisions in the retainer that allowed the solicitors to charge above the usual scale rates for the work in question. They were not told that the hourly rate of charging bore no reference to the experience or seniority of the solicitor; they were not told that the hourly rate of charging did not vary according to the task performed, or the level of skill called for.

9.80 Doyle CJ noted, 'it is the solicitor's duty to provide the client with adequate information and advice. In the present case no advice was given at all about the agreement. There are aspects of the agreement that called for explanation and advice.'[17] He continued, 'I consider that the failure of . . . to provide any explanation or advice to the Kasmeridis leads to the conclusion that the agreement was not fair. It leads to

---

[16] *McNamara Business & Property Law v Kasmeridis* (2007) 97 SASR 129.
[17] See *McNamara* at [43].

that conclusion because the Court cannot be satisfied, having regard to the terms of the agreement, that the Kasmeridis understood the operation and effect of the agreement.'[18]

c. Terms and effect of funding

Clients are required to understand and agree the terms of the retainer they are entering into with their solicitors. Equally, in terms of third party litigation funding and the provisions of an LFA, solicitors have a duty to give an explanation of the differing scenarios under the LFA. This includes the terms and their impact upon the net recovery of damages received by the client. It is often useful to ensure that worked examples of different quantum values at different conclusions to the case are agreed with the litigation funder and explained to the client. This is particularly useful for clients if the agreed terms with the funder are staged over time or using staged facilities. 9.81

d. Potential duty to funders and insurers

Solicitors will owe a duty to their clients rather than an ATE insurer or a funder. There are potentially conflicting duties which would make it difficult for a solicitor to owe a duty to both client and funder or insurer. However, most litigation funders will look to impose contractual duties in an LFA which bind the solicitors. Where it is an express, or implied, term of the solicitors' retainer that they are to be permitted to deal with funders in a way that might otherwise amount to a breach of duty, for example by expressing frank views on the case, or passing on confidential information, there will be no breach of fiduciary duty, because the fiduciary duty to avoid conflict has accommodated itself to the terms of the retainer by reference to which it operates; see *Kelly v Cooper* [1993] AC 205, PC. 9.82

Litigation funders review, assess, and conduct due diligence on the cases they consider for funding. If they require legal advice on matters they seek legal advice from their own lawyers. In order to obtain that advice the litigation funder will require all of the relevant pleading, papers, and documentation available to be able to present to the funders' own lawyers, and for their own assessment. 9.83

On occasions counsel who is instructed by the client may prepare an opinion on the merits of cases for use by the funders. In that situation the duty would be clear. 9.84

In a case involving an ATE insurer, the Court of Appeal considered whether their solicitors and counsel had a duty to the ATE insurer. The case of *Greene Wood McLean LLP v Templeton Insurance*[19] related to a failed application for a Group Litigation Order, the consequences of which were that all of the claimants in the 9.85

---

[18] See *McNamara* at [47].
[19] *Greene Wood McLean LLP (In Administration) v Templeton Insurance Limited* [2010] EWHC 279, [2011] Lloyd's Rep IR 557.

action were left with exposure to adverse costs. They had an ATE policy but the ATE provider declared the policy void and refused to pay. The allegation was that the lawyers had been negligent. The court found that the ATE insurers were responsible for paying under the terms of the policy and found that the lawyers were not negligent.

9.86 It was alleged by the ATE insurer that the solicitors had a direct and proximate relationship with the ATE insurer,

> ...by reason of their appointment as Appointed Representative of the insured miners, because Templeton necessarily relied upon GWM to advise upon and conduct the proceedings and because the foreseeable consequence of a failure by GWM to observe the terms of the policy and/or to advise upon or conduct the proceedings with care and skill was that the defendant might be exposed to a liability to indemnify the insured in respect of adverse costs and Own Disbursements which it would otherwise not have incurred. Much the same points are made in alleging a duty on Counsel to advise not only the GLO Applicants but also Templeton upon the form and nature of any proposed proceedings which were to be the subject of a ATE insurance, to advise upon and conduct such proceedings with the skill and care to be expected of reasonably competent Counsel and, if any matters arose that materially affected the prospects of success of the GLO application, to advise of that and as to the prospects of success of the proposed application.[20]

9.87 In these circumstances, if the solicitors were to have owed the duties to the ATE insurer which were claimed, the solicitors could find themselves with a conflict of interest. The court found that there was no duty of care owed by the solicitor or counsel, to the ATE insurer in these circumstances saying, 'It could not be just and reasonable to impose such a duty in such circumstances with the possibility of creating a conflict of interest...'[21]

9.88 Whilst solicitors will have contractual obligations under both an ATE policy and an LFA, their primary duty will be to their client. Under the terms of the LFA the litigation funder discharges the client's legal fees on the client's behalf, in return for a share of the client's damages.

9.89 If the case is dealt with negligently thus causing the client to lose the case, for example a strike-out for missing a deadline, there may be a number of consequences. First, the defendant will seek costs from the client. Ordinarily, on a loss, the ATE insurer would meet the costs order. But if the order was brought about by negligence on the part of the solicitors then they may object to payment. There is very often a term in the ATE policy to this effect. In this case the client remains liable, but will seek reimbursement from the solicitor. The client

---

[20] *Greene Wood McLean LLP (In Administration) v Templeton Insurance Limited* [2010] EWHC 279, [2011] Lloyd's Rep IR 557 at [96].
[21] *Greene Wood McLean LLP (In Administration) v Templeton Insurance Limited* [2010] EWHC 279, [2011] Lloyd's Rep IR 557 at [112].

would thereafter seek damages for loss of opportunity against the negligent solicitors.

In a funded case, the defendant is likely to seek the costs from the litigation funder rather than the client following the principle in *Arkin*.[22] In the usual situation of a non-funded case a client may be reimbursed wasted expenditure on legal fees by way of part of the damages upon a claim against the negligent solicitors. In a funded case the clients will not have paid any legal fees. The litigation funder however has lost not only the fees that have been paid to the solicitors on the client's behalf, but the funder has also lost the opportunity to recover a share in the substantial damages it had anticipated paying the lawyers successfully to recover. **9.90**

This is a situation where there will be a direct relationship between funder and solicitor. In some LFAs the funder, solicitors, counsel, and the client are party to the agreement. In other situations, the funder will ensure that the solicitor agrees that they owe a duty to the funder as well as the client. The LFA or associated document will require that the solicitors owe a contractual duty to the litigation funder to conduct the case with reasonable skill and care and in any event not to act negligently. **9.91**

D. Conclusion

The professional obligations of litigation funders and solicitors are developing continuously. **9.92**

The ALF is the body which is responsible for regulation of the litigation funding industry in England and Wales. After the calls for full independent regulation from some quarters, over the coming years the ALF will be scrutinized as to how effective it is at carrying out its mandate. The updated ALF Code[23] has added to the credibility of members of the ALF. As the organization grows in stature, it is hoped that membership will become the kite mark of reliability in the litigation funding world. **9.93**

The litigation funding industry has attracted interest, due to the potential for high returns, from a wide and varied background of investors. The obligations contained in the ALF Code and membership of the ALF allow solicitors and clients to use membership of the ALF as a simple and effective gauge as to a particular funder's credentials. **9.94**

From the perspective of solicitors, the SRA Code of Conduct sets out clear and unambiguous requirements for what advice should be given to clients. The need **9.95**

---

[22] *Arkin v Borchard Lines* [2005] EWCA Civ 655.
[23] In January 2014.

to advise clients as to all aspects of the funding opportunities available, what the likely costs may be, the risk of paying an opponent's costs, and the potential to insure the risk of paying adverse costs are all essential issues and the failure to advise on them is a matter of professional conduct.

9.96 Quite apart from the professional conduct requirements, solicitors involved in third party litigation funding arrangements will be bound by the contractual relationship they enter into with the litigation funder. These contractual duties to litigation funders should be considered alongside the professional obligations.

9.97 Whilst in some areas there is scope for a conflict to arise in the duties to clients and to the funder, in most situations the interests of both will be aligned.

10

FUNDING AND THE FUTURE

A. Introduction	10.01	D. ABS	10.47
B. Regulation and Self-Regulation	10.16	E. Jurisdictions	10.57
		F. Evolution	10.63
C. Education	10.32	G. Conclusion	10.67

A. Introduction

The third party litigation funding industry has grown significantly in the last three years and bears no resemblance at all to the fledgling litigation funding world of six or seven years ago. **10.01**

The ringing endorsement of litigation funding from Lord Justice Jackson in his *Review of Civil Litigation Costs Final Report*, and the subsequent formation of the ALF in England and Wales, were the first steps towards the litigation funding's industry moving into the mainstream of commercial litigation. Litigation funding has been termed a nascent industry for the last few years, but it has now evolved from that state of immaturity into an important part of the commercial litigation landscape. At the very least, litigation funding should be considered at the outset of any case by the professional advisers with their clients. **10.02**

The industry faces challenges from various quarters. The direct competition from lawyers looking to take more risk and offering different risk based retainers for their clients will continue. New structures for law firms, which allow external investment, may yet provide stiffer competition for the litigation funding world with the larger firms competing in this space against the mainstream funders. The law firm relationship with funders will continue to provide competition and collaboration, with law firms remaining as the main source of referral of work for the funders. **10.03**

Funding has now entered the everyday mainstream legal sphere for several reasons. However, these considerations are very much open to influence and **10.04** progress, and the market is changing. The first reason is the nature of the cases that funding is generally used with—funders need to expand the breadth of their available market. There is a narrow band of cases which funders are interested in. Given the very high risks inherent in litigation funding, most funders are still seeking to make a return which is three times, or greater, than their initial investment. For the main funders, the need for a wider pool to explore has seen a greater desire to invest internationally. Emerging markets include India (although not in the domestic courts), where a number of cases involve companies dealing in arbitration work. Along with India, there is set to be growth in Singapore, the Caribbean, the Channel Islands, and the US markets. A big factor in the size of growth rests in part on the second issue being faced by funding: that of education.

10.05 Whilst funding has entered the psyche of many lawyers, there is a far greater number of general counsel and litigators who have not yet grasped the concept. The attractions are many, not least providing risk transfer and the covering of the potential for downside costs exposure. Funding also provides an extra pair of eyes on cases, as contrary to opinion from critics—shockingly—funders will not back a case doomed for failure. With increasing demands, lawyers who are not aware or not passing on their awareness of funding to clients are perhaps not providing the best options available. Costs are always a talking point, and never more so than now.

10.06 But whilst the *Andrew Mitchell*[1] case has underlined how the Jackson reforms will be implemented with rigour by the courts, in reality, so far the reforms themselves seem to have had little effect on litigation funding. Some funders have looked at their product offering in an attempt to assist firms that want to use DBAs, but the appetite for DBAs does not seem to be large.

10.07 Even in those cases, someone needs to fund the disbursements. There has been some interest from lawyers running cases on a DBA, and the option of disbursement and work in progress funding, in much the same way that funders operate with lawyers working under US based contingency fees.

10.08 Funders are sharing risk with firms primarily through funding the non-contingent discounted fees under a hybrid CFA. The ability for law firms to be paid a fee in any event, and a higher fee on success, means that their overheads are covered and their risk is reduced. The ability to guarantee cash flow from a funder means that the firm can offer that type of contingent retainer across a wider range of and number of cases.

10.09 Education is extremely important in bridging the gap between lawyers, funders, and clients.

---

[1] *Andrew Mitchell MP v News Group Newspapers Limited* [2013] EWCA Civ 1537. See, however, the more recent decision of the Court of Appeal in *Denton v T H White & others* [2014] EWCA Civ 906 in which the Court of Appeal revisited the approach to be taken to the failure to comply with rules, practice, directions and orders. Denton suggests that henceforth relief from sanctions will be available unless a breach has been serious, and even then an important consideration will be the interests of justice.

10.10 An increased level of awareness and knowledge would demonstrate that the *Excalibur*[2] case, for all the potential problems and risks that it highlighted, has not eradicated the need for funding or indeed the skills of the recognized funders. Whilst litigation funding is not a panacea for all litigation needs, the development of it will lie in closer collaboration of lawyers with clients with a desire or need for funds, and funders seeking new, winning investments.

10.11 There are some speakers and commentators on litigation, and the future of litigation funding, who believe that in the future there will be a healthy market in the trading of litigation and cases as commodities. In England and Wales this seems an unlikely proposition, given the prohibition of the assignment of a bare cause of action. That does not mean, of course, that there are not circumstances, where there is a sufficient nexus between assignor and assignee, that it could not happen; it is simply that the prospect of a commodities style of exchange for litigation is an unrealistic prospect with the current law.

10.12 However, the perception of litigation as an asset and the understanding it may have value which can be realized by the use of funding, internal or external, by general counsel and in-house legal teams, is something which will become more prevalent as the litigation funding market expands and its use is better understood.

10.13 There are some changes in the litigation funding world that may seem unlikely now, but have a realistic prospect of coming to pass. An example is the issue of control of the litigation. In Australia, in the years prior to the *Fostif*[3] decision, it may have been difficult to see that litigation funders would be given the ability to take over the case in quite the same way that they have done so following that decision. In England and Wales, the current state of public policy allows an arrangement which on its face looks champertous—that is, litigation funding, because, *inter alia*, of its ability to provide access to justice.

10.14 Currently, the prospect of a litigation funder exerting control over the litigation is an abhorrent one to some. The thought of having a funder involved at all is not acceptable to some litigants, even a funder with no ability to exert any control. There are others who would not be concerned, and may well be happy to hand over to the funder the running and decision making of a case in its entirety. In some group litigation that may appeal to certain litigants. However, the prospect of a funder taking control of a piece of litigation currently seems unlikely, yet it is quite possible that the position may change with new funders coming into the market looking to challenge the existing regime and rules.

---

[2] *Excalibur Ventures LLC v Texas Keystone Inc. (1) (2) Gulf Keystone Petroleum Limited (3) Gulf Keystone Petroleum International Limited (4) Gulf Keystone Petroleum (UK) Limited* [2013] EWHC 2767 (Comm).

[3] *Campbells Cash & Carry Pty Ltd v Fostif Pty Ltd* [2006] HCA 41.

10.15 One area where litigation funding has made little or no impact to date is in the field of smaller value claims. The reason for this is simply that the returns available do not justify a funder's risk in being involved. There are ways to accommodate these sorts of cases, by law firm funding or 'portfolio' and 'basket' funding. A funder can finance a law firm directly and allow them to choose, within certain criteria, which case to apply the funds to. Or, the firm can decide to put forward a portfolio of cases in which they propose to invest their time and the funder finances some of the work in progress and disbursements for a return across the portfolio. If there is a client, for example, an office holding insolvency practitioner, with a 'basket' of cases either arising out of the same appointment or across a range of appointments, the funder can fund the cases with returns received across all of the cases. The benefit to the funder in these arrangements is the spread of the investment across the portfolio which reduces the risk as losses in one case are invariably made good from the successful ones.

B. Regulation and Self-Regulation

10.16 The ALF was created in late 2011 and now has seven funder members all of whom are active in the market. There are other funders, who are doing regular business but as yet have not joined the ALF.

10.17 There are at least three[4] mainstream litigation funding brokers that appear to make a significant proportion of their revenue from placing litigation funding business, and who are also associate 'broker' members of the ALF.

10.18 The industry has come a long way in a short space of time. The ALF is tasked with policing the industry in England and Wales. A new and more stringent Code of Conduct and membership criteria, regarding capital adequacy, and a new complaints procedure introduced in January 2014, have given the ALF the tools to deal with errant funder members and a greater degree of credibility.

10.19 As the ALF becomes a more mature entity and its position as the litigation funding industry's self-regulation body in England and Wales becomes better established, one thing that may change is the ALF's remit concerning education and publicity. Whilst it will remain the industry's watchdog, it will no doubt begin to publicize the benefits of litigation funding through a process of education and explanation. It may be the industry policeman, but it is also the trade organization of the funder members. Currently though, the ALF sees itself solely as a regulator.

10.20 It is difficult for any trade organization to perform a dual role. The ALF has to combine the function of industry regulator with being the lobby group for the

---

[4] ClaimTrading, The Judge, and Universal Legal Protection.

litigation funding industry, and must do so without falling into conflict. The risk of this framework for the ALF is that it carries out both roles less well than it would do one or the other only. Equally, the ALF runs the risk of criticism from inside and outside the industry, and may find itself unable to perform either role effectively. For many years, the Law Society was the professional body of the solicitors' branch of the legal profession, and at the same time the profession's regulator. Eventually, change was forced upon the legal profession by the Clementi Report[5] in 2004 and thereafter the Legal Services Act.[6] The Law Society remained the professional body of the solicitors' profession, and the Solicitors Regulation Authority became the regulator. The Bar Council went through a similar process at the same time, with the Bar Standards Board becoming the professional regulator for the Bar.

10.21 The future for the ALF depends upon its performance. So far it has had to concentrate on setting out a robust framework through which to promote best practice in the litigation funding industry in England and Wales. The gauge for the ALF is external perception of how it dealt with its first big test. Anything other than the perception that it has acted promptly and fearlessly in policing the industry will signal 'open season' from the critics of the ALF and of the funding industry and the subsequent demand for formal regulation will be revived.

10.22 In this regard, the ALF's first significant test has been the very public difficulties encountered by the litigation funder Argentum, and its related group companies. Argentum resigned from the ALF in April 2014. The ALF investigated press reports criticizing the fundraising activities of a company connected with Argentum. During those investigations the board of the ALF put a series of questions to Argentum concerning their involvement and their precise role in the activities reported in the press. Argentum offered to resign from the ALF and the resignation was accepted.[7]

10.23 The ALF board appears to have acted swiftly in addressing the problems raised by this issue and resolved it in an efficient and timely manner, thus passing its first significant test.

10.24 The issue of formal regulation as opposed to self-regulation remains an ongoing discussion, and the debate will continue on into the future. Provision has been made, by way of s 28 of the Access to Justice Act 1999, which prospectively would introduce s 58B of the Courts and Legal Services Act 1990, for the introduction of statutory regulation of funders. The provision, not yet in force, would, amongst other things, enable Regulations to provide for a funder to be approved by the Lord Chancellor, or a prescribed person. There is in some areas of the litigation funding

---

[5] Review of the Regulatory Framework for Legal Services in England and Wales 2004.
[6] Legal Services Act 2007.
[7] <http://associationoflitigationfunders.com/2014/04/notice-regarding-argentum-capital-limited/>.

profession a feeling of inevitability as to the ultimate advent of regulation. It will only take one mainstream litigation funder to fail for the scrutiny of the adequacy of the regulatory regime to begin afresh.

10.25 The obvious question which is asked is what does the industry have to fear from outside, or independent, regulation? The answer to that is nothing. Many of the litigation funder members of the ALF are subject to one form of regulation or another. The fund structures are regulated by the financial supervision or conduct authorities of wherever they are based. All the UK based investment advisers are subject to the UK Financial Conduct Authority's regulation.

10.26 The two main concerns voiced by litigation funders over external regulation are, first, the extra layer of consequential and additional costs involved in being subjected to that new regime, whatever it is, and, secondly, the very important question of who would actually regulate the industry. One of the other issues that this raises is the international nature of funding litigation.

10.27 The ALF only operates to deal with litigation funding in England and Wales. If a litigation funder wishes to do business in the jurisdiction, then they are likely to want to become a member of the ALF. However, so far the Code of Conduct from the ALF is the only set of government backed rules adopted in the litigation funding world. There have been attempts to encourage the adoption of a regime based on rules similar to the Code in other jurisdictions, but so far the ALF is the only recognized litigation funding watchdog.

10.28 The critics of the ALF, and supporters of regulation, do not suggest by whom the regulation should be carried out or the manner in which it should be undertaken. They tend to suggest that the ALF is "toothless", in that it can only discipline or regulate a member of its own association and then its punitive powers run only to a fine or expulsion. This is true. But, the litigation funding industry believes self-policing will work on the basis that no funder that wants to stay in business would do anything to attract the attention of the ALF's complaints procedure and risk a public punishment and the ensuing potentially terminal publicity. However, what this ignores is the potential for a rogue funder to operate in a way that is damaging to clients and the funding industry. In other sectors of the funding world there have been high profile failures and allegations of fraud. Whilst that raises the question of outside regulation, those that make that argument do forget that the funders in question were regulated by and audited by the relevant local financial conduct authorities.

10.29 One further point to be considered in the context of the debate concerning regulation, is that the ALF and its members are dealing with commercial clients who strike a commercial bargain with a funder over the terms of their funding arrangements. These are not consumer contracts and there is no consumer protection issue involved.

10.30 The ALF believes that the Code is working and self-regulation is unlikely to change anything. Nothing has happened in the industry to suggest that the position of litigation funders has changed since the Code was produced by the CJC in 2011. Accordingly their view is that there is no reason to change the position on self-regulation. In fact what has changed is the size of the industry and its prominence. It is not always necessary for there to be a disaster or scandal before change and regulation is implemented.

10.31 The calls for regulation will continue. Real litigation funders have nothing to fear from regulation by an independent body, although it seems perfectly clear that the current regime has worked to date. Ultimately, regulation will depend upon the size that the industry grows to become, and whether there is a blurring of the boundary between consumer and commercial litigation funding.

C. Education

10.32 The education of the legal profession is the largest issue facing the litigation funding industry. The concept of litigation funding is not a difficult one to grasp. Somebody other than the client pays the lawyers' legal fees, on the client's behalf, in return for a share of the proceeds, if the action is successful. It is a simple transaction in principle.

10.33 The majority of commercial litigation solicitors in England and Wales are aware of litigation funding. There are still those who are not, but they are now very much in a minority. In the main, once the concept of litigation funding has been explained to them, there are very few claimant-side litigation lawyers who do not see the potential benefits of litigation funding to them and to their clients. There are, of course, cases for which funding might not be appropriate, either because of the nature of the case, or because of the resources of the client, or because of a combination of factors. In a very substantial case, where the award may be very much greater than any costs likely to be incurred, a well-resourced client might well consider that funding would be not only unnecessary, but unattractive because of the potential overall cost.

10.34 However, understanding what litigation funding is as a concept, and understanding how litigation funding works are two entirely separate issues. There is a definite distinction between having heard of litigation funding and having had experience of using it and appreciating the benefits of it. As with anything, there are those who have already judged the subject, and have decided that the use of funding is not their preferred method of financing a piece of litigation. Those lawyers may have to use funding, in some situations, albeit reluctantly.

10.35 Where lawyers lack interest in the subject of funding, it is primarily due to the size of the cases that they deal with and their view that funding is appropriate only in a very small number of high value cases every year. Whilst that was the case, things are changing in that regard, with increasing flexibility from funders, and with the understanding from lawyers of the ratios needed to make a funding arrangement work.

10.36 Additionally, lawyers and therefore their clients have concerns over the element of control exercised by a litigation funder. The lawyers do not wish to serve two masters, or run into conflict and ethical issues. This is obviously something that the lawyers should be acutely aware of. In the United States the conflict and ethical issues are very much at the forefront of the campaign against the litigation funding industry. The issue of privilege is also a real problem in the funding industry in the United States. Clearly, any situation where there is potential for conflict between the client's wishes and the funder's wishes can place a strain on the arrangement. However, this is, in the author's experience, a very rare occurrence (as is perhaps demonstrated by the paucity of litigation on the issue), and, in any event, the lawyer's duty will always be to their client, and not to the litigation funder. That said, the lawyer will almost certainly be contractually obliged to disclose any relevant adverse material to a funder, but this will be the basis of the arrangement between the funder and the client, and therefore the client cannot complain concerning such disclosure. The contractual arrangements, considered in Chapter 5, always work on the basis of the solicitor's primary duty being to their client and ensuring that there is no conflict. In any piece of litigation the main objective for any funder is for the client to win the case and to be awarded the level of damages that were anticipated or expected. The client's interests and the funder's interests are usually aligned.

10.37 The only time that there is a difficulty is where the client wishes to take an uncommercial approach or there is a disagreement over the merits or prospects of success. In both these situations there are contractual provisions in force in the funding arrangements to provide a framework for the process of dealing with those disagreements. In a situation where the funder is an ALF member the process will follow the ALF Code of Conduct in these matters.

10.38 In England and Wales, funders cannot exercise control over the litigation. Whilst that message can be transmitted regularly and consistently to the legal profession and to prospective clients, the only way for lawyers to be convinced is to experience running a piece of litigation financed by a litigation funder. The experience should not be too dissimilar to the level of interaction between the lawyers and the ATE insurers in a case run with the benefit of an ATE policy. There will be greater interaction because of the need to seek monthly payment of invoices, but the necessity to report any offers received, and to advise on any significant change in circumstance or prospects of success are the same as with a litigation funder. The key area of difference will be a funder's requirement for a regular update of the situation—most ATE insurers have a fairly 'laissez-faire' attitude to ongoing monitoring and assessment of how cases are run, being more

10.39 One of the issues that litigation funders face in their challenge of educating the legal profession about the benefits of litigation funding is their tendency to operate in secrecy. There is more litigation funding undertaken in England and Wales, and there are more funded cases being run through the English High Court than many commentators would suggest, or, perhaps, of which they are aware. Nobody is able to give an accurate figure, because no litigation funder gives out the details of all the cases they are funding, or have funded.

10.40 In many funded cases, the opponents will not know that the claimant has the benefit of funding unless there is a need to address a security for costs issue, and even then it may not be necessary to divulge the client's funding arrangements. In many group litigation cases the fact that a funder is involved is likely to emerge at an early stage. In some cases, the client or the funder may feel that the opponent's knowledge of there being a funder involved will assist in accelerating settlement discussions. That is not always the case.

10.41 Most of the cases which involve litigation funding and where the issue reaches the public domain are cases where something has not gone to plan or the case has not been successful. The two largest cases in recent years *Innovator One*[8] and *Excalibur*[9] are good examples of this point. Both cases hit the headlines in the legal press due to the fact that they were cases where the claimants were defeated, and they had the benefit of litigation funding.

10.42 When a large case is successful, it may be reported but there are few, if any, cases reported in recent years where the issue of litigation funding has been highlighted. The subject of litigation funding in these matters is only made public where something has gone wrong and the funders are being pursued for adverse costs, or there is something worthy of comment in the funder's losing their money. Publicity is either shunned, or the issue is not newsworthy, when funders win large cases. Whilst the mention of the use of funding in high profile litigation has begun to happen, with several mentions in the press of matters being funded, it is not yet commonplace.

10.43 For this reason, there is a general view that funding is not for the majority of cases, clients, or lawyers. This demonstrates the need for greater education and publicity from the litigation funding industry, including the ALF on the industry's behalf. In the author's experience, once a litigation lawyer has used funding in a case, their understanding of the process and appreciation of the benefits, not only of the prompt monthly payment, means that they will consider the use of funding in

---

[8] *Brown v Innovator One plc* [2012] EWHC 1321 (Comm).
[9] *Excalibur Ventures LLC v Texas Keystone Inc. (1) (2) Gulf Keystone Petroleum Limited (3) Gulf Keystone Petroleum International Limited (4) Gulf Keystone Petroleum (UK) Limited* [2013] EWHC 2767 (Comm).

their other cases. Experience also enables lawyers to learn how to anticipate and handle any problems that might arise from funding arrangements.

10.44 The challenge of education is a real and difficult one for litigation funders. As mentioned above, not every case is right for funding. Litigation funders must do all they can to ensure that members of the legal profession fulfil their professional obligations and, at the very least, consider the relevance of funding in every case.

10.45 The best way for lawyers to learn the benefits of litigation funding is for them to use it, or, at least, talk to funders about using it. To do so they need to be aware of it and understand it. In recent years, there has been a general increase in conferences and seminars where litigation funding is discussed. These have often been associated with the Jackson reforms and the changes to litigation costs. There are very few litigation costs conferences held now where the issue of litigation funding is not addressed.

10.46 Litigation funding has established itself on the Continuing Professional Development landscape, and has become a topic to discuss and talk about. The future will see those theoretical discussions become a more regular practical assessment. Simply by being talked about, the use of litigation funding has increased and will continue to do so. The more litigation funding is talked about, the more it will seep into the psyche of litigators and establish itself. This promotion and discussion will continue to educate the legal profession.

D. ABS

10.47 The term 'litigation funding' has become the standard description for all types of legal financing arrangements from traditional third party litigation funding to a range of finance facilities provided to law firms. Whilst there has been significant growth in litigation funding and changes in the funding landscape, there have also been fundamental changes in the legal profession in the last couple of years.

10.48 The Legal Services Act[10] has altered the way in which law firms can be owned, and ended the old regime that provided for law firms to be owned by lawyers only. Whilst there have been legitimate methods to take limited external investment into law practices in England and Wales for some years, the introduction of alternative business structures (ABSs) into the legal framework is a significant step in transforming the landscape of law firm ownership.

---

[10] Legal Services Act 2007.

10.49 Historically, the process of lending to law firms for use across a portfolio of cases relied upon funds being allocated by individual case, or lending directly to the partners in the firm. The problem with lending to the individual partners is that few lawyers want to take on the financial obligation, and there is no practical alternative for the funder, given the law firm structure. Few law firms hold substantial assets or cash balances.

10.50 Lending to lawyers, or law firm schemes managed and operated by the lawyers and allocated to specific cases, is a proven way of financing a high volume of lower value cases. The method is similar to traditional third party litigation funding but the pricing arrangements are different. The process enables lawyers to seek finance from a funder who understands litigation and finance and is used to the vagaries of litigation, the potential uncertainties involved, and most importantly the timescales and length of time a case takes to conclude. Litigation and law firm finance is not easily comprehended and more importantly cannot be administered in a cost efficient way for any high street or commercial lender. Whilst banks have specialists who focus on the professional and legal sectors, the financing of cases, work in progress, or disbursements are a specialist area and not large enough in size and volume to make it worthwhile for the banks to work with.

10.51 The new ABS regulations have changed the potential for the legal marketplace. There are suggestions that law firms will list on the stock exchange and in Australia there is already a listed law firm.[11]

10.52 Currently, there are venture capital firms who have acquired legal based businesses and there are other larger organizations who are looking to integrate smaller entities, including in law firms, to ensure that they provide the entire legal service from one group.[12] Traditional law firms will begin to face competition from new market entrants. Large and well known brands[13] have already entered the legal market with the changes that allow employed solicitors to offer their services to the public rather than the historic position where they could only offer legal advice to their employer.

10.53 With the change in regulations there comes an opportunity for litigation funders to consider new and different approaches to law firm financing. Equally, it is possible that litigation funders will look at different structures for their own organizations. The most obvious change brought about by the ABS regime is the ability for a litigation funder to take an equity stake in a law firm. The litigation funder's business model is to invest in one-off pieces of large litigation. That is very high

---

[11] Slater & Gordon, listed on ASX in May 2007.
[12] Quindell PLC through Quindell Legal Services acquired the legal practices of Silverbeck Rymer, Pinto Potts, and The Compensation Lawyers in December 2012. During April and May 2013 Quindell Legal Services acquired the brands Accident Advice Helpline, Fast Claim PPI, and the legal costs practice of Compass Law.
[13] 'Wait for ABSs is over: Tesco law is here': Neil Rose, *The Guardian*, 2 April 2012.

risk investment. In order to spread the risk, the litigation funder will invest across a portfolio of different types and size of case with the intention that a large success in one case pays for several unsuccessful investments and that the majority of cases create large returns. On the whole this method has been adopted successfully by members of the industry.

10.54 However, the ability to invest in a law firm itself and to take an equity stake in the firm has several benefits for the litigation funder. First, the funder has spread the risk of investment across the entirety of the law firm's caseload (possibly across the contentious and non-contentious practices). This provides the significant reduction in risk from the portfolio approach. Additionally, though, the investment in the law firm also creates the ability to fund large and small value cases as the returns to the funder are across the entire business, whilst their investment can be used for any type or size of case. Equally, the investment in the firm is very likely to guarantee a commitment to the funder to the exclusion of other funders.

10.55 The investment in an ABS law firm does also raise further questions which were considered in Chapter 8. This highlights the possible use by a litigation funder of an ABS law firm to make investments. Obviously the law firm would be subject to the DBA Regulations and caps on returns, but it is at least debatable whether the ABS would be able to rely on the principle of 'Hodgson immunity'[14] to avoid the risk of adverse costs. It is, though, unlikely that any client would venture into litigation without ATE cover, once armed with the appropriate advice on the subject.

10.56 Ultimately, ABS law firms with the financial backing and investment of a third party litigation funder would enable the funder to be involved in the whole process of a piece of litigation. They would not 'control' the litigation in terms of decision making but, from a risk perspective, the funder would have eradicated some of the risks as the case would be run by lawyers who are the subject of the funder's direct investment. It is possible that this style and type of investment, or a 'Tesco Law' type of arrangement, from funders will become more commonplace.

E. Jurisdictions

10.57 Most common law jurisdictions have a similar approach to litigation funding to that of England and Wales.[15] Whilst litigation funding is not prevalent in all of those jurisdictions there are reported decisions which confirm the acceptability of the process in the places such as the British Virgin Islands, Cayman Islands, Canada, South Africa, and New Zealand. The spread and continued acceptance

---

[14] From *Hodgson & Ors v Imperial Tobacco Ltd & Ors* [1998] 2 All ER 673, [1998] 1 WLR 1056, [1998] EWCA Civ 224, [1998] 1 Costs LR 14, [1998] WLR 1056.
[15] Litigation funding has also met with judicial approval in the Royal Court in Jersey; see *Re Valetta Trust* [2011] JRC 227 (Michel Birt, Bailiff, sitting with jurats).

of litigation funding across the world will undoubtedly see more jurisdictions confirm the validity of the use of funding.

10.58 The litigation funding world has tended to focus on England, the USA, and Australia but there are established markets already in Germany and the Netherlands. There are also emerging markets for litigation funders with expansion beginning in Switzerland, Belgium, and France in Europe and elsewhere in jurisdictions such as Dubai, Qatar, and Brazil.

10.59 Two jurisdictions where the use of funding will certainly increase following confirmation of its legitimacy will be in Hong Kong and Singapore. Currently those jurisdictions do not see a regular use of litigation funding due to concerns over the legality of its use. Over the next few years, both jurisdictions will see that position change.

10.60 The use of litigation funding is specifically permitted in arbitrations in Hong Kong and more recent decisions suggest that there is a steady and increasing recognition of litigation funding's legitimacy within the jurisdiction. So far litigation funders have been reluctant to test out the local courts but the general consensus is that, in time, funding will become accepted.

10.61 The concerns in Singapore are that litigation funding will increase the size of damages claimed and not add anything to the litigation process. However, litigation funding agreements have been recognized where the funder has a commercial interest in the proceedings. The issues of maintenance of champerty are very much of concern to the Singaporean courts.

10.62 The jurisdiction remains an area where litigation funding will eventually grow. Singapore's push to be a recognized centre for international arbitration has commenced a review of the issues raised in litigation funding by the Singapore government. Litigation funding will undoubtedly take hold in Hong Kong and Singapore in the coming years, and both jurisdictions will become areas of significant litigation funding activity. A driving consideration for the courts in those jurisdictions is likely to be that if funding is not held to be acceptable, draftsmen of commercial contracts may provide for disputes to be resolved in other jurisdictions.

F. Evolution

10.63 Currently, the term 'litigation funding' is associated with a one-off large value piece of litigation where a litigation funder pays the legal fees and receives a return based on the successful outcome of the case. It is a non-recourse loan with returns of somewhere between 2 and 5 times the investment or a percentage of the recovered award, or both.

10.64 This is the most basic form of litigation finance. Over time, litigation funders have had to adapt to a more competitive marketplace. In jurisdictions where there are still only a handful of funders in existence, the evolution of funding arrangements and the innovation of available products has been slower than in the more competitive arenas. However, this will change and the flexibility of funding arrangements will improve.

10.65 Over time the attraction to funders of the lower value cases has increased. The understanding of case capture and forming relationships with firms has become better understood. There are significant returns available to investors who operate on a larger volume portfolio basis as described in Chapter 3. These schemes may not be of interest to all of the existing funders, but undoubtedly, given the plethora of lower value claims available, some existing funders will be attracted and there will be new entrants into that market drawn by the financial incentives. The funding of lower value claims lends itself neatly to the use of portfolio funding.

10.66 However, the evolution of litigation finance is not going to be confined to the size of cases that one-off case funding can be used with. Funders are already looking at ways to be innovative in the manner they deploy their capital. The difficulty for some funders is their structure—they are not currently set up to be able to create funding arrangements which differ greatly from the one-off funding or portfolio funding methods. Other funders have more flexibility and lend in novel ways. For example, the perception of a piece of litigation as an asset, much like any other is not a commonly held view. Yet, using litigation finance a business may be able to use that litigation asset to raise money, rather than seeking funds for the purposes of paying legal fees. There are already publicly reported cases where a corporation has raised finance from a litigation funder secured on the claim or case.[16]

G. Conclusion

10.67 Without question, funding is here to stay but it will face many challenges including whether it should be subject to voluntary, self-regulation as opposed to a regime of independent regulation, and the degree to which it becomes an indispensable part of the litigator's toolbox. Consolidation will also be a likely feature of the future litigation funding market, with fewer but larger players competing with non-traditional funders and competition direct from law firms.

10.68 Currently many banks and other financial institutions are on the receiving end of the use of litigation funding. The banks' large financial resources mean that where there is a case with merits against a financial institution the question of whether

---

[16] <http://m.londonstockexchange.com/exchange/mobile/news/detail.html?announcementId=11972069> and <http://www.litigationfutures.com/news/burford-uses-arbitration-claim-offer-aim-listed-company-9m-debt-facility>.

they are able to meet any award is easily confirmed. It has been suggested that banks and finance houses may see the asset class of litigation funding as an attractive alternative investment. Whilst that is possible, it seems unlikely that banks will come into the litigation funding sector. The only bank that was involved in the industry[17] decided to come out of the market, as did a large insurer that had been involved in litigation finance, possibly because of the regular conflicts[18] it would have faced with other aspects of its business.

10.69 There are likely to be a range of changes and developments in the litigation finance world over the coming years. Traditional litigation funding is for claimants and relates primarily to the payment of lawyers' fees. The use of funding to pay other outgoings for the claimant is something funders have done but it is something more likely to be used in the future. For example, the payment of the overhead of a business would ensure its survival to the conclusion of a piece of litigation—something of great importance to any funder involved in funding a case.

10.70 Another area of potential change is the growth in the acquisition of claims. Currently that process is limited, particularly in England and Wales, by the inability to acquire a bare cause of action. It has been suggested that there may be growing market in this area. The general trading of claims seems entirely implausible but the acquisition of companies with valid claims is entirely feasible and has been done by some funders. The pricing mechanism is very different from traditional funding but the principle is well used in the insolvency world with assignments of rights of action from office holders to connected directors or shareholders. Very often, funders are presented with a claim that is the only asset of a company. The acquisition of the company by the funder is often a simple option.

10.71 The view of litigation as an asset will also become a more prevalent position. The ability of any claimant to realize the asset of a case by the use of funding will change the perception of what a piece of litigation is. Whilst there is no immediate likelihood of a trading market in these litigation assets, they do have value to a business. The use of funding allows a case with merit to be pursued with little or no risk to the claimant. The perception of a claim, or a piece of litigation, as an asset will become a more prevalent point of view.

10.72 The issue of control of the litigation remains a sensitive one. As has been discussed earlier, the prospect of losing control of the direction of a case or the ability to decide when to stop is a concern for many potential litigants. The law in England and Wales is clear on the subject, and public policy prevents litigation funders from taking over a case. The ALF Code of Conduct is also clear as to the matter—that is, a

---

[17] Credit Suisse pulled out of the litigation funding market in January 2012.
[18] 'Litigation finance struggles to overcome conflicts': William Hutchings, *Financial News*, 5 November 2012.

litigation funder must 'not seek to influence the Funded Party's solicitor or barrister to cede control or conduct of the dispute to the Funder'.[19] Control of the litigation by a funder is not permitted currently and there seems to be no appetite within the current professional litigation funding community to seek to change that.

10.73 However, it is by no means certain that this view on the subject will prevail in the future. It would take a material change of judicial thinking and a rethink on the issues of maintenance and champerty to allow a litigation funder to exert control over a case. But, a well funded challenge backed by the litigation funding world, or a significant litigation funding entity may see a change in this respect. If the example of Australia is considered, then the change is possible, albeit unlikely. The decision in *Fostif* [20] was a watershed. In the majority of cases the issue of control does not really feature.

10.74 Large one-off commercial litigation cases require ongoing and open discussions between the funder, the client, and the lawyer. There is no need for the funder to be in control. However, a different sort of case, for example a very large group action, may benefit from a different approach to funding, and from the funder. In a group, or class, action the number of clients involved means that individual interaction between each and every client and the lawyers or the funder is impossible. A steering committee is formed and delegated authority is granted to that committee to make decisions on behalf of the entire group. In Australia in this sort of litigation it is often the case that control of the matter is handed over to the funder who will seek to maximize the best recovery for the entire group of claimants and the funder. Obviously, critics will suggest that there is a potential, or actual, conflict of interest. That is possible, but it is equally likely that the interests of the funder and the clients are exactly aligned—after all, the funder is taking all of the risk in this situation.

10.75 It would be surprising if the boundaries on the issue of control are overturned in the next few years and in any event most funders are content with the current position. However, it would be no surprise if a litigation funder, with a slightly different mindset, were to challenge the rules.

10.76 The litigation funding landscape will not remain static in the coming years, and it will continue to be an interesting and innovative area of the law. There are many areas and jurisdictions where litigation funding has a lot to do to become part of the mainstream of commercial litigation practice. However, in the world of commercial litigation in England and Wales, litigation funding is very much a fixture. It does not claim to work for every case, but the use of litigation funding will continue to grow. Whilst it is not yet an essential tool for every commercial litigator, it will become so soon.

---

[19] ALF Code of Conduct clause 9.3.
[20] *Campbells Cash & Carry Pty Ltd v Fostif Pty Ltd* [2006] HCA 41.

APPENDIX 1

LITIGATION FUNDING AGREEMENT

(1)   THERIUM (UK) HOLDINGS LIMITED
(2)   [CLAIMANT   ].

DATE: 2014

PARTIES:

(1) THERIUM (UK) HOLDINGS LIMITED (Company Number 7213330) of 78 Duke Street, Mayfair, London, W1K 5LR ('Therium'); and

(2) [   ] whose address is [
                                    ] ('Claimant');

RECITALS:

(A) The Claimant wishes to bring the Claim against the Defendant and has taken legal advice on the merits of the Claim from the Solicitors and Counsel.

(B) In order to facilitate access to justice, the Claimant has sought the agreement of Therium to provide funding in respect of the Claimant's costs of pursuing the Claim as set out in the Project Plan and on the terms of this agreement ('Agreement').

(C) The Claimant and Therium have therefore agreed that Therium will provide funding in respect of the Claim in accordance with the terms of this Agreement.

OPERATIVE PROVISIONS:

1. Interpretation

    1.1. In this Agreement the following definitions shall have the following meanings:

        'Adverse Costs Order' means any order of a Court requiring a party to pay some or all of the costs of any other party to the Proceedings;

        'Appeal' means an appeal of a judgment or award in the Proceedings, including any cross-appeal of the Claimant and the Claimant's response to any appeal of a Defendant.

        'Application' means any application form submitted to Therium by the Claimant together with all materials and documents submitted to Therium prior to the Commencement Date in connection with the Claimant's application;

        'Business Day' means a day on which banks generally are open in the City of London for the transaction of normal banking business (other than a Saturday);

        'Challenge Notice' means written notice setting out the grounds of a challenge to the fees billed which are payable by Therium pursuant to this Agreement;

        'Claim' means the claim, details of which are set out in the Schedule;

        'Claim Proceeds' means any and all value due to and/or received by, on behalf of, or in lieu of payment to, the Claimant in connection with or arising out of the Claim as a result of any judgment, award, order, settlement arrangement or compromise, (including payment of any damages, compensation, interest, restitution, recovery, judgment sum, arbitral award, settlement sum, compensation payment, costs and interest on costs), whether in monetary or non-monetary form, whether actual or contingent, and before deduction of any taxes which the Claimant may be liable to pay in respect of the Claim Proceeds;

'Claim Proceeds Account' means an account prepared by Therium setting out how any Claim Proceeds are to be distributed to the parties under the Priorities Agreement;

'Commencement Date' means the date specified in the Schedule;

'Committed Costs' means, in relation to each tranche of funding incepted, the Committed Costs for that tranche of funding as detailed in the Schedule;

'Contingency Fee' means, in respect of all tranches of funding incepted, the greater of:

(i) the multiple of the total Committed Costs for all tranches of funding incepted, and

(ii) the percentage of the balance of all Claim Proceeds after payment to Therium of the Reasonable Costs Sum and any other sums payable in priority to the Contingency Fee under the Priorities Agreement at the rate applicable to the last tranche of funding incepted,

as specified in the Schedule, together with any VAT payable on such amount;

'Costs' means legal costs and disbursements, including any premium payable for Legal Expenses Insurance, where specified in the Project Plan;

'Counsel' means the barrister identified in the Schedule who has been instructed to represent the Claimant in respect of the Claim;

'Court' means the court, arbitration panel or tribunal which has conduct of the Proceedings;

'CPR' means the Civil Procedure Rules and supporting Practice Directions;

'Defendant' means the defendant specified in the Schedule;

'Legal Expenses Insurance' means an after the event legal expenses insurance policy in favour of the Claimant in respect of its potential liability for an Adverse Costs Order on terms and with an insurer approved by Therium, such approval not to be unreasonably withheld;

'Notice' means a notice given in accordance with clause 23;

'Notice of Interest' means a notice of interest given pursuant to clause 12.3;

'Notice of Release of Interest' means a notice of release of interest given pursuant to clause 15.6;

'Party' means a party to this Agreement;

'Priorities Agreement' means a priorities agreement substantially in the form appended to this Agreement as Appendix 3, to be executed by the Claimant in accordance with clause 6.1;

'Proceedings' means the litigation or arbitral proceedings relating to the Claim including any pre-action correspondence, settlement negotiations or mediation and any enforcement proceedings to enforce payment of any judgment, order, award or settlement agreement, brief details of which are included in the Schedule and any other proceedings which Therium agrees in writing shall be the subject of this Agreement pursuant to clause 4.3. For the avoidance of doubt 'Proceedings' does not include an Appeal unless specifically agreed by Therium pursuant to clause 4.2;

'Project Plan' means the project plan for the Claim, including the Solicitor's estimate of Committed Costs required to pursue the Claim and an outline timetable, appended to this Agreement as Appendix 1, as may be varied by agreement between the Parties from time to time in accordance with clause 19;

'Reasonable Costs' means the Committed Costs in respect of each tranche, to the extent that those costs are reasonably incurred by the Claimant in accordance with the terms of this Agreement;

'Reasonable Costs Sum' means a sum equal to the total of all Reasonable Costs paid by Therium pursuant to this Agreement;

'Recovery' means the recovery of any Claim Proceeds;

'Solicitors' means the firm of solicitors instructed by the Claimant to act on its behalf in connection with the Claim and identified as such in the Schedule;

'Tranche 1' means the steps in the Proceedings and the funding requirement, as detailed in the Project Plan, up to the maximum of the Committed Costs in respect of that first tranche;

'Tranche 2' means the steps in the Proceedings and the funding requirement, as detailed in the Project Plan, up to the maximum of the Committed Costs in respect of that second tranche;

'Tranche 3' means the steps in the Proceedings and the funding requirement, as detailed in the Project Plan, up to the maximum of the Committed Costs in respect of that third tranche;

'Tranche 4' means the steps in the Proceedings and the funding requirement, as detailed in the Project Plan, up to the maximum of the Committed Costs in respect of that fourth tranche;

'Trust Period' means the period of 80 years from the date of this Agreement; and

'VAT' means value added tax at the rate for the time being in force (as may be varied from time to time by HM Revenue & Customs).

1.2. Any reference to a Recital, Clause, Schedule or Appendix is to the relevant Recital, Clause, Schedule or Appendix of or to this Agreement and any reference to a sub-clause or paragraph is to the relevant sub-clause or paragraph of the Clause or Schedule in which it appears.

1.3. Except where the context requires otherwise words denoting the singular include the plural and vice versa, and words denoting any one gender include all genders.

Appendix 1

1.4. Any reference to 'persons' includes natural persons, firms, partnerships, companies, corporations, associations, organisations, governments, states, foundations and trusts (in each case whether or not having separate legal personality).

1.5. Any reference to a statute, statutory provision or subordinate legislation shall be construed as referring to it as from time to time amended, extended or re-enacted.

1.6. Any phrase introduced by the terms 'including', 'include', 'in particular' or any similar expression shall be construed as illustrative and shall not limit the sense of the words following those terms.

2. Agreement to Fund

2.1. Subject to clause 2.2 below, in return for the Claimant's agreement to pay, where there is a Recovery, the Reasonable Costs Sum and the Contingency Fee in accordance with the terms of this Agreement, Therium agrees with effect from the Commencement Date to pay the Claimant's Reasonable Costs incurred in respect of Tranche 1 in accordance with the terms of this Agreement.

2.2. If the Recovery is insufficient to pay the Reasonable Costs Sum and the Contingency Fee in full then the Recovery shall be applied in accordance with the priority as set out in the Priorities Agreement until the Recovery has been fully applied, after which no further sum shall be payable pursuant to this Agreement.

2.3. At the option of Therium, exercisable on the completion of the stages of the Proceedings secured by Tranche 1, and at Therium's sole discretion, Therium shall have the exclusive right but not the obligation to fund Tranche 2 on the terms set out in this Agreement.

2.4. At the further option of Therium, exercisable on the completion of the stages of the Proceedings covered by Tranche 1 and Tranche 2, and at Therium's sole discretion, Therium shall have the exclusive right but not the obligation to fund Tranche 3 on the terms set out in this Agreement.

2.5. At the further option of Therium, exercisable on the completion of the stages of the Proceedings covered by Tranche 1, Tranche 2 and Tranche 3, and at Therium's sole discretion, Therium shall have the exclusive right but not the obligation to fund Tranche 4 on the terms set out in this Agreement.

2.6. It shall be a condition precedent to the exercise of the options at clauses 2.3, 2.4 and 2.5 above that Therium shall confirm to the Claimant that it has sufficient funds to meet its obligations in respect of that Tranche.

2.7. The option set out as clauses 2.3, 2.4 and 2.5 above shall be exercisable from the date they arise and remain open and exclusive for 2 months from that date. If the period of 2 months expires without Therium exercising the option, the Claimant may enter into alternative funding arrangements for that and any subsequent tranche, save that Therium shall continue to be entitled to exercise that option at any time up until the Claimant enters into a binding obligation which puts alternative funding in place for the whole of the Committed Costs for that and any subsequent tranche, at which point the option shall lapse.

3. Payment Terms and Interest

   3.1. The Reasonable Costs Sum and Contingency Fee shall become payable in the event that the Claimant achieves a Recovery and shall be paid in accordance with clause 13.5.

   3.2. In the event that any sum payable under this Agreement is not paid by its due date, interest will be payable on such sum at the rate of 4% per annum above National Westminster Bank Plc's base rate for the time being in force, compounded annually, from the date on which payment was due to the date payment is received, or for such other period as may be specified in this Agreement.

4. Changes to the Project Plan

   4.1. In the event that the Defendant brings a counterclaim in the Proceedings, then the Claimant may request Therium to fund the Costs of defending the counterclaim. If Therium consents to this request, then the Costs of defending the counterclaim shall form part of the Committed Costs and be incorporated into the Project Plan (which, along with the Schedule, shall be amended accordingly).

   4.2. In the event of an Appeal, then the Claimant may request Therium to fund the Costs of dealing with the Appeal. If Therium consents to this request, then the Costs of dealing with the Appeal shall form part of the Committed Costs and be incorporated into the Project Plan (which, along with the Schedule, shall be amended accordingly).

   4.3. In the event that proceedings involving the Claimant and relating to the Claim, other than the Proceedings, are begun, the Claimant may request Therium to fund the Costs of any or all of such proceedings. If Therium consents to this request (and for the avoidance of doubt Therium may consent to providing funding in respect of the Costs of any or all of such proceedings (or none of them)) the Costs of the proceedings shall form part of the Committed Costs and be incorporated into the Project Plan (which, along with the Schedule, shall be amended accordingly).

5. Excluded Costs and Liabilities

   5.1. Therium will not pay nor be liable under this Agreement for any of the following costs, sums or liabilities incurred by the Claimant:

      5.1.1. Costs and/or other sums incurred as a result of the Claimant's failure (on any one or more occasions) to co-operate with or to follow the advice of the Solicitors and/or Counsel;

      5.1.2. Costs and/or other sums incurred as a result of any default by the Claimant;

      5.1.3. any liability for costs arising under CPR Part 44 or the Claimant's liability for fines or penalties;

      5.1.4. Costs and/or other sums incurred as a result of any unreasonable failure by the Claimant to comply with the CPR or an order of the Court during the Proceedings;

5.1.5. Costs and/or other sums incurred as a result of any unreasonable failure by the Claimant to comply with a pre-action protocol;

5.1.6. Costs and/or other sums incurred prior to the Commencement Date (save to the extent that those costs are included in the Project Plan) or after termination of this Agreement;

5.1.7. any element of VAT where otherwise recoverable by the Claimant;

5.1.8. any Costs incurred in excess of the Reasonable Costs; or

5.1.9. save if and to the extent ordered by the Court, any adverse costs incurred as a result of steps taken before the Commencement Date or after the date of termination of this Agreement;

5.1.10. save to the extent set out in the Project Plan, any premium for costs insurance including the Legal Expenses Insurance.

6. Conditions Precedent and Warranties

   6.1. This Agreement shall not come into force unless and until the Claimant has executed the Priorities Agreement and the Legal Expenses Insurance policy is on risk.

   6.2. The Claimant acknowledges and accepts that Therium's decision to enter into this Agreement is solely based on the information and materials provided in and with the Application (which shall include copies of all legal advice to the Claimant relating to the Claim and all correspondence with the Defendant relating to the Claim) and other documents and materials provided to Therium prior to the Commencement Date and that if any such information, documents and/or materials are inaccurate, untrue, incomplete or have not been disclosed to Therium, this may affect Therium's decision to provide or continue to provide funding under this Agreement. The Claimant confirms that to the best of its knowledge and belief, the information and materials provided in and with the Application, and the documents and materials provided to Therium prior to the Commencement Date are accurate, complete and true in all material respects and that the Claimant has not failed to disclose any information, document and/or material which would be relevant to Therium's decision to enter into and remain bound by this Agreement.

   6.3. Except as may already have been fully disclosed in writing to Therium prior to the execution of this Agreement, the Claimant warrants that:

      6.3.1. as at the Commencement Date the Claimant has not granted (or purported to grant) any charge, lien or other security in favour of a third party over the Claim Proceeds (or otherwise dealt with the same in any way); and

      6.3.2. it will not grant (or purport to grant) any such charge, lien or other security until all payments due to Therium under this Agreement have been met or otherwise extinguished.

   6.4. Therium and the Claimant each warrant that the execution and performance of, and compliance with, their respective obligations under this Agreement is fully authorised by each of them and the persons executing the Agreement have the necessary and appropriate authority to do so.

6.5. The Claimant warrants and acknowledges that it has taken legal advice from the Solicitors or otherwise on the terms of this Agreement prior to entering into it.

7. Payment of Reasonable Costs

7.1. The Claimant shall instruct the Solicitors and any other suppliers of services provided for in the Project Plan to address invoices relating to the work described in the Project Plan to the Claimant but marked payable by Therium and to deliver those invoices to Therium (copied to the Claimant) for payment. In the case of the Solicitors' own costs, these shall be paid monthly or on such other terms as are agreed between the Claimant, Therium and the Solicitors.

7.2. If in the reasonably held opinion of Therium, any Costs invoiced by the Solicitors or any other supplier of services are not Reasonable Costs, Therium shall serve a Challenge Notice on the Claimant, with a copy to the relevant supplier, within 20 Business Days of delivery of the relevant invoice.

7.3. In the event of a Challenge Notice being served, the Claimant agrees to raise any queries identified in the Challenge Notice with the relevant supplier with the aim of reaching an agreement as to the disputed Costs. Where an agreement, satisfactory to Therium, cannot be reached within 10 Business Days of service of the Challenge Notice, the decision as to whether such Costs are Reasonable Costs shall be taken by an independent legal costs draftsman within 20 Business Days of his appointment. The Costs draftsman so appointed shall be a member of the Association of Law Costs Draftsmen (the 'Draftsman') and shall be appointed by Therium. Therium and the Claimant agree to be bound by such decision, and the Claimant shall procure the agreement of the relevant supplier to be bound by such decision. Unless the Draftsman directs another person to pay his costs, Therium agrees to meet his costs which shall be treated as part of the Reasonable Costs.

7.4. Pending resolution of a Challenge Notice, Therium shall pay all Costs that are not subject to challenge.

7.5. Within 5 Business Days of receiving the Draftsman's decision, Therium will pay any sum owing to either the relevant supplier and/or the Draftsman if directed by the Draftsman.

8. Adverse Costs Orders

8.1. Unless agreed by the Parties in writing, the Claimant shall take out and maintain a Legal Expenses Insurance policy sufficient throughout the Proceedings to meet any risk of any Adverse Costs Order in favour of the Defendant or any third party relating to the Claim and the Proceedings.

8.2. Nothing in this Agreement shall confer any liability on Therium for any Adverse Costs Order and the Claimant shall indemnify Therium against any such Adverse Costs Order as may be made against Therium.

Appendix 1

8.3. Nothing in this Agreement shall prejudice:

8.3.1. Therium's right to such an indemnity or contribution from the Claimant in respect of any Adverse Costs Order; or

8.3.2. Therium's contentions in relation to any application by any party to the Proceedings for an order for costs against Therium.

9. Claimant's Obligations

9.1. The Parties recognise that the Solicitors must at all times comply with their duties under the SRA Code of Conduct 2011 to act independently and in the best interests of the Claimant and in accordance with their other professional duties. Nothing in this Agreement entitles Therium to interfere in the conduct of the Claim and/or the Proceedings.

9.2. The Claimant shall:

9.2.1. instruct the Solicitors to provide Therium, prior to execution of this Agreement, with a reliance letter substantially in the form of that annexed to this Agreement at Appendix 2;

9.2.2. instruct the Solicitors and Counsel to conduct the Proceedings in accordance with the procedural rules applicable in the Court and comply with any judgment, order or award made in the Proceedings;

9.2.3. instruct the Solicitors to provide Therium with any documents or information relating to the Claim and Proceedings as may be reasonably requested by Therium;

9.2.4. instruct the Solicitors to provide Therium, insofar as is reasonably practicable and proportionate, with copies of draft pleadings, witness statements and significant correspondence, prior to issue;

9.2.5. through instructions to the Solicitors and/or on its own account:

(a) keep Therium promptly informed of any significant developments in the Proceedings (including any settlement discussions, any offers received and any information, evidence or advice coming to the attention of the Claimant or the Solicitors which may be material either to the prospects of success of the Claim or of enforcing any judgment or award); and

(b) make a monthly summary report to Therium regarding the overall progress of the Proceedings and the Costs incurred against the Project Plan;

9.2.6. comply with the terms of the Legal Expenses Insurance (including as to payment of any premium as and when due) and any duty owed to the insurer providing such cover and to supply to Therium a copy of any correspondence from the Legal Expenses Insurance provider threatening to or withdrawing cover;

9.2.7. take and follow the legal advice of the Solicitors and Counsel at all appropriate junctures, including whether it would be appropriate to make or accept any offer to settle the Claim;

9.2.8. co-operate fully and at all times throughout the proceedings with, and promptly provide such instructions and assistance to the Solicitors and Counsel as they may require for pursuing the Claim, including providing, or procuring the provision of, documents in the possession or control of the Claimant or any subsidiaries or associated companies of the Claimant and, in so far as advised by the Solicitors or Counsel, including providing access to witnesses for the purpose of preparing witness statements and procuring the attendance of those witnesses at trial to give evidence on the Claimant's behalf;

9.2.9. give reasonable notice of and permit Therium, where reasonably practicable, to attend as an observer at internal meetings which include meetings with Counsel and experts and send an observer to any mediation or hearing relating to the Claim; and

9.2.10. pay any element of VAT contained in the invoices referred to in clause 7.1 monthly unless the invoice is subject to a Challenge Notice, in which case the VAT shall be paid within 30 days of either:

(a) a Draftsman decision being issued in accordance with clause 7.3 or

(b) agreement having been reached between the Claimant and the supplier of services.

9.3. The Parties agree not to do or permit to be done anything likely to deprive each other of any benefit for which the other has entered into this Agreement.

9.4. Therium acknowledges the Claimant's right to seek advice in relation to the Claim from whichever solicitors or counsel they may choose. In the event, however, that the Solicitors and/or Counsel cease to have conduct of the Claim, then the Claimant shall obtain Therium's consent to the instruction of any alternative solicitors and/or counsel proposed by the Claimant before they are instructed.

9.5. The Claimant agrees that if Therium requires any advice given by the Solicitors to the Claimant in respect of the Claim and/or the Proceedings to be confirmed by Counsel, the Claimant will instruct the Solicitors to instruct Counsel to provide an opinion to the Claimant on such advice and to provide a copy of such opinion to Therium. Therium agrees to bear the costs of such opinion.

9.6. For the avoidance of doubt, subject to Therium's rights to termination pursuant to clause 15, nothing in this Agreement shall permit Therium to override any advice given by the Solicitors or Counsel to the Claimant. This includes any opinion given pursuant to clause 9.4 of this Agreement.

10. Appeals

10.1. If Therium agrees to provide funding in respect of an Appeal (there being no obligation on it to do so), then the Claimant agrees to instruct the Solicitors and Counsel to act on the Appeal.

10.2. Where Therium elects not to provide funding in respect of the Costs of any Appeal:

10.2.1. the Claimant shall not be obliged to pursue or defend the Appeal but, if it does so, shall comply with its obligations set out in clause 9;

10.2.2. subject to any contrary order of the Court, Therium shall have no liability for any Adverse Costs Order made in relation to the Appeal; and

10.2.3. if the Appeal was brought by the Claimant and the Claim Proceeds are reduced as a result of the Appeal, the Contingency Fee shall be calculated by reference to the amount of the Claim Proceeds immediately prior to the Appeal.

10.3. Where Therium elects to provide funding in respect of the Costs of any Appeal;

10.3.1. clause 10.2.1 will apply;

10.3.2. Therium shall be liable for any Adverse Costs Order made in relation to the Appeal to the extent, if any, set out in clause 8.1;

10.3.3. if the Claim Proceeds are reduced as a result of the Appeal then the Contingency Fee due to Therium shall be recalculated to reduce the amount due to Therium following the Appeal; and

10.3.4. following recalculation in accordance with clause 10.3.3, Therium shall repay any sums paid to it in excess of its entitlement under this Agreement.

11. Recovery

The Claimant shall use its best endeavours to cause any Claim Proceeds to be recovered as quickly as possible.

12. Security for costs

12.1. Where specified in the Project Plan or as otherwise agreed, in the event of an order of the Court that the Claimant shall provide security for the costs of a party to the Proceedings, Therium will discharge that order to the satisfaction of the Court.

12.2. The Claimant agrees to hold the Legal Expenses Insurance policy and all proceeds payable under it on trust for Therium throughout the Trust Period on terms that Therium shall be entitled to such part or all of any proceeds of the Legal Expenses Insurance which become payable as a consequence of an Adverse Costs Order as shall be equal to the amount of any security posted by Therium pursuant to clause 12.1 used to discharge the Claimant's liability (either entirely or in part) in respect of any Adverse Costs Order.

12.3. The Claimant agrees that within 2 Business Days of whichever is the later of:

12.3.1. the date on which this Agreement is executed; or

12.3.2. the date on which the Legal Expenses Insurance policy comes on risk, the Claimant will send to the insurer providing the Legal Expenses Insurance a written Notice of Interest in duplicate for noting on the insurer's records and will provide a copy of such Notice of Interest, duly acknowledged by the insurer, to Therium within 5 Business Days of receipt of the same by the Claimant.

13. Treatment of Claim Proceeds

13.1. The Claimant agrees to hold any Claim Proceeds received by it or by the Solicitors on its behalf, upon trust for Therium throughout the Trust Period on terms that Therium shall be entitled to such part of the Claim Proceeds as shall be equal to the total of all amounts due under the terms of this Agreement to Therium (as the same may be reduced in accordance with the Priorities Agreement).

13.2. The Parties agree that any Claim Proceeds received in monetary form shall be paid into the Solicitors' client account immediately upon receipt. In the case of any Claim Proceeds received in non-monetary form, the Claimant shall either deliver the Claim Proceeds to the Solicitors or pay to the Solicitors as soon as is reasonably practicable the market value of the Claim Proceeds determined in accordance with clause 13.3.

13.3. In the case of any Claim Proceeds received in non-monetary form, the Parties agree that the non-monetary element shall be valued by an independent valuer agreed by the Parties with the cost of that valuation to be met by the Claimant. Where the Parties cannot agree on the identity of the independent valuer, the President of the Law Society from time to time shall be requested to recommend a valuer who shall be the independent valuer for the purposes of this clause.

13.4. On notification of receipt of Claim Proceeds by the Solicitors, Therium shall prepare a draft Claim Proceeds Account and shall deliver that draft Claim Proceeds Account to each of the parties to the Priorities Agreement for agreement.

13.5. Once the draft Claim Proceeds Account is agreed or deemed to be agreed pursuant to the Priorities Agreement (whichever is the earlier), the Parties agree that the Solicitors shall forthwith pay out the Claims Proceeds in accordance with the agreed Claim Proceeds Account.

13.6. Any damages awarded against the Claimant in respect of a counterclaim funded pursuant to clause 4.1 shall be deducted from the Claim Proceeds for the purposes of calculating the distribution under the Claims Proceeds Account. For the avoidance of doubt, such deduction of damages shall not apply where Therium has not funded the cost of defending the counterclaim.

13.7. If any payment due to Therium from the Claim Proceeds is delayed due to action or failure to act on the part of the Claimant, the Claimant shall compensate Therium for the delay in making payment by paying to Therium interest on the sum delayed for the period of the delay calculated in accordance with clause 3.2.

14. Confidentiality

14.1. The Parties agree to keep confidential and, where appropriate maintain any privilege belonging to the Claimant, in all documents and information supplied by the Claimant, Therium or the Solicitors, including (unless otherwise agreed) the existence and / or terms of this Agreement. It is agreed that the provision of privileged documents does not amount to any waiver of privilege, and the Parties shall not use these for any purpose other than in respect of this Agreement, except a purpose to which the Parties have consented or as required by law or regulation. The Claimant agrees that Therium may disclose such documents and information:

14.1.1. to its advisers, including auditors, brokers, legal advisers, investors and potential investors, insurers and potential insurers;

14.1.2. where Therium is under a legal or regulatory obligation to make such disclosure, but limited to the extent of that legal obligation;

14.1.3. to the extent that it is already in the public domain (other than as a result of Therium's breach of this Agreement);

14.1.4. with the prior written consent of the Claimant; or

14.1.5. to the extent necessary to take legal action to enforce Therium's rights under this Agreement or to defend such action.

14.2. Therium shall procure that any persons receiving confidential documents or information pursuant to sub-clause 14.1.1 shall comply with the obligations imposed on Therium pursuant to sub-clause 14.1.

14.3. Nothing in this Agreement shall prevent Therium instructing one or more agents to undertake any action or review documents, evidence or information which Therium would be entitled to undertake pursuant to this Agreement save that Therium shall procure that any agent acting on its behalf shall comply with the obligations imposed on Therium by clause 14.1.

14.4. Therium will immediately inform the Claimant of any request or order to disclose its privileged documents or any other privileged information held by Therium, except where informing the Claimant would contravene any law or regulation.

15. Termination

15.1. Without prejudice to clause 6.1 and subject to earlier termination of this Agreement pursuant to clauses 15.2 to 15.6, this Agreement shall continue in full force and effect until payment of any and all sums due to Therium pursuant to this Agreement and in any event clauses 1, 3.2, 6.2, 6.3, 6.4, 8, 12.2, 14 to 17, 20 to 23, 25 and 26 shall continue in full force and effect notwithstanding termination of this Agreement. For the avoidance of doubt, the options at clauses 2.3, 2.4 and 2.5 above shall not remain open for exercise by Therium after termination of this Agreement.

15.2. The Claimant and Therium may at any time agree, by mutual consent in writing, to terminate this Agreement in which event they shall serve Notice of such termination on the Solicitors.

15.3. If, Therium reasonably ceases to be satisfied as to the merits of the Claim or Therium reasonably believes that the Claim is no longer commercially viable, then Therium shall be entitled to terminate this Agreement by giving 5 Business Days' Notice to the Claimant. Following such termination Therium shall have no further liability to fund the Reasonable Costs but shall remain entitled upon Recovery to the Reasonable Costs Sum together with interest calculated in accordance with clause 3.2 from the Commencement Date until the date of payment. For the avoidance of doubt, following such termination Therium shall have no future entitlement to the Contingency Fee.

15.4. In the event that Therium reasonably considers that there has been a material breach of this Agreement by the Claimant, Therium shall notify the Claimant that Therium requires the Claimant to remedy the breach within 20 Business Days. In the event that the breach is not remedied within that period, Therium shall be entitled to terminate this Agreement forthwith by giving Notice to the Claimant, copied to the Solicitors. Within 5 Business Days of such termination the Claimant shall pay to Therium the Reasonable Costs Sum calculated as at that date, together with interest calculated in accordance with clause 3.2 from the date of this Agreement to the date of payment. Following such termination Therium shall remain entitled to the Contingency Fee upon Recovery and, for the purpose of calculating this, Therium shall be deemed to have exercised the options set out above at clauses 2.3, 2.4 and 2.5. For the purposes of this clause 15.4, a material breach shall include, but not be limited to, any breach of any of the warranties set out in clauses 6.2 to 6.4.

15.5. In the event of a material breach of this Agreement by Therium, the Claimant shall notify Therium that the Claimant requires Therium to remedy the breach within 20 Business Days. In the event that the breach is not remedied within that period, the Claimant shall be entitled to terminate this Agreement forthwith by giving Notice to Therium, copied to the Solicitors. Following such termination Therium shall remain entitled to the Reasonable Costs Sum, calculated as at the date of termination, upon Recovery. For the avoidance of doubt, following such termination Therium shall have no future entitlement to the Contingency Fee.

15.6. In the event of termination of this Agreement pursuant to clauses 15.2 to 15.5, the Claimant shall within 20 Business Days put in place alternative arrangements to discharge any order for security for costs and, at the end of the 20 Business Days period, Therium shall be entitled to terminate any such arrangements made on the Claimant's behalf pursuant to clause 12.1. Therium shall, on payment by the Claimant to Therium of an amount equal to the amount (if any) of any security for costs posted by Therium which has been used to discharge the Claimant's liability in respect of any Adverse Costs Order, provide the Claimant with a written Notice of Release of Interest in respect of the Legal Expenses Insurance.

15.7. Termination of this Agreement shall not affect any accrued rights or liabilities nor will it affect the coming into force or the continuance in force of any provision which is expressly or by implication intended to come into or continue in force on or after such termination.

Appendix 1

16. Contracts (Rights of Third Parties) Act

    A person who is a party to this Agreement has no right under the Contracts (Rights of Third Parties) Act 1999 or otherwise to enforce any term of this Agreement.

17. Data Protection

    In performing their respective obligations and exercising their respective rights under this Agreement, the parties agree to comply with the terms of the Data Protection Act 1998 and all regulations published pursuant to that Act.

18. Assignment

    18.1. The Parties agree that Therium shall be entitled to assign to a third party any or all of its rights, interests and obligations pursuant to this Agreement upon giving 5 Business Days' Notice of its intention to do so to the Claimant.

    18.2. Save as provided in clause 18.1, a Party shall not assign or transfer this Agreement or any of its rights under it, or purport to do any of the same, nor sub-contract any or all of its obligations under this Agreement without having first obtained the prior written consent of the other Party.

19. Variation

    No variation to this Agreement shall be valid unless it is in writing and signed by the Parties' authorised signatories.

20. Waiver

    No forbearance or delay by a Party in enforcing its rights shall prejudice or restrict the rights of that Party, and no waiver of any such rights or of any breach of any contractual terms will be deemed to be a waiver of any other right or of any later breach.

21. Invalidity and severability

    If any provision of this Agreement shall be held to be illegal or unenforceable whether in whole or in part or in relation to either of the Parties to the Agreement, the validity and enforceability of the remainder of the Agreement, or its validity and enforceability as against other parties, shall not be affected and each Party shall take any step required, including executing any further or other document, in order to give effect to the Parties' intention in entering into this Agreement.

22. Succession

    This Agreement shall be binding on the Parties, their successors and assigns and the name of a Party appearing herein shall be deemed to include the names of any such successor or assign.

23. Notices

    23.1. Any Notice to be served under this Agreement shall be in writing and may be delivered by hand or sent by pre-paid first class recorded delivery post to the Party to be served at the relevant address set out in this Agreement or any such other address as the Party to be served may have notified to the other Party for the purposes of this clause 23.1.

23.2. For the purpose of service of Notice or other documents on the Claimant, the Claimant agrees that service on the Solicitors shall be valid and adequate service on the Claimant.

23.3. Any Notice shall be deemed to have been served:

23.3.1. If delivered by hand, at the time of delivery to the Party or Solicitors; or

23.3.2. if posted, at 10.00am on the second Business Day after it was posted to the Party or Solicitors.

23.4. In proving service of a Notice it shall be sufficient to prove that delivery by hand was made or that the envelope containing the Notice was properly addressed and posted as a pre-paid first class recorded delivery letter.

24. Counterparts

This Agreement may be signed in any number of counterparts, each of which taken together shall be deemed to constitute one and each of which individually shall be deemed to be an original, with the same effect as if the signature on each counterpart were on the same original.

25. Dispute Resolution

25.1 The Parties agree that in the event of any dispute between Therium and the Claimant relating to:

25.1.1 settlement of the Claim; or

25.1.2 termination of this Agreement under clause 15;

either party shall be entitled to direct the Solicitors to refer the dispute to an independent Queen's Counsel, whose identity is to be agreed between the Parties or, in lieu of such agreement, to be nominated by the Chairman of the Bar Council. Such Queen's Counsel shall be deemed to be jointly instructed by both parties.

25.3 In the event of a dispute over settlement of the Claim, the Queen's Counsel shall be instructed to provide an opinion as to the appropriate level of settlement. The Parties agree that the Queen's Counsel's opinion on settlement shall be final and binding on each one of them and the Claimant shall instruct the Solicitors and Counsel accordingly. In the event of Therium making a reference to Queen's Counsel in respect of settlement, the Claimant shall not take further steps to settle the Claim without the consent of Therium until the Opinion is obtained.

25.4 In the event of a dispute over termination of this Agreement, the Queen's Counsel shall be instructed to provide an opinion on the rights and entitlements of each of the Parties. The Parties agree that the Queen's Counsel's opinion on this issue in dispute shall be final and binding on each one of them.

25.5   In giving any opinion pursuant to clauses 25.3 and 25.4 above, Queen's Counsel shall also be instructed to determine which one or more of the Parties should bear Queen's Counsel's fees of giving the Opinion (and, if more than one Party, the shares in which they are each to bear those fees) and the Parties agree to be bound by this determination as to liability for the Queen's Counsel's fees.

26. Law and jurisdiction

This Agreement is governed by and is to be construed in accordance with the law of England and Wales. Save for any dispute resolved finally pursuant to clause 25 above, any dispute arising out of or connected to this Agreement, including the validity or termination thereof, shall be finally resolved by a sole arbitrator under the arbitration rules of the London Court of International Arbitration (the 'LCIA'). The seat of the arbitration shall be London, the language of the arbitration shall be English and the arbitrator shall be a practising member of the English Bar. The arbitrator shall be appointed by the agreement of the Parties provided that, if the Parties cannot reach agreement on the appointment of the arbitrator within 30 days, then any Party may apply to have the arbitrator appointed by the LCIA.

IN WITNESS of which the Parties have each executed this Agreement on the date shown above

Signed..
For and on behalf of THERIUM (UK) HOLDINGS LIMITED

Signed..
For and on behalf of [CLAIMANT]

SCHEDULE

Claim: [ ]

Commencement Date: The date of this Agreement.

Claimant's Solicitors: [ ]

Claimant's Counsel: [ ]

Defendant: [ ]

Committed Cost and Contingency Fee:

Tranche:	Committed Costs:	Contingency Fee:
Tranche 1	£[ ]	[ ] × the Committed Costs for Tranche 1 or [ ]%
Tranche 2	£[ ]	[ ] × the Committed Costs for Tranches 1 and 2 or [ ]%
Tranche 3	£	[ ] × the Committed Costs for Tranches 1, 2 and 3 or [ ]%
Tranche 4	£[ ]	[ ] × the Committed Costs for Tranches 1, 2, 3 and 4 or [ ]%

APPENDIX 1

Project Plan

APPENDIX 2

Specimen letter from Solicitors

APPENDIX 3

Specimen Priorities Agreement

PRIORITIES AGREEMENT

(1) THERIUM (UK) HOLDINGS LLP;

(2) [CLAIMANT];

(3) [SOLICITORS]; and

(4) [INSURER].

THIS AGREEMENT is made this   day of   2014

BETWEEN:

(1)   THERIUM (UK) HOLDINGS LIMITED (company number 7213330) of 78 Duke Street, Mayfair, London W1K 6JQ ('Therium');

(2)   [CLAIMANT] of [address] ('the Claimant');

(3)   [SOLICITORS] of [address] ('the Solicitors'); and

(4)   [INSURER] of [address   ] ('the Insurer').

individually a 'Party' and together the 'Parties'.

WHEREAS:

A.   The Claimant has a legal claim against [   ] ('the Defendant') for inter alia [   ]. The Claimant has issued legal proceedings against the Defendant in the [   ] Division of the High Court of Justice of England and Wales under claim number [   ] ('the Proceedings').

C.   Pursuant to an engagement letter dated [   ] ('the Engagement Letter') [and a conditional fee agreement dated [ ]] ('**the CFA**'), the Solicitors act for the Claimant in relation to the Proceedings.

D.   The Claimant has taken out an Adverse Costs Insurance Policy number [   ] dated [   ] underwritten by the Insurer ('the Policy') whereby the Insurer agrees to provide cover to the Claimant up to £[   ] in the aggregate.

E.   In consideration for Therium entering into a funding agreement ('the Funding Agreement') with the Claimant to enable the Proceedings to progress, the Parties wish to set out in this Agreement the priority order for paying the sums due to each of them from the proceeds of the Policy (if any) and from any recoveries made in the prosecution of the Claim.

NOW IT IS AGREED AS FOLLOWS:-

Definitions

1.   In this Deed the following definitions shall have the following meanings:

'Agreements' means all of the Appointment, the Policy, the Engagement Letter, the CFA and the Funding Agreement collectively;

'Base Costs' means the base costs referred to in the CFA, any of the Solicitors' profit costs (excluding uplift) remaining unpaid under the terms of the Engagement Letter and any of the fees (excluding uplift) remaining unpaid of Counsel (or any other counsel retained by the Solicitors in the case);

'Claim' means the Claimant's claims and causes of action against the Defendant in the Proceedings (and any amendment of those claims or causes of action) and any enforcement action or subsequent proceedings relating thereto;

'Claim Proceeds' means all and any value due to and/or received by, on behalf of, or in lieu of payment to, the Claimant in connection with the Claim as a result of any judgment, award, order, settlement or compromise whatsoever, including payment of any damages, compensation, interest, restitution, recovery, judgment sum, arbitral award, settlement sum, compensation payment, costs and interest on costs, whether in monetary or non-monetary form, before deduction of any taxes which the Claimant may be liable to pay in respect of the Claim Proceeds and any sums payable to the Claimant pursuant to the terms of the Policy;

'Claim Proceeds Account' means an account prepared by Therium, setting out the share of any Claims Proceeds due to the Parties and the order of payment;

'Independent Counsel' means an independent barrister of not less than 10 years call who is not and has not otherwise acted for any of the Parties in connection with the Proceedings;

'Notice' means a notice given in accordance with Clause 6 of this Agreement; and

'Notice of Disagreement' means a notice setting out in reasonable detail the scope, nature of and reasons for a Party's disagreement with a draft Claims Proceeds Account.

2. Time of the essence

It is agreed that, in relation to any time period specified in this Agreement, time shall be of the essence.

3. Priority for payments from Claim Proceeds

   3.1. It is agreed that all sums due to any of the Parties pursuant to the Agreements shall be paid out of any Claim Proceeds in accordance with the terms of this Agreement until all such sums are discharged or until the Claim Proceeds are exhausted.

   3.2. It is agreed that the Claim Proceeds shall be distributed in the following priority order:-

      3.2.1. First, to pay the Solicitors such sum as are necessary to bring them up to 100% of their Base Costs;

      3.2.2. Secondly, to reimburse Therium for all and any sums paid pursuant to the Funding Agreement;

      3.2.3. Thirdly, to reimburse the Insurer for all adverse costs it has paid out pursuant to the terms of the Policy.

      To the extent that the Claim Proceeds are insufficient to discharge in full all sums referred in sub-clauses 3.2.1 to 3.2.3 above, the Claim Proceeds shall be applied between the Solicitors, Therium and the Insurer pari passu on a pro rata basis in proportion to their entitlement to sums under those sub-clauses.

      3.2.4. Fourthly, any further sums due to the Solicitors, Therium, and the Insurer until all their entitlements pursuant to the Agreements as at the date of distribution have been discharged in full. To the extent that the Claim Proceeds are insufficient to discharge sums payable pursuant to this sub-clause in full, the Claim Proceeds after payment of all sums referred in sub-clauses 3.2.1 to 3.2.3 above shall be applied pari passu on a pro rata basis to pay the Solicitors, Therium and the Insurer any other sums due to them under the Agreements in accordance with this sub-clause.

  3.2.5. Fifthly, any further Claim Proceeds remaining after deduction of the sums referred to at clauses 3.2.1 to 3.2.4 above shall be paid to the Claimant or as it may direct from which the Claimant shall discharge any further liability it may have to any other person in such manner as the Claimant and that person shall agree, without further reference to the other Parties.

3.3. This Agreement is intended to determine the priority order for distribution of sums recovered in the Proceedings. In the event of conflict between the terms of this Agreement and any of the Agreements, the terms of the Agreements shall take precedence save that nothing in this Agreement shall affect the underlying liability of the Claimant to pay all sums which may fall due for payment to the Solicitors, the Insurer and/or any other suppliers or experts instructed in relation to the Claim under the terms of the Agreements or any other agreement.

4. Determination of the Parties' rights and entitlements to the Claim Proceeds

4.1. As soon as reasonably practicable after receipt of any Claim Proceeds (including any payment made pursuant to the Policy), by or on behalf of the Claimant, Therium shall prepare a draft Claim Proceeds Account and deliver a copy to each of the other Parties.

4.2. Unless, within 14 calendar days from the date of service of the draft Claim Proceeds Account, a valid Notice of Disagreement has been served on Therium by any one or more of the Parties, the draft Claim Proceeds Account shall be deemed to be agreed by each of the Parties and any part of a draft Claim Proceeds Account not the subject of a valid Notice of Disagreement served pursuant to this Clause shall similarly be deemed to be agreed.

4.3. In the event that a valid Notice of Disagreement is served in accordance with clause 4.2 above, the Parties agree to seek to resolve that disagreement within a further period of 14 calendar days, failing which any remaining matters not agreed shall be referred to Independent Counsel who shall be instructed to determine the rights and entitlements of each of the Parties to the Claim Proceeds pursuant to the Agreements and this Agreement. The Parties agree that Independent Counsel's determination on this issue shall be final and binding on each one of them.

4.4. In making any determination as to the rights and entitlements of each of the Parties pursuant to clause 4.3 above, Independent Counsel shall also be instructed to determine which one or more of the Parties should bear Independent Counsel's fees of making the determination (and, if more than one Party, the shares in which they are each to bear those fees) and the Parties agree to be bound by this determination as to liability for Independent Counsel's fees.

4.5. Pending any draft Claim Proceeds Account or any part of it being deemed to be agreed, or pending resolution of any disputed matter by Independent Counsel, the Solicitors shall hold the Claim Proceeds, or such part as is

Appendix 1

not agreed, in their client account. The Parties agree that the whole or any part of any draft Claim Proceeds Account which is deemed to be agreed pursuant to Clause 4.2 above, and any determination of Independent Counsel pursuant to Clauses 4.3 and 4.4 above, constitutes a binding and irrevocable instruction to the Solicitors to distribute that element of the Claim Proceeds forthwith in accordance with that whole or part of the Claims Proceeds Account or determination. Where a Party is directed by Independent Counsel to meet the fees of Counsel in making a determination under Clause 4.4, then the amount of those fees, and any VAT payable thereon, shall be deducted by the Solicitors from any amount of the Claims Proceeds due to that Party.

5. Warranty

The Claimant warrants that there are no persons other than the Parties who have any right or claim or interest whatsoever over the Claim Proceeds in priority or ranking equally with any of the Parties, either in whole or part and that the Claimant has obtained all consents, waivers or releases as may be required in order to validly confer on the Parties the rights as set out in this Agreement.

6. Notices

   6.1. Any Notice to be served under this Agreement may be delivered by hand or sent by pre-paid first class recorded delivery post to the Party to be served at the relevant address set out in this Agreement or any such other address as the Party to be served may have notified to the other Party in accordance with this Clause 6, marked for the attention of the individuals as follows:

      6.1.1. in the case of the Solicitors, [ ];

      6.1.2. in the case of the Claimant, [ ];

      6.1.3. in the case of Therium, [ ];

      6.1.4. in the case of the Insurer, [ ].

   6.2. Any Notice shall be deemed to have been served:

      6.2.1. if delivered, at the time of delivery to the Party; or

      6.2.2. if posted, at 10.00am on the second Business Day after it was posted to the Party.

   6.3. In proving service of a Notice it shall be sufficient to prove that delivery by hand was made or that the envelope containing the Notice was properly addressed and posted as a pre-paid first class recorded delivery letter.

   6.4. If Notice is served by means of a pre-paid first class recorded delivery letter, the Party serving such notice shall, on or before posting the Notice, send a copy of it by email to the receiving Party's usual email address.

7. Successors and assignments

This Agreement shall be binding upon and enure for the benefit of the successors-in-title and permitted assignees of the Parties hereto.

8. Waiver and forbearance

No failure to exercise or delay in exercising any right or remedy under this Agreement shall constitute a waiver thereof and no waiver by any of the Parties of any breach or non-fulfilment by any of the other Parties of any provision of this Agreement shall be deemed to be a waiver of any subsequent or other breach of that or any other provision hereof and no single or partial exercise of any right or remedy under this Agreement shall preclude or restrict the further exercise of any such right or remedy.

9. Variation

No variation of this agreement shall be valid unless it is in writing and signed by or on behalf of each of the Parties hereto.

10. Counterparts

This Agreement may be executed in any number of parts each of which, when executed by one or more parties hereto, shall constitute an original document but all of which shall together constitute one and the same instrument.

11. Good Faith

Each party shall at all times deal with every other Party in good faith.

12. Choice of law and jurisdiction

This Agreement is governed by and is to be construed in accordance with the law of England and Wales. Any dispute arising out of or connected to this Agreement, including the validity or termination thereof, shall be finally resolved by a sole arbitrator under the arbitration rules of the London Court of International Arbitration (the 'LCIA'). The seat of the arbitration shall be London, the language of the arbitration shall be English and the arbitrator shall be a practising member of the English Bar. The arbitrator shall be appointed by the agreement of the Parties provided that, if the Parties cannot reach agreement on the appointment of the arbitrator within 30 days, then any Party may apply to have the arbitrator appointed by the LCIA.

SIGNED FOR AND ON BEHALF OF THE PARTIES:

Signed for and on behalf of...

THERIUM (UK) HOLDINGS LIMITED

Signed by ....

[THE CLAIMANT]

Signed for and on behalf of ....

[THE SOLICITORS]

Signed for and on behalf of ....

[THE INSURER]

APPENDIX 2

Preamble

The SRA Code of Conduct dated 17 June 2011 commencing 6 October 2011 made by the Solicitors Regulation Authority Board under sections 31, 79 and 80 of the Solicitors Act 1974, sections 9 and 9A of the Administration of Justice Act 1985 and section 83 of the Legal Services Act 2007, with the approval of the Legal Services Board under paragraph 19 of Schedule 4 to the Legal Services Act 2007, regulating the conduct of solicitors and their employees, registered European lawyers and their employees, registered foreign lawyers, recognised bodies and their managers and employees and licensed bodies and their managers and employees.

1st Section: You and your client

Chapter 1: Client care

This chapter is about providing a proper standard of service, which takes into account the individual needs and circumstances of each *client*. This includes providing *clients* with the information they need to make informed decisions about the services they need, how these will be delivered and how much they will cost. This will enable you and your *client* to understand each other's expectations and responsibilities. This chapter is also about ensuring that if *clients* are not happy with the service they have received they know how to make a *complaint* and that all *complaints* are dealt with promptly and fairly.

Your relationship with your *client* is a contractual one which carries with it legal, as well as conduct, obligations. This chapter focuses on your obligations in conduct.

You are generally free to decide whether or not to accept instructions in any matter, provided you do not discriminate unlawfully (see Chapter 2).

The outcomes in this chapter show how the *Principles* apply in the context of client care.

Outcomes

You must achieve these outcomes:

O(1.1)   you treat your *clients* fairly;

O(1.2)   you provide services to your *clients* in a manner which protects their interests in their matter, subject to the proper administration of justice;

O(1.3)   when deciding whether to act, or terminate your instructions, you comply with the law and the Code;

O(1.4)   you have the resources, skills and procedures to carry out your *clients'* instructions;

O(1.5)   the service you provide to *clients* is competent, delivered in a timely manner and takes account of your *clients'* needs and circumstances;

O(1.6)   you only enter into fee agreements with your *clients* that are legal, and which you consider are suitable for the *client's* needs and take account of the *client's* best interests;

O (1.7)	you inform *clients* whether and how the services you provide are regulated and how this affects the protections available to the *client*;
O (1.8)	*clients* have the benefit of your *compulsory professional indemnity insurance* and you do not exclude or attempt to exclude liability below the minimum level of cover required by the *SRA Indemnity Insurance Rules*;
O (1.9)	*clients* are informed in writing at the outset of their matter of their right to complain and how *complaints* can be made;
O (1.10)	*clients* are informed in writing, both at the time of engagement and at the conclusion of your *complaints* procedure, of their right to complain to the *Legal Ombudsman*, the time frame for doing so and full details of how to contact the Legal Ombudsman;
O (1.11)	*clients' complaints* are dealt with promptly, fairly, openly and effectively;
O (1.12)	*clients* are in a position to make informed decisions about the services they need, how their matter will be handled and the options available to them;
O (1.13)	*clients* receive the best possible information, both at the time of engagement and when appropriate as their matter progresses, about the likely overall cost of their matter;
O (1.14)	*clients* are informed of their right to challenge or complain about your bill and the circumstances in which they may be liable to pay interest on an unpaid bill;
O (1.15)	you properly account to *clients* for any *financial benefit* you receive as a result of your instructions;
O (1.16)	you inform current *clients* if you discover any act or omission which could give rise to a claim by them against you.

Indicative behaviours

Acting in the following way(s) may tend to show that you have achieved these outcomes and therefore complied with the *Principles*:

Dealing with the client's matter

IB (1.1)	agreeing an appropriate level of service with your *client*, for example the type and frequency of communications;
IB (1.2)	explaining your responsibilities and those of the *client*;
IB (1.3)	ensuring that the *client* is told, in writing, the name and status of the person(s) dealing with the matter and the name and status of the person responsible for its overall supervision;
IB (1.4)	explaining any arrangements, such as fee sharing or *referral arrangements*, which are relevant to the *client's* instructions;
IB (1.5)	explaining any limitations or conditions on what you can do for the *client*, for example, because of the way the *client's* matter is funded;
IB (1.6)	in taking instructions and during the course of the retainer, having proper regard to your *client's* mental capacity or other vulnerability, such as incapacity or duress;
IB (1.7)	considering whether you should decline to act or cease to act because you cannot act in the *client's* best interests;
IB (1.8)	if you seek to limit your liability to your *client* to a level above the minimum required by the *SRA Indemnity Insurance Rules*, ensuring that this limitation is in writing and is brought to the *client's* attention;

IB (1.9)	refusing to act where your *client* proposes to make a gift of significant value to you or a member of your family, or a member of your *firm* or their family, unless the *client* takes independent legal advice;
IB (1.10)	if you have to cease acting for a *client*, explaining to the *client* their possible options for pursuing their matter;
IB (1.11)	you inform *clients* if they are not entitled to the protections of the SRA Compensation Fund;
IB (1.12)	considering whether a *conflict of interests* has arisen or whether the *client* should be advised to obtain independent advice where the *client* notifies you of their intention to make a claim or if you discover an act or omission which might give rise to a claim;

Fee arrangements with your client

IB (1.13)	discussing whether the potential outcomes of the *client's* matter are likely to justify the expense or risk involved, including any risk of having to pay someone else's legal fees;
IB (1.14)	clearly explaining your fees and if and when they are likely to change;
IB (1.15)	warning about any other payments for which the *client* may be responsible;
IB (1.16)	discussing how the *client* will pay, including whether public funding may be available, whether the *client* has insurance that might cover the fees, and whether the fees may be paid by someone else such as a trade union;
IB (1.17)	where you are acting for a *client* under a fee arrangement governed by statute, such as a conditional fee agreement, giving the *client* all relevant information relating to that arrangement;
IB (1.18)	where you are acting for a publicly funded *client*, explaining how their publicly funded status affects the costs;
IB (1.19)	providing the information in a clear and accessible form which is appropriate to the needs and circumstances of the *client*;
IB (1.20)	where you receive a *financial benefit* as a result of acting for a *client*, either: (a) paying it to the *client*; (b) offsetting it against your fees; or (c) keeping it only where you can justify keeping it, you have told the *client* the amount of the benefit (or an approximation if you do not know the exact amount) and the *client* has agreed that you can keep it;
IB (1.21)	ensuring that *disbursements* included in your bill reflect the actual amount spent or to be spent on behalf of the *client*;

Complaints handling

IB (1.22)	having a written *complaints* procedure which: (a) is brought to *clients'* attention at the outset of the matter; (b) is easy for *clients* to use and understand, allowing for *complaints* to be made by any reasonable means;

	(c)	is responsive to the needs of individual *clients*, especially those who are vulnerable;
	(d)	enables *complaints* to be dealt with promptly and fairly, with decisions based on a sufficient investigation of the circumstances;
	(e)	provides for appropriate remedies; and
	(f)	does not involve any charges to *clients* for handling their *complaints*;

IB (1.23)   providing the *client* with a copy of the *firm's complaints* procedure on request;

IB (1.24)   in the event that a *client* makes a *complaint*, providing them with all necessary information concerning the handling of the *complaint*.

Acting in the following way(s) may tend to show that you have not achieved these outcomes and therefore not complied with the *Principles*:

Accepting and refusing instructions

IB (1.25)   acting for a *client* when instructions are given by someone else, or by only one *client* when you act jointly for others unless you are satisfied that the *person* providing the instructions has the authority to do so on behalf of all of the *clients*;

IB (1.26)   ceasing to act for a *client* without good reason and without providing reasonable notice;

IB (1.27)   entering into unlawful fee arrangements such as an unlawful contingency fee;

IB (1.28)   acting for a *client* when there are reasonable grounds for believing that the instructions are affected by duress or undue influence without satisfying yourself that they represent the *client's* wishes.

In-house practice

Outcomes 1.1 to 1.5, 1.7, 1.15 and 1.16 apply to your *in-house practice*.

Outcomes 1.6 and 1.9 to 1.14 apply to your *in-house practice* where you act for someone other than your employer unless it is clear that the outcome is not relevant to your particular circumstances.

IHP (1.1)   Instead of Outcome 1.8 you comply with the *SRA Practice Framework Rules* in relation to professional indemnity insurance.

Notes

(i) The information you give to *clients* will vary according to the needs and circumstances of the individual *client* and the type of work you are doing for them, for example an individual instructing you on a conveyancing matter is unlikely to need the same information as a sophisticated commercial *client* who instructs you on a regular basis.

(ii) Information about the Legal Ombudsman, including the scheme rules, contact details and time limits, can be found at www.legalombudsman.org.uk.

APPENDIX 3

A Procedure to Govern Complaints Made against Funder Members by Funded Litigants

Definitions

1. Save where otherwise provided, terms adopted herein shall have the same meaning as defined in the Code of Conduct of Litigation Funders in England & Wales, the Articles of the ALF, and the Rules of the ALF, and references to an 'Article' or a 'Rule' shall be construed accordingly.

2. The following terms shall have the following meanings in this procedure:

'Associated Entity'	any entity for which a Member is responsible by virtue of Rule 3.4.
'Code of Conduct'	the prevailing Code of Conduct for Litigation Funders in England & Wales as applies at the time of the events which are the subject of any complaint under this procedure.
'Complaint'	a complaint made against a Member or any Associated Entity of the ALF pursuant to the provisions of paragraph 5 below.
'Independent Legal Counsel'	a Solicitor of the Senior Courts of England and Wales holding the position of partner or equivalent in a firm in England and Wales and specialising in litigation or a Queens Counsel in self-employed practice specialising in litigation, and in each case independent of both the parties to the Complaint and the ALF.
'Litigant'	any person or entity who has entered into a Litigation Funding Agreement with a Member or any Associated Entity.
'Previous Procedure'	means the complaints procedure of the ALF in force immediately prior to the adoption of this procedure.
'Responsible Member'	in respect of an Associated Entity, the Member which has taken responsibility for that Associated Entity by virtue of Rule 3.4.

General

3. A Funder Member, by joining the ALF, consents to the complaints procedure set out herein, and as it may be varied from time to time in accordance with the Articles of the ALF and the Rules of the ALF.

4. Wherever a period of time is prescribed below for the taking of a particular step, the Board may for the purposes of any particular Complaint abridge or extend that period of

time by such length as it sees fit, where to do so appears to the Board desirable to ensure the fair and proportionate disposition of the Complaint. Any extension of time under this provision may be granted after the original time for compliance has elapsed if to do so would be fair and proportionate.

5. This procedure shall govern any Complaint made after the adoption of this Procedure and which concerns an act or omission on the part of any Member or any Associate Entity which relates to:

   (1) a dispute and/or the funding of a dispute within England and Wales in respect of which the Member or Associated Entity has entered into a Litigation Funding Agreement; and where

   (2) the Litigation Funding Agreement referred to in (1) above was:

      a. entered into after November 11 2013; and

      b. made between the Member and/or Associated Entity and the Litigant making the complaint (provided for the avoidance of doubt that this procedure shall continue to apply regardless of whether any other person or entity is also a party to that Litigation Funding Agreement).

6. Any Complaint made prior to the adoption of this procedure by the ALF shall be resolved pursuant to the provisions of the Previous Procedure.

Instigating a Complaint

7. A Complaint is instigated by a Litigant ('**the Complainant**'):

   (1) sending a letter of complaint only to the General Counsel of the ALF. The General Counsel shall hold the letter of complaint confidentially, without initial disclosure to the Board; and/or

   (2) otherwise contacting the ALF in writing by any method authorised by the Board from time to time for the bringing of complaints;

   (in either case '**the Initial Complaint**').

8. An Initial Complaint should so far as possible:

   (1) identify the Member and/or Associated Entity ('**the Subject**') in respect of which it is made;

   (2) identify and provide details of the Litigation Funding Agreement in respect of which the Complaint is made;

   (3) identify the provision or provisions of the Code of Conduct said to have been breached by the Subject;

   (4) set out, as concisely as possible, the facts and matters said to constitute such a breach; and

   (5) append any relevant documents.

   save that, for the avoidance of doubt, a failure to include any or all of the matters indicated above shall not invalidate the Initial Complaint.

The Initial Complaint

9. On receiving the Initial Complaint, the General Counsel of the ALF ('**the Investigator**') shall have charge of the Complaint. The Investigator shall thereafter take no part in determining the Complaint save as provided for in this procedure.

10. If on receiving the Initial Complaint it appears to the Investigator that the Initial Complaint fails to include any or all of the information listed in paragraph 8 above, the Investigator may write to the Complainant (on as many occasions as he/she thinks fit) requiring the provision of all and any such further information as appears to the Investigator to be necessary within 28 days, or such other time period as the Investigator may stipulate.

11. The Investigator shall, on reviewing the Initial Complaint (together with any additional information obtained pursuant to paragraph 10 above), prepare and submit a short report to the Board ('**the Preliminary Report**') identifying whether the Initial Complaint appears to disclose any breaches of the Code of Conduct.

12. In the event that the Investigator is of the view (and records in his/her Preliminary Report) that the Initial Complaint, or part of it, fails to disclose any breach, or any arguable breach, of the Code of Conduct (for whatever reason, including by reason of a failure on the part of the Complainant to respond to reasonable requests for additional information) he/she may recommend to the Board that it dismisses the Initial Complaint, or part of it, summarily in accordance with paragraph 13 below. In these circumstances there will be no need for the Investigator to invite a Response from the Subject pursuant to paragraph 14 below.

Summary Dismissal of an Initial Complaint

13. Where the Investigator has prepared and submitted a Preliminary Report to the Board recommending summary dismissal of the Initial Complaint, or part of it, the Board may summarily dismiss the Initial Complaint, or part of it, if it appears to the Board that the facts set out in the Initial Complaint, or part of it, cannot arguably be said to be a breach of the Code of Conduct as alleged or at all.

The Response

14. Where:

    (1) the Investigator has prepared and submitted a Preliminary Report to the Board identifying a ground or grounds in the Initial Complaint on which it is arguable that a breach or breaches of the Code of Conduct has occurred; or

    (2) the Board has decided not to dismiss the Initial Complaint, or part of it, summarily,

    the Investigator shall immediately proceed to take the steps identified in paragraph 15 below.

15. The Investigator shall write to the Subject (and where the Complaint is made against an Associated Entity, the Responsible Member) identifying the nature of the Complaint, the alleged breaches of the Code of Conduct and the facts upon which the Complainant relies and requiring the Subject, within 28 days, or such other time period as the Investigator may stipulate, to respond to the Complaint in writing ('**the Response**'):

Appendix 3

- a. admitting or denying the breaches of the Code alleged in the Complaint (and if more than one breach is alleged, specifying which alleged breaches are admitted and which are denied);

- b. agreeing or disagreeing with the facts set out in the Complaint, and, in the case of facts with which it disagrees, stating its account of the facts;

- c. setting out as concisely as possible any further factual matters which may be relevant either to whether or not it has breached the Code of Conduct or to any sanction that the Board may impose for any of the alleged breaches;

- d. appending any relevant documents; and

- e. stating what the Subject says the appropriate sanction should be in respect of any admitted breaches.

Duties of the Investigator on receiving the Response

16. On receiving a Response, or once the period of time for receiving a Response has elapsed without a Response being received, the Investigator shall proceed to investigate the circumstances of the Complaint and the Response, insofar as may be necessary, in order to provide the report to the Board provided for by paragraph 17 below ('**the Report on Charges**'). In order to conduct such an investigation, the Investigator shall have power to:

    (1) request any information or document from either the Complainant or the Subject (and in the case of an Associated Entity, Responsible Member) which it appears to the Investigator may be relevant to the investigation;

    (2) interview witnesses in person or by telephone;

    (3) ask the Complainant, the Subject (and in the case of an Associated Entity, the Responsible Member), or any witness any question which it appears to the Investigator may be relevant to the investigation;

    (4) invite further written representations on any relevant matter (including evidence obtained during the course of these investigations) from the parties.

The Report on Charges

17. Having conducted such investigation as appears to the Investigator to be necessary in all the circumstances of the Complaint, the Investigator shall provide his/her Report on Charges to the Board. The Report on Charges shall identify each and every charge against the Subject which the Investigator identifies in light of his/her investigation as falling for determination. In the case of each such charge the Report on Charges shall identify whether:

    (1) in the Investigator's opinion, it is suitable for summary determination; or

    (2) it ought to be referred to Independent Legal Counsel.

18. A charge is suitable for summary determination if:

    (1) in the case of a summary determination to dismiss a charge:

		a.	either there is no relevant factual dispute or there is no reasonable prospect that Independent Legal Counsel would resolve any relevant factual dispute in favour of the Complainant; and

             b.   there is no reasonable prospect that Independent Legal Counsel would find that the facts alleged, including any fact which is disputed, constitute the breach of the Code of Conduct alleged in the charge.

    (2)   in the case of a summary determination to uphold a charge:

             a.   either there is no relevant factual dispute or there is no reasonable prospect that Independent Legal Counsel would resolve any relevant factual dispute in favour of the Subject; and

             b.   there is no reasonable prospect that Independent Legal Counsel would find anything other than that the facts, including any fact which is disputed, constitute the breach of the Code of Conduct alleged in the charge; and

             c.   the nature of the charge does not give rise to the potential for suspension or expulsion of the Subject (or in the in the case of an Associated Entity, the Responsible Member) from membership of the ALF for any period of time by way of sanction (and for the purposes of this sub-paragraph it is to be assumed that any other charge contained in the Complaint and not dismissed summarily will be determined against the Subject).

19.   If the Investigator intends to recommend to the Board in his or her Report on Charges that it summarily determines a charge or charges, the Investigator shall write to the party against whom it intends the charge to be summarily determined informing it of that intention, giving reasons for the recommendation, and offering the opportunity to that party to make written representations within 14 days (or such longer time as the Investigator may deem appropriate in the circumstances of the case) as to why the charge should not be summarily determined. The Investigator shall take any representations made within such time into account when providing its recommendations to the Board in the Report on Charges.

The Powers of the Board following receipt of the Report on Charges

20.   Having received the Investigator's recommendations in the Report on Charges, the Board shall consider each charge and shall either:

    (1)   if the charge is suitable for summary determination and the Investigator recommends summary determination, summarily determine the charge; or

    (2)   refer the charge to Independent Legal Counsel for determination.

21.   If the Board summarily upholds a charge, it may either:

    (1)   impose any of the sanctions provided for in paragraph 25 below (with the exception of suspension or expulsion) as is appropriate having regard to all relevant matters including without limitation the circumstances and severity of the charge; any other charge contained in the Complaint which is also upheld summarily; and any previous charges upheld against the Subject;

(2) refer the question of what would be the appropriate sanction for the charge to Independent Legal Counsel.

Reference to Independent Legal Counsel

22. Where a charge is referred by the Board to Independent Legal Counsel for determination (whether as to the substance of the charge or only as to the sanctions to be imposed) he or she shall be provided with all the material collected by the Investigator (including the Preliminary Report and the Report on Charges), and shall have power to conduct his or her own investigations in accordance with any procedure which he or she deems fit and proper, provided that:

    (1) Independent Legal Counsel will without limitation have the same powers of Investigation as provided above for the Investigator;

    (2) Independent Legal Counsel will not reach a determination without offering all parties (including for the avoidance of doubt in the case of a Complaint against an Associated Entity, the Responsible Member) the opportunity to make written representations to Independent Legal Counsel.

23. Having considered the evidence, conducted any further investigations which appear necessary, and considered any representations provided by the parties, Independent Legal Counsel shall provide an opinion ('**the Opinion**') containing his or her conclusions as to:

    (1) whether each of the charges referred to Independent Legal Counsel should be upheld or dismissed; and

    (2) in the event that one or more of the charges is upheld, or the question of sanctions alone is referred to Independent Legal Counsel, which of the sanctions provided for in paragraph 25 below should be imposed. In determining the appropriate sanction, Independent Legal Counsel will have regard to all relevant matters including without limitation the circumstances and severity of the charge; any other charge contained in the Complaint which is also upheld whether summarily or on referral to Independent Legal Counsel; any previous Charges upheld against the Subject; and any sanctions which have already been imposed against the Subject by the Board following the summary determination of any charge contained in the Complaint.

24. Unless it is satisfied that there has been some serious procedural irregularity in the procedure adopted by Independent Legal Counsel (in which case it shall refer the charges to a different Independent Legal Counsel), the Board will, on receipt of the Opinion, impose the sanctions recommended therein.

Sanctions available in respect of breaches of the Code

25. The following sanctions may be imposed against a Member:

    (1) a private warning (including where appropriate recommendations as to future practice);

    (2) a public warning (including where appropriate recommendations as to future practice);

    (3) publication of the Opinion (subject to any redactions which Independent Legal Counsel shall identify in order to ensure that no matter confidential to the parties is disclosed);

(4) suspension of membership of the ALF for any identified period of time;

(5) expulsion from membership of the ALF;

(6) the imposition of a fine payable by the Member to the ALF, up to a limit of £500;

(7) the payment of all or any of the costs of determining the Complaint. For the avoidance of doubt, sanctions under this paragraph 25 will only be applied and (to the extent applicable) made public after the period for any appeal under clause 28 has expired, or, where an appeal has been made, it has been finally determined.

26. Any of the sanctions may be imposed individually or together with other sanctions, as is appropriate to all the circumstances of the case.

27. Where the Subject is an Associated Entity and is found to have breached any provision of the Code of Conduct, any sanction in respect of that breach shall be imposed against the Responsible Member, and the sanction imposed shall take into account the degree of control the Responsible Member has over the Associated Entity, its responsibility for any breach of the Code of Conduct, and any charges previously upheld against the Responsible Member.

Appeal against determination of a charge or imposition of a sanction

28. A party against whom a charge has been upheld by the Board and sanctions imposed pursuant to clause 25 above ('**the Appellant**') may appeal by writing to the Board within 28 days of receipt of that decision setting out the reasons why any determination of a charge or imposition of a sanction should be set aside or varied and indicating that it is their intention to pursue this appeal procedure.

29. The Board shall forthwith write to the Appellant requiring it to undertake in writing to the ALF within 14 days that it agrees to be liable for the ALF's costs of the appeal in the event that it is ordered to pay those costs as below ('**the Undertaking**'). In the event that no Undertaking is received in the required time, the Board may dismiss the appeal.

30. If an Undertaking is received, the Board shall refer the appeal:

(1) in the event of an appeal against a summary determination, to Independent Legal Counsel (not previously involved in the Complaint);

(2) in the event of a decision reached following an Opinion, a Queens Counsel (if Independent Legal Counsel was a Queens Counsel, of greater seniority than Independent Legal Counsel[1]);

(in either case, '**the Appeal Tribunal**').

31. An appeal shall constitute a review of the original decision, and in particular an appeal against a decision reached following an Opinion shall only be granted if the Appeal Tribunal is satisfied that:

(1) there was a serious procedural irregularity in the procedure adopted by Independent Legal Counsel which rendered that procedure unfair; or

(2) Independent Legal Counsel erred in his or her interpretation of the Code of Conduct or otherwise erred in law; or

(3) the conclusions of Independent Legal Counsel were conclusions which no reasonable tribunal could reasonably reach on the evidence before it.

32. If the Appeal Tribunal is satisfied that an appeal should be granted, it may recommend to the Board in a short report setting out its reasons that the Appeal be disposed of as it sees fit, including:

    (1) in the case of a summary determination by the Board:

        a. that the summary determination be set aside in whole or in part and the charge or charges be referred to Independent Legal Counsel (not previously involved in the Complaint); and/or

        b. that any sanction imposed be set aside or varied, or a different sanction or sanctions be imposed;

    (2) in the case of a decision reached following an Opinion:

        a. that the findings in the Opinion be set aside in whole or in part and that any or all of the original charges be referred to different Independent Legal Counsel to be re-determined;

        b. that all or any of the charges be dismissed or upheld;

        c. that any sanction imposed be set aside or varied, or that any sanction or sanctions be imposed, or that sanctions be referred to Independent Legal Counsel;

33. The Board shall, on receipt of the Appeal Tribunal's decision, forthwith enact its recommendation.

34. If the Board dismisses an appeal following receipt of the decision of the Appeal Tribunal, it shall (unless the justice of the case requires otherwise) order the Appellant to pay the ALF's costs of the appeal, in accordance with the Undertaking.

Confidentiality of proceedings

35. Unless otherwise provided for by this procedure or the Board, the fact of and all matters concerning any Complaint shall be kept strictly confidential by the parties. Without limitation to that, the ALF (which expression includes the Investigator for the purposes of this paragraph) shall not disclose any information provided by any party ('**the Disclosing Party**') to the dispute to any other party ('**the Receiving Party**') which is confidential to the Disclosing Party as against the Receiving Party without first obtaining a legally enforceable undertaking from the Receiving Party in favour of the Disclosing Party not to disclose that information to any third party without the consent of the Disclosing Party.

APPENDIX 4

Articles of Association of
the Association of Litigation Funders of
England & Wales

A private company limited by guarantee, November 2011

Appendix 4

Index

Part 1: Interpretation, objects, powers, application of income and limitation of liability

1. Defined terms
2. Objects
3. Powers
4. Application of income
5. Liability of members

Part 2: Directors

Directors' powers and responsibilities
6. Directors' general authority
7. Directors may delegate
8. Committees

Decision-making by directors
9. Directors to take decisions collectively
10. Unanimous decisions
11. Frequency of directors' meetings
12. Calling a directors' meeting
13. Participation in directors' meetings
14. Quorum for directors' meetings
15. Chairing of directors' meetings
16. Casting vote
17. Conflicts of interest
18. Records of decisions to be kept
19. Directors' discretion to make further rules

Appointment of directors
20. Methods of appointing directors
21. Officers of the company
22. Composition of the board of directors
23. Termination of directors' appointment
24. Directors' remuneration
25. Directors' expenses

Part 3: Members

Becoming and ceasing to be a member
26. Eligibility for membership
27. Applications for membership and annual subscription
28. Register of members
29. Representatives
30. Termination of membership

Organisation of general meetings
31. Annual general meetings
32. Extraordinary general meetings

33. Quorum for general meetings
34. Chairing general meetings

Part 4: Administrative arrangements

35. Minutes
36. Dissolution

Directors' indemnity and insurance
37. Indemnity
38. Insurance

1. Interpretation, objects, powers, application of income and limitation of liability

Defined terms

1. In the articles, unless the context requires otherwise:

'application fee' means the fee payable on application for membership of the company;

'articles' means the company's articles of association;

'bankruptcy' includes individual insolvency proceedings in a jurisdiction other than England and Wales or Northern Ireland which have an effect similar to that of bankruptcy;

'chairman' has the meaning given in article [15];

'chairman of the meeting' has the meaning given in article[34];

'Code of Conduct for Litigation Funders' means the prevailing code of the same name, as varied from time to time.

'Companies Acts' means the Companies Acts (as defined in section 2 of the Companies Act 2006), in so far as they apply to the company;

'company' means the Association of Litigation Funders of England and Wales;

'director' means a director of the company, and includes any person occupying the position of director, by whatever name called;

'document' includes, unless otherwise specified, any document sent or supplied in electronic form;

'electronic form' has the meaning given in section 1168 of the Companies Act 2006;

'funder' has the meaning given in the Code of Conduct for Litigation Funders and 'funding', 'funded' and any derivative thereof shall be construed accordingly;

'member' has the meaning given in section 112 of the Companies Act 2006;

'membership fee' means the fee payable upon becoming a member of the company;

'officer' has the meaning given in article [21];

'ordinary resolution' has the meaning given in section 282 of the Companies Act 2006;

'participate', in relation to a directors' meeting, has the meaning given in article [13];

'special resolution' has the meaning given in section 283 of the Companies Act 2006;

'subsidiary' has the meaning given in section 1159 of the Companies Act 2006; and

'writing' means the representation or reproduction of words, symbols or other information in a visible form by any method or combination of methods, whether sent or supplied in electronic form or otherwise.

Unless the context otherwise requires, other words or expressions contained in these articles bear the same meaning as in the Companies Act 2006 as in force on the date when these articles become binding on the company.

Objects

2. The objects of the company are:

(a) the promotion of best practice in litigation funding, including by seeking adherence to the Code of Conduct for Litigation Funders; and

(b) improving the understanding of the uses and applications of litigation funding by providing education, training and information on litigation funding.

Powers

3. The company has the power to do anything which is calculated to further its objects or is conducive or incidental to doing so.

Application of income

4. (1) The income and property of the company shall be applied toward the promotion of the objects.

(2) A director may:

(a) in accordance with articles 25, be reimbursed from the property of the company or pay out of such property reasonable expenses properly incurred by him or her when acting on behalf of the company;

(b) benefit from insurance in accordance with article 38;

(c) receive an indemnity from the company in the circumstances set out in article 37; and

(d) receive remuneration in accordance with article 24.

(3) None of the income or property of the company may be paid or transferred directly or indirectly by way of dividend, return of capital or otherwise by way of profit to any member of the company. This does not prevent a member from receiving reasonable and proper remuneration for any goods or services supplied to the company.

Liability of members

5. The liability of each member is limited to £1, being the amount that each member undertakes to contribute to the assets of the company in the event of its being wound up while he is a member or within one year after he ceases to be a member, for—

(a) payment of the company's debts and liabilities contracted before he ceases to be a member,

(b) payment of the costs, charges and expenses of winding up, and

(c) adjustment of the rights of the contributories among themselves.

Part 2: Directors

Directors' powers and responsibilities

Directors' general authority

6. Subject to the articles, the directors are responsible for the management of the company's business, for which purpose they may exercise all the powers of the company.

Directors may delegate

7. (1) Subject to the articles, the directors may delegate any of the powers which are conferred on them under the articles—

    (a) to such person or committee;

    (b) by such means (including by power of attorney);

    (c) to such an extent;

    (d) in relation to such matters or territories; and

    (e) on such terms and conditions; as they think fit.

    (2) If the directors so specify, any such delegation may authorise further delegation of the directors' powers by any person to whom they are delegated.

    (3) The directors may revoke any delegation in whole or part, or alter its terms and conditions.

Committees

8. (1) Committees to which the directors delegate any of their powers must follow procedures which are based as far as they are applicable on those provisions of the articles which govern the taking of decisions by directors.

    (2) The directors may make rules of procedure for all or any committees, which prevail over rules derived from the articles if they are not consistent with them.

Decision-making by directors

Directors to take decisions collectively

9. (1) The general rule about decision-making by directors is that any decision of the directors must be either a majority decision at a meeting or a decision taken in accordance with article 7, save that proposed amendments to the Code of Conduct for Litigation Funders must be made by a two-thirds majority of members at an annual general meeting or extraordinary general meeting.

    (2) If:

    (a) the company only has one director, and

    (b) no provision of the articles requires it to have more than one director,

    the general rule does not apply, and the director may take decisions without regard to any of the provisions of the articles relating to directors' decision-making.

Unanimous decisions

10. (1) A decision of the directors is taken in accordance with this article when all eligible directors indicate to each other by any means that they share a common view on a matter.

    (2) Such a decision may take the form of a resolution in writing, copies of which have been signed by each eligible director or to which each eligible director has otherwise indicated agreement in writing.

    (3) References in this article to eligible directors are to directors who would have been entitled to vote on the matter had it been proposed as a resolution at a directors' meeting.

(4) A decision may not be taken in accordance with this article if the eligible directors would not have formed a quorum at such a meeting.

Frequency of directors' meetings

11. A meeting of directors shall take place not less than twice in each calendar year.

Calling a directors' meeting

12. (1) Any director may call a directors' meeting by giving 21 days' notice of the meeting to the directors or by authorising the company secretary (if any) to give such notice.

(2) Notice of any directors' meeting must indicate:

(a) its proposed date and time;

(b) where it is to take place; and

(c) if it is anticipated that directors participating in the meeting will not be in the same place, how it is proposed that they should communicate with each other during the meeting.

(3) Notice of a directors' meeting must be given to each director, but need not be in writing.

(4) Notice of a directors' meeting need not be given to directors who waive their entitlement to notice of that meeting, by giving notice to that effect to the company not more than 7 days after the date on which the meeting is held. Where such notice is given after the meeting has been held, that does not affect the validity of the meeting, or of any business conducted at it.

(5) Each director consents to the use of the following means of communication for calling or holding a directors' meeting:

(a) video;

(b) telephone;

(c) electronic mail; or

(d) any other technology (or combination thereof) that permits each director to communicate with every other director in attendance.

Participation in directors' meetings

13. (1) Subject to the articles, directors participate in a directors' meeting, or part of a directors' meeting, when:

(a) the meeting has been called and takes place in accordance with the articles, and

(b) they can each communicate to the others any information or opinions they have on any particular item of the business of the meeting.

(2) In determining whether directors are participating in a directors' meeting, it is irrelevant where any director is or how they communicate with each other.

(3) If all the directors participating in a meeting are not in the same place, they may decide that the meeting is to be treated as taking place wherever any of them is.

Quorum for directors' meetings

14. (1) At a directors' meeting, unless a quorum is participating, no proposal is to be voted on, except a proposal to call another meeting.

(2) The quorum for directors' meetings shall be at least three directors, save under clause 30 (4) where the quorum shall be the board of directors.

(3) If the total number of directors for the time being is less than the quorum required, the directors must not take any decision other than a decision:

(a) to appoint further directors, or

(b) to call a general meeting so as to enable the members to appoint further directors.

Appendix 4

Chairing of directors' meetings

15. (1) The directors shall appoint a director to chair their meetings.

(2) The person so appointed for the time being is known as the chairman.

(3) The directors may terminate the chairman's appointment at any time.

(4) If the chairman is not participating in a directors' meeting within ten minutes of the time at which it was to start, the participating directors must appoint one of themselves to chair it.

Casting vote

16. (1) If the numbers of votes for and against a proposal are equal, the chairman or other director chairing the meeting has a casting vote.

(2) But this does not apply if, in accordance with the articles, the chairman or other director is not to be counted as participating in the decision-making process for quorum or voting purposes.

Conflicts of interest

17. If a proposed decision of the directors is concerned with an actual or proposed transaction or arrangement with the company in which a director is interested, that director must declare such interest to the participating directors.

Records of decisions to be kept

18. The directors must ensure that the company keeps a record, in writing, for at least 10 years from the date of the decision recorded, of every unanimous or majority decision taken by the directors.

Directors' discretion to make further rules

19. Subject to the articles, the directors may make any rule which they think fit about how they take decisions, and about how such rules are to be recorded or communicated to directors.

Appointment of directors

Methods of appointing directors

20. (1) Any person who is willing to act as a director, and is permitted by law to do so, may be appointed to be a director by a decision of the directors.

Officers of the Company

21. The company will have three officers appointed either by ordinary resolution or by a decision of the directors, being:

(a) the chairman;

(b) the secretary; and

(c) the treasurer.

Composition of the board of directors

22. The board of directors shall consist of:

(a) the officers; and

(b) two members appointed as directors by resolution.

save for the first 12 months following incorporation of the company, during which the board may consist of only the officers.

Termination of director's appointment

23. A person ceases to be a director as soon as:

(a) that person ceases to be a director by virtue of any provision of the Companies Act 2006 or is prohibited from being a director by law;

(b) a bankruptcy order is made against that person;

(c) a composition is made with that person's creditors generally in satisfaction of that person's debts;

(d) that person ceases to be a member of the company;

(e) a registered medical practitioner who is treating that person gives a written opinion to the company stating that that person has become physically or mentally incapable of acting as a director and may remain so for more than three months;

(f) by reason of that person's mental health, a court makes an order which wholly or partly prevents that person from personally exercising any powers or rights which that person would otherwise have; or

(g) notification is received by the company from the director that the director is resigning from office, and such resignation has taken effect in accordance with its terms.

Directors' remuneration

24. (1) Directors may undertake any services for the company that the directors decide.

(2) Directors are entitled to such remuneration as the members may determine at a general meeting:

(a) for their services to the company as directors, and

(b) for any other service which they undertake for the company.

(3) Subject to the articles, a director's remuneration may:

(a) take any form, and

(b) include any arrangements in connection with the payment of a pension, allowance or gratuity, or any death, sickness or disability benefits, to or in respect of that director.

(4) Unless the directors decide otherwise, directors' remuneration accrues from day to day.

(5) Unless the directors decide otherwise, directors are not accountable to the company for any remuneration which they receive as directors or other officers or employees of the company's subsidiaries or of any other body corporate in which the company is interested.

Directors' expenses

25. The company may pay any reasonable expenses which the directors properly incur in connection with their attendance at:

(a) meetings of directors or committees of directors,

(b) general meetings, or

(c) separate meetings of the holders of debentures of the company,

or otherwise in connection with the exercise of their powers and the discharge of their responsibilities in relation to the company.

3: Members

Becoming and ceasing to be a member

Eligibility for membership

26. (1) Membership of the company shall be open to persons or entities that:

    (a) are funders within the meaning of the prevailing Code of Conduct for Litigation Funders, as varied from time to time;

    (b) have previously funded or at the time of application for membership are funding disputes within England and Wales; and

    (c) can demonstrate to the directors' satisfaction their compliance with the prevailing Code of Conduct for Litigation Funders, as varied from time to time

    (d) are not statutorily regulated in respect of their litigation funding activities.

(2) Any question of eligibility for membership shall be determined by the directors.

Applications for membership and annual subscription

27. (1) No person shall become a member of the company unless:

    (a) that person has submitted a completed application for membership in a form approved by the directors together with the application fee;

    (b) the directors have approved the application; and

    (c) the membership fee has been paid.

(2) Each member and associate member shall pay annually a subscription to the company. Such payment shall be made within 28 days of the subscription being requested by the company.

(3) The application fee, membership fee and level of subscription shall be fixed, from time to time, by the directors, who may in their absolute discretion raise, lower or waive such fees or subscription.

Register of members

28. (1) The secretary shall maintain a list of names and addresses of all members, which may be inspected on reasonable notice by any member.

(2) The secretary may keep such list on any medium as is deemed convenient, whether in soft or hard copy, and each of the present and past members shall be deemed to have given consent to their details being so kept unless they have given written notice to the contrary to the secretary.

Representatives

29. (1) Any member that is not a natural person may by written notice to the secretary:

    (a) appoint a natural person to act as its representative in all matters connected with the business of the company; and

    (b) remove a representative.

(2) A representative is entitled to:

    (a) exercise at a general meeting all the powers to which the appointing member would be entitled if it were a natural person;

    (b) stand for election as a director; and

    (c) be counted towards a quorum on the basis that the member is to be considered personally present at a general meeting or directors' meeting by its representative.

Termination of membership

30. (1) A member may withdraw from membership of the company by giving 7 days' notice to the company in writing.

(2) Membership is not transferable.

(3) A person's membership terminates when that person dies or ceases to exist.

(4) A person's membership may be terminated by the directors if they determine at a meeting of the board of

directors, at their discretion in accordance with clause 9 hereof, that that person has:

(a) ceased to be eligible for membership; or

(b) failed to comply with the prevailing Code of Conduct of Litigation Funders or other rules of the company as have been notified to members from time to time; or

(c) engaged in any conduct likely to bring the company into disrepute; or

(d) failed to pay to the company the annual subscription for 30 days after it becomes due, has received from the secretary notice of the fact, and has still failed to pay the subscription fee after 21 days from the date of that notice.

(5) A person's membership shall not be terminated by the directors unless at least 21 days' notice has been given to that person of:

(a) the directors' meeting at which the question of expulsion of that person shall be considered; and

(b) the reason for the proposed expulsion.

(6) If a person's membership is terminated by the directors, the secretary shall as soon as practicable give written notice of that decision to the expelled member.

(7) When a member is expelled, the secretary shall strike that person's name off the register of members.

Organisation of general meetings

Annual general meetings

31. (1) An annual general meeting of the company shall be held once in each calendar year on such day and time and at such place as the directors shall determine.

(2) At least 28 calendar days' notice of an annual general meeting shall be given to all members by the secretary.

(3) The venue of an annual meeting shall be in London, unless otherwise determined by the chairman.

(4) Any member wishing to raise any matter at the annual general meeting shall give notice in writing thereof to the secretary no later than 21 calendar days before the date on which the meeting is to take place.

(5) The chairman of the meeting may permit other persons who are not members of the company to attend and speak at a general meeting.

Extraordinary general meetings

32. (1) An extraordinary general meeting can be called by any two directors or members. At least 21 calendar days' notice of an extraordinary meeting shall be given to all members by the secretary specifying:

(a) the place, date and time of the meeting; and

(b) the matters to be dealt with at the meeting.

(2) The venue of an extraordinary meeting shall be in London, unless otherwise determined by the chairman.

(3) Any member wishing to raise any matter at the annual general meeting shall give notice in writing thereof to the secretary no later than 21 calendar days before the date on which the meeting is to take place.

(4) The chairman of the meeting may permit other persons who are not members of the company to attend and speak at a general meeting.

Quorum for general meetings

33. No business other than the appointment of the chairman of the meeting is to be transacted at a general meeting if the persons attending it do not constitute a quorum.

Chairing general meetings

34. (1) If the directors have appointed a chairman, the chairman shall chair general meetings if present and willing to do so.

(2) If the directors have not appointed a chairman, or if the chairman is unwilling to chair the meeting or is not present within ten minutes of the time at which a meeting was due to start:

(a) the directors present, or

(b) (if no directors are present), the meeting, must appoint a director or member to chair the meeting, and the appointment of the chairman of the meeting must be the first business of the meeting.

(3) The person chairing a meeting in accordance with this article is referred to as 'the chairman of the meeting'.

4: Administrative arrangements

Minutes

35. (1) The secretary shall record in a minute book the proceedings of all general meetings and directors' meetings.

(2) Such records shall be kept for no less than 10 years, and shall be open to inspection by members on reasonable written notice to the secretary.

Dissolution of the company

36. (1) The company shall be dissolved with immediate effect if:

(a) the number of members shall at any time fall below two; or

(b) the directors shall pass in a meeting by a two-thirds majority a resolution of their intention to dissolve the company.

(2) In the event that the company is dissolved, its available funds shall be transferred to such charitable institutions as:

(a) have objects similar to those of the company; and

(b) have been selected by the directors from time to time.

Directors' indemnity and insurance

Indemnity

37. (1) Subject to paragraph (2), a relevant director of the company or an associated company shall be indemnified out of the company's assets against:

(a) any liability incurred by that director in connection with any negligence, default, breach of duty or breach of trust in relation to the company or an associated company,

(b) any liability incurred by that director in connection with the activities of the company or an associated company in its capacity as a trustee of an occupational pension scheme (as defined in section 235(6) of the Companies Act 2006),

(c) any other liability incurred by that director as an officer of the company or an associated company.

(2) This article does not authorise any indemnity which would be prohibited or rendered void by any provision of the Companies Acts or by any other provision of law.

(3) In this article:

(a) companies are associated if one is a subsidiary of the other or both are subsidiaries of the same body corporate, and

(b) a 'relevant director' means any director or former director of the company or an associated company.

Insurance

38. (1) The directors shall decide to purchase and maintain insurance, at the expense of the company, for the benefit of any relevant director in respect of any relevant loss.

(2) In this article:

(a) a 'relevant director' means any director or former director of the company or an associated company,

(b) a 'relevant loss' means any loss or liability which has been or may be incurred by a relevant director in connection with that director's duties or powers in relation to the company, any associated company or any pension fund or employees' share scheme of the company or associated company, and

(c) companies are associated if one is a subsidiary of the other or both are subsidiaries of the same body corporate.

APPENDIX 5

Code of Conduct for Litigation Funders
January 2014

1. This code ('the Code') sets out standards of practice and behaviour to be observed by Funders (as defined in clause 2 below) who are Members of The Association of Litigation Funders of England & Wales ('the Association') in respect of funding the resolution of disputes within England and Wales.

2. A litigation funder:

    2.1 has access to funds immediately within its control, including within a corporate parent or subsidiary ('Funder's Subsidiary'); or

    2.2 acts as the exclusive investment advisor to an entity or entities having access to funds immediately within its or their control, including within a corporate parent or subsidiary ('Associated Entity'), ('a Funder') in each case:

    2.3 to fund the resolution of disputes within England and Wales; and

    2.4 where the funds are invested pursuant to a Litigation Funding Agreement ('LFA') to enable a party to a dispute ('the Funded Party') to meet the costs (including pre-action costs) of resolving disputes by litigation, arbitration or other dispute resolution procedures.

    In return the Funder, Funder's Subsidiary or Associated Entity:

    2.5 receives a share of the proceeds if the claim is successful (as defined in the LFA); and

    2.6 does not seek any payment from the Funded Party in excess of the amount of the proceeds of the dispute that is being funded, unless the Funded Party is in material breach of the provisions of the LFA.

3. A Funder shall be deemed to have adopted the Code in respect of funding the resolution of disputes within England and Wales.

4. A Funder shall accept responsibility to the Association for compliance with the Code by a Funder's Subsidiary or Associated Entity. By so doing a Funder shall not accept legal responsibility to a Funded Party, which shall be a matter governed, if at all, by the provisions of the LFA.

5. A Funder shall inform a Funded Party as soon as possible and prior to execution of an LFA:

    5.1 if the Funder is acting for and/or on behalf of a Funder's Subsidiary or an Associated Entity in respect of funding the resolution of disputes within England & Wales; and

5.2   whether the LFA will be entered into by the Funder, a Funder's Subsidiary or an Associated Entity.

6. The promotional literature of a Funder must be clear and not misleading.

7. A Funder will observe the confidentiality of all information and documentation relating to the dispute to the extent that the law permits, and subject to the terms of any Confidentiality or Non-Disclosure Agreement agreed between the Funder and the Funded Party. For the avoidance of doubt, the Funder is responsible for the purposes of this Code for preserving confidentiality on behalf of any Funder's Subsidiary or Associated Entity.

8. An LFA is a contractually binding agreement entered into between a Funder, a Funder's Subsidiary or Associated Entity and a Funded Party relating to the resolution of disputes within England and Wales.

9. A Funder will:

9.1   take reasonable steps to ensure that the Funded Party shall have received independent advice on the terms of the LFA prior to its execution, which obligation shall be satisfied if the Funded Party confirms in writing to the Funder that the Funded Party has taken advice from the solicitor or barrister instructed in the dispute;

9.2   not take any steps that cause or are likely to cause the Funded Party's solicitor or barrister to act in breach of their professional duties;

9.3   not seek to influence the Funded Party's solicitor or barrister to cede control or conduct of the dispute to the Funder;

9.4   Maintain at all times access to adequate financial resources to meet the obligations of the Funder, its Funder Subsidiaries and Associated Entities to fund all the disputes that they have agreed to fund and in particular will;

    9.4.1   ensure that the Funder, its Funder Subsidiaries and Associated Entities maintain the capacity;

        9.4.1.1.   to pay all debts when they become due and payable; and

        9.4.1.2.   to cover aggregate funding liabilities under all of their LFAs for a minimum period of 36 months.

    9.4.2   maintain access to a minimum of £2m of capital or such other amount as stipulated by the Association;

    9.4.3   accept a continuous disclosure obligation in respect of its capital adequacy, including a specific obligation to notify timeously the Association and the Funded Party if the Funder reasonably believes that its representations in respect of capital adequacy under the Code are no longer valid because of changed circumstances;

    9.4.4   undertake that it will be audited annually by a recognised national or international audit firm and shall provide the Association with:

        9.4.4.1.   a copy of the audit opinion given by the audit firm on the Funder's or Funder's Subsidiary's most recent annual financial statements (but not the underlying financial statements), or in the case of Funders who are investment advisors to an Associated Entity, the audit opinion given by the audit firm in respect of the Associated Entity (but not the underlying financial statements), within one month of receipt of the opinion and in any case within six months of each fiscal year end. If the audit opinion provided is qualified (except as to any emphasis of matters relating to the uncertainty of valuing relevant litigation funding investments) or expresses any question as to the ability of the firm to continue as a going concern, the Association shall be entitled to enquire further into the qualification expressed and take any further action it deems appropriate; and

9.4.4.2. reasonable evidence from a qualified third party (preferably from an auditor, but alternatively from a third party administrator or bank) that the Funder or Funder's Subsidiary or Associated Entity satisfies the minimum capital requirement prevailing at the time of annual subscription.

9.5 comply with the Rules of the Association as to capital adequacy as amended from time to time.

10. The LFA shall state whether (and if so to what extent) the Funder or Funder's Subsidiary or Associated Party is liable to the Funded Party to:

10.1 meet any liability for adverse costs;

10.2 pay any premium (including insurance premium tax) to obtain costs insurance;

10.3 provide security for costs; and

10.4 meet any other financial liability.

11. The LFA shall state whether (and if so how) the Funder or Funder's Subsidiary or Associated Entity may:

11.1 provide input to the Funder Party's decisions in relation to settlements;

11.2 terminate the LFA in the event that the Funder or Funder's Subsidiary or Associated Entity:

11.2.1 reasonably ceases to be satisfied about the merits of the dispute;

11.2.2 reasonably believes that the dispute is no longer commercially viable; or

11.2.3 reasonably believes that there has been a material breach of the LFA by the Funded Party.

12. The LFA shall not establish a discretionary right for a Funder or Funder's Subsidiary or Associated Party to terminate a LFA in the absence of the circumstances described in clause 11.2.

13. If the LFA does give the Funder or Funder's Subsidiary or Associated Entity any of the rights described in clause 11, the LFA shall provide that:

   13.1 if the Funder or Funder's Subsidiary or Associated Entity terminates the LFA, the Funder or Funder's Subsidiary or Associated Entity shall remain liable for all funding obligations accrued to the date of termination unless the termination is due to a material breach under clause 11.2.3;

   13.2 if there is a dispute between the Funder, Funder's Subsidiary or Associated Entity and the Funded Party about settlement or about termination of the LFA, a binding opinion shall be obtained from a Queen's Counsel who shall be instructed jointly or nominated by the Chairman of the Bar Council.

14. Breach by the Funder's Subsidiary or Associated Entity of the provisions of the Code shall constitute a breach of the Code by the Funder.

15. The Association shall maintain a complaints procedure. A Funder consents to the complaints procedure as it may be varied from time to time in respect of any relevant act or omission by the Funder, Funder's Subsidiary or Associated Entity.

16. The Code (as amended) applies to LFAs commencing on or after the date hereof.

14th January 2014

APPENDIX 6

The Association of Litigation Funders of England and Wales

Rules of the Association

January 2014

1. DEFINITIONS

    1.1. In these Rules, unless the context otherwise requires:

    'Association' means The Association of Litigation Funders of England and Wales (a company limited by guarantee and registered in England and Wales with registered number 07858647);

    'Associated Entity' and any derivative thereof has the meaning given in the Code of Conduct;

    'Articles' means the articles of association of the Association;

    'Associate Member' and any derivative thereof has the meaning given in the Code of Conduct;

    'Board' means the board of directors of the Association from time to time;

    'Code of Conduct' means the prevailing Code of Conduct for Litigation Funders as adopted by the Association and varied from time to time;

    'Directors' means the directors of the Association;

    'Funder' and any derivative thereof has the meaning given in the Code of Conduct;

    'Funder's Subsidiary' and any derivative thereof has the meaning given in the Code of Conduct;

    'Litigation Funding' means the funding of the resolution of disputes in England and Wales within the meaning of the Code of Conduct;

    'Litigation Funding Agreement' has the meaning given in the Code of Conduct;

    'Member' and any derivative thereof has the meaning given in section 112 of the Companies Act 2006;

    'Officer' has the meaning given in article 21 of the Articles;

'Rules' means the rules set out below which shall apply from 14th January 2014.

2. THE ASSOCIATION

    2.1.   The Association promotes best practice in Litigation Funding, including by seeking adherence to the Code of Conduct and by improving the understanding of the uses and applications of Litigation Funding.

3. MEMBERSHIP

    3.1.   Membership of the Association is open to those persons or entities that satisfy the eligibility requirements set out in the Code and the Articles and comply with these Rules.

    3.2.   Associate Membership of the Association is open to any person or entity that has an interest in Litigation Funding in their capacity as any of the following:

        3.2.1.   Litigation Funding Broker;

        3.2.2.   Costs/Adverse Costs Insurer;

        3.2.3.   Law Firm;

        3.2.4.   Barrister;

        3.2.5.   Overseas Funder;

        3.2.6.   Academic;

        3.2.7.   Overseas Academic.

    3.3.   All applications for Membership or Associate Membership shall be made in writing on the form provided by the Association for that purpose and accompanied by the relevant application fee. By completing such a form, each Member and Associate Member shall be deemed to have agreed to these Rules (as amended from time to time).

    3.4.   When a Funder ('the Applicant') applies for Membership or renewal thereof the Applicant shall:

        3.4.1.   provide confirmation that the Applicant accepts responsibility to the Association for compliance with the Code of Conduct by a Funder's Subsidiary or Associated Entity on whose behalf the Applicant acts in respect of Litigation Funding within England and Wales; and

        3.4.2.   identify, from time to time, any such Funder's Subsidiary and/or Associated Entity

        in both cases to the Association's General Counsel from time to time, to hold on a confidential basis without disclosure to the Board, save where there is a complaint and subject to the complaints procedure then prevailing.

Appendix 6

3.5. No person or entity shall become a Member or Associate Member of the Association until their application has been approved by the Directors and they have paid the relevant Membership or Associate Membership fee ('the Membership fee').

3.6. Each Member and Associate Member shall pay annually a subscription to the Association. Such payment shall be made within 28 days of the subscription being requested by the Association.

3.7. The application fee, Membership fee and level of subscription shall be fixed, from time to time, by the directors, who may in their absolute discretion raise, lower or waive such fee or subscription.

3.8. Once paid, an application fee, a Membership fee and a subscription shall become the property of the Association.

3.9. Every Member and Associate Member shall notify timeously the Association of any change of address or other contact details and any changes in respect of Clause 3.4 above.

3.10. Each Member and Associate Member consents to the Association maintaining and processing personal information for Membership and marketing purposes and credit control.

3.11. The Directors may, in their complete discretion, invite persons to become honorary Members of the Association. Honorary Members shall not be required to pay a Membership fee or a subscription but such honorary Membership may, in the complete discretion of the Directors, be terminated at any time.

3.12. Members may terminate their Membership (or have their Membership terminated) in accordance with article 30 of the Articles.

3.13. Associate Members may resign at any time by giving written notice to the Association. The Directors, in their complete discretion, may terminate at any time a person's or entity's Associate Membership of the Association.

3.14. Any Member or Associate Member who ceases (for whatever reason) to be a Member or Associate Member of the Association shall not be entitled to the return of their Membership fee or subscription (or any part thereof).

3.15. A Funder, whether applying for Membership or renewal thereof and at all material times:

    3.15.1. shall maintain access to a minimum of £2m of capital or such other amount as stipulated by the Association;

    3.15.2. accepts a continuous disclosure obligation in respect of its capital adequacy, including a specific obligation to notify timeously the Association and all counterparties to its Litigation Funding Agreements if the member reasonably believes that its representations in respect of capital adequacy under article 2 or article 9.4 of the Code of Conduct or otherwise are no longer valid because of changed circumstances;

3.15.3. undertakes that it will be audited annually by a recognised national or international audit firm and shall provide the Association with:

   i. a copy of the audit opinion given by the audit firm on the Funder's or Funder's Subsidiary's most recent annual financial statements (but not the underlying financial statements), or in the case of an Associated Entity, the audit opinion given by the audit firm in respect of the Associated Entity advised by the member (but not the underlying financial statements), within one month of receipt of the opinion and in any case within six months of each fiscal year end. If the audit opinion provided is not unqualified (except as to any emphasis of matters relating to the uncertainty of valuing relevant Litigation Funding investments) or expresses any question as to the ability of the firm to continue as a going concern, the Board shall be entitled to inquire further into the qualification expressed and take any further action it deems appropriate; and

   ii. reasonable evidence from a qualified third party (preferably from an auditor, but alternatively from a third party administrator or bank) that the Funder, Funder's Subsidiary, or Associated Entity satisfies the minimum capital requirement prevailing at the time of annual subscription, currently £2m as per rule 3.15.1 above.

3.15.4. accepts that, in the event of a failure by a Member to produce the external verifications by the relevant deadline prescribed and in a form that is reasonably satisfactory to the Board, the result will be:

   i. at the discretion of the Board, immediate suspension of the Member's membership of the Association, such suspension to remain confidential to the Board prior to the expiry of the period in rule 3.15.4 ii below; and

   ii. in the event the default has not been cured within three months of the prescribed deadline, automatic expulsion of the Member from the Association.

3.15.5. accepts the following factors in assessing whether it has adequate financial resources within the meaning of these Rules and the Code of Conduct:

   i. the need for Members to be both conservative in assessing what is counted as capital and pessimistic about the timing and level of any expected returns under existing Litigation Funding Agreements.

   ii. the quality, source and certainty of a Member's capital, as well as the timing and extent of the aggregate financial commitments made by a Member under Litigation Funding Agreements and other commitments (actual or contingent); and

iii. the uncertain nature of litigation in particular with respect to the merits, realistic claim value, budgeted costs (including overruns), enforcement and collection risks and timing of a case, and the professional experience of the litigation team and the Member.

3.15.6. shall test its exposures whenever it makes a new commitment under a Litigation Funding Agreement and thereafter at least monthly with respect to on-going commitments, and rule 3.4 is repeated expressly herein.

4. OFFICERS AND DIRECTORS

Retirement and removal of Directors

4.1. At least two Directors shall retire with effect from the Annual General Meeting in each year and shall be eligible for re-election. Those to retire shall be those who have been Directors longest since their last election.

4.2. A Director shall retire at the Annual General Meeting occurring three years after he took office as a Director of the Association and shall be eligible for re-election.

4.3. A person shall cease to be a Director of the Association if:

4.3.1. He ceases to be employed by a Member;

4.3.2. By notice in writing to the Administrator of the Association, he resigns his membership of the Board;

4.3.3. He (i) absents himself from three consecutive meetings of the Board or absents himself in any year from one-half in number of the meetings of the Board and (ii) the Board resolves that he ceases to be a Director;

4.3.4. He ceases to be a Director pursuant to the Articles;

4.3.5. The Members so resolve at a general meeting of the Association, such resolution to be proposed by not less than 50% of the Members.

4.4. If a casual vacancy occurs, the Board shall by resolution appoint a person to fill such vacancy until the next Annual General Meeting when that Director shall retire and his place be offered up for election.

Election of Directors

4.5. Candidates for election as Directors at the next Annual General meeting may be proposed by any Member and/or by the Board by notice in writing to the Administrator of the Association not less than 21 days prior to the date of the Annual General Meeting.

4.6. Notice of the candidates duly proposed shall be circulated by the Administrator of the Association within 5 days from the last day for proposal of candidates.

	4.7.	If no more candidates are proposed than will be required to be elected as Directors at the next Annual General Meeting, such candidates as are proposed shall be deemed to be elected as Directors.
	4.8.	If more candidates are duly proposed than will be required to be elected as Directors at the Annual General Meeting, the Administrator of the Association shall ballot the Members by inviting votes by email to the Administrator of the Association by no later than 24 hours in advance of the Annual General Meeting.
	4.9.	The election shall be conducted by Single Transferable Vote until all vacancies have been filled. Any vote not cast by the time prescribed in the preceding paragraph shall be void.
	4.10.	The Administrator of the Association shall act as returning officer and shall determine all questions regarding the validity of any vote. No election of any Director shall be invalidated by reason of any defect in or invalidity of any vote used thereat or by reason of any error however occasioned in the tally of votes cast.
	4.11.	A return of the persons elected as Directors shall be made by the Administrator of the Association at the next Annual General Meeting.
	4.12.	The elected Directors shall take office with the effect from Annual General Meeting at which they are elected.
	4.13.	Any Director may appoint an alternate to act and vote in his place at any meeting of the Board. A person may not be appointed or thereafter act as such alternate unless, at the date on which he is appointed and on every occasion on which he so acts, he is employed by a Member.

Officers

	4.14.	The Association shall have three officers (a chairman, a secretary and a treasurer).
	4.15.	The officers of the Association shall be appointed from amongst the Directors by resolution of the Board at the first Board meeting following the Annual General Meeting to take place not later than 30 days after the Annual General Meeting and at the first Board meeting following the retirement of any officer in respect of that office.

5. MEETINGS

   5.1. The Association shall hold general meetings in accordance with its Articles.

   5.2. Notice of such meetings shall also be given to Associate Members, in such fashion as the Directors consider expedient.

   5.3. The chairman of a general meeting may allow Associate Members to attend and speak at such meetings.

6. CODE OF CONDUCT

   6.1. Every Member shall abide by the Code of Conduct.

7. AMENDMENT AND VARIATION

7.1. The Association may, at the discretion of the Directors, amend or vary these Rules from time to time. Such amendments and/or variations shall be communicated to Members and Associate Members in such fashion as the Directors consider expedient.

8. COMPLAINTS PROCEDURE

8.1 Every Member agrees to be bound by the complaints procedure as approved by the Association in general meeting from time to time.

9. LAW AND JURISDICTION

9.1. These Rules shall be governed by, and construed in accordance with, English Law.

9.2. Any dispute arising out of or in connection with these Rules, including any question regarding their existence, validity or termination, shall be referred to and finally resolved by arbitration under the LCIA Rules and the LCIA Rules are deemed to be incorporated by reference into this clause.

The number of arbitrators shall be one.

The seat, or legal place, of arbitration shall be London.

The language to be used in the arbitral proceedings shall be English.

14th January 2014

INDEX

acquisition of claims 10.70
acquisition cost 7.40
adverse costs 1.63, 2.132, 5.105, 6.67
   after-the-event (ATE) insurance 5.90, 6.07–6.13, 6.56
   alternative business structures (ABSs) 8.122–8.123
   Association of Litigation Funders (ALF) Code of Conduct 9.25
   Australia 3.112, 3.119
   Canada 3.129
   conduct rules for solicitors 9.51
   costs and insurance 6.01–6.05
   costs risk of funders 6.57–6.59
   costs of setting up funding 6.56
   damages-based agreements (DBAs) and Jackson reforms 8.126–8.128, 8.131
   Excalibur 2.122, 6.66
   Germany 3.134
   group litigation 7.03, 7.19, 7.22, 7.24, 7.38–7.43, 7.47–7.48
   Hodgson immunity 8.115–8.116, 8.119–8.121
   insurance premium payment 6.14, 6.15
   Jackson reforms, effect of 8.111
   liability and *Merchantbridge v Safron* 2.73
   protection and *Cecil v Bayat* 2.100
   Stoczania Gdanska SA v Latreefers 2.27, 2.30
   United States 3.95
   see also **adverse costs order**
adverse costs order 1.60, 2.27, 2.36
   damages-based agreements (DBAs) and Jackson reforms 8.05
   reasons for funding 3.15
   Sibthorpe and Morris v Southwark London Borough Council 2.87
after-the-event (ATE) insurance 1.39, 5.26, 5.90, 6.07–6.13, 6.56
   adverse costs 5.105
   Association of Litigation Funders (ALF) Code of Conduct 9.25, 9.34–9.35
   brokers or direct approach to funders 5.16, 5.19, 5.22
   Burford Capital 4.67
   claimant's obligations 5.106
   conditional fee agreements (CFAs) 8.11
   conditions precedent and warranties 5.102
   confidentiality 5.112
   costs and insurance 6.67–6.68

   costs of setting up and funding 6.56–6.61
   damages-based agreements (DBAs) and Jackson reforms 8.05–8.08, 8.82
   deposit premium 6.27–6.29
   education 10.38
   ending of recoverability of 1.87
   fully deferred premium 6.31, 6.35–6.38
   group litigation 7.42–7.43, 7.49
   insurance premium payment 6.14–6.17
   intake review and assessment 5.44
   Litigation Funding Agreement (LFA) 5.92
   lower value cases 3.58, 3.60, 3.62
   merits of the case 3.42
   'own sides costs and disbursements' 4.25–4.27
   payment in full on inception 6.18–6.22
   priorities agreement 5.124
   reasons for funding 3.12–3.13
   recoverability 8.12, 8.21, 8.23
   restrictions or cancellation clauses 6.55
   security for costs 5.108–5.109, 6.42, 6.47–6.55
   solicitors' conduct rules 9.52, 9.56–9.57
   solicitors' duties 9.58–9.59, 9.64, 9.66–9.69, 9.71–9.75, 9.85–9.89
   term sheet 5.59
   Tinseltime v Eryl Roberts 2.106
agreement to fund *see* **funding agreement**
alternative business structures (ABSs) 3.61, 3.90–3.91, 8.122–8.124, 8.128, 10.47–10.56
alternative methods of funding 3.70–3.91
   alternative business structures (ABSs) 3.90–3.91
   'basket' of cases 3.83–3.85
   hybrid damages-based agreement (DBA) funding 3.86–3.89
   portfolio approach 3.72–3.82
American Bar Association White Paper 3.101
annual interest rate 3.78, 5.50
appeal/appeals 1.54, 5.133
approval of settlements 9.26–9.35
arbitration 1.54, 3.35–3.36
   after-the-event (ATE) insurance 6.11
   forum/venue/jurisdiction/applicable law 3.50
   funding 10.04
   international 1.54, 5.70
   Singapore 3.148
   United States 3.99
Argentum 10.22
Arkin v Borchard Lines 2.59–2.67
assessment 5.44–5.49

Index

assignment or sale of rights 7.04
associated entities 9.12–9.16
Association of British Insurers 8.18, 8.20
Association of Litigation Funders (ALF) 3.129, 3.131, 9.02–9.42
   alternative business structures (ABSs) 8.123
   associate members 9.05
   board 10.23
   'broker' membership 4.09
   Code of Conduct 1.41, 9.03–9.04, 9.06–9.42, 9.93
     capital adequacy of funders 9.20–9.24
     complaints 9.38–9.42
     conduct and control 9.17–9.19
     costs, other 9.25
     dispute resolution 5.118, 9.36–9.37
     education 10.37
     family office 4.39
     formalities 9.09–9.11
     funder models 4.04
     lower value cases 3.65
     subsidiaries and associated entities 9.12–9.16
     termination and approval of settlements 9.26–9.35
   education 10.43
   family offices 4.34
   funder members 9.05
   funder models 4.01
   funding 10.02, 10.72
   Litigation Funding Agreement (LFA) 5.91
   membership 9.05–9.07
     criteria 10.18
     family office 4.39
     fund raiser funders 4.21
     investment fund 4.55
     one-off funders 4.19
   performance 10.21
   pricing 5.76
   regulation and self-regulation 10.16–10–30
   solicitors' duties 9.60
   Therium Capital Management 4.74, 4.80
Association of Personal Injury Lawyers 8.18–8.19
Australia 1.09, 1.24–1.26, 2.63, 2.129, 3.92–3.93, 3.112–3.123, 3.148
   alternative business structures (ABSs) 3.90, 10.51
   brokers or direct approach to funders 5.14–5.16
   costs risk of funders 6.59
   evolution of litigation funding 10.73–10.74
   forum/venue/jurisdiction/applicable law 3.49
   funding 10.13
   High Court 1.26
   insurance premium payment 6.15
   jurisdictions 10.58
   Law Council 3.117, 3.122
   Law Institute of Victoria 3.117
   reasons for funding 3.19
   Securities and Investment Commission 3.121
   solicitors' duties 9.78

bankruptcy 2.17
Bar Council 9.36, 10.20
Bar Standards Board 10.20
barratry 2.04, 2.08
base costs 1.93, 8.84, 8.87, 8.99, 8.105–8.107, 8.130
'basket' of cases 1.46, 3.83–3.85, 10.15
before the event (BTE) insurance 9.67
Belgium 10.58
bilateral investment treaty case 5.70
Birmingham Mercantile 8.54
'book building' 7.29
'both sides' cover 3.12
Bramden Investments 4.83
Brazil 10.58
British Virgin Islands 3.49, 10.57
brokers 5.11–5.24
budget 5.36–5.41
   for counsel and leading counsel 1.79
   final 5.07
   'full rate' 3.12
   funding process 5.08
   pricing 5.84
   see also costs budgeting
Burford Capital 4.57, 4.64–4.72
'buy into' the case 5.07

Canada 3.129–3.131, 8.126, 10.57
   Ontario model 8.82–8.83, 8.87, 8.99, 8.123
capital adequacy 9.20–9.24
   Association of Litigation Funders (ALF) Code of Conduct 9.08
   family office 4.39
   fund raiser funders 4.21
   investment fund 4.55
   lower value cases 3.65
   pricing 5.76
   regulation and self-regulation 10.18
capital guarantee 4.25–4.27, 4.29
capped fee basis 3.82, 5.87
caps on returns 10.55
Caribbean 3.49, 3.135–3.138, 10.04
   Bahamas 3.135
   Bermuda 3.136
   British Virgin Islands 3.137
   Cayman Islands 3.138
   insurance premium payment 6.15
   one-off funders 4.13
cartel actions 3.133–3.134, 7.02–7.03
case assessment 5.45
'case by case' funding 4.10–4.20, 4.21–4.32
case funding limit 3.12
case law 2.19–2.122
   Arkin v Borchard Lines 2.59–2.67
   Cecil v Bayat 2.95–2.101
   Eurasian Dream (No 2) 2.31–2.34
   Excalibur/Keystone 2.115–2.122
   Factortame (No 2) 2.43–2.53
   Flatman v Germany 2.109–2.110

Index

Giles v Thompson 2.20–2.25
Gulf Azov Shipping v Idisi 2.54–2.58
Hamilton v Al-Fayed (No 2) 2.35–2.42
Harcus Sinclair v Buttonwood Legal Capital 2.111–2.114
Jennifer Simpson v Norfolk & Norwich University Hospital NHS Trust 2.88–2.94
London & Regional (St George's Court) v Ministry of Defence 2.68–2.72
Merchantbridge v Safron 2.73–2.80
Sibthorpe and Morris v Southwark London Borough Council 2.81–2.87
Stocznia Gdanska SA v Latreefers 2.26–2.30
Tinseltime v Eryl Roberts 2.102–2.108
case studies *see* Burford Capital; Therium Capital; Vannin Capital
cash flow planning and budgeting 1.78
causation 2.62
Cayman Islands 3.49, 10.57
Cecil v Bayat 2.95–2.101
champerty 1.08, 1.23, 1.27
  abolition of crimes of 1.33
  Arkin 2.65–2.67
  Australia 3.116, 3.118
  Canada 3.130
  Caribbean 3.135, 3.138
  Eurasian Dream (No 2) 2.32
  evolution 2.14–2.18
  Factortame (No 2) 2.45, 2.47, 2.49, 2.53
  funding 10.13
  Giles v Thompson 2.20, 2.24
  history and development of litigation funding 2.04–2.13, 2.123–2.124, 2.128, 2.131–2.132
  hybrid damages-based agreements (DBAs) funding 3.87
  Ireland 3.143
  Jennifer Simpson v Norfolk & Norwich University Hospital NHS Trust 2.88, 2.91–2.94
  jurisdiction 10.61, 10.73
  London & Regional v Ministry of Defence 2.69–2.70
  reasons for funding 3.08, 3.18–3.19
  Sibthorpe and Morris v Southwark London Borough Council 2.83–2.87
  Singapore 3.148
  South Africa 3.126–3.127
  Stoczania Gdanska SA v Latreefers 2.26–2.28
  United States 3.100
Chancery Division 7.15, 7.17, 8.55
Chancery Modernization Review 3.08
changes to project plan 5.99–5.100
Channel Islands 3.139–3.140, 10.04
  forum/venue/jurisdiction/applicable law 3.49
  Guernsey 3.140
  investment fund 4.49
  Jersey 3.139
Civil Justice Council (CJC) 8.111, 9.02, 9.04, 10.30

Working Group on Third Party Funding 9.03
Working Party on Damages Based Agreements 8.113
civil litigation 8.97
Civil Litigation Costs Review 8.02
claimant's obligations 5.106–5.107
class action 3.131
Clementi Report (2004) 10.20
clients 3.37–3.39
clinical negligence cases 6.14
Code of Conduct *see* Association of Litigation Funders (ALF); Solicitors Regulation Authority (SRA)
Commercial Court 1.63, 7.05, 7.18, 8.69
commercially motivated funders and pure funders, distinction between 8.116–8.117
common costs 7.24, 7.40, 7.48
Competition Appeal Tribunal (CAT) 7.07–7.11
complaints procedures 9.08, 9.38–9.42, 10.18
conditional fee agreements (CFAs) 1.63, 1.73, 2.127, 8.11
  alternative business structures (ABSs) 8.124
  Arkin 2.59–2.60
  and damages-based agreements (DBAs) 8.03–8.06, 8.78–8.79, 8.91, 8.94, 8.101, 8.130
  Factortame (No 2) 2.46, 2.49
  Gulf Azov Shipping v Idisi 2.54, 2.56
  Hamilton v Al-Fayed (No 2) 2.37
  Hodgson immunity 8.114–8.115, 8.118–8.121
  indemnity and *Sibthorpe and Morris v Southwark London Borough Council* 2.82–2.87
  Litigation Funding Agreement (LFA) 5.93
  lower value cases 3.58–3.59
  one-off funders 4.10
  partial 5.07, 5.88
  portfolio approach 3.78, 3.80–3.81
  reasons for funding 3.10–3.11
  reforms 8.02
  Simmons v Castle 8.20, 8.22
  solicitors' duties 9.67–9.68
  Tinseltime v Eryl Roberts 2.102–2.107
  see also discounted; hybrid; success fees
conditions precedent 5.102–5.103
conduct and control 9.17–9.19
conduct rules for solicitors 9.49–9.57
  see also Solicitors Regulation Authority (SRA)
confidentiality 5.112–5.113
conflict 10.36
consolidation 10.67
'Consultation Paper Reforming Civil Litigation Funding and Costs' 8.84–8.85
consumer credit agreement (CCA) 3.58
Consumer Rights Bill 7.06–7.07, 7.11
contingency fees 1.93
  alternative business structures (ABSs) 8.123
  Arkin 2.65
  brokers or direct approach to funders 5.22

contingency fees (*cont.*)
  Eurasian Dream (No 2) 2.33
  Factortame (No 2) 2.45, 2.49, 2.50–2.51, 2.53
  funding 10.07
  Hong Kong 3.146
  hybrid damages-based agreements (DBAs)
    funding 3.87–3.88
  model 8.87
  payment terms and interest 5.98
  portfolio approach 3.82
  Therium Capital Management 4.80
  United States 3.95–3.99
  see also **damages-based agreements (DBAs)**
Continuing Professional Development 10.46
control over litigation 9.17–9.19, 10.13–10.14, 10.72–10.75
costs budgeting 1.62–1.64, 8.72–8.76
  costs management orders 8.60–8.63, 8.65
  group litigation 7.50
  reasons for funding 3.12
costs capping 8.51–8.52
costs, excluded 5.101
costs and insurance 6.01–6.69
  costs risk of funders 6.57–6.61
  Excalibur 6.62–6.66
  security for costs 6.39–6.55
  see also **after-the-event (ATE) insurance;**
    payment of insurance premium
costs judgment in *Excalibur* 2.118–2.120
costs management conference 8.75
costs management orders 8.50–8.76
  costs budgets 8.72–8.76
  essential elements of costs
    management 8.53–8.54
  making an order 8.69–8.71
  new rules 8.55–8.64
  practical aspects 8.65–8.68
costs orders:
  after-the-event (ATE) insurance 5.90
  Arkin 2.63
  costs risk of funders 6.57–6.58
  Gulf Azov Shipping v Idisi 2.54, 2.58
  third party in *Flatman v Germany* 2.109
  see also **costs management orders**
costs sharing, claimants 7.22
costs shifting 2.62, 8.82–8.83
county courts 8.56
Courts and Tribunals Service website 7.17
credibility 9.24

damages-based agreements (DBAs) 1.91–1.94
  alternative business structures (ABSs) 10.55
  funding 10.06–10.07
  hybrid or discounted 1.73
  portfolio approach 3.80–3.81
  Tinseltime v Eryl Roberts 2.106
  see also **contingency fees; hybrid damages-based agreements (DBAs)**

damages-based agreements (DBAs) and Jackson Reforms 8.01–8.132
  after-the-event (ATE) insurance premium recoverability 8.12
  alternative business structures (ABSs) 8.122–8.124
  conditional fee agreements (CFAs) 8.11
  general damages, increase in 8.13–8.14
  Hodgson immunity 8.114–8.121
  lawyers' costs immunity 8.113
  practicalities 8.10–8.110
  proportionality 8.31–8.49
  Regulations (mainly 3 and 4) 8.90–8.98
  sanctions, increased (under Part 36) 8.25–8.30
  Simmons v Castle 8.15–8.24
  see also **costs management orders**
damages awards in United States 3.95, 3.111
damages based premium 6.19
declaratory relief 1.50
Deed of Priorities 5.92
definition of litigation funding 1.18–1.22
development of third party litigation funding 2.01–2.04
direct approach to funders 5.11–5.24
disbursements:
  Flatman v Germany 2.109
  funding 10.07
  lower value cases 3.58–3.59, 3.63
  Tinseltime v Eryl Roberts 2.102–2.106
disclosure 2.109–2.110, 8.67, 9.22
discounted conditional fee agreements (CFAs) 1.73–1.75, 1.77, 3.11–3.13
  and damages-based agreements (DBAs) 8.130
  funding process 5.07
  retainers 5.87–5.88
  see also **hybrid conditional fee agreements (CFAs)**
discounted fees funding 1.93
  see also **discounted conditional fee agreements (CFAs)**
dispute resolution 5.118–5.119, 9.29, 9.36–9.37
  services 1.76
  teams 3.11
draft Code of Conduct for Third Party Funding 9.02
'drop hands' settlement 1.43
Dubai 3.141–3.142, 10.58
Dubai International Financial Centre (DIFC) 3.50, 3.141–3.142
due diligence 1.50
  assessment 5.65–5.73
  exclusivity 5.60
  funding process 5.05–5.06
  negotiation 5.55
  retainers 5.87
  security for costs 6.41
  term sheet 5.57–5.59
  Vannin Capital 4.86

Index

duration of cases and pricing 5.82
duties of solicitors 9.58–9.91
  see also Solicitors Regulation Authority (SRA)

education pertaining to funding, importance of 10.04, 10.09, 10.19, 10.32–10.46
electronic disclosure 8.67
Employment Tribunal 8.81, 8.88
enforceability 3.51–3.53
ethical issues 10.36
Eurasian Dream (No 2) 2.31–2.34
Europe and group litigation 7.01–7.02, 7.26, 7.29
evolution of funding 2.14–2.18, 10.63–10.66
Excalibur 2.115–2.122, 6.62–6.66
exclusivity 5.60–5.64
  fund raiser funders 4.22–4.24, 4.28
  funding process 5.05, 5.131
  indicative terms 5.51
expert evidence 8.68
expert witnesses 2.50

Factortame (No 2) 2.43–2.53
family office structure 4.33–4.42, 6.23
fee arrangements 5.21
  capped 3.82, 5.87
  fixed 1.73
  see also conditional fee agreements (CFAs); contingency fees; success fees
fiduciary duty, breach of 1.59
Financial Conduct Authority 4.50, 4.66, 10.25
financing models 3.58, 4.67
fixed fees 1.73
Flatman v Germany 2.109–2.110
formal offer 5.57–5.59
formalities 9.09–9.11
forms and options of funding 1.28–1.44
forum/venue/jurisdiction/applicable law 3.49–3.50
France 3.132, 10.58
fraud and security for costs 6.52
'fund raiser' funders 4.21–4.32
funder models 1.20–1.21, 3.54, 4.00–4.89
  Burford Capital (case study) 4.64–4.72
  family office 4.33–4.42
  investment fund 4.48–4.56
  private equity 4.43–4.47
  publicly listed 4.57–4.63
  Therium Capital Management (case study) 4.73–4.81
  Vannin Capital (case study) 4.82–4.88
  see also 'case by case' funding
funding agreement 1.36, 2.128–2.130
  Caribbean 3.136
  funding process 5.06, 5.08, 5.95–5.97
  Harcus Sinclair v Buttonwood Legal Capital 2.112–2.114
  see also Litigation Funding Agreement (LFA)
funding contract 5.57

funding options 1.58–1.61, 9.66–9.77
funding process 5.00–5.133
  after-the-event (ATE) insurance 5.90
  brokers or direct approach to funders 5.11–5.24
  due diligence assessment 5.65–5.73
  exclusivity 5.60–5.64
  indicative terms 5.50–5.51
  intake review and assessment 5.44–5.49
  negotiation 5.52–5.56
  pricing 5.74–5.86
  retainers 5.87–5.89
  term sheet 5.57–5.59
  see also key areas of funding process; Litigation Funding Agreement (LFA)
funding, terms and effect of 9.81
future prospects and issues for funding 10.01–10.76
  alternative business structures (ABSs) 10.47–10.56
  education 10.32–10.46
  evolution of funding 10.63–10.66
  jurisdictions 10.57–10.62
  regulation and self-regulation 10.16–16.31

general damages, increase in 8.13–8.14
Germany 3.133–3.134, 7.04–7.05, 10.58
Giles v Thompson 2.20–2.25
global approach and proportionality 8.33–8.34
group litigation 1.71, 7.01–7.50, 10.74
  committee or board of directors 7.37, 7.46
  critical mass 7.34–7.36, 7.45
  England and Wales 7.05–7.25
  issues for funders 7.26–7.43
  judgment or order 7.17
  marketing and client acquisition plan 7.35
  register 7.17
  steering committee 7.35
  see also Group Litigation Orders (GLOs)
Group Litigation Orders (GLOs) 7.13–7.19, 7.22–7.24
  confidentiality 5.112
  solicitors' duties 9.85–9.86
Guernsey 4.49, 4.66
Gulf Azov Shipping v Idisi 2.54–2.58

Hamilton v Al-Fayed (No 2) 2.35–2.42
Harcus Sinclair v Buttonwood Legal Capital 2.111–2.114
headline information 5.31
hedge funds 4.13, 4.16
High Court 1.94, 3.08
historical background 1.23–1.27, 2.01–2.04
Hodgson immunity 8.114–8.121, 8.123–8.124, 8.127, 8.131, 10.55
Hong Kong 3.144–3.147, 10.59–10.62
hybrid conditional fee agreements (CFAs) 1.73, 5.07, 5.88, 10.08
hybrid damages-based agreements (DBA) 1.73, 3.86–3.87, 4.68, 8.94, 8.130

Index

'Improved Access to Justice Funding Options and Proportionate Costs' 9.02
increase of third party litigation funding, reasons for 1.56–1.85
indemnity costs and *Excalibur* 2.119
indemnity deed or bond 6.52–6.54
indemnity insurance 1.52, 5.34
indemnity principle 3.87, 8.89, 8.107–8.109
independent legal advice 9.18
India 10.04
indicative behaviour 1.58
indicative terms 5.50–5.51
initial review 5.45
insolvency cases 2.16, 3.85, 3.112, 4.10, 4.13
insurance:
  before the event (BTE) 9.67
  indemnity 1.52, 5.34
  see also after-the-event (ATE) insurance; costs and insurance
intake review and assessment 5.44–5.49
interest payment 5.98
interest rate, annual 3.78, 5.50
intermeddling 3.18
international perspective 3.92–3.149
  Caribbean 3.135–3.138, 10.04
  Channel Islands 3.49, 3.139–3.140, 4.49, 10.04
  Dubai 3.50, 3.141–3.142
  France 3.132, 10.58
  Germany 3.133–3.134, 7.04–7.05, 10.58
  Hong Kong 3.144–3.147, 10.59–10.62
  Ireland 3.143
  New Zealand 3.124–3.125, 10.57
  Qatar 3.50, 3.141–3.142, 10.58
  Singapore 3.148–3.149, 10.04, 10.59–10.62
  South Africa 3.126–3.128, 10.57
  see also Australia; Canada; United States
investment committee 4.71–4.72, 4.86
investment criteria 4.06, 4.35
investment fund 4.48–4.56
Ireland 3.143
Italy 7.01
item by item approach and proportionality 8.33–8.34

Jackson Reforms 1.86–1.94
  see also damages-based agreements (DBAs) and Jackson Reforms
Jennifer Simpson v Norfolk & Norwich University Hospital NHS Trust 2.88–2.94
jurisdictions 5.46, 10.57–10.62
'just and reasonable' requirement 7.10

key areas of funding process 5.25, 5.43
  budget 5.36–5.41
  merits of the case 5.28–5.35
  quantum 5.28–5.35
  strategy 5.42–5.43

Law Society 10.20
  Multi Party Action Information Service 7.17
lawyers' costs immunity 8.113
letter of claim and response 5.30
liability 5.101
  after-the-event (ATE) insurance 5.90
  excluded 5.101
  intake review and assessment 5.44
  merits and quantum 5.28, 5.33
  pricing 5.83
libel actions 3.111
limitation periods 1.54, 2.96–2.98, 5.62
line item approach 8.73
Litigation Funding Agreement (LFA) 1.29, 5.91–5.127, 9.07
  adverse costs 5.105
  agreement to fund 5.95–5.97
  Association of Litigation Funders (ALF) Code of Conduct 9.09–9.15, 9.19–9.20, 9.25–9.27, 9.29–9.33
  changes to project plan 5.99–5.100
  claimant's obligations 5.106–5.107
  conditions precedent and warranties 5.102–5.103
  confidentiality 5.112–5.113
  dispute resolution 5.118–5.119, 9.35
  excluded costs and liabilities 5.101
  Form H 1.79
  payment of reasonable costs 5.104
  payment terms and interest 5.98
  priorities agreement (appendix 3) 5.123–5.127
  project plan (appendix 1) 5.121
  reliance letter (appendix 2) 5.122
  Schedule to agreement 5.120
  security for costs 5.108–5.109
  termination 5.114–5.117
  treatment of claim proceeds 5.110–5.111
Litigation Funding Magazine 3.09
'Litigation Funding: Status and Issues' 2.07
London & Regional (St George's Court) v Ministry of Defence 2.68–2.72
lower value cases 3.54–3.69, 10.15

mainstream professional funders 1.21, 4.04, 4.06, 4.09
maintenance 1.08, 1.23, 1.27, 2.04–2.13, 2.123–2.124, 2.126, 2.131
  abolition of 1.33
  Australia 3.116, 3.118
  Canada 3.130
  Caribbean 3.135, 3.138
  evolution 2.13–2.17
  Factortame (No 2) 2.44, 2.48
  Giles v Thompson 2.23
  hybrid damages-based agreements (DBAs) funding 3.87
  Ireland 3.143
  Jennifer Simpson v Norfolk & Norwich University Hospital NHS Trust 2.87, 2.93

Index

jurisdiction 10.61, 10.73
London & Regional v Ministry of Defence 2.70
reasons for funding 3.08, 3.19
Sibthorpe and Morris v Southwark London Borough Council 2.85
Singapore 3.148
South Africa 3.126–3.127
United States 3.100
Manolete Partners 4.68
material misrepresentation or material non-disclosure 6.52
Mercantile Courts 8.56
Merchantbridge v Safron 2.73–2.80
merits of the case 1.41, 3.40–3.42, 4.31, 5.28–5.35
 Harcus Sinclair v Buttonwood Legal Capital 2.113–2.114
Ministry of Justice 9.04
mixed (damages & non-damages) cases and Part 36 (offers to settle) 8.27
monetary/damages cases and Part 36 (offers to settle) 8.27
multiple facility or percentage structure 5.77
multi-track cases 8.56

necessity standard and proportionality 8.36, 8.43
negotiation 5.52–5.56
Netherlands 3.133, 10.58
 Collective Settlement of Mass Claims Act (2005) 7.01, 7.11
 group litigation 7.03–7.05
new proportionate costs rule 8.47
New York Bar Association 3.101
New York Convention 3.53
New Zealand 2.63, 3.124–3.125, 10.57
Nigeria 2.54
no win no fee arrangement 8.79
 see also damages-based agreements (DBAs); hybrid conditional fee agreements (CFAs)
nominal amount payment 1.43
non-damages cases and Part 36 (offers to settle) 8.27
non-disclosure 9.69
non-party costs order:
 Arkin 2.61
 Flatman v Germany 2.110
 solicitors' duties 9.73–9.75
 Tinseltime v Eryl Roberts 2.102–2.107
non-recourse funding 1.21, 1.28–1.29
 hybrid damages-based agreements (DBAs) 3.88
 indicative terms 5.50
 portfolio approach 3.78–3.81
 United States 3.101–3.102
Novitas Loans 4.77
nuisance payment 1.43

'one-off' funders 10.74
Ontario model 8.82–8.83, 8.87, 8.99, 8.123
opt-in basis 7.08, 7.33
opt-out collective action 7.07–7.12

pain, suffering, and loss of amenity 8.13, 8.16, 8.22, 8.88
panels of third party litigation funders 1.76
payment (definition) 8.93–8.96
payment of insurance premium 6.14–6.38
 deposit premium 6.27–6.29
 fully deferred premium 6.30–6.38
 payment in full on inception 6.18–6.26
payment of reasonable costs 5.104
payment terms and interest 5.98
personal costs liabilities in *Gulf Azov Shipping v Idisi* 2.58
Personal Injuries Bar Association 8.18–8.19
personal injury cases:
 damages-based agreements (DBAs) 8.84, 8.88, 8.92, 8.97
 Flatman v Germany 2.109
 Jennifer Simpson v Norfolk & Norwich University Hospital NHS Trust 2.94
 Simmons v Castle 8.15
 solicitors' duties 9.75
pilot schemes and costs management orders 8.54, 8.65
Poland 7.01
portfolio approach 1.21, 3.72–3.82, 10.65
 fund raiser funders 4.23
 funding 10.15
 lower value cases 3.62
 Therium Capital Management 4.80
pricing 4.29, 5.74–5.86
priorities agreement 1.43, 5.123–5.127
priorities of payments 5.92
private equity structure 4.43–4.47, 6.23
privilege 10.36
pro bono 2.104, 8.114–8.115
professional conduct 2.47
 see also Solicitors Regulation Authority (SRA) Code of Conduct
professional duty, breach of 1.59
professional indemnity insurance 1.52
professional liability insurance 3.52
professional negligence 1.59, 3.52, 9.73–9.77, 9.89–9.90
professional obligations 3.17, 9.01–9.97
 see also Association of Litigation Funders (ALF)
professionalism standards 3.146
project plan 5.96, 5.121
proportionality 8.31–8.49, 8.65–8.67
publicity 10.19, 10.43
 group litigation 7.28–7.29, 7.33–7.34
publicly listed funder 4.57–4.63
 prospectus 4.58
 structure of funder 4.59
 transparency 4.60
'pure assister' 2.58

Qatar 3.141–3.142, 10.58
Qatar Financial Centre (QFC) 3.50, 3.141–3.142

Index

quantum 1.54, 5.28–5.35
  budget 5.37, 5.39
  of costs 8.65
  of damages 2.44
  intake review and assessment 5.44
  pricing 5.83
Queen's Bench Division 8.56
Queen's Counsel 5.119

ratio of costs to likely damages 5.36, 7.34
ratio of quantum of damages to the budget 1.48
'real party' to the proceedings 8.117–8.118, 8.124
reasonableness of costs 5.98, 8.65
reasonableness and proportionality 8.44
reasons for using funding 3.06–3.19
recourse scheme 3.78
recoverability 5.28, 5.33–5.34, 5.44, 5.48
regulation 10.16–16.31
  independent 10.67
  see also self-regulation
reliance letter 5.122
retainer 1.73–1.75, 5.87–5.89
  funding process 5.07
  hourly based 1.73
  reasons for funding 3.16
  risk-based 1.73
  standard 1.72–1.73
  terms and effect of 9.78–9.80
risk 1.02–1.03, 6.57–6.61
  assessment 5.04
  aversion 1.58
  perceived and pricing 5.82
Royal Bank of Scotland 7.05, 7.18–7.19, 7.29–7.32, 7.38–7.41, 7.48

sanctions, increased (under Part 36) 8.25–8.30
satellite litigation 2.113
Schedule to agreement 5.120
Secretary of State approval and fund raiser funders 4.32
security for costs 5.108–5.109, 6.39–6.55, 6.67
  education 10.40
  Excalibur 2.119–2.120
  Hamilton v Al-Fayed (No 2) 2.37
seed capital 7.27, 7.30, 7.33
self-regulation 10.16–10.31, 10.67
Self Regulatory Code for Third Party Funding 9.02
Selling Lawsuits, Buying Trouble (2009) 1.85, 3.106
settlements 9.33–9.34
  approval 9.26–9.35
  'drop hands' 1.43
  negotiation 1.41
Sibthorpe and Morris v Southwark London Borough Council 2.81–2.87
Simmons v Castle 8.15–8.24
Singapore 3.148–3.149, 10.04, 10.59–10.62
solicitors 9.43–9.91
  after-the-event (ATE) insurance 9.43–9.48

  conduct rules 9.49–9.57
  duties 9.58–9.91
  funding options 9.66–9.77
  funding, terms and effect of 9.81
  retainer, terms and effect of 9.78–9.80
Solicitors Regulation Authority (SRA):
  Code of Conduct 1.58, 9.49, 9.53, 9.56–9.58, 9.95
    damages-based agreements (DBAs) 8.131
    solicitors' duties 9.72
  conduct rules 3.60
  Handbook 9.53
  lower value cases 3.59
  regulation and self-regulation 10.20
solvency 9.21
South Africa 3.126–3.128, 10.57
special purpose vehicle 3.133, 9.12
specific performance 1.50
steering committee 10.74
Stocznia Gdanska SA v Latreefers 2.26–2.30
strategy 5.42–5.43
subject matter 3.33–3.36
subsidiaries and associated entities 9.12–9.16
success fees 1.29, 1.47, 1.63
  conditional fee agreements (CFAs) 8.11
  damages-based agreements (DBAs) 8.05–8.08, 8.82, 8.91
  ending of 1.87
  reasons for funding 3.10
  recoverability in *Simmons v Castle* 8.21, 8.23
  retainers 5.87–5.89
summary judgment in *Gulf Azov Shipping v Idisi* 2.54
Sweden 7.01
Switzerland 10.58

tax tribunals 8.81
Technology and Construction Courts (TCC) 8.54, 8.56
term sheet 5.57–5.59
termination 5.114–5.117
  of funding arrangement in *Harcus Sinclair v Buttonwood Legal Capital* 2.111
  and approval of settlements 9.26–9.35
Therium Capital Management 4.73–4.81, 5.91
Tinseltime v Eryl Roberts 2.102–2.108
Tolstoy decision 8.114
tranches or stages of funding 5.79–5.80
transparency 4.24, 4.60, 4.66, 9.24
treatment of claim proceeds 5.110–5.111
tribunals 8.81
types of cases 1.45–1.55, 3.20–3.53
  clients 3.37–3.39
  enforceability 3.51–3.53
  forum/venue/jurisdiction/applicable law 3.49–3.50
  intake review and assessment 5.46
  merits of the case 3.40–3.42
  subject matter 3.33–3.36
  value of likely recovery 3.43–3.48

Index

uberrimai fidei principle 9.64
underwriting 4.69, 4.72
United States 1.09, 1.91–1.93, 2.96, 3.49, 3.92, 3.94–3.111, 10.58
  American Bar Association White Paper 3.101
  brokers or direct approach to funders 5.14–5.16
  Burford Capital 4.68
  Chamber of Commerce: Institute of Legal Reform 1.85, 3.106
  Chambers, Ernie 6.02
  costs and insurance 6.01–6.04
  education 10.36
  Excalibur 6.63–6.64
  funding 10.04
  group litigation 7.26
  hybrid damages-based agreements (DBAs) funding 3.87–3.89
  New York Bar Association 3.101
  New York Convention 3.53
  one-off funders 4.13
  'pants lawsuit' (Pearson) 6.03
upfront payment 5.22
use of funding 3.01–3.149
  lower value cases 3.54–3.69
  reasons for using funding 3.06–3.19
  see also **alternative methods of funding; international perspective; types of cases**

value of likely recovery 3.43–3.48
Vannin Capital (case study) 4.82–4.88

waiver of privilege 3.101
warranties 5.102–5.103
'whitelabelled' products 1.75
witness statements 8.68
work in progress funding 10.07
Working Party on Damages Based Agreements Report 8.120